Soul Light
for the
Dark Night

Soul Light
for the
Dark Night

*Daily Meditations of Healing
from Trauma and Abuse*

Patrick Fleming, M.Div., L.C.S.W., C.S.A.T.

Sue Lauber-Fleming, R.N., M.A., L.C.S.W.

Vicki Schmidt, B.S.

Published by
Gentle Path Press

Gentle Path
P R E S S

Gentle Path Press
P.O. Box 3172
Carefree, Arizona 85377
www.gentlepath.com
Copyright © 2019 by Gentle Path Press

First edition: 2019

For more information regarding our publications,
contact Gentle Path Press at
1-800-708-1796 (toll-free U.S. only)

ISBN: 978-1-7320673-1-8

We dedicate this book to the courageous survivors of trauma now finding their voice, speaking their truth, and empowering all of us to break the cycle of trauma and abuse. To the brave survivors of #MeToo, #TimesUp, and #NeverAgain, and to all survivors who will in their own time and in their own way break their isolation and silence and join the swelling chorus of empowered voices, may the Spirit of Light and Love bless each of you with a new freedom to stand tall and to live your life in all its unique and wondrous glory and power.

"There is a great brokenness in the world and greater still,
an undeniable light moving in all things."
–Paula D'Arcy

Table of Contents

Foreword

Patrick Carnes, PhD.

Over the years, I have listened to thousands of sex addicts and their partners describe the pain and chaos caused by addiction. As I explored their stories further, I also heard the profound suffering and damage caused by their experiences of trauma and abuse earlier in their life. Part of this damage was to their spirituality. Their suffering was not only physical and psychological. It was spiritual as well, because, like addiction, trauma wounds many layers of the individual.

My life's work and mission has been to illuminate the dark, painful, hidden world of sex addiction and the underlying trauma. I have strived to bring both into the light where the suffering can be seen and shared, and recovery and healing can unfold. In *Soul Light*, Pat, Sue and Vicki have furthered this work exponentially. Their meditations provide daily stepping-stones on the heroic journey of transforming what I call "legitimate suffering" into a new vision for your life. As Victor Frankl, a pioneer psychotherapist and concentration camp survivor showed us, even in the horrific trauma of the concentration camps intense suffering can be survived and redeemed by discovering new meaning, purpose and service.

These meditations offer an experiential template for healing, and also a reason for hope. They provide a spiritual GPS to help you find your own way out the darkness of your trauma. They guide you to an inner sanctuary, your waiting soul, which has remained untouched and unharmed whatever your trauma. No matter what your body and mind have endured, your soul remains unassailable. The soul is the wellspring of your healing and recovery. These meditations will help you to reconnect to your soul, to your True Self and repair the damage to your body, mind and spirit.

No one can travel your healing journey for you. However, each day a meditation will lovingly and capably help light the way. Because of their years of experience accompanying counseling clients and from their own journeys of healing, Pat, Sue and Vicki make wonderful soul friends and what I call "fair witnesses" to companion, encourage and challenge you. Many of their meditations arise from their own story of trauma and healing. I have learned from my work with survivors and from my research that two primary requirements of recovery are the reassurance of safety and the power of story. By sharing dimensions of their own story, the authors provide both a safe and sacred space and a new narrative to help you re-write your own story. You are invited and supported to write a new personal narrative. A story no longer of shame, fear and isolation, rather now a story of courage, triumph, love, holy self-pride, and connection to your deepest self and to the "God of your understanding."

The Twelve Steps have long taught us, and my own research has confirmed, that discovering and practicing your own spirituality is one of the key tasks in establishing recovery and personal serenity. These meditations are written in the spirit of the Twelve Steps and the many Twelve Step communities. The authors take great care to assist the reader in discovering or re-discovering their own spirituality. They respect all spiritualities and draw their inspirations from the world's great spiritual traditions and spiritual teachers. There is no one right way. There are many paths. You will be helped and companioned in Soul Light to find, shape, and live your own road. You will also be helped to heal and remove any of the emotional or spiritual trauma blocks that have oppressed your spirit and inhibited your "conscious contact" with your soul and with your Higher Power.

Trauma pain can be very destructive and emotionally and spiritually paralyzing. Pain can also be a teacher. It can provide soul windows to open up the eyes of your mind and your spirit to a new vision of who you are and who you can be. These meditations are soul windows. Day by day, as you open each one, the light of your soul will more and more dispel the darkness of your trauma. The light will flood into the dark corners and illuminate the darkest secrets. You will learn the glorious truth of your inestimable value and worth. The universal soul journey is the path that moves you from being spiritually asleep to becoming fully awake and alive. These meditations are a daily wakeup call that will open up the eyes of your heart and your spirit.

One of my favorite quotes comes from JRR Tolkien's *Lord of the Rings:* "Not all who wander are lost." To heal your spirit after trauma and abuse and to restore your own spirituality, it is often necessary to wander for a time as you explore the byways of your life. These meditations can be a vital part of your search. As you "wander" daily through the meditations, I have no fear that you will get lost. Instead I trust that you will, in fact, be found. You will find your own True Self and the God of your understanding in the light of your soul. You will know a new freedom and happiness, a serenity undiminished by shame or clouded by fear.

Blessings on your journey.
Patrick Carnes, PhD.

Preface

All trauma, all abuse, is an assault on the human spirit. It can feel as if your very soul has been shattered. In truth, your soul cannot be damaged in itself. Your spirit can ultimately never be broken. Even severe trauma and abuse do not hurt your soul, your deepest being and *True Self.* Your soul is an Immortal Diamond that cannot be weakened or broken. What we have observed, however, is that trauma can rob you of your connection to your soul, can obscure your vision of your soul's light within you, and can block you from hearing its deep whisperings of wisdom and guidance. All of this can cloud or even obliterate your experience of your essential and eternal value and worth. This is what makes your spirit feel broken.

What sometimes has not been widely acknowledged is that trauma profoundly wounds the survivor's spirituality as well as their body and mind. Although the psychological work that we do has been crucial to our clients' well-being and recovery, it has often been insufficient for bringing them full healing, peace, and joy. The spiritual wounds of trauma survivors have to be healed as well. Survivors of all types of trauma wrestle with similar spiritual struggles, whether the trauma was verbal, physical, or sexual abuse; violence or war; a mass shooting; harassment; the sudden death of a loved one; or other major traumas.

In response to this spiritual need, we have created a process to help survivors of trauma heal spiritually as well as psychologically. Healing is a journey to reclaim your soul and heal your abused and traumatized spirit. This process developed into the Five Pathways of spiritual healing which we first presented in our second book, *Five Pathways to Healing the Spirit after Abuse and Trauma* (WordStream Publishing, 2011). The Five Pathways are:

- the Pathway of Spiritual Courage,
- the Pathway of Holy Anger,
- the Pathway of Sacred Grief,
- the Pathway of Forgiveness,
- the Pathway of Transformation.

A summary of the pathways is found in Appendix I in the back of this book. We also developed the Spiritual Laundry List" as a way to describe the spiritual wounds caused by trauma and some of the spiritual solutions for those wounds. This is found in Appendix II. We have woven many of the themes of the Five Pathways and the Spiritual Laundry List into the meditations for this book.

This spiritual healing process does not replace the vital psychological healing process every survivor needs to undergo. None of the meditations in this book are intended in any way to substitute for necessary emotional and psychological healing and treatment. The psychological healing process and the spiritual healing journey can go hand in hand. There is a dynamic interplay between the two spheres of our humanity—psyche and spirit—and progress in one dimension can augment healing in the other. So if you are in counseling or treatment, you will find it especially impactful and liberating to use these daily mediations as a healthy supplement for your soul.

It is important to briefly describe our approach to spirituality in this book and in our work. The distinction is sometimes made between spirituality and religion. Spirituality is everything that makes up your experience of the life of your soul. Religion, for some at least, is the more structured set of experiences and beliefs through which the life of the soul is expressed and hopefully nurtured. This book is intended to be a book of soul, of spirituality, not of religion. We, your authors, come from a Catholic Christian background, our spirituality having been shaped and nurtured by its rich spiritual tradition as well as by the Judeo-Christian sacred writings of the Bible. At the same time, for these meditations we have also drawn on the deep wells of wisdom of many other spiritual traditions of the East and West.

In our counseling work, we help our clients tap into and utilize their own spirituality and faith as a part of their healing process, always with great respect for their spiritual path and with no intent to impose our own spiritual beliefs. This is the approach we employ in this book. Our hope is to empower you through these meditations to discover and live from your own spiritual Way. We will help you draw from your own particular faith tradition, as well as from the great riches of other global spiritual traditions, so you can make this healing journey from the depths of your own faith, spirituality, and soul. To paraphrase an AA aphorism, we invite you to taste everything, take only what fits for you, and leave the rest.

A word about God language. The word "God" can be loaded with all sorts of limiting and painful associations. Some survivors have been abused by religious leaders. Others have had their image of God damaged by their trauma experience. Some of you understandably question even the reality and identity of God because of what you have suffered. Or you may react to the misuse of religion in our world where religion has been used to justify hate, discrimination, oppression, and even violence. Our philosophy about God talk is to take the same approach as the twelve-step programs. You are invited in these meditations to discover and deepen your relationship to the God of *your*—not our—understanding. We will alternately use the words "Higher Power," "God," "Lord," or "Spirit;" and "Divinity," "Being," or "Ground of Being." We use these with respect for who or what is your Higher Power, which in AA tradition can be whatever you experience as a power beyond and greater than yourself. We also operate out of the humble realization that no one can or has ever been able to capture in mere words the Great Mystery that is beyond the comprehension of our limited human minds.

These meditations were inspired by our healing work with thousands of survivors over the past thirty-five years of counseling. We have been blessed to listen to their sacred stories, to walk with them in their pain, and to rejoice with them as they experience freedom from fear and shame. We have been thrilled to watch survivors find their voice and their holy anger as they speak out against the abuse they and their sisters and brothers have experienced. We have been so blessed to watch the brilliant light of their souls emerge from the dark cloud of trauma and shine brightly in their world. In recent years we have been heartened to observe the growing movements in our society to end abuse and prevent trauma. These meditations arise from all of these survivor stories, which encompass the struggles and triumphs in breaking free from the emotional and spiritual bondage of trauma.

Our own trauma stories have also contributed to the creation of these meditations. Reflecting on our own pain, learning from our own struggles and victories, and listening to our own souls on our personal paths to healing have been additional sources of inspiration. We are on the same healing journey that we invite you to embark upon. You will hear parts of our trauma story in some of the meditations. (Sue and Vicki's stories are told in full in our two other books, *Shattered Soul?* and *Broken Trust: Stories of Pain, Hope, and Healing from Clerical Abuse Survivors and Abusers.*) Each meditation is illuminated by our own soul struggles and triumphs. We are all on a soul pilgrimage of healing together.

So you are not alone. We will be with you in spirit and in prayer each time you read and reflect on a meditation. Not only we three, but an army of survivors all over the world will also be on the road with you. So fear not, we are with you. Fear not, your soul is with you. Fear not, your God is with you. Remember each step of the Way that the darkness and pain of your trauma is no match for the brilliant inner light of your soul. So let's now start on the road of healing together.

Blessings to you for each step and each day of your soul journey through the spiritual landscape of these healing meditations.

Pat, Sue, and Vicki

January 1

Which Way Are You Looking? (Pat, Sue, & Vicki)

Happy New Year! Welcome to *Soul Light for the Dark Night*! We invite you to join us in a yearlong journey of self-discovery and healing through these daily meditations. We hope you will sense that we are traveling with you each day. We will be present to you through the meditations and always with you in Spirit. We hope too that you know that you are joined by your fellow survivors of trauma, your sisters and brothers who, like you, are seeking to find their voice and be set free. You are not alone. You are surrounded and accompanied by a community of Spirit, "a cloud of witnesses," as you make this pilgrimage.

The month of January is named after either the Roman God Janus or the Latin word *janua,* which means door. Both capture some of the spiritual significance of this day. Janus is pictured with two faces, one looking to the past, one to the future, which is what we do on New Year's. It's a good day to reflect on which way you are looking. Many survivors have only a face for the past. You may tend to focus primarily on the past traumatic events of your life. You find it difficult to be fully present to the great gift of Now and struggle to envision a hopeful future. We are inviting you this year to develop three faces and look in three directions: to the present moment, to a hope-filled future, and to your sacred center deep within where your soul abides and meets the God of your understanding.

We also invite you to join us in opening the door of this New Year. Open the door to new beginnings and new possibilities for healing and freedom. Open the gate to the love and light of your soul. Come with us each day—one day at a time, one moment at a time—to open yourself to wondrous self and soul discovery.

My Spiritual Practice for Today

We recommend that you *do not* make any New Year's resolutions. They are generally a setup for failure and shame. Instead, ask yourself which direction you are looking. Choose today to turn from the past and focus your gaze on the present moment, on the possibilities of your future, and within to the light of your soul.

January 2

What Google Doesn't Know and Siri Won't Tell You (Pat)

If you Google, "What is the meaning of life?" you get thousands entries and answers. If you ask Siri, "What will make me happy?" she will do a web search for you, again returning a million different memes. You may find some helpful wisdom in various websites, as you might in some great books. However, in the end, none of it will bring you the answers and the serenity you seek. The truth is that with the deepest spiritual questions, you can't look up the answers; you can only look within.

Peace is an inside job. Personal spiritual wisdom comes from within you. Thankfully, your soul's voice can teach and guide you to deep personal wisdom if you learn to listen. You possess a place within you that Virginia Satir called your "wisdom box" where your soul and the Spirit speak to you as you reflect on the events in your life. It is part of every person's birthright. It is where your personal life lessons are stored, ready to be tapped by your gut feelings, your intuition, and your mind.

The difficulty for survivors is that you have so much painful noise in your head that you can't hear the small, still voice inside that is your soul speaking to you. Or you so distrust yourself as a result of abuse that if you hear your inner voice, you mistrust it and don't believe you possess a wisdom box or have anything in it. Healing grows when you discover that you have a wise voice inside, and you listen to it. It comes when you realize that your smartphone provides lots of information, but only your own wise soul can nourish you, guide you, and bring you a peace that surpasses all understanding, all websites, all search engines.

My Spiritual Practice for Today

Recall instances in your life where your gut told you something and it was true; or where your intuition knew that you knew something, but you didn't know how you knew it. This is your soul speaking in your own personal wisdom box. Choose today to trust it. Use your mindfulness tools to quiet your mind and listen to yourself amid the events of the day. What wisdom do you hear?

January 3

A New Year: Write a New Story of Your Life (Pat & Sue)

Making New Year's resolutions to change something about yourself often doesn't work. It fact, it backfires. Resolutions are frequently not implemented or soon forgotten. They lead to frustration and self-judgment, and actually block personal change. For survivors, resolutions increase shame and self-anger.

Perhaps the best resolution this year is to make no resolutions at all! Instead, at the start of this new year, work to accept and embrace yourself as you are. For now, don't change a thing about yourself. This self-acceptance can include rewriting the story you have told yourself about yourself based on your trauma, and writing a new story from what you discover as you listen to your soul over this upcoming year of meditations. Unlike resolutions, this can bring real and surprising change in your life.

We are all storytellers. Whether you are conscious of it or not, you compose, edit, tell, and retell a story about your life all the time. Your mind plays a running narrative and video that expresses who you believe you are and what the events of your life mean in your ongoing tale. This shapes how you feel about yourself and influences your life choices. For survivors, your personal story is often shaped by the experience and perception of your trauma. It is colored by shame, fear, pain, and self-rejection. You may be allowing your trauma or your abuser to write your story.

This year, and this meditation book, can be an opportunity to become the author of your own story. You can rewrite your life script from the viewpoint of your strengths, your resilience, and the creative, life-giving ways you found to survive. Listening to the wisdom of your soul, you can see yourself in a new light. Instead of starting the new year with resolutions, begin it with a new story.

My Spiritual Practice for Today

I will start a journal today for this year of meditations. Part of my journaling will be to rewrite my personal life story from a new viewpoint. I will question my assumptions about myself and my life, especially those formed by my trauma or written by my abuser. I will start to listen each day to my heart and my soul as they tell a new story about my life.

January 4

A Courage Like No Other (Vicki)

We all have more courage than we believe we do. Fear can drive us away from an awareness of the inherent courage that lies within our soul. The fear of being judged harshly about something very intimate can be a colossal and oppressive barrier in every endeavor. It invades family life, work life, and social life.

How do we take the first steps to release obstacles to our fearfully held courage? We do so with a small courageous act today and another tomorrow; we take small steps until we can run. Often we feel so broken that we have no inner resources to call forth, but we do. They are locked deep inside.

Sometimes a first courageous act can be to pick up the phone and call a therapist or decide to tell a trusted friend a secret you have been carrying. This effort can be the first step toward reclaiming your life. It can be the first step toward understanding your life and how events that occurred affected it. Our lives can be a complicated puzzle that needs an objective guide to help us see our way through.

Every life contains experiences that leave scars on us. Some are small bumps along the way, and some are life draining. The life-draining experiences can leave you shattered and lacking hope. The courage to tell your story will be the first step in reclaiming your life. Once you summon your courage, you can move forward with the next steps in the healing process. Having the courage to tell your story means you are ready to face the secrets that have held you captive for so long. In the healing journey, uncovering the masks that you hide behind is an essential step toward healing. The need for courage will present itself often. Every step toward wholeness requires a new level of courage. It is there, waiting to be summoned. If you can trust it is there, you can take the first steps toward healing your life.

My Spiritual Practice for Today

I commit today to finding the first ounce of courage that will allow me to take a first, second, or third step in my healing process.

January 5

Becoming Visible (Sue)

Abuse, for me, equated with being seen and getting hurt. Finding spiritual courage meant becoming visible and breaking through the fear of being noticed or acknowledged. I identified with "Mr. Cellophane Man" in the musical, Chicago., Just like that character who was unseen and invisible, I felt the same, and my fear kept me that way.

One of the most life-changing acts of courage that healed this was when I became a cheerleader in high school. Talk about becoming visible! It scared me to death, yet something in me pushed me to try out. Something inside had to be seen. Before I went to the try-outs, I stopped by my parish church, and, within child-like faith, I told God how much I wanted to be a cheerleader. I asked for God's help at the audition. I made it! I had a strong pair of lungs and an ocean of energy and enthusiasm that was waiting for this opportunity to surge forth. I broke though my fear and became visible.

My hidden talents began to emerge, a process that has continued through my adult life. I discovered strengths and gifts within me that I had never guessed were there. With God's help, I found the courage to become more visible, and I gradually weakened the vise grip of my fear and shame. I heard an inner voice urging me to step out of the shadows. My job has been to listen and to respond with the courage to grab onto whatever rope was offered me, pulling myself past my fear and into the light.

Sometimes, still, when I do public speaking, the fear of being visible returns. I think, "Do I have the right to stand before this audience?" I want to run and hide. Yet when I see the audience and feel a warm connection with them, something shifts inside. The fear evaporates, and I hear God whisper, in a quiet voice: "You are my precious child. You are loved, you matter, you count, you are you, celebrate you!" Then the words begin to flow.

My Spiritual Practice for Today

Listen to the inner voice of your soul inviting you to step out of your own shadows. How are you being called to become more visible? What inner gifts are yearning to blossom? How can you pull yourself past your fear today and let your light shine?

January 6

When the Fox Poops, Stop and Listen (Pat)

One morning as I was racing to my mammogram appointment (men get breast lumps too—mine was suspicious and worrying), I rounded a curve, and there was a small red fox in the middle of the road. He just stood there motionless watching me, so I stopped the car and watched back. I was intrigued, but also pretty irritated because I was anxious to get to my appointment and find out what was happening with my body. The fox didn't move, just kept staring at me. Then very nonchalantly it squatted and proceeded to poop in the middle of the road! Just as nonchalantly, it got up and sauntered off the road to the left. I started to drive on when the fox darted back across the road right in front of me, forcing me to stop again. Now on the right shoulder, the fox looked back as if to say, "Did you get the message?"

The message? What was the message? I wrestled with this the whole day as I went through a couple rounds of tests and consultations. My soul often speaks to me through nature, although I don't mean this in a magical or fairy-tale kind of way. What was my soul—and the wise young fox—trying to tell me?

Reflecting during the day, this is what I heard: "Stop, slow down, listen to the soothing voice of your soul and your God saying, 'Fear not, I am with you.'" I also heard, "You are carrying a lot of poop inside right now"—I was both terrified and furious about the lump—"let it out, and let it go." So that's what I did, and gradually I felt a growing peace as the day wore on, even though I still had no medical answers.

Late in the day, I realized another message: "Poop or get off the pot." I had been stalling about a major decision in my professional life. Was it time to make the decision? Did the fox say all of this to me? I do know that he got me to stop and listen, and that proved very wise.

My Spiritual Practice for Today

If a fox stops and poops in your path today—in whatever guise that may take—simply stop and listen.

January 7

A Life Interrupted (Vicki)

We can only appreciate the miracle of a sunrise
if we have waited in the darkness.
–Anonymous

Life happens. A sibling dies in a terrible auto accident; another sibling is diagnosed with a tumor on his spine; parents grieve; a Catholic priest with his own unhealed wounds takes advantage of a grieving family and holds power over them. Each one of us could make a list of the difficult things that have happened in our family.

Life wasn't going well. I was obsessed with work, spending as many as eighteen hours a day on the job. We were developing a continuing care retirement community, so the workload was heavy, and I was involved in every aspect of its development. I could bury myself in this project, and no one would notice. What I was hiding was gnawing at me. I could not see how I could extricate myself from the abusive man who I worked for; I felt a bondage to him. What I didn't understand is that his power over me started the minute he walked into my hospital room after the car accident that killed my sister, Becca, and injured my mother, two brothers, and me. I could never have connected that dynamic from the age of eight to what I was feeling in my early thirties.

I was referred to a therapist who lived two hours away from my home. I was so petrified of anyone knowing my story that I felt I had to go out of town to get help. I feared my abuser. I didn't want him to know I was speaking to anyone, and living in a small town of 1,500 people, I was afraid of the story being made public.

A life interrupted is an invitation to explore the mystery of darkness. Darkness does not have to be evil or feared. We've associated darkness with evil throughout history and in many sacred texts. Nancy Schreck, OSF, writes, "Knowing how to walk in the dark takes time. When we do so, we sign a waiver that allows us to bump into some things that frighten us at first. But all we need do is to ask the mystery of darkness to teach us, to follow the darkness wherever it leads, and to become intimate with darkness."

My Spiritual Practice for Today

Reflecting on the darkness that seems to be coating you with fear, take the first step in recognizing that out of darkness comes healing. Coming out of darkness signifies you will see the light of a new day.

January 8

Telling Your Story (Pat & Sue)

One of the greatest acts of courage for a survivor is finding your unique and holy voice. This happens the day you break free from the iron grip of fear and shame, break the dark silence and secrecy of abuse, and bring your trauma into the healing light by telling your story to trusted individuals.

Telling your story shatters the power of fear and shame over you. It breaks the poisonous, debilitating, shaming power of secrets and activates the spiritual process of bringing darkness into the light where God's love can heal and redeem it. Years ago, we heard this universal spiritual principle at a workshop, and we have seen it validated in the lives of many of our clients: "Love—especially God's love—brings up everything unlike itself for the purpose of healing." And secondly, whatever is brought up to the light itself becomes light.

When you courageously tell your story, you are working with love, with God, to activate this principle to free you from fear and shame and move you farther along the road to your healing. Perhaps you have already experienced this and have found the courage to share your story with someone. Congratulations!

If you have not yet done so, do not indict yourself. It may not be time yet. Love will bring your story into the light ready to be told in love's time. When your story wants out, you will know it. Do not be afraid. It will feel scary and painful at first. However, remember it is love and light at work for the purpose of your healing. It is the restoration of your own strong voice and the voice of your soul so you can proclaim your truth and be free.

My Spiritual Practice for Today

If you have not yet shared your story, consider whether it is time. Carefully consider whom you can trust with your story. Often it is wisest to first share it with a professional. If you have already told your trauma story, reflect on how it felt to reclaim your voice and what changed for you, especially spiritually.

January 9

Serenity Prayer, Reflection 1 (Pat & Sue)

"God grant me the serenity to accept the things I cannot change…"

This is the first line of the famous Serenity Prayer, written by the theologian Reinhold Niebuhr and adopted by AA and the twelve-step movement. It is a powerful and liberating prayer for many, and it outlines a program for healthy choices. It's frequent use and application is one of the keys to inner peace.

Although it describes a whole and interconnected spiritual process, we will reflect on it in three parts. In this first part, you are asking God to give you the grace of serenity that comes when you accept the things in your life that you cannot change. You seek a grace, a gift, a new spiritual power. When you receive this gift and accept your powerlessness over things you cannot change, despite your furious efforts, you will experience a deep inner peace arising within you.

It seems to be a human trait to want to control things. You feel safer when you think you are in control of everything in your life. This is especially true for survivors. Part of trauma is the awful feeling of helplessness because you could not prevent or control what happened to you. The understandable response is to try harder to hyper-manage every aspect of your life. Unfortunately, this just makes things worse. There are so many things in your life that you cannot control: people, situations, changes in the world, and even aspects of yourself. Attempting to control them creates the illusion that you are safer. Accepting that there is much you cannot change feels threatening, and yet paradoxically it brings serenity. Acceptance yields an inner peace that leads to trust. Trust leads to a deeper connection with your inner power and resources, with your soul and your Higher Power. These are the deepest sources of your safety and serenity.

My Spiritual Practice for Today

List five things that you try to control. Choose one to focus on today. Ask for the soul power to surrender control of this, and accept that you cannot change it—and ask for the grace to experience that this is okay. Be aware that you may at first feel greater fear. Be open to the serenity that will come.

January 10

Serenity Prayer, Reflection 2 (Pat & Sue)

"Courage to change the things I can…"

Powerlessness is not helplessness. Even though there is much that you cannot change or control, in every situation there are things you can change if you summon the courage to do so. Sometimes the only things you can change are your attitude and reaction to the situation. Often those are the most powerful changes you can make. One of our mentors, Virginia Satir, taught that you always have at least three choices in every situation. The process of courage then is to identify at least three things you can do. Choose one, ask for the courage to do it, and then put your choice into action. You will experience the inner power and resources that you possess in your mind, heart, and soul. You will tap into strengths you thought you did not have or believed your trauma had destroyed.

Courage is not the absence of fear. Courage, especially the spiritual courage arising from your soul, is the determination to push through and past fear, to move forward, and to not allow fear to paralyze you and prevent you from changing what you can. Fear says, "Don't act, don't move, danger, danger everywhere; above all, safety first." Your soul says, "Have courage, trust, grow, be open, risk, explore, take action, and change what you can. You can do it. I believe in you, and I will give you what you need to move forward." Often the first step is the most important in the process of change. Taking the first step toward some needed change sets the process in motion and creates a new energy and momentum that will empower you to effect the change that you are called to. Ask for the courage, feel it well up within you, and take that first powerful step.

My Spiritual Practice for Today

List five things that you can change in your life or yourself that would benefit you. Especially be aware of changes that you have been resisting out of fear. Choose one that you can start to implement today. What is the first step? Do your best to make this change begin to happen.

January 11

Serenity Prayer, Reflection 3 (Pat & Sue)

"And wisdom to know the difference."

Ah, there's the rub! Sometimes it's difficult to discern between the things you can change and the things over which you are powerless. So you ask for wisdom to know which is which.

You may think you lack this wisdom and can't develop it. Actually, you already possess this wisdom deep inside. You only need to learn how to listen for it and use your courage to act on it. Virginia Satir had another wonderful concept that she called your "wisdom box." Everyone has one. It is a place within you where your soul and mind meet and talk to each other. It is an energy spot where intuition and deep knowing are developed and refined. It is where your learning from different life experiences is stored, ready to be tapped into as needed. You need to believe you possess or can develop that wisdom. You can learn to open your wisdom box to see and listen to what you already know and trust it. This is also called "trusting your gut" or "following your intuition."

At times, you have to fight your own resistance to listening to your inner wisdom. You may not want to know what you need to let go of and what you can actually change. You may want to hold onto something or someone and try to stay in control by manipulation, aggressive or passive-aggressive tactics, or even by worry (which is a mental attempt to be in control). You may not want to face the changes that you can and need to make. So part of praying for wisdom is asking for the grace and courage to want to know. The key spiritual action is to request the wisdom and then quiet your mind enough to hear your soul and your mind speaking to you in your own personal wisdom box. The sign that you are listening well will be the serenity you experience as the answer comes to you.

My Spiritual Practice for Today

List five things in your life that you are unsure of whether you can change or whether you are powerless over them. Choose one and pray for the wisdom to know the difference. Spend quiet time with your soul and imagine looking into your wisdom box for the answer.

January 12

Toward Gentleness and Love (Vicki)

Today I am drawn to reflect on thoughts of love and gentleness. To live a spirit of gentleness, I am called to live a life of love for all creation. When I make a commitment to consciously love, it calls me to live a gentle life, respecting all that God has created in this world. When we love with respect, gentleness becomes a way of life, and we see life and our relationship to it as a pure gift.

The poet Rumi shares this about the power of love and its potential to transform.

I was dead, then alive.
Weeping, then laughing.
The power of love came into me,
and I became fierce like a lion,
then tender like the evening star.

On a visit to Mexico, I went with a small group to visit a mother and daughter who were living in a small adobe house with a dirt floor and a tin roof. They had no electricity and no running water. The only furniture in their humble home was a bed with soiled blankets, a rickety table with two chairs, and a small wooden cabinet. The mother was blind, and her daughter was blind and mentally handicapped. They were given scraps of food left over from a son who lived nearby. Chickens roamed in and out of their small home.

Their greatest possession was their loving relationship, "tender like the evening star." When we arrived, they were sitting on the edge of their bed clinging to each other. I was at once aware of their gentle spirits and the beauty of their interdependence. Their gentleness with us was a beautiful gift in that moment. In their desperate poverty, they relied on one another for everything. Their hospitality to us that day was humbling. It was a reminder of how important interdependence is for every human being.

Gentleness and respect for all living things is what God is calling us into every moment. We must open our hearts to an awareness of these sacred times in the course of our days.

My Spiritual Practice for Today

On my journey toward becoming gentler, I want to be more attuned to and grateful for the beauty and gentleness that is a present in the world around me. I want to have a gentle spirit to share with others.

January 13

Religion (Pat)

Religion can be like sex: wondrous, beautiful, ecstatic, and potentially dangerous, to be deeply enjoyed and closely watched. Religion can be a powerful force for good in the world—think of the Dalai Lama or Pope Francis—or it can be misused to justify control and oppression, hate, and even violence. We have seen many examples of this in our time with too many instances of terrorism or persecution based on a purportedly religious ideology arising from a misinterpretation and misuse of religious belief. All of this is an abuse of religion, and an abuse of God as well. I have fantasized sometimes that we need to set up a God Abuse Hotline where abuses and misuses of God could be reported and investigated (we also need a Bible Abuse Hotline). This misuse of religion reminds me of a bumper sticker I saw a few years ago: "Lord, save me from your followers!"

Many survivors have become alienated from religion by a personal experience of the abuse of religion. You may be a victim of direct religious abuse, where a religious leader or group has employed religion to control, brainwash, or intimidate. You may have been raised in a fear-and-shame-based church that has left you with a damaged image of yourself and God. A religious leader, who misused their spiritual position, may have emotionally, physically, or sexually abused you. Or you might be turned off by religion because of what you have observed in some of its followers. All of this is based on a tragic misuse and abuse of religion.

Religion is meant to be a community of belief and love that nurtures spiritual growth and brings forth "the better angels of our nature." Although spirituality certainly can flourish outside of organized religion, there is much spiritual richness in all religions that could nurture your spiritual path and your healing.

This is, of course, a very personal matter. Each of you will make your own choice about your relationship to religion. It will be helpful in your discernment to heal any way that religion has hurt you.

My Spiritual Practice for Today

Reflect on your experience of religion. Is there anything in need of healing that alienates you? What role do you want religion to play in your healing and your spirituality?

January 14

Have A Bad Day (Pat)

Everyone has a bad day once in a while. These are days when everything seems to go wrong, when the forces of the universe seem aligned against you. Or there are days when you wake up tired and cranky, and a mood sets in that permeates the whole day. Survivors' bad days can also be tinged with sadness about the losses incurred by your trauma or agitated by anger at your perpetrator or the "fate" that made you a victim.

On many of these bad days, it will be best to work your way out of the negative mood using the tools you have developed to change your thoughts and focus on gratitude. However, sometimes it is therapeutic to let yourself have a really good bad day. These are days in which you need to grieve and lament about what was done to you. You may need to feel your sacred anger to help empower and heal you. These are days that you will want to answer the ubiquitous, artificially cheery greeting "Have a good day" with "No, thanks. I'm having a really bad day, and I intend to enjoy it!" (Notice the person's reaction).

Letting yourself feel the emotions, the colors, and the shadings of your recovery process is paradoxically healing. So occasionally allow yourself to have a really fine bad day, and relish it! However, don't let your bad day devolve into a full-fledged pity party, saying to yourself, "Poor me what a dismal life I have" and "What a lousy person I am."

Whenever you are tempted to go there, take a deep breath, and remember that your soul says you are a person of infinite value. Then realize that it's just a bad day, not a bad life. Whether it's a bad day, a bad week, or a bad month, it doesn't mean that you have a bad life lived by a bad person. It's simply a bad day—perhaps one you need—and forecasts nothing about tomorrow or the day after.

My Spiritual Practice for Today

If it seems right for you, declare today a "bad day." Allow yourself the healing luxury to feel your anger or grief and lament what happened to you. If not today, give yourself permission to have a truly good bad day sometime in the future.

January 15

Living in the Circle of Value, Part One (Sue)

There is a saying, "Wherever you go, there you are!" A key to living with serenity and joy is knowing who you truly are. It is the awareness that your soul, your True Self, is who you actually are. It is the knowledge that because of this, you, all of you, are of inimitable and infinite value, and nothing—including trauma and abuse—can add to or subtract from that value. It just is. If you carry this awareness with you wherever you go, whatever you experience in each moment, then no matter what is happening, you can be at peace. This is living in the Circle of Value. Living each day in this circle, the circle of God's eternal love for you, in each now of your life, is the ultimate goal for your healing journey.

It means living from your center, your soul, no matter where your life's journey takes you. It means knowing nothing can rob you of your magnificence and worth. It is defining yourself not by any external surface measures of self-esteem, but by the image of God that you were created to be and by the soul-esteem your soul bequeaths to you—just because you are you. It is living from an inner sanctuary free from fear or shame in the complete knowledge that you are loved and sustained by infinite love and that love will never forsake you. And it is, in the inner sanctuary of the circle of value, understanding that your very essence is such that it cannot be harmed, abused, controlled, or shattered, and it is already perfect.

My Spiritual Practice for Today

Wherever you go today, remember who you are. Especially in moments that you feel out of balance, threatened, or less than, pause, go inside, image yourself stepping back into the circle of value, and say to yourself: "I am God's precious child, a magnificent person of infinite value."

January 16

Living in the Circle of Value, Part Two (Sue)

Abiding in the Circle of Value frees you from having to fight each day to defend your small self, your fearful, limiting ego. There is no need. You are not that little self. You are a magnificent person of infinite value. No one and no event can take that from you. You can live from your larger self, your True Self, your soul. Living in the circle means you can enjoy the externals of your life and the characteristics of your persona in the world, but you do not have to be defined by them or work so hard to protect them. You no longer need to expend and waste so much psychic energy in the psychological self-defense of enhancing and protecting your self-image in the world. You live in the sound of your True Self whispering, "I am, I am here, I am now, I am I. I am a person (always and everywhere) of magnificent and infinite value."

Living in the circle frees you, then, to live from your Truest Self. It frees you to be the unique, individual word that is spoken by the Eternal Word. You exist in the formless world of soul because that is who you are, and yet you are able to live peaceably in the world of material form. You are capable of being at home in many places because you have a home deep within yourself, your inner sanctuary of communion with your soul. You can be at home always with yourself and know that you are never alone in anything. You experience yourself to be the dance of the "Great Dancer" as you make and create your own unique moves and steps in the dance of life.

My Spiritual Practice for Today

Imagine today living inside a circle of light, a light emanating from a fiercely glowing center point inside you, which is your soul. Pick a color for the light that surrounds you. Visualize that light all around as you go about your day. Notice the difference it makes, especially in your interactions with others, being aware of living from your True Self.

January 17

Courage to Be (Vicki)

Often at the beginning of a healing journey, one can feel lost. We can get so caught up in the cycle of abuse that nothing feels real any longer. Life, although rich in many ways, can feel empty. Going through the motions every day can feel meaningless. Imagine stepping into your therapist's office and feeling for the first time that there is hope for your aching soul.

It was a struggle to identify my true self; yet it was my deepest desire. I wanted to be able to look in the mirror and love the image I saw. As a young woman discerning what my career and future would be, I found myself stuck in a place that was dictated by the abuse. Despite tremendous patriarchal obstacles that worked to stifle my feminine spirit, I have found my identity as a woman in the acknowledgment of my truth as a woman of God. Through the discovery of my core values and truth, I have come to recognize the feminine gifts I have to be a compassionate, loving, and nurturing person. Our truth is the awareness of the inherent qualities we have to love, to intuit, to communicate, to bond and love, to befriend and embrace, to gather, and to seek intimacy in healthy relationships. My identity as a woman has been molded as a potter shapes clay, slowly and gently molding and then tested by fire.

Becoming a woman is never a journey walked alone. Women's friendships and desire for openness and life-giving intimacy provide the support needed to come to an understanding of who we are as women. My growth toward a mature feminine spirit has been nurtured because of the women who have journeyed with me through the joys and sorrows of life. When we find ourselves at an impasse and cannot find an opening to walk through, courage allows us to reach out and ask for help. It is there if we but summon it. It seemed that every step of my healing process was a confirmation that I was being led by a power outside of myself, that my willingness to say the first courageous yes resulted in calling my therapist, which brokered the first grace. And then saying yes to each new tiny step confirmed the action of God's grace toward becoming whole.

My Spiritual Practice for Today

Today, I will envision my first step toward healing and make a plan to reach out for help.

January 18

Cancer Gives Me the Hiccups (Pat)

Many things about my cancer journey were weird. Instead of getting a normal male cancer like prostate, I got breast cancer. Some of the side effects I experienced from the treatment were unusual too.

Most people struggle with nausea during chemo. My treatment gave me the hiccups. At first it seemed sort of funny, but after hours of nonstop, convulsive hiccups every minute or two, I was getting exhausted and concerned. Can you hiccup to death? I tried all the usual remedies. I googled for solutions. Nothing worked. I called my oncologist, who confirmed that my hiccups were unusual and prescribed some meds. None of them worked.

I felt desperate after several days of this. I prayed for relief. It came in an equally unusual manner. Sue had been to a party and had brought home several helium balloons. That evening, while hiccupping nonstop, out of the blue it came to me that helium might do the trick. So I breathed in the helium and sang to Sue in a silly high-pitched helium voice, "You are my sunshine, my only sunshine; you make me happy when skies are gray…" It was a strangely romantic moment. We both laughed and held each other. And then the hiccups stopped. After that I always kept helium balloons on hand. It worked each time the hiccups came back.

Every moment in life can teach you. This moment taught me that even in painful and desperate moments, you can find humor, laughter, and joy. Was it the laughter or the helium that cured my hiccups? Probably both. I also learned that difficult times offer an opportunity to bond more deeply. Our helium moment was one of many times during my treatment that Sue and I cried together, grieved together, or laughed together—or all three at once. Each time drew us even closer. The helium episode also taught me that even during high stress, if you listen deeply enough and are open to crazy, out-of-the-box possibilities, solutions appear.

My helium idea was a soul- and Spirit-inspired deep intuition. Your soul will do that for you too. So, remember that in any circumstance, humor, laughter, love, and inspiration can always be found.

My Spiritual Practice for Today

Recall a stressful time. What did you learn? How did your soul help to redeem the situation?

January 19

An Army of Survivors (Pat & Sue)

Over seven historic days in January 2018, 156 survivors courageously confronted their abuser, Dr. Larry Nassar, in their victim-impact statements. Judge Rosemarie Aquilina called them an "army of survivors." Each of them spoke their truth about their sexual abuse at the hands of Dr. Nassar, who had abused his victims under the guise of phony medical treatment for more than twenty years.

One woman, a gymnast and lawyer, Rachael Denhollander, started this amazing army. She had the courage to speak up as a lone voice against Dr. Nassar and his enablers. Gaining courage from her and each other, other survivors found their voice and came forward with their stories. Each of them became a hero in that powerful army. Olympic gymnast Ally Raisman expressed it well: "Imagine feeling like you have no power and no voice. Well, you know what, Larry? I have both power and voice, and I am only just beginning to use them."

You are a part of this army of survivors. You know your truth, and you can find your voice. You may serve in a different way than these courageous female athletes, but you are just as much a part of the army and just as important in the battle. If you ever feel you are alone, remember that, at least in spirit, you are part of this growing army of survivors.

What can hearten you further is to know that, although the war against abuse is far from being over, the battle is being won. It is now widely agreed by prominent researchers that the rates of sexual, physical, and emotional abuse have gone down substantially in the last twenty years. A large part of this decline has come from survivors speaking up and bringing this traumatic issue into the light. So you are part of a winning army, though there are many more battles to be fought.

Judge Aquilina's final words to the army of survivors are a powerful call to arms: "Leave your pain here, and go out and do your magnificent things."

My Spiritual Practice for Today

Picture yourself as a member of the army of survivors. How does it feel to be comrades in the battle with your fellow sister and brother survivors? If you are hesitant, hear your soul say to you, "Enlist today."

January 20

The Anniversary Effect (Pat & Sue)

Periodically a client will come in for a counseling session and report to us that, out of the blue, they had a sudden onset of old feelings of dread or depression, or pervasive sadness and tearfulness. It is puzzling and alarming to them because they cannot connect these emotions to any current event in their life. When we explore the feelings with them, we often discover that it is the anniversary of some major loss or trauma. They are usually relieved to hear that they are unconsciously remembering and feeling what happened to them on that particular date or time of year.

The anniversary effect is your body and your mind remembering so you can memorialize and honor your loss and your pain. The spiritual energy is God's love bringing up anything unlike itself for the purpose of healing. It can be helpful for you to be aware of the anniversary effect so you will not be blindsided by a sudden and unexpected eruption of emotion and pain.

Even more helpful is to use the anniversary of your trauma to consciously work to further your healing and celebrate your progress. Every time you remember with heart and soul what you have suffered, you rework the memory and the pain to a new place in your mind. You create a new and more positive story about your trauma and your loss that becomes a further step in your healing pilgrimage.

Don't be afraid of your trauma anniversary. Use it to honor and commemorate what you survived. Look at whatever further healing is needed, and celebrate how far you have come.

My Spiritual Practice for Today

Note on your phone's calendar or somewhere else the anniversary date of your trauma. Set an alarm for a few days prior. When the anniversary comes, be prepared to relive and re-grieve what you experienced. Also make a conscious plan of self-care, commemorating and celebrating your healing as your anniversary approaches.

January 21

Mindfulness (Pat & Sue)

Mindfulness is an important spiritual practice for healing and recovery from trauma. Learning to be mindful of the eternal now of the present moment gives you a powerful tool to move away from negative or disturbing thoughts. It calms the famous "monkey mind," the chattering, jumping, and scattered part of the mind that can afflict us all.

Mindfulness quiets the monkey mind and even the trauma mind, and gently and powerfully draws you away from this mental noise to a deep still-point at your center in your soul. This is especially vital for survivors. Your trauma may have left you with a hyperactive mind, always buzzing with depressing and anxious thoughts or painful memories and flashbacks.

When we are working with a survivor, and he or she has a strong flashback or frightening memory, we use mindfulness to help them calm and refocus themselves. We have them open their eyes, stand up, and look intently around the office at the bookshelves, the art, the light streaming in from the windows, and at us. This brings them back from the painful past into the present moment. We also have them consciously focus on their breathing, and change its anxious, shallow, and rapid pace to deep, slow, cleansing breaths that calm and bring them to center.

As you can see, mindfulness is a valuable tool to put in your recovery tool kit. You can teach it to yourself. You can also find many resources to learn it online or in your local community. The practice is simple. You can choose to make the focus your breath, the repetition of a short prayer (just a few words is best), or meditation word or phrase. Sitting in a quiet place, you focus your mind on your chosen centering tool. If it is your breath, you consciously breathe in and breathe out with your awareness on your breathing. Various thoughts and feeling inevitably impinge and try to grab your attention. Don't fight them, don't judge them; simply bring your focus back to your breath.

Mindfulness is simple, yet quite powerful, and your soul thrives on it.

My Spiritual Practice for Today

The key to mindfulness is practice. Set aside 10 to 20 minutes a day, and try it for thirty days to see if it works for you. You can start today.

January 22

Seeing in the Dark (Pat)

There will always be times of darkness in your life. Survivors know that better than most. You are not promised a life always filled with bright light. There are long nights when darkness seems to surround and envelop you. The darkness can be a period of depression and hopelessness or a time in which everything seems to go wrong or appears to be lined up against you. The darkness of trauma can return with a flashback or a painful memory. Such dark times can leave you seemingly blinded and staggering around in the dark, bumping into things and skinning your shins.

This is why it is helpful to develop the spiritual ability to see in the dark. Your soul wants to equip you with spiritual night vision goggles. You can, with soul help, develop the capacity to see and navigate by all the available light that you cannot ordinarily see. And there is always available light. You will sensitize your spiritual vision to see the light that is always there, though not at a wavelength you can see without your soul. There is always more light than you think. You can find it and learn to look in the right places for it. There are always hidden, brilliant blessings in the dark shadows of seemingly totally dark situations. Like walking in the woods on a night with a full moon, you will be able to see and navigate by the soul light that is always shining, even in the dark nights.

My Spiritual Practice for Today

Think back to a time that was particularly dark for you. What light and which blessings can you now perceive that were hidden in the dark? Take a situation that appears dark to you now. Try out your spiritual night vision goggles. Look at the situation with soul light. What light and hope could possibly be there that at first sight is hidden in the dark corners? What solutions or changes are available that you are not yet seeing? How might your soul or God be at work lighting a path for you?

January 23

Cling To or Move On? (Vicki)

What makes us cling to suffering even when it is time to let it go? Is it our unfinished business? Sometimes we cling to anger because we have not yet thought of how we might forgive that person who has deeply hurt us. At times, the thought of forgiveness is so far removed from where we find ourselves that we can't even think about the word. We can't see how it might possibly feel if we made a conscious decision to forgive. To be sure, every soul must take the journey to forgive perpetrators of violence; to forgive those who have emotionally abused us requires understanding. And yet, every spiritual practice calls us to forgiveness. An unforgiving heart is a sorrowful heart, a heart that is overwhelmed with sadness.

The poet Rumi says;

> Sorrow prepares you for joy. It violently sweeps everything out of your house so that new joy can find space to enter. It shakes the yellow leaves from the bough of your heart so that fresh, green leaves can grow in their place. It pulls up the rotten roots so that new roots hidden beneath have room to grow. Whatever sorrow shakes from your heart, far better things will take their place.

Whatever forgiveness "shakes from your heart, far better things will come to take their place." To forgive is to open up the expansiveness of the heart to allow it to love again. Forgiveness is change, and change is a conscious choice to move from one space, either physically, mentally, or emotionally, to another. Moving from status quo to a place of change can be likened to leaping over a deep ravine, hoping to reach the other side. Fear holds us in place where we feel safe and comfortable, even though the place we are in may not be what is best for us. The fear of the unknown within that place of change is sometimes too difficult to face. With courage and trust we are called to holy movement toward that which is best for us.

My Spiritual Practice for Today

Today may I practice forgiveness in small ways so that when it is time to forgive the larger issues, I will be prepared to authentically forgive all.

January 24

S.H.A.M.E. (Pat)

The spiritually corrosive power of toxic shame can be summarized in an acronym: S.H.A.M.E, which stands for "Shit Happening Appears to be ME" (based on the famous bumper sticker "Shit Happens"). Abuse and trauma leaves survivors with a strong emotional belief that what happened to them was somehow their fault or revealed some horrible inner truth about them. Shame from abuse feels real. It feels true that you are bad, defective, unlovable, etc.

The belief is deeply engrained in your mind, your emotions, and even your body. It becomes personal dogma, difficult to shake. When shame becomes so much a part of your self-image, it colors and filters all of your perceptions about yourself and your life. When bad stuff happens, you think it reveals some badness in you. You are constantly seeing what looks like confirmation about your shame in your life situations and in people's reaction to you.

It is vital to realize that shame is always a lie. Shit happening only appears to be you. The shit is not you. Your abuse gave you the appearance and the false feeling that it was an indictment of you. Your soul desperately seeks to free you from this lie. The abuse was not your fault, nor was it a reflection of who you are. Your shame lens distorts your spiritual sight so you can't see who you truly are: a magnificent person of great and infinite value. This is your soul's truth about you. Spiritual healing comes when you can label shame thoughts as lies and hear your soul—or God—whisper the truth of who you are deep within you. The healing continues as you bit by bit embrace this truth as your new creed and dogma.

My Spiritual Practice Today

Draw a line down the middle of a page in your journal. On the left side write all of the shame-based negative thoughts you have about yourself. Write the word "lie" next to each. On the right side, opposite each shame lie, write the truth that you hear from your soul or from God about each shame belief. Write "my eternal truth" next to each. Every time a shame lie pops into your head, label it a lie and speak your soul's truth to that lie.

January 25

Living in the Circle of Value (Pat & Sue)

A key to living your life's journey with serenity and joy is to know and live who you truly are. It is the awareness that your soul, your spiritual essence, is your True Self. Because of this, you are of inimitable and infinite value and worth, and nothing—including trauma and abuse—can add to or subtract from that value. It just is. If you carry this awareness with you wherever you go, whatever you experience, then every moment is a blessing. We call this living in the Circle of Value. Living each day in the circle of value, the circle of God's eternal love for you, is our ultimate goal for your healing journey.

Living in the Circle of Value means abiding in your center, in your True Self. It means knowing that nothing can diminish, tarnish, or separate you from your infinite magnificence and value. It is defining yourself not by any external measures of self-image or self-esteem, but by the image of God you were created from and by the soul-esteem your soul bequeaths to you—just because you are you. It is living in your inner sanctuary in the knowledge that you are loved and sustained by Infinite Love. In your inner sanctuary your essence cannot be harmed, abused, controlled, or shattered and is already perfect. Abiding in the Circle of Value frees you from fighting to defend your small self, your fearful, limiting ego. There is no need. You are not that little self. You are a magnificent person of infinite value. No person or event can take that from you. You can live from your big self, your True Self, your soul. You no longer need to expend and waste so much psychic energy in your self-defense, constantly striving to build up your self-image in the world. You live in the awareness that "I am a magnificent person (always and everywhere) of infinite value."

My Spiritual Practice for Today

Draw two concentric circles on a piece of paper or on your smartphone. In the inner circle write "True Self," your name, and the phrase, "I am a magnificent person of infinite value." Carry this with you to remind you to live each moment in your sacred Circle of Value.

January 26

Hatching Out of Helplessness (Vicki)

Don't do daily prayers like a bird
pecking, moving its head
up and down. Prayer is an egg.
Hatch out the total helplessness inside.
–Rumi

Whatever your religious tradition or choice of belief, this metaphor of prayer or pleading to a power much bigger than yourself can be a call to action. It's a reminder that you are required to be the active player in your own healing. Perhaps you think you can sit back, and something amazing will happen to make you feel better. Sorry, folks, it doesn't work like that—ever!

As Rumi writes, you have to hatch out of the total helplessness inside. You have a deep desire within you that wants what is best for you, that wants you to pursue your true purpose. Prayer and action go hand in hand. Your pleading and prayer can lead to the courage you need to break free of the chains that bind you, that keep you from saying yes to life! There is no room for playing the victim role.

Walking away from the debilitating feeling of helplessness is one of the most courageous steps you can take. Can you count the number of small situations in life that you have overcome? These are baby steps that prepare you to take the big steps of finding the strength and character of the True Self. As Richard Rohr writes:

> *"If we do not discover a prayer practice that invades our unconscious and reveals what is hidden, we will actually change very little over our lifetime."*

My Spiritual Practice for Today

Today the word "victim" will not be used to describe me! I choose to be a person of courage and conviction who seeks only to grow and overcome issues that have held me back from becoming my True Self. I am no longer a victim.

January 27

Being Childlike (Pat & Sue)

Jesus said, "Unless you change, and become like a little child, you will not enter the kingdom of God." (Matthew 18:3) Think of a little child who you know. Notice his or her childlike wonder and excitement about the world. Everything is fresh and new to them. Each day is a new adventure. They are open and curious. They are busy each day gobbling up new experiences, growing their brain, and expanding their spirit. Children are naturally spiritual.

You were like this at one point in your life. We all lose this to some degree and have to rediscover it in adulthood. Survivors often have their childlike spirit ripped away from them prematurely by their trauma. It is another loss and spiritual wound inflicted on you. You can recover your inner child and its delightful capacity for wonderment and transcendence. Jesus is saying that this will bring you into God's kingdom, Jesus's vision of how humans live in community with each other and God, here and in the hereafter.

Buddhists call this way of being "beginner's mind." They too recognize that this is natural in childhood and has usually been lost. They teach that beginner's mind is necessary to become awakened and mindful and that it can be relearned. It involves having an attitude of openness, eagerness, and a lack of preconceptions or prejudgment when studying spiritual teaching or entering meditation. Beginner's mind is an awakened mind; it is being childlike in spirit and open and alive to all the beauty, wonder, and mystery that is all around and inside you. Your soul says, "Be a child again, each day anew."

My Spiritual Practice for Today

Go for a walk in a natural setting. Look at everything you see as if you are seeing it for the first time. Adopt the eyes of a child and the mind of the beginner. Be alive and present to all that is around you. Take delight in the light on the branches and leaves of the trees. Stop for colorful flowers and smell their fragrance. Feel the air, warm or cold, brushing by your cheeks. If you encounter another person, look at them like a walking mystery and a living miracle. Carry this childlike wonder to everything you encounter all day.

January 28

Find the Good and Praise It (Pat)

Two of my survivor clients have favorite sayings that describe their attitudes about people and relationships: "Find the good and praise it" and "Believe the best; forgive the rest." Their philosophy is to look for what's right with people rather than what's wrong with them. It's to believe in the core goodness of people, look for it, and then strengthen that goodness by affirming it. You assume the positive rather than automatically judging the negative, and you are open to forgive the hurtful mistakes. This is a transformative perspective about the people in your life.

These two sayings can also be applied to yourself: look for the good in yourself and praise it; believe the best about yourself, and forgive the rest. In fact, if you do this with yourself, it will be easier to apply to others.

Some survivors may resist and even scoff at these philosophies. Your instinct might be to assume the worst about people and furiously scan for what's wrong or dangerous about them, even in your close relationships. This is understandable. You were badly hurt. Your trust was manipulated and betrayed. It's hard to believe in the best of humanity when you have experienced the worst. The only safe policy seems to be to assume the worst about people and make them prove their goodness and trustworthiness to you. You keep your abuse radar on high alert at all times. It is an understandable reaction, yet it will lead you to live in constant fear and skepticism, and remain distant and isolated.

However, you can do both. You can keep your abuse radar on and still look for and believe in the good. Yes, of course, stay on the lookout for abuse, but at the same time see and trust the good in yourself and in the people in your life.

My Spiritual Practice for Today

Reflect on the two sayings from my clients. Act today as if they are your philosophy about people as well. Notice how you feel.

January 29

F.E.A.R. (Pat)

F.E.A.R. is an acronym that stands for False Evidence Appearing Real. Abuse and trauma can fill you with so much fear that it distorts your vision, including your spiritual vision, and you begin to see fear everywhere and about everyone. Even when there is no reason to be afraid, your hyper-vigilance—which developed to protect you—can see danger even when it is not there. It finds "evidence" that appears to confirm your fears and feels real and dangerous sometimes when it is not. Certainly, some fears are realistic—there are some scary situations and some scary people out there—and a healthy level of concern for self is an important part of self-care. However, a fear that is all consuming and that sometimes sees danger when it is not there is unhealthy and debilitating.

Fear then becomes become a spiritual illness, a sickness of the soul. This is beyond the feeling of fear or the experience of anxiety, which we all have, and which can be a healthy, self-protective emotion. Fear becomes a soul sickness when it is a way of life, when it is your basic stance in and against life. Fear freezes you into paralysis, controls you, and robs you of joy, peace, serenity, and connection. Fear constructs a frozen fortress around your soul, which becomes its prison. Fear becomes a life script and a self-fulfilling prophecy, which blurs and distorts your vision, keeping you from seeing what is safe and loving and trustworthy in your life.

Patrick Carnes writes in *Recovery Zone,* "All therapy and recovery is about coming to terms with fear." How do you need to come to terms with the fears your trauma created in you?

My Spiritual Practice for Today

Meditate on this saying that comes out of the twelve-step programs: "Fear knocked at the door; faith answered and no one was there." When are your fears based in real concern and healthy self-care, and when are they false readings of a person or situation based in a mind traumatized to see danger everywhere? How can you use your faith—in God, in your soul, in the fundamental goodness of the universe—to see when the fear that seems to always knock at the door of your mind is not really there?

January 30

From Vulnerability to Strength (Vicki)

Author and lecturer Brene Brown writes, "Owning our story can be hard but not nearly as difficult as spending our lives running from it…Only when we are brave enough to explore the darkness will we discover the infinite power of our light."

I can't imagine where my life would be today if I hadn't embraced the darkness of grief and abuse. As a young girl, I lost my sister, Becca, age 5, in a terrible auto accident. Our parish priest entered our lives then, visiting often, and began acting as a surrogate father to my brothers and me. I remember him coming to the hospital to see us. My brother Steve and I shared a room. Seeing Father walk into our hospital room is the only vivid memory I have of the hours after the accident. It felt like God had just walked into the room. After we returned home, Father dropped in to see us often. Over time our allegiance to him grew, and I felt especially close to him. His frequent visits to our home were highlights for us. I loved my dad, but Father held a special place in all of our hearts.

Although no one saw it, he was reeling me into an emotional dependence on him, and by the time I was in my late teens, the sexual abuse had begun.

Owning this story is the hardest thing I have ever done. The bravery it took to speak out and shed light on what was going on was monumental. I didn't see a bright light at the end of the tunnel for a very long time. Slowly, as I had the courage to share my story, I began to see glimmers of hope that my life could be different. We must stay the course and see our way through to the light. There is no other way but through.

My Spiritual Practice for Today

The unknown answers can weigh us down. Continuing to ask the questions that lead to healing answers and outcomes is essential. Today I promise myself that I will not be afraid of telling my story so the answers to my questions can bring about the healing I so desperately seek. Today I know that in my deepest vulnerability, the questions are there to be asked. The solutions that point to a new understanding are waiting for me.

January 31

FF (Pat & Sue)

Your soul's triumph over fear, and the healing of these spiritual wounds caused by traumatic fear, is the gift or grace of spiritual courage. One day fairly early in our relationship, we were taking a drive along country roads outside of St. Louis. We were talking intensely about the many uncertainties and fearful choices that were confronting us. In that moment, we were both filled with and paralyzed by our fears. We turned a corner of the winding road and suddenly came to a T intersection with a new road, County Road FF.

We sat there for a moment silently contemplating this sign. One of us, probably Sue, said, "That road sign stands for Fuck Fear. Let's turn onto it." (Pardon the language here, but no other words fit so well or capture the force of our experience—besides, that's what we said! If you prefer you could use "Fie on Fear!") So we did.

FF became a code word for us, a reminder to find the courage our God had given us to push through our fears and not allow them to control us. Spiritual courage became the choice, determination, and grace to travel the FF highway. This did not mean we did not feel fear—courage is not the absence of fear; it meant we would not live defined and confined by fear. So **FF!**

My Spiritual Practice for Today

You can find your own FF moment! Say the words to yourself: "FF." They can be as empowering and fear dispelling for you as they were for us. You are saying, "I renounce fear and all of its works and all of the ways it binds me emotionally and spiritually." This does not make it go away. You will still feel fear and its negative energy, yet you will start to dip your toe into the more powerful current of your soul's courage and begin to move through and against your fear. Your soul applauds and rejoices! Let FF be your mantra today. Repeat it over and over, and feel its power to loosen and dispel the grip your old fears have on you.

February 1

The Mountain Meditation: Your Fear (Sue & Pat)

My Spiritual Practice for Today

We invite you to do a powerful guided meditation that we call the Mountain Meditation. To enter into this meditation, find a comfortable sitting position. As you read, pause, close your eyes, and imagine the scenes described.

Picture yourself on a beautiful beach. See the waves, the sand, the brilliant color, and the vastness of the ocean. Feel the sun and the wind on your skin. Hear the crash and whoosh of the surf. Turn around now, and face away from the sea. Looking down, you see a backpack. In it are your fears, the fears that control your mind and sap your spirit. Pick it up and place it on your back. Notice how it feels to carry your fears.

In front of you is a beautiful forest. See yourself walking along a trail into the forest. Appreciate the coolness and the shaded light. You reach the edge of the forest and see an open meadow filled with multicolored wildflowers. The trail leads you through the meadow to a clear, flowing stream with a bridge across the dancing water. Stop for a moment to enjoy the light sparkling on the water.

Now look up from the bridge and see a shining mountain before you. Following the trail, you ascend the mountain. You climb through the clouds, above the timberline to the top of the peak. Look around you at the glory of creation. Then you notice a large boulder to sit on and rest. You take off your backpack and unload your fears.

Then, from the other side of the peak, your spiritual being and mentor comes and sits down with you on the boulder. You can discuss whatever you want. Be sure to give the being your fears and ask for the gift of peace. Hear your spiritual guide say to you, "Be not afraid. I am with you always."

When you are ready to leave, thank your guide. Remember what was said to you. Slowly hike back down the mountain, over the bridge, through the meadow, through the forest, to the beach, and to the edge of the vast ocean. Open your eyes. Journal what you experienced and what the being at the top of the mountain said to you.

February 2

Groundhog Day: Seeing Your Own Shadow (Pat)

Today is Groundhog's Day. Punxsutawney Phil, the most famous groundhog of them all, did not see his shadow. This means we will have an early spring, which sounds like great news, but the poor groundhog actually has it all backward. As it pertains to human beings, only when we see our shadow can spring come.

The idea of the shadow part of our personality comes from psychiatrist Carl Jung. Jung taught that the shadow is the darker side of our personality that we are unaware of and resist seeing. When we fail to see our shadow, these parts of us will act up in our life. They will disturb our peace, distort our perceptions, and often get projected onto other people in hurtful ways. The idea of the shadow is similar to the twelve-step program's idea of "character defects" that Steps 6 and 7 challenge us to identify in ourselves and then "humbly ask God to remove." They are unhealed, unredeemed places, patterns of darkness, and artifacts of our ego that are not bad in themselves, and yet can stir up trouble for us.

The springtime of your heart and soul comes when you see your shadow and face it honestly, fearlessly, and with great self-compassion and the knowledge of God's warm, merciful embrace. This feels scary, especially for survivors, so the temptation is to turn away. Yet if you see your shadow, embrace it, and bring it into the light of God's love, humbly asking God to remove it, it will be transformed and become a gift for you and others. Then the forecast for you is an early and glorious spring bursting with new life.

My Spiritual Practice for Today

Reflect on some part of you that you have been afraid to face. Don't shame yourself for this. We all have a shadow. Bring this part of you into meditation and imagine the light of your soul or the light of God enveloping and embracing that part of you with great love and acceptance. Be aware of what you feel as you experience this.

February 3

Through The Eyes of A Child (Sue)

One day many years ago, my oldest grandson, Jason, and I went for a walk. Jason was three. We had walked only a few steps down our street when Jason got very excited and said, "Granny, do you hear it?" I didn't hear anything. Jason pulled my hand to walk faster toward a small strip of woods between houses about a half a block away. He said again, "Do you hear it? It's a waterfall." Now I heard a little trickle of water. Jason pulled me toward a small creek flowing through the woods. "Do you see the waterfall now, Granny?" I didn't see any waterfall. Then Jason pointed to a spot in the creek where the water fell about two feet over a couple of rocks. This was Jason's waterfall. I joined him then in his excitement over the beauty of the waterfall before us, the water glistening and musically trickling down at our feet.

I always remember this story when my eyes have gone dull, when I have stopped seeing the natural and spiritual miracles all around me. Little children see with a freshness and natural awe that most of us grownups have lost. They see things we don't even notice. We can learn, though, to see again as children see. I do this daily by noticing the small beauties: the light on the white bark of a sycamore in winter; the delight in Pat's voice when we share a laugh; the light in a grandchild's eyes when she achieves a new skill; the color of the sunset each day; the excitement of looking for a rainbow on a rainy day.

I know it is even harder for survivors to keep fresh eyes. Trauma has clouded and darkened your vision. My grandchildren and great-grandchildren have helped me relearn to see. You can do the same. Either with your children or grandchildren, or with your own inner child, you can see the world of wonders brand new through the eyes of a child.

My Spiritual Practice for Today

See everything today through the eyes of your inner child. Look for all of the small "miracles" that surround you that normally only little children see. Walk about in wonder and delight today.

February 4

Shame as a Turning Point (Vicki)

It seems everyone is ashamed of something. From small childhood lies and the accompanying penance after getting caught to the larger shame that comes from getting older and carrying more responsibility. Do we want to feel shame for years, or do we want to get over it quickly and move on? I would guess that many of us, depending on the issue, would rather wallow for a time in private shame rather than muster up the courage to speak the truth. Why is the truth so difficult? Perhaps it's the fear of being judged too harshly or that our lives would be forever stained by that judgment.

Carrying the shame of abuse can feel like a thousand pounds on your back. We seem so ready to carry that weight as we put off addressing the secret. It's easy to bury those thoughts deeply so we only think of them occasionally in the middle of the night or when something we read rings true to our own personal story. We all want to be stellar human beings, and admitting our hidden secrets seems like losing control of our lives.

I felt shame because I had allowed this relationship with an abusive man to take control of my life. I should have known better; I should have stopped it when it started. I should have told a responsible adult. Why didn't I? Because I felt special and appreciated? All these thoughts continued to feed my shame. I kept telling myself it was my fault. That is, until I looked at the relationship that our pastor had with my entire family, until I began to understand that I had been groomed to always say yes to Father since I was 8 years old. Then I was able to begin to let go of the shame and say it wasn't my fault. I did not initiate his sexual advances. I didn't have the knowledge I needed to say no.

We know so much more today about sexual abuse and how devastating it can be. We know how damaging it can be to the souls of children, adolescents, and even young adults when there is no equality of power.

My Spiritual Practice for Today

I will pay attention to my inner knowing. Today I know fully what is appropriate and what is not. I know I have the ability to say no to whatever is unhealthy for me. I will protect myself to the best of my ability from those who wish to do me harm.

February 5

Wounds of the Spirit (Pat & Sue)

To help our survivor clients become aware of the spiritual wounds caused by their trauma, we developed the Spiritual Laundry List for Adult Children from Dysfunctional or Abusive Families. *Read through these and pick three that most affect you. These can be the focus of your healing through the upcoming year.*

The Grease, Grit, and Grime: We seem to have several spiritual characteristics in common as a result of being raised in a wounded, dysfunctional, or abusive household.

- We have imaged our Higher Power, the God of our understanding, in a distorted way because of our childhood experience of our dysfunctional, addicted, or abusive parent (or other significant adult).
- We find it difficult to discover and experience the God of our understanding or, at times, even perceive within us the existence of a Higher Power at all.
- We have come to believe that God is not faithful, that God is as unpredictable and untrustworthy as our wounded and abusive parent or other abuser.
- We have come to believe that God's love is conditional and that we have God's acceptance only if we are perfect.
- We think our Higher Power demands more of us than we can give or handle, just as we once felt overwhelmed by the needs of our dysfunctional families or by the trauma of our abuse.
- We find it difficult or impossible to trust our Higher Power.
- Our spirituality is grim and lacks hope, joy, or serenity; we find it difficult to be hopeful or trust in the gift of love available to us.
- We are consumed with the past, anxious about the future, and unable to simply be in the moment with God, with another person, or with God's creation.
- We fear being abandoned by our Higher Power and so resist being drawn closer to God.
- We struggle with major commitments, or even becoming aware of our life-vision, purpose, and journey.

- Our spirituality is based on a sense of shame and unreasonable guilt, and is dominated by "shoulds."
- We find it difficult to be grateful.
- We have become addicted to religion.

February 6

Images of Your Higher Power (Pat & Sue)

We have imaged our Higher Power, the God of our understanding, in a distorted way due to our childhood experience of our dysfunctional, addictive, or abusive parent (or other significant adult).
–The Spiritual Laundry List

Because God is within you, in the light of your soul, God was abused when you were abused. Part of the abuse of God is that God's image gets distorted. It is a tragic effect of abuse that your picture of God so often becomes damaged, and as a result, your potential for a healing and meaningful relationship with God is inhibited or blocked. Damage to a survivor's image of God is especially pronounced when there is clerical sexual abuse, religious abuse, or abuse by a parent. Trust is destroyed, shame and fear are injected, and abandonment and rejection are experienced. Often, this gets projected onto God. You come to believe that God has abandoned and rejected you as well. It becomes difficult to trust God, to believe God is with you, loves you, and wants to draw close to you to comfort you and heal your pain.

The first step in resolving the problem is to identify how your abuse has influenced your image of God. Who is God for you? What is your picture of God? What parts of this picture have been shaped by your trauma or abuse? Does your perception of God facilitate a relationship, or does it inhibit or even block a relationship? When you go to God in prayer, meditation, or worship, what do you feel? Do you experience peace, love, strength, closeness, healing? Or do you feel guilt, shame, fear, distance, rejection, abandonment, or nothing at all? What adjectives would best describe who God is for you: loving, close, caring, nurturing, transcendent, awesome, or distant, cold, uncaring, punishing, vengeful, rejecting, condemning? Whose face do you have on God? Is it the true God of your faith, or is it the face of your abuser?

My Spiritual Practice for Today

Reflect on the above questions until you have a good idea of how you perceive God. How does your image make you feel, and how does it affect your spirituality?

February 7

A New Image of God (Pat)

Part of your healing journey is to search for new positive, life-giving images of God, free from the effects of your abuse. There are many resources available to help you find God anew. The Bible contains more than forty images of God. Go on a Bible search for them. Other spiritual traditions offer images of God you may find appealing. Talk to your soul friends about this. Who is God for them? The richest resource, though, is within you: Your own soul will guide you to a new vision of who God is for you. Listen to your soul quietly speaking to you in meditation, in nature, in dreams, in reading, in soul-searching reflection. Your soul will use all of these and more to help you in your search. Be awake to any new sense of a presence of something beyond you that yields peace, serenity, joy, freedom, or love. These experiences will help you put together a new puzzle that in time will look like the God of your understanding.

You will need to tap into your soul's courage to enter into this search for God. It is always challenging to leave behind your old beliefs and venture forth for new ones, even if the old ones made you miserable. They are familiar, secure, and paradoxically comforting. That is why letting go of them is so intimidating. If you are courageous and open to searching, you will find a new image of God, a divine and loving presence beyond your previous imagining. Then one day, you will experience a new kind of presence. You will feel that your God is truly with you, by your side, holding you in the palm of his loving hand. You will find a new peace and joy. You will experience being wanted, loved, cherished, and accepted. This comes to different people in different ways. Then you will be ready to let go of the false gods inflicted on you by your abuse and discover the true God of your understanding. Let your soul surprise you.

My Spiritual Practice for Today

In your journal write a description of the God of your new understanding. All day act as if you fully believe that this is truly your God and notice the difference this makes.

February 8

God Dwells within You (Pat)

God dwells within you as You! This is a paraphrase from a line spoken by Julia Roberts in the movie, *Eat, Pray, Love.* It is a stunning statement with equally stunning implications. It means you have divinity within you, a divine spark of sacred energy and light, and that divinity abides in you as your True Self. It means that God is not out there somewhere beyond reach; God is right here, right now, reachable, touchable within you. You do not have to seek God elsewhere. Seek God within you. Do you want to know God? Get to know yourself. The more you know and love your True Self, the more you know and love God.

None of this is to say that God is not a being who is also transcendent; that is why we use the term "Higher Power." We need to be in relationship to a being that is beyond us. However, this doesn't mean we can think of ourselves as God. We all know people who think they are God. They are arrogant and superior. They suffer from what could be called Deity Delusion Disorder.

Words are insufficient to fully capture the meaning of Julia Roberts's statement. Perhaps it is best said like this: You are not God, and yet you are divine, and God shows up within you as You! All of these stunning spiritual truths can be incredibly healing for survivors. Because you are where God chooses to pitch his tent, you are of eternal and infinite value and worth. The more you absorb this reality, the more you will push out and evaporate your shame. If you accept that getting to know yourself will also lead you to know God, no longer will you run away from your inner emotions, intuitions, and inspirations. You will learn to trust yourself, and thus trust God. Because of your shame, it may be difficult for you to believe these spiritual realities about yourself. And yet your True Self knows the truth of who you are: Simply divine!

My Spiritual Practice for Today

Meditate on Julia Roberts's statement and what it means to you and your healing. How does it change your spirituality? How does it change your view of you?

February 9

Grief, the Price of Love (Vicki)

"Grief never ends…but it changes. It's a passage, not a place to stay. Grief is not a sign of weakness, nor a lack of faith…It is the price of love."
–Source unknown

Loving myself was difficult for many years. Besides, who ever talked about self-love in their early adult years, even though there is plenty of self-indulgence? Loving oneself is something we begin to understand at a more mature age, isn't it? It's difficult to think of healthy self-care in the midst of a busy life with school, friends, and an active, fun social life. Life is lived at a more frenetic pace in those early years of adulthood with that sense of invincibility. I wasn't willing to stop and realize how stuck I was in that unhealthy relationship in those years of adulthood. For lack of anything better, we stay where we are, hoping it will get better. It wasn't until I took some courageous steps toward seeking help that my life began to unravel, and then it could be sewn back together again in a more positive way.

The grief of having lost so many formative years to a secret and abusive relationship was painful. It changed over the years, though. All grief changes with time; we hope to find a place to hold it without it consuming us. It somehow buoys us to endure the next sadness or loss.

What can we learn from this darkness? Many spiritual writers refer to the darkness of grief as liminal space; it can be a time of great understanding if we allow the grief to speak its wisdom. Rather than hold on to the grief, can we be aware that it is there to teach us and allow the wisdom to wash over us? Loving self means we are willing and capable of enduring the sadness that is sure to come into every life. It is love that carries us forward to new life. And love begins within our own hearts.

My Spiritual Practice for Today

Grieving the losses of life means getting in touch with the love I carry for myself. Today I will be aware that grief is the bridge to a new life built on love, which starts in my own heart.

February 10

Resisting Happiness (Sue)

Over the years I have witnessed some of my survivor clients fight and resist their own happiness even when it is readily available to them. I call this, "The fear of having it good." It at first was puzzling that some of my clients exhibited this. They wanted to be happy, yet they often fought the opportunity to be happy. What's going on here?

I soon realized that this is another trauma wound that creates this fear of allowing happiness, peace, and pleasure into your life. The wound takes several forms. You desperately want to be happy or have peace, yet when you approach it, you feel you do not deserve it, so you stop it. You resist because feeling miserable feels normal; feeling good feels new and strange, and you don't know what to do with it, so you return to familiar misery. Your trauma has led you to want to always be in control; happiness requires letting go of control. So it feels safer to be unhappy. It also feels safer to hold onto being "right" that you're wrong and bad and undeserving of feeling good. When you have a moment of happiness, you are afraid to trust it because you fear that it will be snatched away from you and you will be left worse off than before. The "solution" is to not let yourself be happy! You can see how this fear of having it good can lead to what I call an "addiction to misery."

God and your soul do not want this misery for you. God and your soul desire an abundance of happiness, peace, joy, and healthy pleasure for you. They invite you to a life banquet of the nourishing soul food of joy and delight. They invite and lovingly challenge you to trust them and trust happiness. Let go of your fear of being happy. Stop fighting it. Allow yourself to fully feel and receive the happiness offered, and know that you are safe in enjoying it. As the song says, "Don't worry! Be happy!"

My Spiritual Practice for Today

Look for opportunities to be happy, joyful, or at peace today. Resist your impulse to run away. Choose to risk and embrace your moment of happiness. Tell yourself you are safe, and simply enjoy.

February 11

Give Me the Life I Was Meant to Live (Vicki)

Opening the Heart
Paula D'Arcy

Please help me.
I want to keep opening my heart.
I'm healing at my own pace
and in my own way, and yet
I share this life/death cycle with all creation.
I'm beginning to look beyond myself.
I've focused only on these losses
for so long. But many people suffer,
and there is so much to think about
if I really want to live in the world differently.
My life before this grief was so innocent.
I had no idea what heartache felt like,
or how strong the waves of grief could be.
I had no idea, really, about you.
I kept you in a compartment
and only thought of you
when I wanted something.
I don't know what it is like to live
from a heart that is truly open,
and to love from that freedom.
But I want to know.
Please, transform the old me.

Could these heartfelt words from Paula D'Arcy speak to our grief, our loss? We can remain trapped in the sorrow of our grief, whether from the loss of a loved one or the loss of the life we had always hoped for. It felt as though I was enslaved to this man who only wanted to use me for his own pleasure, for his own vision of life. I was trapped and could not imagine how to walk away. It was a brainwashing for sure. I grieved the loss of the life I wanted for myself.

I ask my Higher Power for the courage to transform the old me into the woman that I want to become. Give me the strength to move out and away and into life, the life I was meant to live.

My Spiritual Practice for Today

What is enslaving me or holding me back from living the life I was meant to live? Today I want to think and write about those things that are holding me back. Give me the courage to unblock what is keeping me from living my life.

February 12

Love Your Body (Pat & Sue)

We proclaim today National Love Your Body Day! Your body needs and deserves this from you.

Many trauma survivors find it difficult to feel good about their bodies. Some even feel alienated, detached, or distant from their bodies. This is particularly true if you are a survivor of sexual or physical abuse where your body itself was the target of the abuse. You may feel ashamed of parts or the whole of your body. Some survivors of sexual abuse even feel that their body betrayed them because it responded to the abuse with natural sexual responses.

Maybe you were verbally body shamed by family, by kids at school, or even by societal stereotypes: "You're too fat. Too thin. You're skin is too dark. Too light. Wrong hair. Wrong shape, etc." All of this can make it difficult to love and take good care of your body.

So today befriend your body. Nurture and indulge your body. Love your body, and reclaim it from abuse. See the magnificence of each and every part of your body. It is an amazing organism, an astoundingly beautiful creation. Thank your body today for serving you so well. Remind yourself that your body is the sacred temple that embodies and expresses your divinity, your soul. It is where God and the material world meet and commune. So enjoy your body and all its delights today. Feed it tasty and healthy food. Exercise and stretch your body, put it through its paces, and feel the joy of how your body performs for you. Put your hand over your heart or pulse, and feel the miracle of life coursing through your arteries and veins. Pamper your body by taking a long soaking bath or shower, getting a massage, or simply giving it some extra rest.

Celebrate your body today and shower it with love. Your body will thank you.

My Spiritual Practice for Today

Spend 10 to 15 minutes in front of the mirror and look at each part of your body. See the beauty and the miracle of your body. Affirm each part of your body and thank it for its service. Then pick one way to nurture your body today and gift your body with it.

February 13

Love Your Sexuality (Pat & Sue)

Human sexuality is a wondrously complex gift involving our bodies, brains (our main sex organ), relationships, the creation of new life, and even our relationship with our soul and with God. Sexuality has been called a "Holy Longing." This powerful longing lifts us out of our small ego selves to unite with the beloved other and beyond to divinity. Sex is a school of love where we are challenged to learn how to give and receive love, how to lose our self in pleasure and ecstasy, and how to communicate love and open ourselves to intimacy ("In To Me You See"). Sexuality and sexual imagery has been used in many sacred scriptures and spiritual writings to express a deep desire for and union with God.

Healing your sexuality after sexual trauma is often one of the most difficult parts of the healing journey for survivors. You are not alone in your struggle with sex. It's depth and complexity are what make sexuality so glorious and all humans so prone to make mistakes with its power. Your sexuality is powerful, beautiful, and holy. However, your sexual trauma likely has left you ashamed of your sexuality and afraid of its power.

The central part of sexual healing is to counter that shame and fear by learning to love your sexuality and trust its goodness and power to kindle love and spirit. You love your sexuality by accepting your sexual self as you are, including some of your sexual wounds. You love your sexuality by affirming and loving every inch of your body, especially the sexual parts. You love and heal your sexuality by giving yourself permission to enjoy its excitement and pleasures. You love your sexuality by reclaiming your sexuality as yours alone and developing a voice that can freely say no or yes to sexual requests. You heal your sexuality each time you dress yourself attractively.

The depth of healing comes when you embrace your own sexuality as a holy, divine fire whose heat and light, passion and pleasure are a gift, a grace from your soul and your God.

My Spiritual Practice for Today

Reflect on what you feel about your sexuality. Recall the messages positive and negative you received about your sexual self. Choose one way to reclaim and love your sexuality today.

February 14

A World Without Love (Pat)

Let's do a thought experiment together on this Valentine's Day. Thought experiments are carried out in scientists' imaginations to test their theories.

Einstein used them in developing his Theory of Relativity. Imagine that gravity has suddenly stopped working. What would happen? We would start floating around in our homes or offices and start bumping into each other. We would all have to operate like astronauts on the International Space Station, catching our food, our tools, and our children in midair. Nothing would stay put, things would start to fall apart, and the universe would start to unravel. The moon would wander off. The earth would sling out of orbit and head off to the deep reaches of space, if it didn't smash into Jupiter. The sun would explode, cease to warm and light us, and spew out its fierce gasses to incinerate us. We can't see gravity and don't think much about it. Yet we know how much we need and depend on its invisible force.

Imagine now a world without the invisible force of love. What if Infinite Love stopped working in the universe? What would happen to us and to our world? Something similar and even more devastating would happen. Love is what ultimately binds us together. Love attracts us to each other and holds us close. Love guides and empowers us to compassionate and healing choices. Love is *the* life force that brings all life into being and maintains it in existence. Without love the world would fly apart into chaos, coldness, and total darkness. Picture Europe during World War II under Hitler's domination—a world without love. Hate, violence, darkness, and evil reigned.

What theory does this thought experiment suggest? Love is an invisible force that is infinitely more powerful and necessary than gravity. It is the ultimate force that holds all things together. For some survivors it is difficult to believe in love or see it in their life. This is understandable because you were a victim of a loveless act. Yet, even when you don't see love, it is present, doing its work, and drawing us to itself. Don't give up on gravity! Don't give up on love!

My Spiritual Practice for Today

Be aware today of the invisible force field of love. Be open to see its effects in your life. The force is with you always!

February 15

Whose Beloved Are You? (Vicki)

"Whose beloved are you?" I asked,
"You who are so unbearably beautiful?"
"My own," he replied,
"For I am one and alone
Love, lover and beloved
Mirror, beauty, eye."
–Fakhruddin Iraqui

Self-esteem wasn't a phrase I spent much time thinking about. I was young and giving my life away to a degree that was unhealthy. Being a workaholic and stuck in an unhealthy relationship that I was hiding from everyone who loved me, even my best friend, was beginning to take its toll. Healthy self-care wasn't something I understood. Keeping my abuser happy was all that needed to happen. Anything he asked of me would be achieved. Being stuck in a cycle of workaholism can be deadly. Using it to hide something else exacerbates the unhealthiness of it. I wasn't eating or sleeping well. I was jumpy and always felt tremendous pressure to deliver.

Talking to a trusted friend and counselor allowed me to look at this unhealthy lifestyle and question why I was hurting myself this way. I began to see that I wasn't just being abused, I was being used to achieve someone else's vision. Did I love myself? I couldn't answer that question. What did that mean? Whose beloved was I? These were all challenging questions to reflect on. Of course, I had to love myself. If I didn't care enough to take care of myself, then who would? That is the ultimate question.

"For I am one and alone, love, lover and beloved." We are all these expressions of love. Love is the ultimate healer; love is the binder of all wounds. When we abandon ourselves to a higher love, we turn ourselves over to a greater healer who can bind all our wounds. Our reflection in the mirror doesn't always reveal who we believe we are. Working toward loving the beauty we see in the mirror is the work of learning to love ourselves. Loving ourselves is the fruit of deep soul work. We often turn away from the beauty of our true selves because of false perceptions. Only we can peel away the façade and reveal our true beauty.

My Spiritual Practice for the Day

I know today how important it is to learn to love myself, to appreciate the gifts that I have to share with the world. Loving myself is key to taking the steps needed to create a healthy lifestyle.

February 16

Love Your Emotions (Pat & Sue)

Survivors have an uneasy relationship with their emotions. Because painful emotions are connected to your trauma memories, you will either tend to suppress all of your feelings, feel nothing and be numb; or feel your emotions too deeply and be controlled by them.

Either extreme doesn't work very well. The result is that you are robbed of the vital role that your emotions play in giving you energy and information that you need to function well. Your emotions are meant to work with the thinking regions of your brain to process the information from your senses and perceptions and make decisions about how to best respond to your needs. Their purpose is to be an inner barometer of how you are doing at any particular time and how to make it better for you. Emotions are an on/off system. You either allow yourself to feel all of your emotions or none of them at all. To feel joy, you have to allow sadness. If you remain afraid of your emotions and avoid them, you will know little about what you most need, and you will be bereft of the juiciness, color, and energy of life.

Emotions are your friends, even when they make you feel bad for a time. Part of your healing is to gradually rediscover and love your emotional self and learn to listen to it. If you do this, you might feel uncomfortable at first because it is new. Sometimes, too, your feelings come back very strongly. Just breathe and ride them out like you are riding a wave on a surfboard. Allow yourself to feel what is happening inside, and do not be afraid. You are safe to feel your emotions. They will dissipate in time if you don't fight them.

You will come to know your emotions as gifts to open, feel, treasure, and learn from. They are also sources of grace and spiritual energy that will lift you up in ecstasy to the heights of the divine.

My Spiritual Practice for Today

Name your emotions as they bubble up through the day. Allow yourself to feel them. Listen intently to at least one of them, and hear what need it is alerting you to. Respond and take care of that need.

February 17

4.5 Billion... (Pat)

4.5 billion, 13.8 billion, and 10 trillion—staggering, mind-blowing numbers. They represent, respectively, the age of Earth, the age of the universe, and the number of galaxies (with an average of 100 billion stars in each) in the universe. These are the commonly agreed upon numbers from scientists today. Take a moment and contemplate these numbers and the age and the incomprehensible vastness that they represent. When I do this, my mind goes "tilt" like an old-fashioned pinball machine shutting down because it is overwhelmed. What happens to you?

Or contemplate scientists' description of the birth of the universe, called the Big Bang Theory. The whole universe began 13.8 billion years ago as a singularity point of immense density and energy, which exploded and expanded out to become our universe, and eventually you and me. The whole universe was contained in that singular point. Again, this is mind bending. And to that picture add black holes, quasars, pulsars, white dwarf and red giant stars, supernovas, thousands of known planets, hundreds of them possibly similar to Earth.

If your mind cannot fully comprehend all of this, your soul can. You are invited to respond with wonder and awe, deep spiritual states of your whole being as it takes in the magnificence, enormity, and glory of the cosmos as we know it. This cosmological awe can make you feel small and humble—as perhaps it should—and yet lead you to an ecstatic wonderment that expands your mind and spirit like the Big Bang did to the universe.

My Spiritual Practice for Today

Go outside tonight and look up at the night sky. As you gaze at the stars and the planets, and possibly the moon, contemplate the age and vastness of the universe of which you can only see a small and relatively recent part. Be open to any response that your heart and your soul produce in you. Be open to awe and wonder at the miracle and magnificence you behold. Be aware that you are a magnificent and expansive part of this incredible grandeur. Know that you are one with it all.

February 18

The Being at Your Center (Pat & Sue)

The being at your center is you, your True Self, also called your soul. The being at your center is Spirit, by some called God. The being at your center is truly both, the place within you where your True Self and your Higher Power meet and commune. The life of soul and Spirit is about working hard to cut a path to your deeper self that waits patiently for you to arrive, perhaps tired, aching, and out of breath. Once the path to your soul is cleared and the being at your center is discovered, you can return to the external world in intimate relationship to your soul. You will then possess a deeper, more peaceful and serene sense of home, which you will carry with you wherever you are.

For many survivors, the work of cutting a path to your soul is especially difficult, and the path itself may appear dark and obstructed with emotional landmines and giant spiritual boulders. You may be burdened with shame that lies to you and tells you are bad and undeserving of the magnificence with which your soul and Spirit endow you. You may feel abandoned or even wounded by God. You will struggle to reconcile your trauma with a loving soul and a loving God.

No matter what the obstacles are, your soul will light the path. Your soul and Spirit will give you the strength to move aside the boulders. You will be given the vision and courage to defuse and disarm the landmines. This year of meditations will provide you road maps, a GPS, and all the spiritual tools that you need to create this life-giving path to your soul. You will emerge from this year with a new and deeper relationship with your soul and Spirit. You will come home, perhaps for the first time.

My Spiritual Practice for Today

Reflect on your relationship to your soul and your relationship to Spirit. How strong is it? How easily can you connect? What obstacles do you experience to having a clear path and open access to your deepest and True Self? What spiritual practices or actions could you take to light and open up your inner path?

February 19

The Need to Be Loved (Vicki)

God Just Came Near
No
One
In need of love
Can sit with my verse for
An hour
And then walk away without carrying
Golden tools,
And feeling that God
Just came near.
–Hafiz

I traveled to Haiti on mission once and visited an orphanage for abandoned children. Toddlers and infants filled the rooms of this large vessel of love for these babes. Six of us arrived at the front door to offer our help. The sisters who cared for these beautiful children, day in and day out, said only, "Love and hold as many of the babies as you can. They are so hungry for human affection, and we do not have enough hours in the day to meet this need."

Our hearts were immediately broken, and we understood. We initially felt this would be easy, maybe fun. Yet after holding the first baby and feeling them melt into our bodies, we realized how heart wrenching it would be to lay each one down. The babies who had the strength to cling to us like little chimps, with their arms and legs wrapped tightly around us, had to be pried from us so we could hold another child. Many of us wept each time this happened. None of us had ever known the ravenous hunger of needing to be touched, to be loved.

We spent the morning with the babies. On our way back to the mission center, there was only silence. Secretly we wanted to bring those babies home with us to love. That evening we shared what that experience meant. We felt that God had walked near to us that day and that feeling would remain with us for a long time.

Grief comes to us as the fruit of many lived experiences of sorrow and joy. We grieved for the babies we held. Sharing ourselves with those who need us is a way of healing our own grief. Tears flow easily for me, a gift I suppose. That day, holding so many babies, I grieved the loss of not having my own children to love. The abusive relationship I was in kept me from getting married and starting my own family.

My Spiritual Practice for Today

Today I will reflect on the ways I can grow through my grief by being present to those around me. Can I nurture my grief, heal my grief, by giving to others?

February 20

Abandonment (Pat & Sue)

We fear being abandoned by our Higher Power
and so resist being drawn closer to God.
–The Spiritual Laundry List from *Shattered Soul,* p. 36–37

Many survivors were emotionally or physically abandoned when they were young. This is very painful and frightening. Children cannot care for themselves, so abandonment feels like it is a matter of life-and-death survival.

A deep fear of abandonment is created that continues into adulthood. This has a profound effect on relationships. You fear being abandoned again, so you keep people at a distance. You practice preventive abandonment by pushing people away before they can even start to get close. This creates great barriers in human relationships.

It also affects your relationship to your Higher Power. If you felt abandoned by your human parent, you will project this onto God. You may have felt abandoned by God in the midst of your trauma, wondering where God was when it happened. Don't feel bad about feeling this way; during his trauma on the cross, Jesus cried out, "My God, my God, why have you forsaken me." In reaction, you will keep your distance, fearing to let God come close. You may even totally reject God.

Healing this fear of abandonment can be scary. You fear letting down your guard, even with God. Your healing task is to muster the courage to begin to dismantle the barriers to love that were built up in you. You can gradually invite your Higher Power closer. You develop spiritual vision and see how God is there with and for you. You start to trust that grace, blessing, and love are there for you. For some it involves realizing that although your parents may have abandoned you, God did not. You stop projecting your parent's face onto God and believe that God is faithfully there for you. You rethink your history and can to see how God was with you all along.

My Spiritual Practice for Today

If you suffer from fear of abandonment, look at how this has affected all of your relationships, including with God. What first steps can you take to overcome that fear and let your God come closer?

SOUL LIGHT FOR THE DARK NIGHT

February 21

Baby Terese (Sue)

Oh, sweet Baby Terese, on this day in 1963, you blessed me with 45 minutes of your precious life. At that time, as an Rh-negative mother, the odds were slim, and yet you were born alive. How filled with blessings your short life was for me. My water broke in the lobby of the hospital, splashed on Dr. B's polished shoes! He immediately fetched a wheelchair, and zoom, off we went to the delivery room. You were born very quickly.

How beautiful you were. They wanted to whisk you off to the nursery to begin treatment. I said, "STOP!" I stretched out my arm and was able to cup and cuddle your sweet head in my hand. I can feel the softness and roundness of your tiny head to this moment. Then you were taken away.

In the recovery room, I had the most amazing and sacred experience. I dreamed each of your birthday celebrations from 1 to 21: Grandma's hot milk cake, candles, the circle of family singing "Happy Birthday," your siblings loving you—a beautiful life. Then, when your 21st celebration was complete, the pediatrician woke me and said you were now in heaven with your brother Billy (Billy also died soon after birth, the year before). I said, "I know, the angels have taken her home."

Terese, you were in my life so briefly, yet how deeply you touched my life. It's true, you only lived 45 minutes, and for 9 months we were so beautifully close. I'd caress my bulging belly and talk to you. I'd delight in your aquatic gymnastics as you swam around inside of me. Even now I am connected when I feel again your soft, smooth head and your peaceful energy. You came from God, breezed by with a sweet hello, and returned to God.

To this day I think of you, my sweet little girl, and know that you watch over me. You taught me that every life is precious, no matter its length or what happens during its span. You taught me that every moment is sacred, even the sad ones, because in each moment there is the seed of grace and blessing, of learning and transformation.

My Spiritual Practice for Today

Reflect today on the losses in your life. Allow yourself to mourn, and yet look too for the blessings and lessons that are seeded in the soil of your grief.

February 22

Soul Muscle (Pat)

Obviously your soul, being a personal, nonmaterial energy, does not have muscle. Yet muscle is a good metaphor to help reflect on the strength of your connection to your soul.

Imagine that connection as a muscular system that links your soul to your heart and mind and energizes them. How strong are your soul muscles? How much do you exercise them? Are any of them weak or even atrophied? We all know that our muscles weaken if unused, especially if we rarely exercise them. You have heard the sayings "Use it or lose it!" and "No pain, no gain" as applied to exercising your body. How much are you exercising your soul muscles?

This can be a difficulty for many survivors. Because of your pain, you may be afraid to go inward where the soul muscles lie. Or your trauma may have led you to reject religion and spirituality, so you avoid any spiritual practices. Or, like all of us, you may simply go through periods of spiritual laziness and self-neglect.

However, do you really want your soul muscle, your soul connection, to atrophy (your soul itself can never actually weaken or grow slack)? The following are ways to exercise and make your soul muscle strong. These can make you a soul muscle super bod, spiritually buff and ripped (what's the spiritual equivalent of a six-pack?).

Great Soul Muscle Exercises:
- daily meditation or prayer (e.g., starting off your day)
- daily spiritual reading of some kind (e.g., scripture, poetry)
- annual retreat week or weekend
- regular periods of solitude and silence
- listening to music
- walking in nature
- looking deeply into your lover's eyes
- being with a child and being a child with that child
- praying a grateful list each day
- pausing during the day to consciously make contact with God

These are just a few ways to build gorgeous and life-giving soul muscles. There are infinite other ways. Your spiritual workout program will be unique and personal to you. Enjoy your workout!

My Spiritual Practice for Today

Reflect on how strong your soul muscle is today. Review and perhaps update your daily and weekly spiritual exercise program.

February 23

The Magic of Love (Vicki)

Love causes magic.
It is the final purpose of the world story,
The Amen of the Universe.
–Novalis, poet and philosopher, 1772–1801

The love of family and friends buoyed me through the years I was trudging through the difficult part of my journey. There simply is no other way through the pain of it all other than walking through it, crying through it, stepping in the shit, and then moving forward. It can be a gut-grinding experience for sure. But the love of family and friends was an absolute. Sometimes families are so dysfunctional that there can be no real support, so we search among our friends for that support. We're not meant to carry these things alone. Sometimes we have to ask for what we need. Sometimes even our friends can't give us the support we need. Perhaps it touches on something deep within them that needs to be healed. Keep reaching out.

The priest who abused me had a high profile in the community where I lived. We lived in a small town but within a few miles from the capital city. For some reason, he remained in the small semi-rural parish for thirty-six years and developed great power. This exacerbated my fear. It was even more important that I wrap myself with a circle of friends I could trust.

The magic of love brought healing, friendship, courage, endurance, right relationship, a deeper love than I had ever known, authenticity, and acceptance. This magical love created a clear understanding of healthy boundaries and catapulted me into a level of spiritual awareness about myself.

We don't learn these kinds of lessons in universities with advanced degrees or in isolation. I earned an advanced degree about my life. Answers weren't given to me. I was led to answer my own questions in my own time by a skilled therapist. It is one of the greatest gifts of my life. "Love brings up anything unlike itself for the purpose of healing," my therapist would say to me over and over.

My Spiritual Practice for Today

Today I want to allow love to use its magic to bring up all that needs to be healed from my life experiences. I want to trust that this magical love held deep within my own soul has the ability to heal my stories.

February 24

Addiction: No Blame, No Shame (Pat)

Many survivors not only feel shame about their trauma; they are ashamed if they also suffer from an addiction. This self-blame game is totally unnecessary.

Modern brain research validates the original insight of AA that addiction is a disease. This is true whether your addiction is a chemical addiction, like alcoholism or drug addiction, or a behavioral addiction, like gambling, sex addiction, or compulsive overeating. Addiction is a disease of your brain, just like depression or bipolar disorder. Addiction is a "circuit disorder" in which the wiring (neurons) of your brain gets scrambled and short-circuited. As a result, your brain gets hijacked by the addiction. You, your brain, and your life suffer a hostile takeover. Addiction becomes something you cannot not do. Your reward center becomes hyperactive, spewing out excessive amounts of the pleasure chemical dopamine. The survival mechanisms of your brain are also hyperactivated, so it feels like holding on to your addiction is life and death. Meanwhile, the thought and moral reasoning sections of your brain, your cerebral cortex, get turned off and go dark. This all happens unawares, growing like a silent cancer that emerges only when it has metastasized and is out of your control.

Many make the judgment that an addict is just weak, lacking willpower and perhaps even the right morals. You might be making that same judgment with yourself. Addiction is not a moral disorder! It is a disease that survivors are particularly prone to because of the trauma.

When the severe pain of your trauma hits, it is natural to try to find a way to lessen the pain. Some survivors seek relief by medicating their emotional pain with whatever helps them feel better. Eventually this can evolve into a full-blown addiction, even though their original intention was to simply get pain relief. This dynamic is especially powerful in survivors who have a family, genetic history of addiction, which predisposes them to this disease. The bottom line is there is no blame and no shame to being an addict.

My Spiritual Practice for Today

If you suffer from the disease of addiction, do you shame and blame yourself? Focus on being compassionate and understanding with your addiction and yourself today.

February 25

Addiction: The Spiritual Path to Recovery (Pat)

AA describes addiction as a "cunning, baffling, and powerful" disease. Part of what makes it so baffling is that addiction works—at first. Your addiction starts out by making you feel better, and then it turns on you and makes your life much worse.

This is true not only psychologically, but spiritually as well. Addiction can start as a way to seek connection with your soul and God. You are seeking to transcend your ego and your pain to experience being absorbed into something greater. Except that it backfires. The attempt to escape and transcend leads to spiritual numbness that pulls you away from your soul and God. Your spiritual senses become dulled, and it becomes more difficult to hear your soul's whispers or see its light shining within you. The addiction molds itself into your golden calf and becomes the god that you unconsciously worship. Addiction is a form of idolatry because it replaces your true Higher Power and becomes a false god to whom you are compelled to bow each day.

This is why recovery from addiction needs to be spiritual and include turning to a power greater than yourself and your addiction. No addict can recover from their disease by their own efforts. You need to acknowledge that you are powerless over your addiction and decide to turn your will and your life over to the care of God, as you understand him. In doing so, you reverse the spiritual side effects of your addiction. You put yourself into the hands of a True God, your Higher Power. You tap into the power of Spirit to gradually disempower your false god, your addiction, and expel it from your life. You reconnect with your soul and renew your spiritual sensitivities. You become alive again in your spirit. To paraphrase St. Irenaeus from the second century A.D.: The glory of God is man and woman fully alive—and fully in recovery.

My Spiritual Practice for Today

If you are in recovery, reread the first three steps of the twelve-step program and reflect on their spiritual meaning for you. If you are not yet in recovery, do the same, and then please choose recovery today and ask your Higher Power to give you the grace and courage to step onto the path of recovery.

February 26

This Wild and Precious Life (Vicki)

In the final analysis, the questions of why bad things happen to
good people transmutes itself into some very different questions,
no longer asking why something happened, but asking how we
will respond, what we intend to do now that it happened.
–Pierre Teilhard de Chardin, 1881–1955

Life happens to all of us. As Mary Oliver says in her poem, "Tell me what is it you plan to do with your one wild and precious life?" How do we respond? Our history is filled with survival stories from the beginning of time.

What is central to us, though, is what happens to us. It's difficult to think big when we're stuck in our own pain. It feels next to impossible to think beyond the next day, when all we can do is put left foot, right foot in front of us to get through the day. We are at once experiencing our own piercing pain and the pain of the universe, the pain of every human being who has suffered before us and who will suffer after us.

It is the universal story of humanity. Each time we can climb out of our own personal nightmare and lay claim to our lives to live another day is a time to rejoice! How we take our suffering and transform it into something that is life giving for others is a testament to the resilience of humanity.

You can do this with the help of those who love you and surround you with support. I am stronger today because of the people who walked with me through the joy and sorrow of the journey. As cliché as it is, the saying "What doesn't kill you makes you stronger" is as true as the day is long. What most defeats us is also what most fills us with strength. We can all take comfort in knowing this is a universal truth.

My Spiritual Practice for Today

Today I want to consider what I plan to do with this one wild and precious life I have been given. What is my life's bucket list? What steps do I need to complete in my healing journey that will allow me to fulfill that list of adventures?

February 27

Moral Injury (Pat)

A growing body of clinical and research evidence strongly suggests that the near epidemic of PTSD experienced by our soldiers returning from war in Iraq and Afghanistan—and Vietnam as well—is triggered as much by their guilt about their role in battle as the direct trauma they experienced in combat. Mental health professionals who treat veterans are calling this "moral injury." This is a new and important insight that acknowledges that the spiritual wounds caused by trauma and abuse are real and damaging, and are as vital to address in the healing process as the physical and psychological wounds. This, of course, is the central premise of these meditations.

The moral injury that so strongly contributes to PTSD in soldiers is their guilt about having to kill in battle, or their survivor's guilt if a comrade from their unit was killed. This guilt creates what some call "a shadow on the soul" that must be addressed in the therapy if the veteran is going to have a chance for healing and freedom from their deep psychic pain. A part of this healing comes through psycho-spiritual experiences that facilitate self-forgiveness because these veterans are haunted by what they had to do in combat and feel morally diminished.

The equivalent of moral injury in victims of abuse and noncombat trauma is the shame and false guilt you have about your abuse. Many of you blame yourself for the abuse, or feel that the abuse has morally compromised you, and has made you bad or even evil. Self-forgiveness is not the answer here because you did nothing to create the abuse or trauma. What is needed is for you to embrace your innocence, to move to self-acceptance, and to have an experience of total acceptance from your soul and your God.

My Spiritual Practice for Today

The court of the universe has declared you not guilty, innocent, and totally blameless for what was done to you. The verdict of your soul and your God is the same. Focus your thoughts today on your innocence, and be aware all day of how you carry yourself differently as an innocent person.

February 28

The Cone of Shame (Pat)

You have probably seen a dog wearing "the cone of shame." It is a large plastic cone-shaped device put around a dog's neck after surgery to prevent the dog from scratching stitches around its head. Most dogs seem very miserable wearing the cone of shame. They fight it to no avail. It bumps into objects in their path and makes it more difficult to run, play, rest, and sleep. Some dogs seem to give up fighting the cone of shame and try to act as if isn't there, which proves impossible. All of this makes for a very unhappy dog until the cone of shame is removed.

Like many survivors, you might be wearing an invisible cone of shame around your neck, put there by your abuser. Like the dog's, this shame cone is quite uncomfortable and makes it difficult to navigate through your life. It creates a strong emotional belief that you are not worthwhile, of no value, or even worse, that you are innately defective and bad. You may feel you are unworthy to have a blessed life. You are not good enough to succeed. No one could possibly love you or want to get close to you, including God.

It's vital that you begin to realize that your human cone of shame is not real; it is a distortion and a lie inflicted on you by the trauma. It is false evidence appearing real that unfortunately feels powerfully true. But the truth of who you are resides in your soul, untouched by your trauma: You are a beloved person of infinite value, worthy to love and be loved, and to delight in all the gifts of life. In other words, the cone of shame is not, and never was, hanging about your neck, even though it felt real and true. Part of the healing from shame is to accept this and then to metaphorically take the (nonexistent) cone off your neck and be free.

My Spiritual Practice for Today

Imagine your shame as a cone around your neck. Notice what it's like to live with it. Next picture yourself removing the cone or realizing that it was never actually there. Go through your day with this realization and enjoy your new freedom.

March 1

The Mountain Meditation: Your Shame (Sue & Pat)

My Spiritual Practice for Today

We invite you to do another version of the Mountain Meditation. To enter into this meditation, find a comfortable sitting position. As you read, pause, close your eyes, and imagine the scenes described.

Picture yourself on a beautiful beach. See the waves, the sand, the brilliant color, and the vastness of the ocean. Feel the sun and the wind on your skin. Hear the crash and whoosh of the surf. Turn around now, and face away from the sea. Looking down, you see a backpack. In it are your shame feelings, the beliefs that you are somehow bad or defective. Pick it up and place it on your back. Notice how it feels to carry your shame.

In front of you is a beautiful forest. See yourself walking along a trail into the forest. Appreciate the coolness and the shaded light. You reach the edge of the forest and see an open meadow filled with colorful wildflowers. The trail leads you through the meadow to a clear, flowing stream with a bridge across the dancing water. Stop for a moment to enjoy the light sparkling on the water.

Now look up from the bridge and see a shining mountain before you. Following the trail, you ascend the mountain. You climb through the clouds, above the timberline to the top of the peak. Look around you at the glory of creation. Then you notice a large boulder to sit on and rest. You take off your backpack and unload your shame.

Then, from the other side of the peak, your spiritual being and mentor comes and sits down with you on the boulder. You can discuss whatever you want. Be sure to give the being your shame and ask for the gift of freedom from all shame. See your spiritual guide take your shame and throw it off the side of the mountain into a deep abyss. Hear the words, "You are not this. Those are lies. You are a magnificent, beloved person of infinite value."

When you are ready to leave, thank your guide. Remember what was said to you. Slowly hike back down the mountain, over the bridge, through the meadow, through the forest, to the beach, and to the edge of the vast ocean. Open your eyes. Journal what you experienced and what the being on the mountain said to you.

March 2

The Lady in White (Sue)

At 19 I had my appendix removed. I reacted to the anesthetic and didn't regain consciousness for a couple of days. This is what I remember from the time I was gone.

I was walking through a beautiful meadow with very green, soft grass and could hear the soothing sound of a babbling brook. Colorful wildflowers were all around with a vibrant blue sky and stately, lovely trees. Sunlight danced on the water as it flowed under a footbridge. On the other side of the bridge I saw a lovely lady in a flowing white gown with long, wavy, blond hair and a radiant, loving smile.

She motioned for me to come. I started crossing the bridge, but part way across I stopped and said that I wanted to turn around and return. The invitation to cross the bridge and stay was a gentle beckoning, and it was my choice either way.

The next thing I knew I was waking up, and Sr. Mary James was offering me a sip of tea. I said, "No thank you, Sister, I don't care for tea." She responded, "I didn't ask if you cared for it. I want you to drink it." Her Irish wit and the tea did the trick. That moment began my recovery. Since then I've never feared death and have been committed to embracing life. As a survivor I have had my share of fears, and yet this experience gave me an ultimate peace that abides in my core, never really shaken.

In recent years, near-death experiences like mine have been widely studied. The similarity in survivors' stories is remarkable. What is even more amazing is that nearly everyone reports that their fear of death is gone. I wish that peace and absence of fear on everyone, especially you survivors of trauma.

This same peace is possible for you, even without undergoing a near-death experience (which, by the way, I don't recommend). Your freedom from fear may come more gradually. It can flow from your soul's daily invitation to experience, as I did, that at the heart of the universe is an incredible force of Perfect Love. And as scripture says, "Perfect Love casts out all fear." (1 John 4:18)

My Spiritual Practice for Today

Reflect on Sue's story and its meaning for you. Listen to your soul's invitation to cross the bridge to inner peace.

March 3

No Time to Wait (Vicki)

If something must be done, waiting won't make it easier.
But it can certainly delay our own development. To grow, it's
necessary to do what must be done—sooner rather than later.
Otherwise we miss all the opportunities that go with it.
–Joan Chittister

It's good to listen to voices of wisdom, men and women who have been through the hard stuff of life and who know from their experience what a difference it makes to get on with healing. Getting stuck in the darkness that life can bring can feel like quicksand. The more we dwell in it, the deeper it drags us down into that sense of helplessness.

The wisdom of others is necessary to show us the way out. The heroes and heroines of life are those men and women who have climbed out of their own quicksand pits and then shown others how to do so. It takes a community of people around us to give us the blessed assurance that there is hope. Or as Julian of Norwich proclaimed with great trust, "All shall be well, all manner of things shall be well."

Spiritual Practice for Today

Are you stuck in quicksand? Do you feel you are sinking deeper into a sense of hopelessness? Who can you call today who will throw you a rope and begin to pull you up?

March 4

#MeToo (Sue & Pat)

Abuse happens wherever there is the tragic intersection of power and vulnerability, sickness, and silence. The recent stories of the powerful Hollywood movie producers, directors, and stars are a prime example of how abusers employ their power to abuse the vulnerable and feed their own sickness. Thankfully, it is also a story of the empowerment of survivors when they break their enforced silence and join together to challenge the powerful and the sick.

#MeToo has emboldened many victims around the world to speak out about their abuse. Today we invite you to focus on two lessons from this story: the power of your voice to break the silence and end abuse; and the healing awareness that you are not alone.

Your abuser coerced your silence by intimidation and emotional manipulation, by shaming and threatening. You became convinced that no one would believe you or you would be judged. Do not feel ashamed if you have not yet broken your silence. It is incredibly difficult. It took decades for #MeToo victims to speak up. Now witness their power as they do so, including their power to stop the cycle of abuse. If you have broken your silence, celebrate how this has liberated you. If you still struggle to tell your story, ask yourself if you are ready to add your voice to the chorus of #MeToo. You can tell your story to anyone whom you trust, whoever will hold your story sacred: a therapist, a soul friend, your life partner, or a family member.

#MeToo also says, "You are not alone." Survivors all over the world are sharing their story. Abuse engenders the belief that you are set apart and shamefully unique. Instead, you are a part of a swelling chorus moved by the Spirit to break the isolation and the silence. At least 1 in 4 women and 1 in 6 men has been sexually abused. In the U.S. population, that is 81,303,836 women and 55,086,609 men!

Your soul is gently insisting, "Be not afraid. Be not ashamed. You are not alone. If it is your time, break your silence, and add your story to the growing chorus of empowered voices."

My Spiritual Practice for Today

Meditate today on these two truths: You are not alone, and your voice has great power.

March 5

You Are Not Alone (Pat)

As every survivor knows, you are not promised that everything in life will go well or that you will be spared suffering. Actually, suffering is guaranteed! Perhaps the only thing that you are promised is that you will never be alone. No matter what happens in your life, you will never have to face it alone. Anything is more bearable—or more joyful—if someone shares your experience and walks through it with you by your side with an arm around you and a listening ear. The promise is that there will always be a Presence, subtlety abiding, available to listen and share the burden. One of the most common phrases in the Judeo-Christian scriptures is this message from God: "Fear not, for I am with you." You are not alone. You never have been, and you never will be alone.

As many survivors know, it is difficult to believe this at times. It often feels as if you are alone, especially during the trauma and its painful aftereffects. You likely have felt abandoned by God. Shame from abuse may leave you feeling that you don't deserve divine presence. It is understandable to feel this way—and it is vital that you don't believe the lie of shame or your feeling of abandonment.

A loving Presence is always with you, always available. It doesn't promise to save you from traumatic events. Life, after all, is a rose garden with many beautiful, fragrant flowers—and lots of thorns right there with them.

Our colleague Paula D'Arcy presents a two-person play that imagines this promise very well. She relates the story of her emotional and spiritual struggles after the terrible deaths of her husband and young daughter in a drunk-driving accident. As she acts out her anguished journey to healing, she depicts God—played by an actor with a Texas accent—as always being present: in the shadows behind her, to her left, to her right, before her, behind her, usually unseen, sometimes sensed, sometimes not, but always there.

That's the promise: Presence will always be present.

My Spiritual Practice for Today

In every moment today, practice awareness of the Presence. Sense divine omnipresence in every circumstance, person, instance of beauty, and all kindness given or received. Notice Presence and notice what you feel.

March 6

A Vision of Your Spiritual Healing (Pat & Sue)

The second part of the Spiritual Laundry List is designed to help you have a clear vision of what spiritual gifts your healing journey will grace you with. *Read through these and pick three that you most want and need, or perhaps already have.*

The Wash, Rinse, and Polish: By choosing the spiritual healing journey, we learn that we can live our lives in a more meaningful manner; we can learn to change our attitudes, habits, and old patterns, including our old patterns of relating to our Higher Power, to find serenity, purpose, and happiness.

- We learn that God is good and loving after all. We discover that our Higher Power does not possess any of the negative characteristics that we experienced in our abuser.
- We learn to see our abusers as human beings, let go of the anger and bitterness we once projected from them onto our Higher Power, and choose forgiveness.
- We choose to surrender our lives and will to the God of our understanding.
- We accept that we are accepted by God; we accept that we are accepted and loved not for what we do—simply because we are!
- We let go of the delusion and control of shame and perfectionism, stop "shoulding" upon ourselves, and begin to adopt personal values, which are reasonable and lead to balance and wholeness.
- Through a balanced program of prayer and meditation, we develop an authentic and personal relationship with our God and invite God into every area of our lives.
- We learn and experience the gift of being in the present moment with our God and with God's creation.
- We recover a childlike sense of wonder, joy, and awe about the magnificence of ourselves and all of creation.
- We develop a grateful heart and live in thankfulness for the many gifts that we have been given and that surround us always.

- Our spirituality reveals to us that we are a person of great and infinite value; this knowledge about ourselves leads us to more fully value and love others in our life.
- Our soul leads us to live in a new sense of purpose and mission that enhances and deepens our lives and the lives of all with whom we come into contact.

March 7

Trusting the Silent Mystery (Vicki)

The soul knows the geography of your destiny. Your soul alone has the map of your future, therefore you can trust this indirect oblique side of yourself. If you do, it will take you where you need to go, but more important, it will teach you a kindness of rhythm in your journey.
—John O'Donohue, *Anam Cara*

It matters not what your faith tradition is. The soul knows the great potential that is held deep within you. Again, it is the wisdom of retrospect that allows me to reflect on this quote. I could never have guessed the map of my future when I was walking through my healing work. I could only see what was right in front of me. Painful for a time, I could only see and feel what I was going through on any given day. I did not have the vision to see where I was going, other than small incremental steps that seemed interminable

We are being asked to trust that the soul knows where it is leading us. We're being asked to trust the invisible mystery around us and that it knows where we're headed, even though we haven't a clue. This is trust of the finest kind. And trust we must. If you can find one shred of courage to share your story, if you can find one person who believes you and trusts your experience, then you can move forward and trust this silent mysterious guide that is beginning to reveal the rhythm of your journey.

Indeed, there is a rhythm to the healing journey. I felt its stride once I got past the first few speed bumps: the telling of the story, the brutal truth of the story. It was then that I could let out a huge sigh and begin to piece together the puzzle of why. Trust the process, and it will take you where you need to go. Then you will begin to see your authentic self emerge, and the roots of your authenticity will go deep, creating an emotional strength like you have never known. Those deep roots will support you throughout your life and help you weather all of life's storms.

My Spiritual Practice for Today

I want to trust the silent mystery that is my soul. I believe that the strength of my soul will guide me in this journey, and I trust in it. I am not afraid of this mystery for it is my strength.

March 8

It's the Thought that Counts (Pat)

The main cause of stress is not the situation itself, but the way in which you think about it. It's been estimated that 90 percent of what makes you depressed or happy, stressed or peaceful, are the thoughts you have about yourself and the events in your life, not the events themselves.

Our thoughts are powerful and yet ephemeral and sometimes misleading. I recently had a dramatic experience of this. For months my mind was hyperfocused on a serious health scare. I had round after round of anxious thoughts swirling in a high-speed loop in my brain. Anxious thought fed anxious thought. Fear and depression grew exponentially. Until one day after praying and meditating—as best I could with my agitated brain—I took a walk in a nearby nature preserve. It was a sparkling early fall day with brilliant blue skies, crisp air, and even crisper light.

As I focused on the beauty around me, I suddenly realized that my brain was quiet; there were no anxious thoughts. They were all gone. I was relieved and stunned. What had happened to all of the fearful thoughts that had dominated my life for months? And if they were gone, what did that mean about the thoughts themselves? Were they ever real? Was there anything to be so desperately fearful about? I decided that they had been grossly exaggerated—probably by about 90 percent! My situation had not changed, but my thoughts had.

Trauma often leaves survivors with a barrage of negative thoughts about themselves and their life. Each new situation is viewed through a darkened lens of past trauma-based beliefs. It is powerfully freeing to realize that these are just thoughts, and most likely not true. In mindfulness meditation you are invited to see all of your thoughts as clouds passing through your mind. You are encouraged not to attach or focus on any of them. Just let them float by and recenter on your breath or your prayer phrase and the Presence within you. Later ask yourself: How real are your thoughts, especially the negative ones?

My Spiritual Practice for Today

Reflect on these questions. Are your thoughts mainly self and life enhancing, or mainly self and life negating? What is the single most negative thought in your mind? What affirming thought does your soul want to replace it with?

March 9

Love Thy? (Sue & Pat)

Jesus was once asked which commandment was the greatest. His response is called the "Great Commandment." The first part of the commandment is about loving God with your whole self. The second part is actually two further commandments: "Love thy neighbor—*as* thyself." Jesus says this summarizes all of Jewish and Christian teaching.

It has been our experience that many of our clients only hear the first part, "Love your neighbor," and totally miss or dismiss the second part, which commands you to love yourself. As a result, many survivors become proficient at loving others and quite good at forgetting and neglecting themselves. One term for this is codependency, which is the compulsive tendency to always put others' needs first and your own needs dead last. This causes serious problems in close relationships and contributes to depression and anxiety.

So it is vital to hear both parts of Jesus's commandment. We interpret it by starting with the second part: Love yourself first, and then you will be empowered and freed to love your neighbor. If you don't love yourself, your love for others will be distorted and out of balance.

What Jesus is encouraging is a balanced and fluid love that flows out of love of self into love of the other and back again—an unbroken circle of love. If you only love yourself, you may turn into an isolated egotist; if you only love your neighbor, you might become an overextended, resentful, and compulsive care-taker. The teaching is "*Love thyself*", and then let it flow out from you to others.

The airlines provide us with an excellent example of this. During the preflight safety speech, the flight attendant instructs, "If there is a sudden drop in cabin pressure, oxygen masks will drop down. If you are traveling with children (or others in need), secure your own mask first *before* helping them with their masks." If you don't give yourself enough oxygen, how can you help or love anyone else?

My Spiritual Practice for Today

Reflect on Jesus's words. Which part of the commandment do you struggle with? What blocks your self-love? How can you bring your love into balance? How can you love yourself more fully? Decide on one act of self-love and carry it out today.

March 10

Channels of Love and Healing (Vicki)

It is difficult for us to grasp that we are the channels of love and healing, by virtue of our very being here as creation-come-to-consciousness-and-love.
–Barbara Fiand, *Awe-filled Wonder, The Interface of Science and Spirituality*

As I moved through many counseling sessions and explored different alternative healing treatments such as massage, reiki, healing touch, meditation and centering prayer, I came to understand that each of us has the ability to be channels of love and healing. As Barbara Fiand says so beautifully, "our very being here as creation-come-to-consciousness-and-love" is the very gift we have all been given to be a healing presence to one another.

My therapist and close friends who had been through their own healing process were that creation-come-to-consciousness for me. They channeled love to me and worked to bring me to the wholeness I was seeking. As I've said in other meditations, we are wounded healers offering our wisdom and love to others who are embarking on their own journey.

Consciousness means "knowing with." We know that our presence with one another is a healing presence. When my friend, Rhonda, was dealing with a very serious illness, she asked me to share reiki with her. My friend and I arrived and set up the massage table. Rhonda's son, who was 6 at the time, asked if he could help us. In the process of reiki, we lay hands on nineteen positions on the body as vessels for God's healing energy. We guided little Dylan to lay his hands on his mother wherever he felt she needed it. Dylan stayed with us for a long time, laying his little hands on his mother's body. Even Dylan knew the power of his conscious love. His mother experienced a profound healing that night.

If we all carry this healing love within us, then we can call that forth to initiate our own healing. It is there for each of us if we can attune ourselves to it.

My Spiritual Practice for Today

Today explore the possibility of learning about alternative healing therapies that are available in your area. Consider adding them to your counseling experience as a way to enhance your healing.

March 11

Unwanted Grace (Vicki)

I came across the words "unwanted grace," and their coupling appeared an oxymoron. Could anything unwanted be considered a grace or a gift? It required some time to reflect about how something uncalled for, unwanted, could ever be something that would be a teachable moment. Once again we find its truth in the wisdom of retrospect.

Discovering my truest self was painfully brought forth because of the trauma I experienced in an abusive relationship. Would I have come to understand my truest self if I had not experienced the trauma? Maybe in a different way. I choose not to think of it that way. I choose to believe that the gift of my trauma was the catalyst that led me to a deeper understanding of my purpose in life. Spending time wondering if I would have gotten there on my own is wasted time. This was part of my life story, and I choose to accept it as a small part of the story of my big, wonderful life and move on.

Our trauma does not have to define us. It will always be a part of us. Understanding that this small piece of the largesse of life was just that, a small part. Significant, yes, and still a small part of the big picture. Brene' Brown writes: "When we deny the story, it defines us. When we own the story, we can write a brave new ending."

My Spiritual Practice for Today

Today, in a spirit of forgiveness and letting go of the past, I want to begin to think of the trauma that has so occupied my consciousness for some time and begin to write a new ending to the story. I choose to begin thinking of this part of my life as a small portion of the larger life I want to live.

March 12

The Power of Your Point of View (Pat)

Everyone's story has a point of view, a place from which you view, interpret, and write your personal narrative. Because you are the director of your own movie, you choose the camera angles. Where you stand determines what you see. I had a powerful experience of this while on retreat at a monastery at the foot of the Sangre de Christo Mountains of Colorado. If I looked out the back window of my hermitage, I saw a dry desert ravine covered with scrub bushes and rock. If I looked out the front window, I had a spectacular but narrow picture of high mountains bathed in a constant play of light and shadow. If I climbed to the top of a nearby hill, a vast scene of mountains, desert, and valley, with an almost endless horizon, opened before me.

Changing your point of view can be powerfully liberating. That is why experiences such as a spiritual retreat or meditation can be so life changing. You temporarily change your point of view from your usual, busy, day-to-day camera angle. You stand in an unaccustomed place and look at your life differently. You may even see yourself from the point of view of your soul or of God. It is important to discover that you can tell and retell your story from different points of view as you trek the different pathways of your healing journey.

In our work with victims, we have discerned five points of view from which victims can retell their story. All five are necessary at different phases of the healing process. The five points of view are:

Victim

Survivor

Thriver

Your Soul

Your God or Higher Power

Each of these points of view possesses the power to move you along your healing journey to a new story about your trauma and yourself, a story that can progressively free you emotionally and spiritually.

My Spiritual Practice for Today

If you have never written down the story of your abuse or trauma, you will find it helpful to do so now. Reread your story. Reflect on it and discern from which point of view it is told. How does that point of view feel? How would it feel to tell your story from another point of view?

March 13

Point of View: The Victim Story (Pat)

The first point of view is from the perspective of the victim. It is usually the first story you write in your mind and heart, once you are ready to let go of the shame-based story of your abuse or trauma. It is an absolutely necessary story. You are saying to yourself, to the world, and to your abuser:

"This was done to me. You did it to me. It was not my fault.
I was and I am innocent. I was vulnerable and powerless to stop the abuse.
I was a victim."

You are shedding your shame in the victim story. You are stating that what was done to you was wrong and harmful. You are putting the responsibility where it belongs, on your abuser. The anger expressed in the victim story is a powerful antidote to the poison of shame. You are saying:

"I am not bad, sick, dirty, or evil. What you, my perpetrator, did was wrong, sick, and even evil. What you did to me does not define me. Nor will I let it any longer obscure my God-given light, glory, and magnificence."

The victim story, though, has limitations. It can become a trap if you stay there too long. It can re-enforce a sense of helplessness and fear. It can make you believe that you do not have the inner strength to take charge of creating and shaping your life. The victim story is a narrative to eventually leave behind.

My Spiritual Practice for Today

Rewrite or reflect on your story from the victim viewpoint. Bring this story to prayer or meditation and notice what you experience. How does this story change things for you? What happens to old feelings of shame or false guilt about your abuse or trauma? Can you sense the empowerment that this perspective starts to engender in you?

March 14

Point of View: The Survivor's Story (Pat)

The second narrative about trauma and abuse is the story told as a survivor. In this story you assert:

"Yes, this was done to me, and it was wrong and deeply hurt me.
Yet I am still here. I'm making it. I'm getting by and gradually getting
through what the abuse did to me. I am feeling stronger.
I will overcome and transcend this. I am learning how to protect and
care for myself. I am even starting to love myself. I am a survivor."

You will still feel wounded, but you also will feel a growing inner strength that comes from telling your abuse story from the survivor's point of view.

You can increasingly assert your personal power to protect yourself and determine the course of your life. You are starting to get past the pain of your trauma and can see beyond it to a life out of the shadow of your abuse. You can see that there is more to you and your life than the trauma. You are learning new life tools to better care for yourself. You are experiencing more and more moments of serenity and joy. You are discovering gifts in yourself and in your life that you never imagined were there for you. There is new hope and new vitality. Sometimes you have a bounce in your step and lightness in your heart. It is easier to be grateful. This is a big breakthrough. Yet even more is possible.

My Spiritual Practice for Today

Rewrite or reflect on your story from the survivor viewpoint. Bring this story to prayer or meditation and notice what you experience. How does this story change things for you? What happens to your old feelings of depression, weakness, and helplessness? Can you sense the freedom, serenity, and even joy that this perspective creates in you?

March 15

Point of View: The Thriver's Story (Pat)

When you are ready to write the thriver story, you have progressed to the place where you can see your abuse and yourself in a profoundly different light. You can now say to yourself and to the world:

> "Yes, I was abused. It was wrong, and it hurt me. Yet the abuse no
> longer defines or controls me. I have risen above it, transcended it,
> and even grown stronger because of it. I am learning to transform my
> abuse experience into something life giving for myself and for others.
> I am thriving! I am victorious!"

This is a powerful, transformative story about abuse that sets you largely free from the power of the shame and fear that your abuse had over you. You are not just surviving. You are now thriving and are victorious over the wounds and limitations from your trauma. There may still be residual scars, but you know now that they are not you. In fact, you can see them as victory trophies, not marks of shame, and they no longer define you.

You are discovering new self-definitions, new purpose, and new meaning for your life. You have transformed your suffering in the alchemy of your healing journey to a precious metal. You no longer regret or are bound by the past. You are able to be mindfully present in the moment, in the power of now, and are unafraid of the future. You live with passion and a desire to give back to those still suffering. You glow at times with a new fire and a new light.

My Spiritual Practice for Today

Rewrite or reflect on your story from the thriver viewpoint. Bring this story to prayer or meditation and notice what you experience. How does this story change things for you? What new spiritual energy do you feel within you? Can you perceive the new light, purpose, and life meaning that this perspective creates in you? Also, read and reflect on the "Wash, Rinse, and Polish" section of the Spiritual Laundry List (in Appendix II). These are spiritual characteristics of spiritual wholeness you are likely experiencing as you move through the survivor and thriver stories.

March 16

Point of View: Your Soul's Story, God's Story (Pat)

Your soul's story, as well as God's story, about your abuse will powerfully transform your relationship to your abuse. We cannot write a script for your soul's story or God's story. We cannot predict what that would be, for "the Spirit blows where it wills." We wouldn't presume to speak for God. Only you and your soul can discover this together.

We do know that the story will be one of compassion, love, transcendence, grace, and strength from your soul. Your soul's point of view will be very different from the victim's story or even the survivor's story and closest to the thriver's story. Ask your soul to tell her story of your abuse. Ask your God for the divine point of view. These two new narratives will set you free and let your spirit soar far beyond the oppressive gravity of your abuse.

Hopefully you have experienced a series of revelations as you move from victim to survivor to thriver and now to your soul's story. In the process, you progressively free yourself and discover your inner resilience, strength, power, worth, and magnificence.

Changing your point of view as you retell your abuse story can feel challenging and threatening. For some, it is particularly difficult to get past the victim story. It has taken courage to let go of what has become familiar to you and move to a higher story. Affirm yourself for your spiritual courage and offer a prayer of gratefulness for all of your new and healing stories.

My Spiritual Practice for Today

In meditation, envision your story of trauma like a movie projected on a screen. Imagine that God and your soul are your only audience. Let your spiritual imagination open you to hear and see how your soul and God respond to your abuse. How do they see and understand your experiences? Write the new story in your journal. Another way to hear your soul's story is to write a prayerful dialogue with your soul (or God). Ask your soul how she views you and your abuse. What different light does your soul shine on your trauma? What spiritual questions remain unanswered for you? Ask your soul whatever you need to ask.

March 17

Understanding Our Story (Vicki)

As we conform our lives to our stories, we find that we are transformed. Our individual stories, when interconnected with a world of stories, become part of the historical underpinnings of life on earth. When I think of how small my life is within the vastness of the universe, it is easy to think how inconsequential it is. Think of the millions of stories of human life, love, and struggle that happen every day. To recognize that our story is just as important as every other story is to give our lives a deeper meaning than we may otherwise have done. Life is a compelling story. Each soul brought into this world is literally a bright star of potential. The light grows dim at times, and sometimes we make choices that keep that light from shining.

Recently I completed a series of counseling sessions that brought me to a new understanding of my own story. Using Eye Movement Desensitization and Re-Processing (EMDR) methods of bringing unhealed PTSD issues to the fore from the limbic portion of the brain, where much of our trauma is stored, I was able to release some long-held negative thinking and appreciate the value of my story more dynamically.

Imagine if no one shared their stories of love, pain, and healing. How would we be able to understand the human condition and see our life as a gift? It doesn't matter that there are billions of stories. It simply matters that ours is among them, adding to the kaleidoscope of humanity.

Your story has value. Every human story has inherent value that can indeed change the world. We have too many inspiring instances of it to doubt that it is possible. Not only is telling our story important, we must heal the hurtful parts so we can continue living. Then the full story of who we are can be fully lived.

Spiritual Practice for the Day

Today I will reflect on my own story to clarify, to understand, and to heal whatever difficult things my life has encountered. Today I will reflect on what I need to do to become fully who God has called me to be.

March 18

Should (Pat & Sue)

"Should" (or "shouldn't") is the most dangerous word in the English language. *Should* is the vocabulary of shame. *Should*, when used about yourself, says you *shouldn't* be the way you are. You *should* be something different. *Should* is a word of self-judgment. When you say to yourself that you *should* be such and so, or you *shouldn't* be this or that, you create shame in yourself. You are not okay. You *should* be other than who you are, presumably better.

Should is also the lexicon of self-limitation, even self-imprisonment. When you say you *should* do something, you are trapping yourself into believing that you have no choice but to do what say you *should* do. It's the one right way— which it usually isn't. You are wrong and bad if you want to pursue other choices.

Should and *shouldn't* are the verbal manifestations of your trauma. They re-shame and re-traumatize you every time you think or utter them. Think of one of your *should* statements and see how you feel saying it out loud. For example, if you tell yourself, "I *should* be a better parent, partner, or friend, so I *should* do this particular thing," your first instinct might be to react with, "Well, of course, I *should* be better. How else am I going to improve myself?" If you look deeper, you will see that you have left out how you are already good, and you have given yourself only one course of action. How does that feel? We find that it feels shitty, shameful, and restricting.

Fortunately, you can live very well without *should* in your vocabulary. You can learn to stop "*shoulding* on yourself" and others. You can systematically root out the word from your speech and thoughts. You can replace it with affirming both–and statements and the language of personal freedom: "I am a good parent, friend, and lover, *and* there is room for improvement. How do I want to go about that?"

By the way, we are not saying you *should* stop saying *should*; we are saying you can, you may, if you want. And we know you will feel stronger and freer if you do.

My Spiritual Practice for Today

Closely observe your speech and your thoughts all day. Notice how often you use *should* or *shouldn't*. Be aware of how you feel. Substitute new words and feel the difference.

March 19

Soul Friends (Pat)

Every survivor needs a soul friend. You need what the Irish call an *anam cara*, Gaelic for a friend of your soul, a person to whom you can reveal the deepest intimacies of your life, someone with whom you share your soul. Early Irish Christians had a saying (adapted from pre-Christian Druid spirituality): "Anyone without a soul friend is like a body without a head."

These special people become the core of your support network. They can be your spouse or life partner, trusted family, close friends, a therapist, a spiritual director, your pastor, or if you are in a twelve-step program, your sponsor. Share your journey of healing. Let your *anam cara* know what you are experiencing as you do these meditations.

Carry reminders of the people who love you and stand with you in Spirit. Keep pictures of your soul friends in your wallet, purse, smartphone, and computer to remind yourself that you are not doing this alone. Don't keep your pain, your struggles, your healing, and your triumphs locked inside. Share them with your *anam cara*, and make sure your soul friend knows you will need their ears, their shoulders, their hands, and their prayers all along your path.

My Spiritual Practice for Today

Choose your network of supportive soul friends. Talk to each of them and let them know you are doing these meditations. Thank them for their love and care, and request that they be available when needed to be with you in prayer and spirit.

On a piece of paper, draw a circle and place your name in the center. Then write all the names of your soul friends in a circle around you. Include everyone who supports you in any way. Use this as a visual reminder that you are not alone. You have a powerful soul circle of support.

March 20

Your Brain on Meditation (Pat)

You probably have seen the famous antidrug commercial of the 1980s, "Your Brain on Drugs." It shows a skillet of hot, bubbling oil. A fresh egg is dropped into the pan. It instantly sizzles, pops, and fries way too fast on its way to burning.

Amazingly, using MRI and other brain scans, we now have actual pictures of how the brain reacts to drugs, alcohol, and the behavioral addictions (such as gambling, sex, and compulsive overeating). They all show similar effects: The reward/dopamine and fear/survival sections of the brain become chronically overstimulated and stressed, and the cerebral cortex, where you do your thinking and moral reasoning, goes off-line and dark, and temporarily stops functioning (which explains a lot). We also have images of the brain reacting to trauma. Among other effects, the amygdala, the emotion, fear, and survival center of your brain, gets chronically hot wired and hypersensitive to any potential or imagined dangers. This is one reason why trauma is one of the main causes of addiction. Your brain tries unsuccessfully to calm itself through the addiction.

Mercifully the brain is "plastic;" that is, it can change and be rewired at any age. Research demonstrates that one of the most powerful tools to reshape and calm the brain is meditation, particularly mindfulness meditation. We even have pictures of the brain on meditation! What they show is fascinating and encouraging. The amygdala is calmed and actually shrinks with regular meditation. The thinking part of your brain, the prefrontal cortex, gets thicker and stronger. Research also shows that meditation is sometimes as effective as antidepressant medication for treating depression and anxiety; it reduces stress and inflammation in the body and increases empathy and compassion. All these benefits and no side effects!

The more regularly you meditate, the more changes are seen, and the more permanent they become. So you actually rewire and heal your brain. Through meditation, you reclaim your brain from trauma and addiction.

My Spiritual Practice for Today

What role has meditation played in your life? Do you make it a part of each day? If not, consider finding 20 minutes a day for meditation. The morning is often the best, but any time will do. Your brain will thank you.

March 21

The Negative Power of Unforgiveness (Vicki)

Forgiveness is part of being human. It's easy to see the ravages of unforgiveness in people's lives. Holding a grudge can eat away our interior lives like a cancer; yet we often let it fester until it becomes an ugly sore that not only damages our health but the relationships around us.

I didn't like the person I was when I was angry at my perpetrator. I had too many hateful thoughts. For a time I only wanted bad things to happen to him; after all he deserved to be punished. That wasn't truly me having those thoughts. It was a perverted form of me. I'm thankful I moved through that phase quickly. Nothing good comes from that kind of animosity toward another human being. That way of thinking was inconsistent with who I thought I was and who I wanted to become.

Ilia Delio, teacher, theologian, and author, wrote about this in an article in *National Catholic Reporter* (March 20, 2015): "We humans can easily fall prey to being 'victimized,' resentful, angry, self-righteous and therefore seldom at peace with one another because we cannot forgive one another. Forgiveness begins in the heart. We cannot forgive others if we cannot forgive ourselves and let go of our divisive thoughts. To heal our inner woundedness is to know God's power of love within us, which is stronger than death, a love overflowing with future life. God is the power of the future, and one who lives in God rests on the future."

I lived the pain of unforgiveness. It manifested itself in my grinding teeth, my clenched fists, my frayed nerves, the sleepless nights, the endless hours of work I used to bury my feelings, and the occasional violent thoughts. I learned that nothing good can come from holding persistent anger, that overriding sense of unforgiveness, which goes against one of the binding commandments of most religious traditions.

For my own healing, I needed and wanted to forgive my abuser. During a retreat with Paula D'Arcy, she reminded those in attendance, "Forgiveness is the fragrance that the violet sheds on the heel that has crushed it."

My Spiritual Practice for Today

We are called to live a life of gracious forgiveness just as we seek the same from others. I want to enter a new phase of life, a life with a forgiving heart for myself and for others.

March 22

Your Inner Philosopher (Pat)

Whether you realize it or not, you are a philosopher. We all are. It is part of being human that you tell a story to yourself and others about your life. A part of that story is your philosophy of life. You have one, whether you can consciously articulate it or not.

You assign meanings to different events and circumstances of your life. You develop certain life lessons and values, beliefs and assumptions about your life. You do this even as a child. Every child is a little philosopher weaving together meanings and beliefs about what they experience and are taught.

Other influences, such as a church, scriptures, and mentors, may help shape your philosophy, yet in the end you create your own personal value and belief system. As you enter into adulthood, your own unique philosophy guides you as you navigate the many situations and choices of your life.

Traumatic events are among the most powerful influences in forming your philosophy. Your inner philosopher, especially when you are young, attempts to make sense of your trauma and somehow find meaning in it.

Sometimes this yields a triumphant, hopeful, and resilient philosophy of life: You have survived and overcome your trauma. You are strong and can handle whatever may come. Life is essentially good; there is always reason for hope and joy.

Often though, trauma leads to a negative, fearful, and shame-based philosophy: Life is dangerous, and you are weak, probably bad in some way. Live defensively, don't expect too much, hope for little, don't trust it or enjoy it too much if something or someone good comes your way. Always play it safe.

Your inner philosopher determines whether you believe that life sucks or life is marvelous. Luckily, you are in charge of your inner philosopher. You can employ your inner philosopher to reexamine and reformulate your life philosophy if it has been distorted by trauma; then you can develop a new one that better reflects who you are now and what you have learned in recovery.

My Spiritual Practice for Today

Write your personal philosophy of life. See how much of it was shaped by your abuse or trauma. What would you like to change now? Tap into your inner philosopher and write a philosophy reflecting your healing journey. How is it different?

March 23

My Fire Truck Epiphany, Part One (Sue)

It took a big red fire truck to wake me up. In many ways my life was very good. I was a full-time mom busy raising five wonderful children. Life was an endless circle of carpooling, homework, sports, theatre, laundry, cooking, and cleaning. It was fulfilling, and yet there were signs that something was wrong, although I was too busy to notice. I was on automatic pilot, rushing through my life at breakneck speed. I had become a human doing, a mom machine. I had little sense of who I was, what I needed, or even why I was doing what I was so furiously doing.

One sunny winter day all of this changed in an instant. Two friends and I were driving, when POW! A giant fire truck pulled out of the firehouse and hit the driver's side where I was seated. I suffered a bad concussion. When people talked, it seemed like they were whispering from the top row of a large sports arena, and I was sitting on the floor. I had a fracture in my back, and muscles and ligaments were torn throughout my body. Every movement was excruciating. My life slowed to a painful crawl.

Three months after the crash, a young woman—a Jane Fonda lookalike—knocked on my back door and asked to use my phone. Although I was in my early forties, I shuffled to the door at the speed of a 90-year-old. She took one look at me and said, "My God, what happened to you?" On leaving she said, "I'll be here tomorrow morning, and we'll walk!" I pleaded, "I can't walk." She simply replied, "I'll see you then."

Sandy—my Jane Fonda angel—became my salvation. She appeared the next morning, and we walked from my back door to the end of my driveway. I cried most of the way with my angel coaching me at every step! We did this every morning, each day walking a bit farther. This routine led by an angel gradually began to heal my physical trauma.

My Spiritual Practice for Today

Angels of all kinds appear during or after traumas to help lead us through to healing. Who or what was your angel? Reflect today on the gift of your own personal angel.

March 24

My Fire Truck Epiphany, Part Two (Sue)

My emotional and spiritual trauma needed another kind of therapy. It came from a nun. A few months after the crash, a sister friend invited me to work as a volunteer chaplain in the hospital that she administered. Still in a lot of pain and concussion fog, I reluctantly said yes.

Chaplaincy presented me with a great dilemma. Having been a human doing machine and a nurse used to attending to physical needs, I didn't know what to do for the patients I was visiting. I confessed my concern to another chaplain, Deacon Ken. He simply replied, "Just bring to each patient the gift of you. This will be God's presence to each one." This was revolutionary. I was just to be present to each patient with love, listening, and sometimes prayer. The fire truck had stopped me in my tracks and left me with so little I could do. Now I was learning to be and love in a whole new way.

This work was a great way to heal! It took my attention off of myself and my pain as I focused on the patients' needs. I was learning so much. Like many survivors of abuse, I did not really know who I was or what I had to offer. Gradually I discovered how to be Sue without all of the doing. I connected with gifts within me that had long been dormant or that I had not been aware of. I learned that I had something to offer the patients that was emotionally and spiritually healing for them.

In this realization, a call—I believe from God—began to awaken in me. It was a call to be a presence of healing for those who are suffering in body, mind, heart, or soul. This eventually led me to return to school and become a psychotherapist, specializing in counseling with survivors of abuse. This is the call that I continue to live.

My Spiritual Practice for Today

Reflect on what you have learned about yourself from your trauma experience. Is there a call for a new way of life that has emerged from your trauma?

March 25

My Fire Truck Epiphany, Part Three (Sue)

Much later I reflected on my experience and the spiritual tradition of trauma leading to spiritual awakening. I recalled the Bible story of Paul being knocked off his horse by an overwhelming light that surrounded and stunned him. He had been busy trying to put down the growing Christian movement. He was blinded by the light, heard Christ speak to him, and then went through a period of quiet prayer and reconsideration of his whole life's purpose. His eyes were opened again with new spiritual vision that gave him a dynamic new passion and focus for his life.

This is what the trauma of the fire truck did for me. I was knocked off my very fast horse and forced to completely rethink and eventually redirect my life. The fire truck led to a spiritual awakening. The pain first blinded me and then opened my eyes in a marvelous and unexpected way. The pain and the concussion immobilized me long enough for me discover the depths that God had created in me and how he wanted to use my gifts.

It is amazing how one is invited by trauma to be still, to listen, and to notice. My fire truck trauma created an environment of quiet and introspection. And lo and behold, I began to give birth, actually a rebirth of the me that was consumed by the busy duties of life. Over the next several years, ever so slowly, I became aware of who I am in God's eyes and who he was calling me to be. For Paul it took a flash of light and a voice. For me it took a fire truck, God's presence to me in the stillness, and several special people.

My body still feels some of the effects of the fire truck. My heart and soul though have flourished and soared. It was a trauma I would not wish on anyone, yet I am now ever grateful.

My Spiritual Practice for Today

Have you allowed your trauma to lead you to stillness and deeper reflection? What spiritual awakening has emerged or is still being born from your own trauma epiphany?

March 26

Check Your Transmission (Pat)

The spiritual teacher Fr. Richard Rohr writes, "Pain that is not transformed is transmitted." Another way to say this is hurting people hurt. Unless you are working to heal and transform the pain from your trauma, you will likely transmit it in some fashion to others, especially to those you love the most: your children, your life partner, and close friends. This can take many forms: outbursts of anger, being emotionally withdrawn and unavailable, projecting a negative view of life, or instilling unnecessary fear, among others. This means that your healing journey is not just for you. It is also vital for everyone in your life. The freer you are from the effects of your trauma, the freer you are to love. You will stop the transmission of pain and break the cycle of trauma and abuse.

It is important that you stop to check your transmission. Are you passing on or transmitting your pain to others? Is your hurt leading you to hurt?

Do not shame yourself about this. All human beings hurt other human beings at times, usually those closest to us. It is universal and inevitable. Perfection is not a human trait. So join the human race and accept that you will hurt someone.

What is crucial is how we respond when we hurt someone. If you admit your mistake, if you make amends and help the other to heal, and most important, if you learn from your mistake and change the hurting behavior, then your actions are redeemed and the vicious cycle is broken. Pain that *is* transformed is *not* transmitted and, in fact, can be a source of healing and new life for yourself and those you love.

My Spiritual Practice for Today

Without shame or self-condemnation, honestly examine your actions and your relationships today. Ask yourself if you are transmitting your pain to others. Resolve to change this. Be patient with yourself; change takes time. Perhaps explore whether you can and need to make amends. Resolve too to rededicate yourself to your healing journey for yourself and for all those in your life.

March 27

Good Grief (Pat)

When you are in the midst of your grief, it is hard to believe that you will ever come out of the pit that you feel you have fallen into. It is equally difficult to trust that any light or goodness will emerge from the darkness of your grief. The delayed grief that victims of trauma often experience about their trauma losses can shake you to your foundation. You find yourself asking: *Who am I now? What is real? What is left? What is meaningful? What is my life purpose now? Where do I go with my life now?* These are deeply spiritual questions. In raising these questions, grief challenges you to eventually reorient and reenergize yourself and your life in relationship to your losses. This is the deep soul work of grief.

These existential questions incubate in the cocoon of your grief. Your soul helps you turn them over and over as they are polished like rough-cut gemstones placed in a rock tumbler until they are smooth and shine in the light. Gradually answers appear out of the gloomy fog of your grief. Some of them will be new answers; some of them will be old answers now seen in a new light with an added dimension or a new twist.

As these answers emerge, and as you start to free yourself from the past, you will find a new energy percolating up from deep within you. This is the energy of your soul stirring you to set out in new directions, to reinvest in your life with new vigor and new vision. The dawn will always follow the night. New life and personal resurrection will in time come forth from the cocooning period of your grief. You can now embark on the journey of restoring the lost pieces of your broken spirit that you have been mourning. You and your soul will make your spirit whole again. Then you can say with Lucy, "Good grief, Charlie Brown!"

My Spiritual Practice for Today

What new energy and vision for your life has emerged or could emerge from your grief? Describe this developing life picture in your journal. What steps can you take to make the vision come true?

March 28

The Soul Cannot Be Enslaved (Vicki)

Freedom is found in discovering the inner identity
of the Soul in us that cannot be enslaved.
–Paula D'Arcy, from "Oneing, An Alternative
Orthodoxy," cacradicalgrace.org

I met a young woman named Leah, who shared a powerful testimony of being abused and tortured from age 6 by a stepfather. At age 20 she met a handsome older man who made her feel special; he bought beautiful clothes for her, and they dined at upscale restaurants. She was falling in love with this kind man. This went on for six months.

Then one day she questioned him, and he beat her into submission. From that point on, he began selling Leah to others ten to fifteen times a day. She was trafficked throughout the United States. She tried to leave many times and was captured, horribly beaten, and chained to a post in their basement.

Leah's story is happening to women everywhere! The rooms where Leah and other girls serviced the men were called stalls, as if they were farm animals.

Finally Leah was arrested with her trafficker, and she met someone who would listen to what she was enduring at the hands of this man. She is now 30 and is working to rebuild her life with a healthy circle of friends to support her.

Leah is a testament to the human resilience that we all inherently possess. If Leah can survive her experience and come out on the other side to tell her story, so can we. She wants to tell her story to help stop human trafficking and to help others coming out of it. Leah knew her soul could not be enslaved. She cried out to God for help during her years of enslavement. The men could use her body, beat her, torture her, but Leah knew her soul was bigger than anything they could do to her. She knew her freedom would come because she trusted this inherent identity as a child of God.

Perhaps Leah's enslavement became her emancipation.

My Spiritual Practice for Today

I want to recognize the inherent resilience I possess. Today I want to begin visualizing my soul as impervious to enslavement.

March 29

Compassion is an Anti-Depressant (Pat)

The famous psychiatrist Milton Erickson was visiting and lecturing in an American city, and a local psychotherapist asked him to visit one of his patients in her home. The woman had been depressed for many years despite medication and intense work with the therapist. The local therapist hoped that the famous psychiatrist would suggest some profound and ingenious therapeutic intervention to help his "hopeless" case.

Erickson met the woman and chatted with her for a bit. Then he noticed that she had a number of thriving, beautiful African violet plants. He complimented the woman on her green thumb and then told her that he wanted her to grow an African violet for every family that had a funeral at the church to which she belonged. She agreed, and he walked out. In three months her depression lifted.

What happened? Erickson simply invited the woman to tap into her capacity for compassion and thinking of others, and take the focus off her own pain. This antidepressant worked.

Depression and anxiety from your trauma can unwittingly pull you into an excessive and negative egocentric focus on yourself, your pain, and your fearful and negative thoughts. Even shame, paradoxically, can lead to a reverse egoism. You can be so absorbed in the negative thoughts about how uniquely bad you are that the whole focus is you. All of this deepens your depression.

Compassion for others moves you out of yourself. Compassion means "suffering with" the other. Surprisingly, feeling and empathetically experiencing others' suffering liberates the ego. Compassion is an antidepressant and an anti-anxiety agent without any side effects except an enlarged heart and freedom from your small, false ego self.

My Spiritual Practice for Today

Try a dose of compassion today. Come out of yourself to empathize with someone in your life who is suffering. In your meditation, picture someone or a group of people you know to be hurting. Imagine what they are experiencing; put yourself in their place. Ask your soul to guide you to do some act of compassion today. Notice how you feel.

March 30

Anger Is an Antidote (Pat)

Imagine that you have been forced to take a toxic poison. Whether you were coerced, manipulated, or seduced, you had poison injected into your system when you were vulnerable and unable to resist. Imagine that this poison is long-lasting and insidious, and brings on a chronic toxicity and illness that effects every part of your system, even sickening your mind and your spirit. This is what the poison of trauma and abuse does to victims.

One treatment approach to a poisoning is to give an antidote to the toxin, a substance that counteracts and reverses the poison's effects. One of the most powerful antidotes to abuse is soul-empowered anger. You can think of your anger as a grace given to you by your soul and by your God to counteract the poisonous effects of your trauma. It might be surprising to think of anger as a grace, yet it is. It is a grace given as an anti-toxin or anti-venom against the shame and fear that abuse or trauma has inflicted on you.

Anger, like sex, is a powerful life energy that can be either life restoring or life destroying. The key is to let your soul guide you to healthfully and lovingly channel your anger. This makes it holy and life affirming. The soul work of anger frees you from the toxic power of shame, fear, and helplessness inflicted by abuse.

Until you are able to tap into this holy energy of anger, your abuse still controls you and defines you. Your abuser lives on in your shame and fear. When you let your soul open your anger, you set yourself free from your abuse and your abuser. You place the anger where it belongs: on your perpetrator. You reverse the direction of your anger away from yourself where it has been so self-destructive. The energy of your anger, now soul-directed, empowers you to be bold on your own behalf. The power of your abuser is broken and no longer controls you.

My Spiritual Practice for Today

If you have not yet tapped into your anger, ask yourself if is time. If so, invite your soul to open up your anger in a healthy way. One way is to write an angry letter you promise not to send. Pray before you write and let your soul inspire you.

March 31

Anger at God (Pat)

Many survivors are angry with God about their abuse. Their anger often makes them feel guilty and afraid. They fear that God will reject them for it, so they bury their anger.

If this is you, you are robbing yourself of a rich spiritual process. Just as anger at your abuser is holy, anger at God about your abuse can be holy and healing. Lightning will not strike you. You will not be judged or condemned. In fact, your soul and your God will rejoice.

When you are able to express your anger at God, you are joining God in his anger at your abuse. God can take your anger. Who better to express it to? God is even nearer when you express your anger, not in spite of your irate words, but precisely because of them. So if you are angry with God, be honest with yourself and with God. Ask your soul how to express your anger. This may feel scary or shocking. It might cause a temporary feeling of distance in your relationship with God. In the end, it will bring you closer.

The Bible tells the marvelous story of Jacob wrestling all night with a mysterious angel of God. Jacob wrestles the angel to a draw, refusing to let go of him until the angel blesses him. The angel renames Jacob "Israel" which means, "You contended with divine beings." This is a marvelous metaphor for what happens when you are angry with God. You are wrestling with God. You are confronting a divine being with questions like why God "allowed" your abuse.

Wrestling is a very intimate contact sport. You are entwined with God even as you fight. So dare to shake your fist at God. Address your anger and your questions to God. You may not get all the answers that you are looking for. However, in time you will be blessed with inner peace about your questions, gain a release for your anger, and develop a more intimate relationship with your God.

My Spiritual Practice for Today

Write an angry letter to God. Bring it to your prayer and read it to God. Imagine God receiving it with great love and compassion. Or use the "angry" Psalms 10, 17, 22, and 142 to pour out your anger at God.

April 1

The Mountain Meditation: Your Holy Anger (Sue & Pat)

My Spiritual Practice for Today

We invite you to do another version of the Mountain Meditation. To enter into this meditation, find a comfortable sitting position. As you read, pause, close your eyes, and imagine the scenes described.

Picture yourself on a beautiful beach. See the waves, the sand, the brilliant color, and the vastness of the ocean. Feel the sun and the wind on your skin. Hear the crash and whoosh of the surf. Turn around now, and face away from the sea. Looking down, you see a backpack. In it is your just and holy anger about your trauma or abuse. Pick it up and place it on your back. Notice how it feels to carry your anger.

In front of you is a beautiful forest. See yourself walking along a trail into the forest. Appreciate the coolness and the shaded light. You reach the edge of the forest and see an open meadow filled with multicolored wildflowers. The trail leads you through the meadow to a clear, flowing stream with a bridge across the dancing water. Stop for a moment to enjoy the light sparkling on the water.

Now look up from the bridge and see a shining mountain before you. Following the trail, you ascend the mountain. You climb through the clouds, above the timberline to the top of the peak. Look around you at the glory of creation. Then you notice a large boulder to sit on and rest. You take off your backpack and unload your anger.

Then, from the other side of the peak, your spiritual guide comes and sits down with you on the boulder. You can discuss whatever you want. Be sure to share your anger with the guide and ask that your anger be pure, empowering, and healing. Experience your spiritual guide receiving and affirming your holy anger. Listen to what he or she says to you about your anger and how to use it for healing.

When you are ready to leave, thank your guide. Remember what was said to you. Slowly hike back down the mountain, over the bridge, through the meadow, through the forest, to the beach, and to the edge of the vast ocean. Open your eyes. Journal what you experienced and what the guide at the top of the mountain said to you.

April 2

A Safe and Sacred Space (Sue)

A comedian playing a slightly deranged therapist will tell you to "Go to your happy place." We invite you to go to your "holy place."

An essential ingredient in spiritual healing for survivors is that you create for yourself a special place of safety and sacredness that you can retreat to when you need solitude for reflection and prayer or when you need a refuge from any pain that arises.

This can be an actual space, like a meditation room that you create in your home, or a retreat center, chapel, synagogue, mosque, or church that is available to you. It can be your bathtub, your shower, or a quiet nook at your office or in your basement. It can be a place in nature that nurtures your spirit and feels safe to you. Some survivors simply maintain a sacred and quiet place in their mind. They visualize a beautiful and deserted beach or a secluded spot in the mountains, or a place they may have travelled.

It does not matter where you locate your holy place of safety. What matters is that you create such a space that you can retreat to, real or imagined, that is sacred to you, that nurtures your soul, and that feels totally safe emotionally and spiritually.

My Spiritual Practice for Today

Take time today to design, decorate, and plan your sacred space. If it is a physical place, how do you want it to look and to feel? What symbols or images do you want to place in it? How will you make it safe and private, a place of soul refreshment? If it is a visualized place, describe it in detail in your journal so you can go to it easily in your mind. Commit to going to your holy place frequently, if not daily.

April 3

The Little Space of the Heart (Vicki)

The little space within the heart is as great as the vast universe. The heavens and the earth are there, and the sun and the moon and the stars. Fire and lightning and wind are there, and all that now is and all that is not.
–The Upanishads

How can one know the vastness of the heart? How can we know the unfathomable depth to which the heart can take us? When I learned to forgive the man who took so much away from my life, I was able to recognize this depth of the heart. There was a freedom that enveloped me and called me to let go of the tightly held angst I carried every day.

I have learned that we are literally the universe. Our DNA can be traced to the same stardust that is found in the billions of stars that light the night sky. Ashes to ashes, dust to dust. We are formed by stardust, and we go back to stardust. The time we have between our creation and our dying is a finite span of time. It becomes our choice to use that time wisely. Do we want to live in a state of anger and unforgiveness, or do we want to live free of the burdens that anger can bring into our lives?

What is keeping us from living fully? What are the barriers that keep us from taking the step toward forgiveness? To be sure, it is a process of growth and understanding. If we are growing through trauma and abuse, it takes time. However, forgiveness will come into your heart if you are faithful to your process of healing. It is a deeply personal journey to come to a spirit of deep forgiveness, and sometimes it seeps in almost unnoticed. Don't give up on forgiveness. The fire, lightning, and wind are here for a purpose beyond what we see in the sky during a storm. They are there to blow through our spirit to help us release all that is blocked by pain. Let your heart guide you.

My Spiritual Practice for Today

Taking baby steps toward a spirit of forgiveness is part of my healing journey. Today I will think about how I might welcome the spirit of forgiveness in my heart. I will trust that small acts of forgiveness will give me the courage to forgive the larger trauma in my life.

April 4

Anger and Nonviolence (Vicki)

While attending a retreat called Engaging Impasse, I learned an important lesson about creating a nonviolent attitude that would reshape the way I felt. It is called the Two Hands of Nonviolence.

With one hand in the stop position, I say, "Stop what you are doing. You may not abuse me. You may not oppress me. I refuse to obey you. I refuse to cooperate with your demands. I refuse to build the walls and the bombs. I refuse to pay for the guns. I will even interfere with the wrong you are doing. I will not submit to this injustice, not merely because it is destroying me, but because it is destroying you as well."

With the other hand outstretched (maybe with love and sympathy, maybe not, but always outstretched), I say, "I won't let go of you or cast you out of the circle of my care and concern. I have faith that you can make a better choice than you are making now, and I'll be here when you are ready. Like it or not, we are part of one another, part of the beloved community, part of the sacred web of creation." (Adapted from Barbara Deming, *Revolution and Equilibrium,* New York: Grossman Publishers, 1971)

Society has programmed us to believe that when something is perpetrated against us, we have to seek retribution. It is true that justice must be served in many cases. An unhealthy attitude that seeks violent retribution can cause us more emotional and physical trauma that only exacerbates our original trauma.

When I let go of the hateful thinking toward my perpetrator, I was able to take the next step on the pathway of forgiveness. Understanding the Two Hands of Nonviolence allowed me to think differently. I thought about his unhealed emotional trauma that must have led him to abuse me. I began to think of him as a human being who also needed healing.

My Spiritual Practice for Today

I want to reflect on the Two Hands of Nonviolence to see if I can begin to think of my perpetrator as a human being who is also in need of healing. I want to move my anger toward grief and forgiveness so my soul can be free of debilitating anger.

April 5

A Sacred Moment (Pat)

One of the most sacred moments I have ever experienced was when I facilitated a meeting between an abusive priest and one of his victims. This priest, now deceased, was then in his late seventies. He had sexually abused several young girls while serving in various pastoral positions. He finally stopped when he was caught and sent to prison. He was grateful that he was arrested and punished because it brought his terrible abusive behavior to an end.

He had been in counseling with me for a little over a year when one of his victims called to ask for a meeting. She was by then a woman in her early fifties. They both agreed that I would facilitate the meeting. The priest began the meeting by again apologizing to his victim (they had met once before) for abusing her and for the tremendous harm he had caused her. She accepted his apology and then expressed her forgiveness to him. He answered her questions about the past to help her further heal. I described to her some aspects of his history and sickness that I thought would also help in her healing.

The most moving moment came when I told her that the priest had also been sexually abused when he was a child—at the same age he abused her. The priest had revealed this information to me for the first time just a few months prior. He had never told anyone before. His victim was deeply saddened to hear that he too had been abused and said to the priest how sorry she was for him.

It is difficult to put into words the feeling that was in that room as we spoke. It was a sacred moment. There was a presence of divine Spirit, a holy and palpable peace. It felt, too, that a great weight of pain had been lifted and an old, rusty chain had been broken and carried away. The awful Gordian knot of abuse had been cut by the priest's apology and by the woman's forgiveness and compassion. They had together broken the cycle of abuse.

My Spiritual Practice for Today

Survivors have a whole range of emotional reactions to this story. Be aware of yours. Whatever you feel is all right and a part of your healing.

April 6

Accepting Acceptance (Pat & Sue)

We accept that we are accepted by God; we accept that we are
accepted and loved not for what we do—simply because we are!
–The Spiritual Laundry List

You are already accepted. You are already loved. You are already acceptable and loveable. It's not because you have been working so hard to make yourself acceptable. It is grace, it is gift. Your Higher Power already sees you as loveable and already accepts you. It just is so. Your only job is to accept your acceptance. You have already won the greatest lottery in the universe. You just have to turn in your ticket! When you accept your acceptance, you will be free of shame, and you will abide in the deep reassurance and confidence that no matter what, you are accepted, you are loved, and you are cherished.

This comes to different people in different ways. For some survivors, it will require a daily conscious choice to accept acceptance until it fully sinks in. You can do this by repeating the mantra, "I am accepted, I am loved." This could be your centering prayer for a time. For other survivors who have experienced acceptance in an intimate, loving relationship, you can transfer that experience to your relationship with God. You can trust that you are loved and accepted even more by God.

Sometimes the acceptance comes in a flash, a deep spiritual experience of being loved. Paul Tillich, the great Christian theologian, describes one such spiritual experience in his book *The Shaking of the Foundations*: "It is as though a voice were saying: 'You are accepted, you are accepted, you are accepted, accepted by that which is greater than you…Do not try to do anything now; perhaps later you will do much. Do not seek anything; do not perform anything; do not intend anything. Simply accept the fact that you are accepted!'"

My Spiritual Practice for Today

Choose to accept the spiritual truth that you are accepted, here and now, just as you are. Make that the focus of your meditation. All day long repeat to yourself: "I am accepted."

April 7

The Circle of Life (Pat)

Nature does not waste anything. Everything gets recycled for a new purpose beyond itself. All matter changes into some new matter, some new life or energy. This is the great "Circle of Life." Dung, which began as food, is transformed into fertilizer. A wounded or dying tree provides housing for owls, woodpeckers, and squirrels, and eventually food for insects and the earth into which it finally falls.

One of my favorite nature metaphors for transformation involves a certain species of palm tree in Africa. It produces a large nut, a seed that can only sprout into new life and produce a new tree if it is eaten by an elephant. It must pass through the elephant's digestive system to be activated and then is ejected onto the ground with the elephant's copious and smelly excrement. This provides an excellent fertilized start for the new tree that sprouts from the nut.

There is a seed of new life in your traumatic experience. Even the dung of your trauma and abuse, transformed in the digestive process of your healing journey, can become fertilizer for a new purpose in your life! As a survivor of abuse, what is the larger purpose of your healing journey? It is no doubt meant first to be a gift for you so you can live more freely and abundantly. However, your soul seeks to bring forth an even higher purpose for you. Your soul has been working in you to transform the oppression and darkness of your abuse into something life giving. This is for your own sake, yet it is not for your sake alone. It is also for the healing and enlightenment of all those in your world.

Your soul invites you to discover a new and transcendent purpose for living as a healed survivor from abuse. Another way to say this is that there is a spiritual call to some new life purpose or mission embedded in the soil of your healing journey. Your soul, your God, wants to play you—even your trauma—like a golden harp to bring unique, beautiful, and healing music to the world.

My Spiritual Practice for Today

Simply be with these questions: What will your call, your life mission be? How does your soul want to transform your healed trauma into a blessing for others?

April 8

The Deepest Freshness (Pat)

The world is charged with the grandeur of God. It will flame
out, like shining from shook foil; it gathers to greatness, like
the ooze of oil crushed...And for all this, nature is never spent;
there lives the deepest freshness deep down things.
–Gerald Manley Hopkins, poet, 1877

When nothing else speaks to you spiritually, when your prayer and meditation feels dry and empty, when people seem to have failed you, or when your smartphone turns stupid and blah, go to nature to be renewed and recharged. Go to the beach and feel the power of the ocean. Go to any lake or stream and sense the energy of water. Take a walk on a cold, clear winter day and see the brilliant white light on the bare branches of the trees. Hike in the mountains and let them lift your heart and spirit into their heights. Go for a long, slow stroll through the woods on a warm spring day and see and feel nature awakening. As the poet says, "there lives the deepest freshness deep down things" of nature. Nature will never fail you. You can always discover her freshness and be refreshed and renewed in body, mind, and spirit.

Nature is also a place to meet God, even when God seems to be nowhere else. Nature is charged with the energy, glory, and grandeur of God. Native American spirituality especially senses God all around in the midst of her creation and her creatures. Native American spirituality sees the divine, the presence of Wakan Tanka (the Sioux name for God) everywhere, infusing all things with divine energy and power.

Urban life has distanced and separated us from the natural world. We are not in tune with the rhythms of the seasons, the change of light, the seasonal behaviors of birds and animals. Reconnecting with nature can be a powerful resource for your spiritual healing and growth. "Nature is never spent," even when you are. Make it part of your spirituality to spend time in nature, and receive the gift of its deep down freshness and grandeur.

My Spiritual Practice for Today

Go for a walk in a beautiful natural place. See, taste, smell, hear, and feel all the goodness of nature that surrounds you. Know that you are one with that goodness.

April 9

A Deeper, Truer Life (Vicki)

Anger can be felt in the hard clenched fist, the knot in the pit of the stomach, the incessant negative thoughts regarding another; perhaps it's the one who has hurt us. Imagine if we could harness the energy it takes to remain stuck in anger and instead spend it on giving and receiving love. It might just transform the world; it might be the key to real peace.

I remember being humiliated in front of a respected group of people once. It was all I could do to not get up and run out of the room. It was brutal, shaming, and highly inappropriate. That one instance remains in my memory; it was a time when I felt consumed by anger. That sleepless night I wept, I swore, and I vowed never to allow anyone to treat me that way again. It was a visceral sensing of the true character of the priest who abused me. People are frozen in time when these things happen. Not one person came to my defense. This experience was the beginning of the courage I would need to walk away from this man who had used me for his own gain.

It's prophetic how a specific experience like this can be the catalyst for change. Because I felt this shaming so deeply, I could see what a broken and abusive man he truly was.

Parker Palmer in his book *Let Your Life Speak* writes: "Everyone has a life that is different from the 'I' of daily consciousness, a life that is trying to live through the 'I' who is its vessel. This is what the poet knows and what every wisdom tradition teaches: There is a great gulf between the way my ego wants to identify me, with its protective masks and self-serving fictions, and my true self. It takes time and hard experience to sense the difference between the two—to sense that running beneath the surface of the experience I call my life, there is a deeper and truer life waiting to be acknowledged."

My Spiritual Practice for Today

Today I want to reflect on the times when I have felt angry. I want to feel the anger, acknowledge it has affected my healing journey, and work on releasing my anger so I can move forward.

April 10

Soul Puzzle (Pat)

This is a puzzle (or koan) from your soul to reflect on. What does it mean to you?

If you have a who and a why,
you can live, even thrive,
with most any what or how.

Before you read the next paragraph take some time to ask yourself how this soul riddle speaks to you.

One interpretation, but only one of many, is along the following lines. If you have a who in your life—a lover, partner, spouse, or friends, or even the who of your God—and if you have a sense of life purpose—your why for living—the circumstances, the what's of your life and how you are going about your life are much less important to the quality of your life.

You may think that you need a certain set of conditions or a certain life history to be happy or do well in life. You may also think that you have to make the perfect choices about how to live your life. Actually, what truly creates deep soul satisfaction are relationships of intimacy, closeness, and support where you are known and loved. This can come from fellow humans, your pets, and/or from your relationship with your Higher Power.

The other key to thriving in your life is to have a sense of life purpose, which is different and unique for each person. If you can say, "This is why I live and take up space and oxygen on this planet. This is why I get up every morning and move with energy and joy through my day." If you are connected to your who and you have a sense of your why, your life purpose, you will thrive no matter the whats and the hows happening now and in your past.

My Spiritual Practice for Today

Continue to reflect on this puzzle from your soul. Do you focus too much on the circumstances of your life or remain stuck in the wish that you had a different personal history without the trauma? How can you better value and cherish the relationships in your life? How can you discover and fully live your life purpose and personal mission?

April 11

Tears Are Holy Water (Sue)

During and after my primal-scream anger period, much grief about my abuse and my life surfaced: loss of an emotionally healthy mom; loss of my childhood in many ways because I became my mom's caretaker; the sadness and humiliation of Mom's erratic, irrational, hysterical outbursts and behavior after our assault; the opportunities that I missed as a child to be open, free, and visible. I began, too, to grieve things missing in my adult life. There were far too many possibilities never realized, too many healthy paths never chosen or that I had allowed to be blocked.

In my forties, I pursued several years of professional training and personal and spiritual growth work with my mentor and pioneer family therapist, Virginia Satir. In a sense, it was a years-long spiritual retreat to allow God to help me discover the hidden person that I always was. There were periods during this time of great joy, of exciting discovery, and personal breakthroughs.

It was also, off and on, a time of great grief, especially about what might have been. I grieved and ended my first marriage. I grieved, for the first time, the deaths at childbirth of two of my children. I grieved the constrained and fearful life that in some ways I had led since I was four.

I shed many tears and learned that tears are holy water. They blessed me with release and healing from my losses. Tears of mourning need to be collected in a sacred vessel and then drunk as a sacrament of healing for heart, mind, and soul. I drank from this cup often during this time. However, I emerged from this long passage of my life a new person—really, though, the person that I had always invisibly been—with a new life.

This is the life that I live now and have been living gratefully, joyfully, for many years. Sacred grief and holy tears helped to prepare the way.

My Spiritual Practice for Today

List all of the losses you have suffered because of your trauma. Allow yourself to feel the grief of these losses. If you shed tears, be grateful and bless them and let them flow. Share your grief with your therapist, spiritual guide, or soul friend.

April 12

The Longest Ten Inches (Pat & Sue)

The longest ten inches in the universe is the gap between your head and your heart. Clients tell us that they know something intellectually in their head, but they cannot move it those ten inches into their heart where we experience emotions. It's like there is a metal trap door lodged somewhere in your throat that blocks your head from convincing your heart. This trap door blocks your head and your heart from uniting.

This same head-heart split can be seen spiritually as well. You might carry one set of spiritual beliefs in your head and a different set of contrasting spiritual beliefs in your heart. It is often the emotionally based beliefs that are the most powerful in forming you spiritually. The heart level of emotional beliefs is where victims experience the spiritual wounds from trauma. The difficulty is that you sometimes are not aware of what is happening to you spiritually at this heart-and-gut level. It is like a spiritual subconscious, unseen yet powerfully influencing you.

For example, imagine that you are in church for a Sunday service. The preacher talks about how much God loves you. Your head assents to the idea of God's love, but deep down you feel unloved. You question how God could love you if he allowed you to be abused. You think that God may love others, but question God's love for you when your shame makes you feel unworthy and defective. Or you believe that God's love comes with major conditions, that God requires you to get an A+ in life, and you think you are getting an F, or at best a D–. You don't feel God's love for you no matter what your head and the preacher says.

It is from this split that many spiritual struggles, and even crises of faith, are born. The solution is to wake up and see what is happening inside of you. Then consciously, patiently bring your head beliefs deeper and deeper into your heart.

My Spiritual Practice for Today

List the emotional spiritual beliefs created by your trauma. How do they affect you? Pick one and work on it today. For example, if you feel you are unworthy of God's love, choose a positive affirmation: "I am worthy, and God loves me." Repeat it like a mantra all day, breathing it each time deep into your heart.

April 13

The Circle of Value (Sue)

In response to the shame I saw in my survivor clients, I developed a process that I named "The Circle of Value." The Circle of Value is based on the spiritual truth that you are a magnificent person of infinite value. That is simply so. It is so because of your True Nature, your True Self, the spark of the divine within that is your soul. The Circle of Value gives a symbolic image and a process for integrating this essential truth into every fiber of your being.

The mental process goes like this: Every time you catch yourself thinking a shame-based thought or any negative self-talk, repeat the negative phrase to yourself and then add, "And I am a magnificent person of value." Then visualize placing that negative thought inside the Circle of Value. Doing this means that this negative thought, true or not, does not subtract from your essential value and worth—which just is. This is your soul's message.

Here is the surprising part. It is just as important that you do the same thing with any positive thoughts that your ego attempts to use to build you up, even if they are true. It is important to realize that the ego contributes to your shame by artificially trying to pump up your self-esteem. Neither strengths nor weaknesses, virtues nor vices can add to or subtract from your infinite value, which is simply your divine truth, totally independent of personal characteristics.

When you think of something positive about yourself, or when you receive an affirmation from someone, take it in, enjoy it, and put it in the Circle of Value. Repeat the positive phrase to yourself and add, "And I am a magnificent person of value." If you regularly use the Circle of Value, you will gradually integrate your soul's truth about your True Nature and infinite worth.

My Spiritual Practice for Today

Draw a circle in your journal. Label it "The Circle of Value." Each day write inside the circle your positive and negative thoughts about yourself, always followed by this mantra: "And I am a magnificent person of infinite value." Make it your daily prayer and your special sacrament.

April 14

Awakening from the Heart (Vicki)

*Your visions will become clear only when you can look into your
own heart. Who looks outside dreams; who looks inside awakes.*
                              –C. G. Jung

It is true that my vision could not become clear until I could see what was
in my heart, hidden deeply away. Many layers of denial, disbelief, and fear
had to be dismantled before I could see clearly the path before me. I was
beginning to dream about what my life could be. However, I hadn't started
the work of dissection yet. This kept me from awakening to the truest part of
myself. It was impossible to know the quality of the meaning of awakening to
myself because I could not see the truth of who I was or even what potential
lay within me. Being mired in such emotional discomfort, it was difficult to
see anything hopeful for the future.

Truly, Jung's words, "who looks inside awakens," couldn't be more true.
The first awareness of the truth of what I had been living for so many years
was the first peek into my heart. And once that initial opening happened,
I was able to begin to lay it all out for dissection and understanding. It may
sound like a science project in those terms, but it really is a systematic way of
opening ourselves to the truth.

The consistent challenge of all that kept me in servitude to a deeply dysfunctional person began to be chiseled away, and his grip began to release.
To be sure, it was a co-dependence that had to be broken, a dependence that
began at the age of 8.

Freedom from dominance, freedom from servitude, freedom from
the clamp wrapped tightly around my person finally began to be released.
Understanding brought clarity and answers to long-held questions. Things
made sense. I could understand the reasons why this happened. I could begin
to see my full potential as a woman and see a vision for a better life ahead.
Thirty years later, I can see the steady path toward fulfilling those visions that
came to me after my heart was awakened.

My Spiritual Practice for Today

Today I want to look deeply into my heart to see what I have buried there for fear of anyone knowing. I want to release the pain so I can begin to see the vision for my own life clearly.

April 15

Grace (Pat & Sue)

Pope Francis says, "Grace is the amount of light in our souls." We say that there is an immense amount of light in the souls of each of you. The difficulty is that the dark night of trauma keeps you from seeing the amount of grace light that exists in you. It is there. We have seen it in many survivors who couldn't see it themselves. We hold up a mirror so they can eventually see it.

Grace is the energy and spark of divinity with you. The word "grace" emphasizes that you do not have to work for or earn your grace. It is given. It is a gift. It is offered you always. All you have to do is receive it. Wow! Christmas or your birthday every day and in every moment! Living in Graceland is learning to open up the opportunities for grace that are always around you and basking in the warmth and light that flows like a luminous spring within you.

Although you do not earn grace, you can do things to enhance its flow and expand its power in you. Grace is kindled especially when you are grateful for the blessings in your life. Every time you express gratitude, your light expands and glows brighter. You energize your grace when you acknowledge the light in someone else and pray that they be blessed. You intensify your grace whenever you choose light over the darkness with which trauma and some forces in the world attempt to surround you. Perhaps grace comes most alive when you see your own grace light and affirm it. This is difficult for many survivors. So perhaps imagine that the words of the angel Gabriel said first to Mary (and repeated in the traditional prayer) are being said to you:

"Hail _____(your name), full of grace, the Lord is with you. Blessed are you among women (and among men)."

Amen! (Which means "So be it!") Repeat as needed.

My Spiritual Practice for Today

Reflect on grace in your life. How easy is it to see it working in your life? Can you discern and count your blessings and give thanks for them? Look for all the opportunities for grace today. Open each gift offered you, embrace it, and enjoy.

April 16

A Precious Wound (Pat)

Once upon a time, there was an Irish king who came into possession of a diamond that became his great treasure. He displayed it in a prominent place in the center of his throne room. It was a large stone with many hints of light and color, but uncut and unpolished.

One morning the king entered his throne room alone and let out a great cry of anguish. When his courtiers rushed in, they beheld the king on his knees before his great diamond, his eyes transfixed on a large, new crack in the heart of the stone. The crack threatened to shatter the diamond into a million tiny pieces. The king frantically called for his experts to save the stone, but no one could figure out what to do to preserve the now-fragile gem.

One day a mysterious bearded monk with long, straggly hair and a tattered robe came into the king's court. The wild-looking man stood silently before the diamond for the longest time, looking deep into its center. Finally, the monk turned to the king and spoke. "I can save your diamond. But you must leave me alone with it for the next three days without any interruptions." At first the king was skeptical and was tempted to throw the presumptuous monk out, but he relented and gave the monk permission to work on his cherished diamond.

At the end of the third day, the king asked to come in. Upon entering, the king gasped and fell to his knees. There before him, reflecting all the light of day, was a magnificent, glittering crystal diamond rose artfully cut by the monk from the king's unpolished stone. Then the real miracle became apparent to him. The monk had ingeniously carved the crack, which had once threatened to destroy the diamond, into the very stem of the gemstone rose, a crystalline stem that now held the rose up firmly into the light.

The moral of the story and the miracle of transformation is that your soul can take even the deep wound of your trauma and shape it into a precious and beautiful gem that will shine brightly for all to see.

My Spiritual Practice for Today

Ponder the fable of the king's diamond. How is the precious wound of your trauma being transformed into something beautiful and sacred?

April 17

Self-Compassion (Pat)

Self-compassion is one of the keys to having a satisfying life. Self-compassion is the ability to have empathy for yourself, to feel for yourself, and to care about yourself no matter what. It is treating yourself with the kindness, care, concern, and understanding that you would give to a loved one. It is realizing and accepting that you are a magnificent personal of infinite value, yet you are imperfect—and that is perfectly all right. You live a wondrous, blessed, and yet imperfect life, and that is just fine as well. Ultimately, self-compassion is loving yourself with all of your gifts, talents, and strengths, as well as your mistakes, messes, and weaknesses. Self-compassion empowers you to believe in yourself, celebrate your successes, and also admit, learn from, and correct your mistakes. Self-confidence and even self-esteem without self-compassion can be brittle, appearing strong, and yet too easily broken by mistakes, setbacks, and suffering.

Self-compassion is particularly essential for survivors, and yet for many it is difficult to achieve. Some survivors were told that the abuse was their fault. Other survivors blame themselves in some fashion for their trauma. This toxic shame blocks self-compassion. Many survivors are left with a merciless inner voice that constantly judges them and keeps them from ever feeling for themselves.

This is unfortunate because self-compassion has been proven to be a factor in overcoming and healing from trauma. For instance, one study of veterans showed that the more self-compassionate they were, the less severe their PTSD symptoms. The ability to have empathy for yourself, especially about your trauma, is vital to healing and will even lessen your pain.

One way to build self-compassion is to imagine how a loved one would speak to you about your trauma or your mistakes and weaknesses. Or how you would speak to your own child if they had experienced something similar. You can learn to give yourself the same compassion and love that you give to others.

My Spiritual Practice for Today

Write a short letter of self-compassion to yourself today. Express your empathy and understanding for what you have been through and for any mistakes you have made. Then choose one act of self-compassionate kindness to do for yourself today.

April 18

Discovering Your Quirky, Wonderful Self (Vicki)

The decisive question for [every human] is: Is he [or she] related to
something infinite or not? That is the telling question of…life.
–Carl Jung

I've known this deep longing for a lifetime. It's the thing that draws me to want to sit quietly with a book of deep spirituality and just let the words sink in so I can reflect on life. It draws me to a focus of what is real and what is just ego language that does not reflect my true self. Perhaps the phrase "It keeps me grounded" fits best here. Always being drawn deeper and deeper into a life of infinite love in the Spirit has always felt true. Wisdom lies there. It is just waiting to be discovered. I longed for that wisdom and saw it as a language that would help me grow and overcome the areas where I felt weak and stuck.

The old adage that says "It's important to always hitch your wagon to something bigger than yourself" rings true with Carl Jung's statement. Are we related to something bigger than ourselves, something infinite? It is a serious question for every life. To what can I attach my gifts, my particular and unique abilities, in order to make a difference in the world?

We can become blind to that vision if we don't wipe away the film of chaos from our true vision. If we don't take care of the unhealed wounds in our lives, we cannot release the true gift of each life. Who we are in this day and time is a precious gift to the world. Each of us is filled with a quirky, fun, genius-like personality that can solve myriad problems in the world. What are we being called to do? What inner gift is waiting to emerge to make this planet a better world?

My Spiritual Practice for Today

Today I want to make a list of all of the wonderful attributes that are uniquely mine. Even if at this moment I don't believe in myself, I'm going to write down the ways my gifts can make a difference.

April 19

Be Your Self (Pat & Sue)

Awoman once became very distraught at one of our workshops because she thought we were telling her she had to change herself, and she felt helpless to do this. We reassured her that this was not what we were teaching. We explained that we were actually saying not to change herself at all. In fact, we invited her to give herself permission to be who she already was, to be the person she was created to be. We encouraged her to simply accept herself, just as she was, and to know that she was already accepted, chosen, and loved by God and the universe. The woman left the workshop very relieved.

All survivors need to hear this message. You need to hear that you are wondrous, sacred, accepted, and beloved just as you are. Your healing journey will certainly lead to changes in your thoughts and beliefs, actions and choices. It will not, however, mean that you need to make a major overhaul of your core self. Who you are is just excellent. The message from your trauma that you are not fine as you are is a lie.

Your healing will empower you to be even more yourself, your True Self, the real you that you were created to be. Your authentic and best self will be brought forth. So don't plan on changing—although much in your life will change. Plan simply to be more of who you already are. Rejoice, celebrate, and revel in your coming-out party, your coming out from the darkness and chains of your trauma to the freedom to be simply and brilliantly who you are right now.

My Spiritual Practice for Today

Celebrate today the goodness of who you already are. Throw a party for yourself. Reward yourself today, not for anything you have done, but simply because you are you. Give yourself some special self-care treat. Celebrate ways that you have already become more yourself, and be conscious of how it will feel to grow into being the best of yourself as your life's journey progresses.

April 20

Naming and Mourning Your Losses (Pat)

As a survivor of trauma, you have a lot to grieve. Trauma has inflicted many losses on you and has, in effect, stolen many things from your life. This meditation is about naming and mourning these losses.

When a loved one dies, the loss is often clear, and the pain is usually focused. With grief about trauma, the pain can be just as intense, but it is often vague and diffuse, and the losses involved are less obvious. Part of your healing work is to name and properly mourn your losses, to fully grieve what was taken from you.

The goal of grief is to free you from the hold and oppression of the past. If you still live controlled and haunted by the events of the past, then you have less energy for your life in the present. You are not living in the *now* of your life. You are trudging through life with heavy baggage that is no longer useful. It simply weighs you down and keeps pulling you back into the past. Grief puts the past in the past and prepares you to move into a new future.

Paradoxically, before you can let it go and be in your now, grief requires you to first revisit the past. I am frequently asked by my clients, "Why do I need to explore my past? I want to forget the pain that I went through. Why dredge it all up again?"

If the past is truly past and it no longer affects you, then, indeed, there is no reason to go back there. However, for many survivors of trauma, the past is still very much present and alive in them, impacting them in a variety of significant ways. Until it is faced, felt, and understood, the past continues to haunt and overshadow your present life and functioning. You are not living in the *now* of your life. You are driving forward through your life by looking in the rearview mirror—a dangerous way to drive! Naming your losses and grieving them is a way to honor your pain, let go, and move into the present.

My Spiritual Practice for Today

Take time to list all of the losses you incurred as a result of your trauma. What was taken from you physically, emotionally, relationally, and spiritually? Choose one loss that you have not fully mourned and allow yourself to grieve it this day.

April 21

Namaste (Pat)

"Namaste" is a beautiful, powerful greeting and gesture that comes from the Hindu spirituality of India. It involves holding your hands in the folded prayer position over your chest, your heart chakra, and slightly bowing to another person. You can either say, "Namaste" or remain silent as you bow. The gesture and word is an expression of the divinity in you acknowledging the divinity in the other. Your soul, your divine spark, recognizes the divine soul in the other. In Hinduism, it means, "I bow to the divine in you." It can be a greeting or a goodbye. It can be a blessing or an expression of deep gratitude for the other. If it is done with deep feeling and with the mind surrendered, it can deepen your connection with the other person.

It can also be a meditation. You can go through your day doing namaste to everyone you encounter. You can do this unobtrusively by simply nodding your head toward each one. Silently acknowledge the divine within each person you meet. Or perhaps visualize each important person in your life, like your family and your soul friends, one at a time and express namaste to them. If you are ready, you could also do namaste to the difficult people in your life. Perhaps even to your abuser. This does not mean that you accept any abuse or wrong done to you. It simply means you know that there is a divine spark within each person, even if it is covered by the darkness of his or her actions.

You can also do namaste to yourself as a meditation. Fold your hands over your heart and bow to yourself. Acknowledge the divinity within you. See with your spiritual third eye the divine spark, light, and energy within your soul. Know what infinite and eternal value this gives to you. This can be incredibly healing. Your abuser did not acknowledge the sacred divinity with you and profaned the sacred temple that you are. Even this could not put out your divine light. Every namaste to yourself restores your awareness of who you truly are. Namaste!

My Spiritual Practice for Today

Either express namaste to everyone you meet today or focus the namaste on yourself. Notice how it changes how you see others and how you feel within yourself.

April 22

The Transforming Power of Love (Vicki)

Obstinate are the trammels, but my heart aches when I
try to break them…I am certain that priceless wealth is in
thee and that thou are my best friend but I have not the
heart to sweep away the tinsel that fills my room.
–Rabindranath Tagore

We often dig our heals in deeply in resistance to letting go of long-held pain. The longer we hold on to pain, the deeper its roots grow. There is a love that is stronger than all of the pain we have endured, all of the heartaches that have befallen us. That love is there for us. We only have to ask for it. And yet, the asking can be such a fearful thing to do.

The unhealthy relationship had been going on for five years. Emotionly I was a mess. Despite my family's fear of me going to India, at 24 I left to spend time with Mother Teresa's community. It was a journey that would open my eyes to the magic of love on a grand scale. It would begin to sweep away the tinsel that was filling my room. I was being led by a love that had the power to unlock the human heart.

I lived with a group of nurses who worked at a mission hospital for the poorest. It was primitive at best, only metal bars on the windows. Birds flew through the hospital frequently. Each morning as I would leave to work with the sisters, I would pass by little Dubuk. He was 7 years old and suffering from tuberculosis of the bone. His legs were greatly diminished, and he could not walk. His mother slept on the floor next to his bed most nights. We couldn't communicate with words, but we communicated with our hearts. I fell in love with this little guy, his sweet smile and his gentle acceptance of his paralysis. His image is still on my heart.

Among the gifts of this journey, the greatest was the softening of my heart. I began to let go of the anger that I harbored. I began to see my life in a larger context and that a different life was possible. The ache in my heart had subsided because I felt the transforming power of love.

My Spiritual Practice for Today

Finding a love that can transform requires a willingness to seek that love. Today I want to consider the ways I can find the power of transforming love and invite it into my life.

April 23

Emerging Consciousness (Vicki)

The secret of change is to focus all of your energy not on fighting the old but on building the new.
–Socrates, from "Charter for Compassion"

Can you sit and feel what is emerging within you? A desire for answers, for clarity? Can you feel within you a divine emergence, something that is drawing you to more?

Emerging consciousness is that calling that comes from deep within that says you can become more of whom you were meant to be. It's a dissonance, a sort of chaos within your soul that says, "I need to fix this chaos in my life." It isn't saying dwell on the past; it is saying look to the future, to all that your life can become. It is saying step out of the past, the hurt, the trauma and embrace a new emerging consciousness.

We can only curse the past for so long before we either decide to stay there for the rest of our lives or choose to embrace the unknown future where hope lies. If we want to be happy, if we want to take control of our lives, now is the time to step away from the past, do the work that is required, and embrace new life. It does not come by simply wishing. It comes through hard, gut-wrenching work. An emerging consciousness is that place within us that is calling for wholeness and authenticity. It is a deep well that is thirsting to be quenched. The answers are there if you seek them.

I didn't know it then, but when my friend suggested calling a counselor she knew, that mere suggestion sparked the emerging consciousness within me. I knew there was something more for me in the world. Every step I took toward fulfilling that emerging consciousness brought me closer, and each step ignited a new level of consciousness that gave me the strength to continue.

We must become who we are meant to become. No one can do this for us. It is our work alone. And there are many competent psychotherapists who can guide us on the journey.

My Spiritual Practice for Today

Today I will reflect on how my consciousness is emerging. I will begin to think about this in terms of my spiritual journey. I will reach out for help and find someone who can guide me as I begin this journey.

April 24

Recycling Your Trauma (Pat)

Your trauma is recyclable. There is a toxic, self-destructive way to recycle and a healthy way that is good for your personal environment. Survivors recycle their trauma destructively every time they step back into the cycle of abuse and allow themselves to be revictimized.

This negative recycling is seen especially when survivors enter and remain in abusive relationships. The promise or hope for love pulls you into a friendship or relationship that turns abusive, emotionally, physically, or sexually. Your original trauma is recycled into a new form of victimization.

These vicious circles are at times difficult to break out of. You keep hoping for love, and you believe that you deserve the abuse or could not get anything better. The new trauma feels all too familiar. The gravity of the past feels incredibly strong.

However, you can break out of the vicious circle by recycling your perceived helplessness and shame into holy anger and self-empowerment. Your soul and God stand with you in your just anger when you say, "Time's up! No more abuse!" to your abuser. You can decide, "I will no longer be my own abuser and revictimize myself." You can even choose to recycle your abuser and move him or her out of your life.

This kind of recycling takes time, patience, and careful, safe strategy. What is most important is that you open your eyes to see abusive patterns in your present life and that you know you have the heart and soul power within you to end that abuse. You can recycle and transform any traumatic situation into a new abuse-free environment for yourself.

My Spiritual Practice for Today

Look at your life today and see if there are any ways that you are still caught in the cycle of abuse and suffering revictimization. Pick one of these patterns or situations to work on. See how you can recycle and change this into something healthy and life giving for you.

April 25

Lamentations (Pat)

Sometimes things are so breathtakingly awful there is nothing to do but lament. And some things are so sad that only your soul can do the lamenting for you. Many spiritual traditions understand this and offer prayers, psalms, and rituals of lamentation and grief to provide expression and solace for the mourning process. Laments bring forth from the depths of your grieving heart and your soul your brokenness, your cries for deliverance, and your desperate need for healing.

There is a time and a season in the healing journey of survivors of abuse to lament the awfulness of what has happened to you. There is a time for grieving what trauma has cost you and what you have lost. You can safely give yourself permission, time, and space to lament.

Be gentle with yourself, however, in your grieving. Be especially attentive to self-care when you are in a time of lamentation because it can be painful. Stop if you feel overwhelmed. You do not need to grieve alone. Share your sadness and your losses with a counselor, a spiritual guide, or your soul friend.

My Spiritual Practice for Today

Read and reflect on any of the sorrowful Psalms from the Old Testament of the Judeo-Christian tradition: Psalms 5, 6, 13, 14, 22, 31, 39, 63, 69, 77, 88, 102, 116, 126, and 139. In your journal, write about how they touch you. What emotions do they invoke in you? How does it feel to bring your sadness before your soul and before your God as the psalmist does?

Or write your own broken-heart prayer expressing your sorrow, sadness, and grief about your abuse. Address it to your soul or to your Higher Power. Make it your primary prayer today, or pray it daily for a week or as long as you need in order to fully access and feel your grief. Share your prayer with a spiritual guide or companion.

April 26

Open the Faucet (Sue)

At times in your healing journey, you will experience, as I sometimes do, a buildup of sadness inside. You feel the sadness whooshing up and the pressure building to let the emotions rise to the surface and flow out of your tear ducts. A part of you though is afraid and ashamed of what you are feeling. Or you are ashamed of crying, especially in front of someone else. These are the times to remember that tears are holy water. They are sacred and healing, and they need to be released.

You can push past your fear and embarrassment and choose to open the faucet and let the tears flow. They may come out as a trickle; they may burst forth as a flood. Don't be afraid, you won't drown! No one has ever died from crying.

Every drop is a blessing. Did you know that every teardrop contains stress chemicals that you release from your body when you cry? A good cry is healing for men (who usually have a harder time with it) and women. Keep the faucet open for as long as you need. Sometimes it is most healing to weep alone—one of my favorite places is the shower—and sometimes it is important to share your tears with another.

One of your fears is probably that someone else will judge you or reject and abandon you if you show the "weakness" of tears. With a true soul friend, it will be just the opposite. Your soul friend will be honored and touched by you sharing your tears. His or her faucet may open as well. It will actually bring greater intimacy and deepened closeness with your soul friend as well as with your soul and with your God.

Then, when you feel a sense of relief, you can close the faucet and dry your tears. Careful, don't close your faucet too tight. You will want it to open easily for the next time.

My Spiritual Practice for Today

Give yourself permission to open the faucet and cry as needed. Then when the emotions build up inside, you will be ready to let them flow and become healing waters for you.

April 27

Rekindling the Light (Vicki)

Sometimes our light goes out but is blown into
flame by another human being.
Each of us owes deepest thanks to those who have rekindled this light.
–Albert Schweitzer

The list of those who helped to rekindle the flame in my soul after several years of therapy and healing is a long one. Our interconnectedness with other people becomes prominent when we go through such a heart-wrenching process. Finally, after the secret was revealed, I was able to ask for the help I needed and then knew that my dear friends and family were there for me. When I finally had the courage to speak, it felt as though I had laid down a heavy burden.

We don't have to go through life suffering silently without support. People who loved me before they knew this secret loved me after they knew. I know that isn't always the case. Thankfully, it was true for me.

Cynthia Bourgeault writes, "When you can lean into yearning, you discover it is not a sign of absence, but a sacrament of connection." Those who love us and want to stand with us through life's challenges are a sacrament of connection. They are our people, a connection of love that wants to make sure that all who are in the circle of connection are cared for and loved. We shouldn't deny them the opportunity to serve, to be present to us.

There was a visible shift in my growth and healing once my family and friends knew what I had been going through. I felt buoyed by their love and support, and it deepened my desire to continue the journey I was taking with my therapist. I had begun to see the light and knew in my soul that I was being re-created into who God was truly calling me to become. I felt excited and encouraged to continue. There were difficult moments still to come throughout the process; however, now I knew that I could endure it all.

My Spiritual Practice for Today

Today I will think about reaching out to a trusted friend or family member to tell them my story and ask for their support. I will be clear about what I will need from them so they can truly be present to me throughout my healing process.

April 28

A Soul Selfie (Sue)

If you had a highly advanced camera with special spiritual technology that could take a soul selfie, what would you see? Since this has never been done, we don't exactly know, but we do know you would see the essential, eternal core of light, love, and energy deep within you that is most truly and essentially who you are. You would see your True Self.

Throughout history, the human species seems to have an intuitive understanding that there is something within that transcends the material, observable world. Whether this understanding is expressed religiously in the great spiritual traditions of East and West, or through art, myth, storytelling, literature, dance, music, theater, or the pursuit of scientific truth, we generally feel that there is something more about us than meets the eye. That which is transcendent within us is named many things in different spiritual traditions: our inner divine spark, our Christ or our Buddha nature, our interior wisdom box, the life breath or life force that animates us, the energy of the universe within, our True Self.

Your soul is both who you most essentially are, your True Self, and the life force within that seeks to move you beyond the limits of your mind, your ego, and your life circumstances. Your soul is untouchable. It cannot be broken, damaged, weakened, or altered—even by trauma or abuse. In your soul, you remain yourself, no matter what is done to you or what you experience. Your sacred worth and eternal value abides despite all that life may throw at you. Your soul's capacity to move beyond yourself and the limits of life remains within you. You may be hurt and significantly affected by abuse or trauma, yet your soul, your truest Self, has not been damaged or diminished. Your soul endures. That is what a soul selfie would reveal to you.

My Spiritual Practice for Today

Take a metaphorical soul selfie today. In your meditation, look at the soul self that you are, and meditate on what that means about the infinite value and power that resides undiminished within you. Download your soul selfie to the "wall" of your mind and heart so you never forget the truth of who you are. Text it to your soul friend so he or she can remind you.

April 29

Grand Canyon of Grief (Pat)

I once hiked from the North Rim to the bottom of the Grand Canyon. The hike opened my eyes to a whole new world deep inside. From the rim the canyon looks to be a fearsome, overwhelming place of dead and arid rock. As you descend, you read the story of millions of years of earth life told in the layers of rock. You also encounter waterfalls and streams, places of intense green growth. At the very bottom the Colorado River runs alternately wild and peaceful, its cool waters refreshing and life giving.

When survivors stand at the edge of feeling the losses incurred by their trauma, it is intimidating. The canyon of your grief seems so vast, foreboding, and painful. The instinct is to turn away and run. But when you do descend into your grief—usually best done with a guide like a therapist or spiritual mentor—you discover layers of the story of your life, places of refreshment, and at the bottom, a river of renewal and new life. There is pain and aridity to be sure, yet also a powerful flow of grace.

The spiritual purpose of grief is to free you from the hold of the past. If you live haunted by the events of the past, you have less energy for life in the present. You are not living in the now of your life. You are driving your life forward by looking in the rearview mirror—a dangerous way to drive. You are also traveling with heavy baggage that you no longer need. Grief puts the past in the past and prepares you to move into your future.

Paradoxically, before you can let the past go, grief requires you to first revisit and mourn the past. You have to descend into the canyon of your grief. It will at times be difficult—my hike into the Grand Canyon was the most difficult I have done—yet you will discover a river of freedom and healing in your grief that you could never have imagined from the overlook.

My Spiritual Practice for Today

In your meditation, peer into the canyon of your grief. Notice what you feel. Pray for discernment about when to enter into your sacred grief. What will you need from your soul friends and from your soul?

April 30

Listen to the Call from Your Soul (Pat)

A spiritual call is hidden in the heart of your healing journey. A call is an invitation, a passion, a desire, a choice, and a commitment all rolled into one. This call from your soul invites you to discover a new purpose for your life, which will use the spiritual gifts your soul has given you for service or ministry to others. Your soul is speaking to you quietly or loudly, always respectful of your freedom to choose to respond or not, calling you to hear and discover what goodness for others can arise from your healing and transformation.

Listen for this call from your soul. Your soul will help you discover your life mission and purpose. It may involve some specific ministry or acts of service. It may lead you to volunteer your time and share your healing and your new freedom in a church or community service project. Or you may be called to reach out in some way to fellow survivors of abuse, personally or through a survivor support or advocacy group. The mission may be to live differently in a life role that you are already committed to. If you are a parent, your main mission may be to stop the cycle of abuse with you, to raise your children in a loving and abuse-free family environment. Your call might be to live from a new heart and spirit in your marriage or friendship. Your work of service may have nothing to do directly with your experience of trauma or abuse.

The form your mission takes does not matter. It matters only that you have listened to your soul and have let it fashion a mission and a new life purpose from the ashes of your abuse.

My Spiritual Practice for Today

In your quiet time, if you are ready, ask how your healing journey might be used for others. Listen for any word or intuition from your soul as it calls you to some new life mission and purpose.

May 1

The Mountain Meditation: Your Sacred Grief (Sue & Pat)

My Spiritual Practice for Today

We invite you to do another version of the Mountain Meditation. To enter into this meditation, find a comfortable sitting position. As you read, pause, close your eyes, and imagine the scenes described.

Picture yourself on a beautiful beach. See the waves, the sand, the brilliant color, and the vastness of the ocean. Feel the sun and the wind on your skin. Hear the crash and whoosh of the surf. Turn around now, and face away from the sea. Looking down, you see a backpack. In it is your sacred grief, a bag of all of your losses suffered as a result of your trauma. Pick it up and place it on your back. Notice how it feels to carry your grief.

In front of you is a beautiful forest. Envision yourself walking along a trail into the forest. Appreciate the coolness and the shaded light. You reach the edge of the forest and see an open meadow filled with colorful wildflowers. The trail leads you through the meadow to a clear, flowing stream with a bridge across the water. Stop for a moment to enjoy the light sparkling on the dancing water.

Now look up from the bridge and see a shining mountain before you. Following the trail, you ascend the mountain. You climb above the timberline through the clouds to the top of the peak. Look around you at the glory of creation. Then you notice a large boulder to sit on and rest. You take off your backpack and unload your grief.

Then, from the other side of the peak, your spiritual guide comes and sits down with you on the boulder. You can discuss whatever you want. Be sure to share your grief and bag of losses with the being. Experience your spiritual guide receiving and affirming your deep sadness. Allow yourself to weep and mourn your losses, held in the arms of your beloved guide. Hear the words of comfort that you receive.

When you are ready to leave, thank your guide. Remember what was said to you. Slowly hike back down the mountain, over the bridge, through the meadow, through the forest, to the beach, and to the edge of the vast ocean. Open your eyes. Journal what you experienced and what the guide at the top of the mountain said to you.

May 2

Healing Waters (Pat)

Your tears of mourning for the losses caused by your trauma are sacred healing waters. They are holy water. Treasure them. They should be collected and later ingested to heal the dryness and fractures of your heart wound.

In the movie *The Shack*, the woman who plays the Holy Spirit collects in a glass vial the tears that the main character sheds about the traumatic death of his young daughter. Later in the movie, when the man is ready to let go of his pain, she takes the vial of his tears and pours them onto a clearing in the garden of his life. Immediately, spectacular colorful flowers and fragrant herbs sprout and grow from the watering of his tears.

Do not be afraid to cry about your losses. Do not be ashamed of your tears. They are sacred. They are healing waters flowing out to help you release your pain. For grief to be healing, it has to be felt. In fact, allowing yourself to mourn and feel your grief can be a key breakthrough in restoring your ability to feel your emotions.

For some victims one of the losses that abuse has taken is the vital human capacity to feel and experience emotions. Grief itself helps to restore this loss. It may seem silly to cry over events that happened long ago, but buried grief is toxic for you, and if not honored and allowed expression, it limits your spirit's capacity for joy, hope, and love.

Many survivors haven't felt their losses. Grieving and crying out your grief is a way to honor your pain, let go of it, and begin to move on. There is no timetable for this, so be patient with your tears, and allow them to flow as long and often as you need. Remember, "Blessed are those who mourn, they shall be comforted." (Matthew 5:4)

My Spiritual Practice for Today

Look inside. Are there any reservoirs of tears that you have not yet released and shed? Have you fully felt your losses? Give yourself permission to be teary-eyed today, or sit down and allow yourself to have a good cry, pouring out whatever tears and grief that want to come forth. You can do this alone, or have someone close hold you, whichever is most comforting for you.

May 3

Sorrow, Forgiveness, Change (Vicki)

What makes us cling to suffering even when it is time to let it go? Is it our unfinished business? Sometimes we cling to anger because we have not yet been able to think about how we might forgive that person who has deeply hurt us. At times, the thought of forgiveness is so far removed from where we find ourselves that we can't even begin to think of the word. We can't see how it might possibly feel if we made a conscious decision to forgive.

To be sure, forgiveness is a journey for every soul to forgive perpetrators of violence against us. To forgive those who have emotionally abused us requires a radical shift of understanding what is necessary to move forward. Every spiritual practice calls us to forgiveness. An unforgiving heart is a sorrowful heart, a heart that is overwhelmed with sadness.

The poet Rumi says, "Sorrow prepares you for joy. It violently sweeps everything out of your house, so that new joy can find space to enter. It shakes the yellow leaves from the bough of your heart, so that fresh, green leaves can grow in their place. It pulls up the rotten roots, so that new roots hidden beneath have room to grow. Whatever sorrow shakes from your heart, far better things will take their place."

To forgive is to open up the expansiveness of the heart to allow it to love again in a new way. Change is a conscious choice to move from one space, either physically, mentally, or emotionally, to another. Moving from status quo to a place of change can sometimes be likened to leaping over a cavernous ravine, hoping to reach the other side. Fear holds us in place where we feel safe and comfortable even though that place we are in may not be what is best for us. The fear of the unknown within that place of change is sometimes too difficult to face. With courage and trust in God's providence, we are called to holy movement toward that which is life giving! Rumi also says, "Why do you stay in prison, when the door is so wide open?"

My Spiritual Practice for Today

I will begin to think about forgiveness in a new framework. I will reflect on how my life could be different if I were able to forgive the person who hurt me. What is my unwillingness to forgive doing to my life?

May 4

Goodness and Wisdom Arises (Vicki)

In *The Bond Between Women*, China Galland speaks eloquently about the goodness and wisdom that arise within us to overcome any number of obstacles:

> *There is a goodness, a Wisdom, that arises, sometimes gracefully, sometimes gently, sometimes awkwardly, sometimes fiercely, but it will arise to save us if we let it, and it arises from within us, like the force that drives green shoots to break the winter ground, it will arise and drive us into a great blossoming like a pear tree, into flowering, into fragrance, fruit, and song, into the wild wind dancing, sun shimmering, into the aliveness of it all, into that part of ourselves that can never be defiled, defeated or destroyed, but that comes back to life, time and time again, that lives—always—that does not die.*

I knew I had to create a greater spaciousness to hold my grief. At times the grief weakened my mind, body, and spirit. Those late-night drives home when I considered running into a bridge abutment with my car were reflective of how grief weakened me during some of the darkest times. It was my faith, though, my deep trust in a loving God that buoyed me during those darkest times.

My therapist played a significant role in giving me hope that I could work through all of the issues that kept me feeling trapped. She affirmed me as a person of value when my abuser mocked me as psychologically unfit. And because of the level of trust between us, because of how she modeled God's unconditional love, I could integrate that solid understanding into my own soul. I could believe that, indeed, I was psychologically sound.

There is a place within us, as China Galland says, "that part of ourselves that can never be defiled, defeated, or destroyed." This is the core value of who we are, and no one can take that away from us. They may try, but we have the strength within ourselves to resist losing that core integrity that is who we are.

My Spiritual Practice for Today

Try to be in touch with your core soul identity. Who are you? What are your strengths? Can you envision your core soul identity that cannot be defiled? How can you hold onto this as you move forward in your healing journey?

May 5

Sailing Through Life (Pat)

Sailing is a wonderful metaphor for how to live life. You are the sailboat itself. You are fitted with spiritual sails to catch and use the wind of the Spirit (*ruach*, the Hebrew biblical word for Spirit, also means wind) to propel you forward. You have a tiller or wheel to determine your direction in response to the winds that are blowing in your life. You have a keel hidden deep in the water that provides stability when the wind blows hard and without which you would be blown over and could not steer. These parts of you represent various spiritual gifts that you are given and can cultivate: the ability in quiet to hear the winds of Spirit blowing in your life and soul; the capacity to discern and choose the direction of your life in each moment; the grace to go deep to your center to experience tranquility and strength.

On the other hand, noisy power boating gives a false sense that you are in control and can muscle through life's waves with strength of will alone.

Sailing is peaceful and presents a more accurate portrayal of life. Being in control is a myth. You are reliant on the wind and the currents. If the wind is blowing the wrong direction, you cannot sail directly to where you want to go. You can learn, though, to skillfully set your sails to harness the wind of the Spirit and use your tiller to turn to the best angle into the wind to catch it just right.

The metaphor of sailing invites you to develop a relationship with the winds of the Spirit, a harmonious and skillful interaction that moves you through the waves, currents, and storms of your life. Letting go of control, yet remaining in charge of your boat and where you desire to steer it, you are the captain of your ship, and the *ruach* blowing into your sails is your propulsion, your life breath, and power.

My Spiritual Practice for Today

Practice sailing through your life today. Take time to listen and see how the wind is blowing. Set your sails and grasp your tiller to catch the winds of the Spirit. Enjoy the ride as you dance across the waves.

May 6

My Forgiveness Story, Part 1 (Sue)

All healing is a process. The forgiveness part of healing is a process as well. God's love brings up everything unlike itself for the purpose of healing. This comes in God's time when the moment is fully ripe for forgiveness.

I had an unusual experience of God's timing. I was speaking in San Francisco with Pat and Vicki to a national conference of victim assistance coordinators, a wonderful group of people dedicated to healing for victims of abuse by Catholic clergy. I was standing at the podium speaking about the healing power of forgiveness when I suddenly experienced a strange sensation in my body and then a fleeting picture of my mother being sexually assaulted by Monsignor (I was 4 at the time and also molested by the priest). I have learned to listen to my body and to honor the sacredness of these experiences. I listened to what was happening within me while continuing to present. Then it really hit me. I had never forgiven the priest for molesting my mom and me, and for the horrendous toll this took on our family. And here I was talking on forgiveness!

I stopped my talk. I took a few deep breaths and shared with the audience what was going on. This broke all my fear rules because I allowed my self to be visible and to have a voice. I acknowledged to the group that I had not yet forgiven Monsignor and then chose right there and then to forgive him with sixty people as my witnesses. I felt a momentary wave of release and lightness, and was ready to go on with the talk.

When I reflected later, I realized that I had been ready to forgive Monsignor for some time. It was sitting on the shelf, so to speak. I had just not picked it up and looked at it until that moment. This choice to forgive Monsignor was the last major piece of the puzzle of my healing process. Much healing had already occurred, and now this piece freed me further to lay the past to rest.

My Spiritual Practice for Today

If you have been able to forgive, write and reflect on your own forgiveness story. If the time is not right for you yet, pray about what might help to move you closer to forgiveness.

May 7

My Forgiveness Story, Part 2 (Sue)

A large part of what brought me to the point of forgiveness was my therapeutic work and personal experience with the priests and brothers of the residential recovery program where Pat and I provide counseling. Listening with sacred listening to their sacred stories of their own abuse and hearing their commitment to healing and recovery for themselves and for their victims had opened my heart, mind, and soul to a new vision of perpetrators of abuse. I could see the woundedness that had spawned their abusive behavior. I could see the sickness and suffering that was behind their abusive actions. I could see their desire to be spiritually free and whole. What they wanted was the same thing I wanted for myself and my other clients who had been abused.

This experience with these men led me to wonder about Monsignor's sacred story. What abuse or other trauma had led him to do the awful things that he did to my mother and me? What sickness had created these behaviors? He clearly suffered from alcoholism. What great pain he must have been in with this sickness and with whatever sexual sickness he also was gripped by. What did he feel in his lucid moments when he realized what he and his priesthood had come to? How awful it must have been for him to be so out of control and to be living in such total contradiction to his calling.

Hearing the stories of the men that we counsel had revealed to me the inner world of intense suffering that many perpetrators experience at the core of their intense and out-of-control sickness. This led me to see Monsignor with a 20/20 spiritual vision that opened my heart to forgive him that day in San Francisco. Sadly, I doubt that Monsignor ever got any help, care, or healing from his sickness as a perpetrator. Tragically, this parallels my mother's life. Neither ever received the healing help that could have set them both free.

My Spiritual Practice for Today

If you are ready, imagine the story of your perpetrator. What do you know about him or her? Do you know if your perpetrator was abused or traumatized in some way? Most have been. What do you feel when you tell their story? Whatever you feel is perfect and will be used by your soul to further your healing.

May 8

Pray for my Abuser? What? (Vicki)

In my involvement with Mother Teresa of Calcutta, I had several opportunities to meet with her over a span of ten years. I hoped that during a meeting with her in Washington, D.C., I would have the opportunity to tell her about the abuse and ask for her prayers. I shared how challenging it was to walk the journey. I'll never forget that 15-minute conversation. I had met with her several times over the years, but this one was special. With a promise of prayers for me, she became more serious and leaned in to me to say, "We must pray for priests. We must pray especially for those who hurt us, for they need someone to pray for them."

Let me just say that really wasn't what I wanted to hear! And yet, something in me knew the wisdom of her words. Our discussion came to a close, and we said our goodbyes. I remember walking away feeling stunned and speechless. I knew something monumental had just touched me. I hadn't let go of my anger and bitterness yet.

Hearing this from Mother Teresa was a lightning bolt of awareness. This was pivotal in my ability to look at the big picture of my abuse. It was the first time I became aware that I could make the shift from anger to understanding. This didn't happen right away, but it washed over me with time. It would come full circle several years later when I visited a residential center for priests who have abused. As I spent the evening with twenty-six men who lived at this facility, I was transported back to that moment with Mother Teresa when she asked me to pray for priests.

I'm aware that it takes a lifetime of hard emotional work to reach an understanding like this. Our stories are all so different and entangled. Yet knowing that we are all born with an inherent gift of human resilience, we have the capacity to get there. I'm confident in knowing that my abuser had his own unhealed wounds that propelled him into his unhealthy behavior with me. The least I can do is to ask God to lead him to seek help for his own healing.

My Spiritual Practice for Today

I want to think about my own human resilience and see where it takes me in beginning to understand and forgive my abuser.

May 9

Brother Sun, Sister Moon, Brother Caterpillar (Pat)

Francis of Assisi has become a universal saint for people of many different spiritual traditions. He is considered the patron saint of modern ecology because of his marvelous relationship to the natural world. Francis saw nature as the mirror of God, and all creatures as his brothers and sisters. He found the holy and divine within everything around him. He showed us the power of nature to heal. He taught deep respect for nature, and called us to become good stewards of the environment.

One of the great stories about Francis is when he stopped along the road to preach to a flock of noisy birds. The birds reportedly fell quiet in rapt attention. He saw God in every person he met. Another wonderful story is when Francis overcame his fear and revulsion, and kissed a leper that he encountered one day. Perhaps Francis can be the patron saint of survivors. His life and teachings invite you to learn to love and be healed by nature and to see yourself and all human creatures as good and beautiful reflections of God.

There is powerful natural healing in what I call Francis moments. I learned about these from my older brother Rocky. Rocky developed schizophrenia at 24 while serving as a pilot in the Air Force. He suffered greatly from his schizophrenia, and yet he eventually achieved a remarkable gentleness and peace. Some of this came from the healing of nature. Rocky loved the outdoors, so we often went for long hikes in the woods. I had many Francis moments with Rocky on these walks. Like Francis, Rocky loved the birds. He didn't preach to them; he talked to them, and they talked to him. Sometimes he would laugh out loud and tell me what the birds were saying. He saw the birds as fellow fliers.

The best Francis moment, though, came one day when Rocky stopped suddenly on a wooded trail, reached down, and picked up a caterpillar. He gently placed it on the side of the trail, saying, "I'm sorry to disturb you, but I don't want you to be stepped on."

My Spiritual Practice for Today

Take time in nature and simply be open to your own Francis moment. See all around you as your relations and mirrors of the divine. Be gentled and healed by what you experience.

May 10

Aging Anger (Pat)

Unlike a good red wine, anger does not age well. More like a cheap wine, anger held too long turns to vinegar of the spirit. Stuck anger over time becomes resentment, bitterness, depression of the mind and spirit, and even chronic hatred and aggression, passive or direct. This can become a dark pall over your spirit that obscures your vision of your soul and can, in the worst case, block your access to your soul entirely.

Persistent, protracted anger is the opposite of the healing, serenity, and love that your soul desires for you; it prevents you from receiving these gifts. Anger, as we have seen, can be holy, healing, and liberating, but it can become unholy when it is obsessive, bitter, and bent on vengeance or hurt for your abuser.

Even wanting for a time to hurt your abuser, or for your abuser to experience pain, is an understandable expression of anger. Really desiring that hurt for your abuser as a permanent life stance is poisonous to your soul. If you turn your heart into a weapon against your abuser, you may get some satisfaction and actually inflict some harm, but you will always end up using the hate in your heart against yourself. This is a spiritual law. Hate kills. It is a slow toxin that poisons and eats away at your spirit. Dwelling on your anger keeps you in your pain until you become the pain.

My Spiritual Practice for Today

You have understandable and justified anger about your trauma. Yet it is important today to examine the current state of your anger. Is it still empowering and liberating for you? Is it still working to make you safe and heal your shame? Do you still need it? If so, embrace it. However, if you are hanging onto your anger beyond its time, it may be time to let your anger go and begin the forgiveness process. Is your anger souring into bitterness or turning into hate and making you a hateful person? Then you are being invited to ask for the grace to move beyond anger and onto the path of forgiveness.

May 11

Moments of Love (Sue)

Holding a newborn.
Nursing or feeding your baby.
Hearing those first words
and the first laugh.
Seeing the first smile.
Experiencing love with your beloved,
Peaceful silence in the afterglow,
Holding hands walking through the woods,
The sunlight dancing on a mountain stream,
Washing your hair in its bracing, cold water.
Praying by candlelight in a quiet chapel.
Watching a sunset.
Hearing a bird serenade the dawn.
Listening to the silence of the desert at twilight.
Sensing the symphonic rustle of aspen leaves stirred by a breeze.
Hearing the wind whistling though pine needles.
Viewing majestic mountains reflected in a crystalline blue glacier lake.
Taking a wild night ride through a mountain valley,
the spectacular light and sound
of a thunderstorm encircling our tiny car.
The full moon rising over the ocean,
blazing a path of light to both of our hearts.

My Spiritual Practice for Today

Recall your own moments of love and enter into each as fully as you can. Feel the love in each wondrous memory.

May 12

Today I Will Honor My Sacred Story (Pat)

Everyone has a story, a sacred story, because it is about you. It is to be told and listened to sacredly and respectfully and held preciously. The gifts of your story are many, although at first it may not feel like it. Telling the story of your abuse or trauma, whether to a trusted other or even to yourself, can, at first, feel intimidating. Ultimately it will be liberating. The truth sets us free. As you tell your story, your soul will illumine the truth of what you have experienced and help you see it in a new and healing light.

At the same time, we are not our story. We are not simply the sum of the events of our lives. We are much, much more. And yet each of our stories is sacred and sheds light on parts of who we are and what has shaped and formed us. Telling and retelling your story will help to free you from the pain and shame of abuse. It will bring into the light what seemed dark and hidden, shameful and scary, and will empower you to see yourself with spiritual 20/20 vision through the loving eyes of your soul, your True Self.

My Spiritual Practice for Today

Write or reread the story of your abuse or trauma experience. Bring your sacred story to a prayer or meditation time. Ask for the grace to see your story in a new and sacred light, perhaps from the viewpoint of your soul or your Higher Power. See what new vision this gives you about your story. Take this in, and rewrite your story from this new spiritual perspective.

May 13

Today I Choose to Be Willing to Forgive (Sue)

Forgiveness is first for the forgiver. Forgiveness is for you. Forgiveness is only secondarily for your abuser, for the one who hurt and traumatized you so deeply. The purpose of forgiveness is to set your heart and your soul free and let them soar above chronic anger, bitterness, and the desire for revenge. Anger, at first, is necessary, healing, and empowering. Held too long it turns into vinegar and turns you into an embittered victim. There is a saying that "Holding onto resentments is like swallowing the poison pill you intended for the one who hurt you." Forgiveness empowers you to let go of toxic resentments and anger that you no longer need.

Forgiveness is a process that takes much soul work and is meant to happen only when the time is right for you. It is vital that there be no pressure or schedule for forgiveness. Forgiveness is not denial of what was done to you. Forgiveness is not forgetting or excusing. Forgiveness does not necessarily mean reconciliation or restoration of relationship with your abuser.

Forgiveness is about choosing to let go of anger that you no longer need and lifting the heavy and corrosive burden of resentments or bitterness from your heart and soul. Forgiveness is for your own healing and freedom.

My Spiritual Practice for Today

Bring the question of forgiveness to your meditation or prayer today. Am I ready to let go of my anger? Is the time for me to forgive getting closer? What emotional and soul work do I yet need to do to prepare my heart to forgive? Ask for the grace or gift of being willing to forgive. Or even the grace to be willing to be willing. Wherever you are now in the forgiveness process is all right as long as there is willingness to be willing to one day forgive.

May 14

The Little Boy Who Touched the World (Vicki)

Who sees all beings in his own Self
and his own Self in all beings, loses all fear.
–The Isa Upanishad

The little boy from Syria who washed up on a shore in Turkey caught the world's attention. So many had already perished in the dangerous trek from Syria or Iraq or northern Africa because of the less than seaworthy vessels they were sailing in; overloaded with passengers, they were sure to capsize. Thousands have died before this child; yet the image of him lying on a beach captured our hearts. His brother and mother perished as well, leaving his father to carry the guilt of not being able to save them. They slipped away from him in the sea.

We struggle to understand such human suffering. Not only the refugee crisis but the individual human suffering that brings us to our knees, asking God to bring an end to this suffering. When things seem beyond our ability to help, beyond our ability to make a difference, we go to the God of our understanding to plead for help. Yet we know that the only help that is available is through our own hands. In the Christian tradition, we pray and sing, "Christ has no body now but yours, no hands, no feet on earth but yours." It is we who respond with compassion and love to the horrific suffering we see and read about day in and day out.

And this is how we respond to our own struggle. We know there is no one who will initiate healing. We are the ones who set out on a journey to heal ourselves. There is no healing from above; it is from within, deep within our own blessed soul. We have been given the wisdom and knowledge to figure it out for ourselves. No matter how stuck we are in our dysfunction, we can find help, we can make our way toward wholeness. We muscle up the courage to stand in our own truth and say, I need help. Can you help me? Will you help me? And we move forward.

My Spiritual Practice for Today

Today I will use the innate abilities I possess to rise up to the challenges of my life. I will begin to ask the questions I need to ask to seek help for the resolution of my issues.

May 15

Tweeting Others (Pat)

"Tweet others as you would like to be tweeted" (a message on a church signboard). This is a wonderful, modern twist on the Golden Rule, "Do unto others as you would have them do unto you" (Matthew 7:12). It challenges us all to look at how we treat each other online in social and other media. It also challenges survivors to look at how they allow themselves to be treated in cyberspace.

This new world, as marvelous and useful as it is, can also be a place for real abuse to occur. There is nothing virtual about the very real emotional and mental damage caused by online verbal abuse, sexual harassment, sexual predation, threats, blackmail and intimidation, and other forms of cyberbullying resulting in cyber-trauma.

The wounds, psychological and spiritual, can be just as damaging as in-person abuse. Even online exposure to some things on the Internet can be quite hurtful. For instance, there is increasing evidence that early childhood exposure to online pornography affects children similarly to actual sexual abuse. Another example is that couples who fight via texting seem to do more damage to each other and to the relationship than if they were in a face-to-face fight. They say very hurtful things to each other that they might not say if they were seeing the pain on the other's face. In fact, it seems that the relative anonymity and emotional distance of various media gives permission to use abusive language and other toxic trolling that we would never do in person.

For survivors the issue is twofold. Do you fall into the same trap as others and misuse virtual communication to channel your anger abusively in some way? Or just as important, how well do you take care of yourself online? Some of you are more vulnerable to further abuse because your defenses have been weakened and shame may make you think that you deserve further mistreatment. It is vital today to learn good online respect and etiquette toward others and to establish healthy online boundaries that protect you.

My Spiritual Practice for Today

Look closely today at your behaviors in various media. Do you use them to build up or tear down? Do you exercise good online self-care and not allow yourself to be victimized, intimidated, or abused?

May 16

The God Problem (Pat)

God has a problem. To be precise, God has a PR problem, an image issue. So many people, including religious people, have misused God, or their perception of God, to pursue and justify their own ego-driven agendas, sometimes even justifying abuse and violence, that God has gotten a bad name in some quarters. Perhaps we need to call the God Abuse Hotline where abuses and misuses of God can be reported and investigated.

God is abused also by abuse. Because God is within you in the light of your soul, God was abused when you were abused. Part of the abuse of God is that God's image often gets distorted by the abuse in the victim's mind and heart. As a result, your desire for a healing and meaningful relationship with God is inhibited or blocked. Sometimes this damage to the victim's image of God is direct, for instance, in clerical sexual abuse. It is also seen in religious abuse, where religion is misused to shame, frighten, control, or brainwash. In these cases, the image of God is a part of the abuse and directly distorts the victim's understanding of God.

Even if your trauma did not involve some overt misuse of religion, there can still be substantial damage to your image of God and your relationship with God. Trust is destroyed; shame and fear, abandonment and rejection are experienced. Often this gets projected onto God. You come to believe that God has abandoned and rejected you as well. It becomes difficult to trust God, to believe God is with you, loves you, and wants to comfort and heal your pain. This is the God problem for many victims of abuse.

My Spiritual Practice for Today

The first step in resolving the God problem is to identify how your abuse has affected your image of God. What adjectives would best describe who God is to you: loving, close, caring, nurturing, awesome, or distant, punishing, vengeful, rejecting, condemning? Is this the God of your faith, the God of love? Or is it an image of God inflicted on you by your trauma? You have a new freedom to discover the God of your own understanding.

May 17

The God Tree Meditation (Sue)

(Adapted from Maureen Halpin's *Imagine That: Using Phantasy in Spiritual Direction*)

Your Spiritual Practice for Today

Take a moment to relax. Assume a comfortable position. If it is comfortable for you, close your eyes; if not, leave them open. Focus on your breathing, slowly in and out. If thoughts come, notice them and gently let them go. Imagine yourself in a beautiful natural setting. It might be a familiar place to you or a place in your imagination. You are alone, and you like being alone.

As you enjoy being in this place, you sense a presence. You realize that God is appearing to you as a tree! Let that tree slowly come into focus.

What kind of tree is your God tree? How does it look? What do you feel in the presence of the God tree? See yourself approaching the God tree. What is this like for you? What do you feel? How close can you get to the God tree?

As you notice the God tree, you slowly become aware that you are a tree as well. What kind of tree are you? What is your tree like? Where is it in relation to the God tree? What does your tree feel like or do in the presence of the God tree?

Come out of the fantasy slowly. Let it fade from your mind's eye.

Focus again for a few moments on your breathing. Gently open your eyes and become present again to your surroundings.

Reflect in your journal on your meditation experience:

What kind of tree was your God tree? What does that mean to you? What kind of image of God might that indicate you have?

How is that image related to your abuse?

How close could you approach the God tree?

What kind of tree were you? What was the condition of your tree?

What did your tree feel like in the presence of the God tree? What does this mean about the effect your abuse has had on your relationship with God?

At some point, you can redo this meditation, visualizing the God you are discovering in your search for new images of God free of the abuse. What kind of tree would that be?

May 18

The Question with No Answer (Pat)

Suffering is difficult to make sense of. All spiritual traditions address the question of suffering. Although many provide partial answers, pieces of the great puzzle, none of them, in my opinion, provide a completely satisfying answer.

As a close observer of human suffering, I have sought to understand the meaning of suffering in my own life and in the lives of my clients. I want to make sense of it, as you probably do, to find some answers and to perhaps develop a grand unified theory of suffering that would put all the pieces of the great mystery together. This has eluded me, and I suspect it always will.

This is the nature of spiritual mystery. It is a phenomenon just beyond our sight, replete with paradoxes and contradictions, yet yielding partial glimpses of an underlying light and liberating truth. In the Jewish tradition, there is the biblical theme of suffering as a purifying, refining force that shapes spiritual character and draws the sufferer closer to God and God's ways. In Christian spirituality, Jesus's suffering on the cross, leading to his resurrection, is the prototype for transforming our suffering and woundedness into new life and freedom. The Buddha found enlightenment, surrendering all attachment and ego, to break the cycle of human suffering.

These insights and my own experience have led me to several conclusions and partial answers about the meaning of the suffering caused by trauma. First of all, suffering is not good in itself, nor does your soul or God sadistically want you to suffer for your own good. What they desperately desire is your healing. At the same time, God and your soul can use your suffering in the process of healing to transform you into a new creation, stronger precisely because of your suffering. This is the paradox and mystery of suffering.

Your suffering then becomes a gift, a precious and sacred wound. Your very brokenness becomes the road to wholeness and holiness. This gives your suffering its spiritual meaning and purpose, even though trauma suffering itself is unjust, unwarranted, and unwanted by you, your soul, and your God.

My Spiritual Practice for Today

What are your questions about your suffering? What answers work for you spiritually? Can you be at peace with no complete answers?

May 19

The Beauty of the Journey (Vicki)

Let beauty heal your parched soul, your depleted self.
Let it replace your ego, your need for an identity.
Let it give back meaning and purpose to your days.
Let it save you from darkness and despair.
Let beauty be your life.
–Esther Elizabeth, 2006

When we are stuck in the cycle of abuse, the word "beauty" is far from our vocabulary. Yet beauty is all around us. It is life giving to spend time in nature, just sitting in silence or walking.

When I spent time in nature, I had the opportunity to remove myself from all that reminded me of the abuse and the consuming dysfunctional cycle in which I was caught. Beauty lured me toward healing and renewal. It was the beauty of wholeness that called to me.

There is a beauty to the process of psychotherapy. It was a deliberate unveiling; it didn't force me to respond or accept thoughts and ideas I wasn't ready to embrace. My therapist was luring me toward my own inner knowledge, always drawing me into a deeper understanding of myself, trusting in my own intelligence and intuitive spirit to know I would be able to answer my own questions with her guidance. In the most difficult of emotional trauma, she reminded me of the inner strength I already possessed.

Speaking truth to the power of abuse was from my True Self, and it was a monumental step toward healing. In time, I could finally look into a mirror and see my own beauty and the gift of my life. The language we hold in our minds is just as important as the language we speak. The truth we hold within is beauty when we can express it with freedom. This is the authenticity of the True Self. To live consistently in the True Self is the true dance of beauty.

My Spiritual Practice for the Day

Today I want to be aware of the beauty that surrounds me. May the beauty that surrounds me become the healing balm that brings me to a deeper understanding of my own inner beauty.

May 20

The Forgiveness Diet (Pat)

One way to implement forgiveness is to go on what the spiritual writer Sondra Ray calls the Forgiveness Diet. It involves creating forgiveness affirmations such as:

I am willing now (or I am willing to be willing)…to forgive my abuser.

I forgive you, (name), my abuser.

I forgive you, (name), I bless you, and I set you free.

I forgive you, God, for my abuse (if you have anger at God about your trauma).

Like every diet, the forgiveness diet also requires you to abstain from "foods" that are unhealthy, especially the spiritually toxic junk food of bitterness, hate, and the desire for revenge.

Work with each affirmation for a week, saying it or writing it seventy times during that week. This will fulfill Jesus's teaching of forgiving "seventy times seven," which actually means to forgive as much and as often as it takes. Repeat the Forgiveness Diet as needed. This will help you to absorb the spirit of forgiveness into your very being.

If you are not ready for this—and again, be patient and gentle with yourself about this because forgiveness is a process whose time and pace is different for each survivor—you can instead ask daily for the gift of being willing and ready to forgive. Ask your soul. Ask your God. It will be given to you in the time it is meant to happen for you, and your inner resistance and fear will melt away.

My Spiritual Practice for Today

If you are ready, start your Forgiveness Diet today. After you have practiced the Forgiveness Diet 70 times 7 for at least one month, reflect on what has changed inside you. How do you feel different? How do you see your abuse differently? What do you feel toward your abuser now?

May 21

The Cleansing Power of Anger (Sue)

At one time I was a true rage-aholic, as my children can sadly testify. The rage was really at myself for allowing abuse to continue into my adult life by being silent and not having a voice.

I firmly believe in this absolute spiritual law: God's love brings up everything unlike itself for the purpose of healing. God was surfacing the anger for my healing. In my early forties, I was able to transform the anger into a primal scream when I was alone in the house. I screamed from some very deep well of hurt and rage at all the abuse that I had experienced in my life. I would scream at the top of my lungs, turning myself inside out, refinishing my inner guts and spirit all the way down to my soul, sanding myself hard to remove the gunk that had accumulated inside me. This was an amazing cleansing.

My screams gave expression to all that had been unsaid because I had no voice. God's love was working through my primal, raging screams to heal me and set me free. Gradually the screaming subsided. There was no longer a need to scream. I felt lighter. I felt alive and, for the first time in a long time, grateful to be alive. I had room now for joy. I had space to receive love and affirmation. I could now see the many blessings in my life and be more deeply grateful. I was freer to let go and let God. I also had the energy to change the things in my life that were unhealthy, even abusive, and change them I did.

With God's help, I live a joyous and abuse-free life today. When I get angry now, it is not from some hidden and deep tank of rage. It is anger that I can channel and harness for good.

My Spiritual Practice for Today

Do you have a hidden tank of anger from your trauma inside? Are you afraid of your anger? Is it time to let love bring this anger to the surface to be released and cleansed? How can you do that safely, for example with a therapist or spiritual guide? Reflect on these questions in your meditation or journal.

May 22

The Beauty of the Blur (Pat)

Out of the blue, with no warning and no risk factors (except never having been pregnant!), I was diagnosed with male breast cancer. This was quite traumatic. The nine months of treatment—mastectomy, two rounds of chemo, and one of radiation—were even more traumatic. Gratefully, I emerged cancer free and healthy.

Every trauma, however, leaves its scars, physical, emotional, and spiritual. One of the most troublesome for me is the change in my vision, possibly a side effect of the chemo regimen. This is what I call the blur. It is like living in an Impressionist painting with everything beyond 10 feet fuzzy and bathed in a diffuse, glowing light, rather than the sharp-edged Realism of my previous vision. My eyesight has improved enough that I can drive, read, and generally function well. But the blur remains, which is quite frustrating and sometimes alarming.

However, the blur has become my teacher, a daily opportunity to learn and grow spiritually. The first lesson is about trust. Each day I am challenged to trust that I will be given sufficient vision to do whatever is required. Each day I have been given the eyesight that I need. I am also called to accept that what I am given is enough, even if it is different and less than I had before.

The blur challenges me to focus on what I can see clearly rather than focus on what I cannot. If I focus on blurry objects, or even the dark floaters in my eyes, everything appears out of focus, and I become anxious. If I focus on what I can see well enough, my vision improves, and the blur doesn't bother me. I can actually choose to some degree how much clarity I have depending on what I choose to focus on.

I have also learned to see the beauty in the blur. As I write on this early spring day, I notice that faces are softened and glowing. I revel in the redbud tree's purple blossoms, the bright yellow pods of dancing daffodils, and the electric spring green of the trees' first leaves. It is all slightly blurry, Monet-like, and it is beautiful.

My Spiritual Practice for Today

Reflect today on what scars or after-effects you have because of your trauma. Of course, you would rather they be healed. At the same time, how might they be your teacher, and how might they even be beautiful?

May 23

The Eye of the Storm (Sue)

As a member of the steering committee of a national event, my dear friend was aware that the committee environment around her was becoming "cyclonic." In the past she would have entered the storm believing that she could fix it. As a result her cortisol levels would go sky high, and she would experience a hurricane of stress. To add insult to injury, she usually failed to remedy the situation, and sometimes the other individuals involved in the cyclone would resent her for her well-intentioned attempts at fixing it.

This time my friend chose to use a simple tool, a true gift from her God. Oh, so simple and so powerful. She stepped back and realized the wisdom in this realization: Aha, I can't change their stress, but by God, I can lower mine. And then she chose to focus in on her secret tool: her breath.

She mindfully breathed in God's love and mindfully breathed out God's love. Over and over for about five minutes. With this as her focus, she entered the eye of the storm where it is silent quiet and calm (when hurricane hunter pilots enter the eye of a hurricane, the winds of the storm may be howling at 150 mph, but in the eye it is so quiet and calm one can hear a pin drop). My friend quieted herself so completely that her husband, who had accompanied her to the event and was aware of the storm swirling in the committee, was astounded at how she appeared when she emerged from the meeting and questioned if she was OK.

"Very OK", my friend replied. "I am totally at peace."

My Spiritual Practice for Today

Whenever you experience any stress storms today—small or hurricane force— use my friend's simple tool. Focusing on your breath, breathe in God's love and breathe out God's love toward everyone involved in your stress. On the wind of your breath, enter into the serenity of the eye of your personal storms.

May 24

Suffering in Silence (Vicki)

As long as I was suffering in silence, I was forced to remain stuck in the intensity of grief. As soon as I was able to speak the pain that was locked in my heart, I could begin to move forward. It was almost ten months into therapy with my counselor before I could begin to tell her what was weighing on my heart.

I was ashamed, that I had allowed a Catholic priest to take total control of my life at age 18 and treat me like a slave. Now, at age 31, I was fearful, in the deepest understanding of the word fearful, of anyone knowing this secret. I had been groomed from early childhood by him. It seemed a natural progression at age 18 when he made his first sexual advances. Every year that went by, I prayed for some way to remove myself from that relationship. Every part of my life was enmeshed with his manipulative persona.

Today I'm watching my siblings and peers enjoy their grandchildren, and I'm reminded once again of what was taken from me: the ability to have my own children and grandchildren. Because of his manipulation and control, the years when I would have married were taken from me. That deep grief shows itself sometimes, and then I remind myself again how much love I am surrounded with from family and friends.

The pathway of grief, like spiral dynamics, finds people at different places on the journey. Long spaces of time can pass when we think we have finally conquered grief. And then one experience, one paragraph in a book, or one story can bring us back to the core issue of our grief. Today, however, I have the tools to accept the grief for what it is, acknowledge it, and move forward without fear. I now know that it is just a small hiccup on the journey.

My Spiritual Practice for Today

I now understand grief as the sacred holder of the pains of my past. Grief is part of the container of my soul where all my sorrow is held. I know today that I can return grief to its container whenever I choose to do so. It will not keep me from living my life fully.

May 25

Your Trauma Wound (Pat)

The wound is the place where the light enters you.
–Rumi

Until I was 25, I struggled with the speech impediment of stuttering. At times it was debilitating, always painful. I was so embarrassed by my stammering that I went mute in the classroom or in social situations. I would know the answer to the teacher's question, but was terrified to raise my hand. I would have a joke to tell my friends, yet I kept it to myself to avoid the risk of stuttering in front of them. I was a bright, funny, likeable kid, but few people knew that side of me. They saw a quiet, shy, reserved young man, never guessing the anxiety and shame inside.

The stuttering completely stopped when I was 25 through a process combining counseling and prayer that even today feels nearly miraculous and somewhat mystifying. I am grateful to be freed of the stuttering.

I have also become grateful, though, for having been a stutterer. I would not be who I am without the trauma of my stuttering. Out of the pain came several gifts. I learned to listen well to others and became an excellent observer of people. I developed the capacity to feel the emotions and pain of those around me. These gifts helped to make me the therapist, friend, and spouse that I grew to become. Perhaps the greatest grace of my stuttering was that it drove me inward to focus more deeply on my inner life. This became the seedbed for my inner spiritual journey.

Love and suffering are the primary gateways to the transformation of your mind, heart, and spirit. These two core life experiences break us open to profound personal change and life-altering grace. It is easy to see how love is life changing. The transformational power of suffering is not so obviously seen. Yet, embedded in every experience of suffering, including my stuttering and your trauma, is a seed of transformation. There are graces and gifts, unpolished diamonds, and other gems hidden in the soil of the pain you endured because of your trauma. Rumi said it best: The light will be discovered in your pain and will shine forth through your wound.

My Spiritual Practice for Today

Reflect on how your trauma wound has been transformed to become a gift of light for you and others.

May 26

Radical Forgiveness (Pat)

Doing an injury puts you below your enemy; revenging one
makes you but even with him; forgiving it sets you above him.
–Benjamin Franklin

Benjamin Franklin's words illustrate the radical power of forgiveness to heal and spiritually transform victims of abuse. If you do not in time move toward forgiveness of your perpetrator, you will remain on the same level spiritually as your abuser. If you forgive—remembering always that the forgiveness process is different for each person—you will rise above your abuser and transcend all that was done to you.

For a time, wishing hurt on your abuser is an understandable expression of anger. Really desiring that hurt for your abuser as a permanent life stance is poisonous to your soul. If you turn your heart into a weapon against your abuser, you may get some satisfaction, but you will always end up using the hate in your heart against yourself. This is a spiritual law. Hate kills. It is a slow toxin that gradually poisons your spirit.

The radical act of forgiveness goes to the root of the circle of abuse and removes any spiritual toxins that the abuse planted in you. Forgiveness is radical because it pulls out the root of bitterness, fear, and shame and stops the cycle of abuse. If you do not eventually, in your own soul-guided time, forgive, you remain in the cycle of abuse. You help to keep the circle turning, becoming a part of it and continuing to transmit and pass the pain and hurt forward.

Remember, forgiveness is first for the forgiver. It is for your spiritual growth and freedom. It is part of building your own spiritual character and radically removing yourself from the power of the abuse over your self and your life.

My Spiritual Practice for Today

In your meditation or quiet time today, check with yourself nonjudgmentally to see where you are in the process of forgiveness. Do you still need your anger? Is it turning into hate or bitterness? Are you ready to go radical and enter into the journey of forgiveness? What spiritual support and tools will you need for this journey? If it is time, thank your anger for its service to you and begin to let it go.

May 27

The Inner Cry of the Soul (Sue)

"I want to be seen!" cries my soul. But the shame of abuse and trauma cries louder: "Don't be seen!" "Hide!" "Don't make eye contact!" "Hang your head low!" "Don't speak up!" "Don't rock the boat!" "Anticipate others' needs." Hopefully these rules will keep me safe. If I'm seen, I will get hurt, yelled at, shamed, belittled. I was caught in a strong inner tug-of-war, the pain of it deep, wretched, and raw. My soul kept whispering to me, "Be visible, come out of your shell, you have so much to share." My fear said, "No way, it's not safe!"

In third grade at Halloween, my school decided to parade each class on stage at an assembly showing off our costumes. My mother thought a gypsy skirt, a peasant blouse, a scarf in my hair, and bangles on my wrists would be lovely. She also had me carry a tambourine so I could shake it as I paraded! Well, I began trembling at the thought of it. As a bed-wetter, I had to hang my sheets outside for the entire world to see. And here I was being instructed to march on a stage in a colorful costume and shake the tambourine. No thank you! I obediently wore the costume and carried the tambourine. But I never looked up. I held the tambourine close to my side without making a sound. It was terrifying and humiliating. I wanted to run and hide.

Despite this trauma I gradually learned to listen to the call of my soul. I broke though my fear and became visible. With God's help I found the courage to make myself more visible bit by bit, weakening the vise grip of my fear and shame. I heard an inner voice urging me to step out of the shadows. My job has been to listen and to respond with the courage to grab onto whatever rope was offered me and pull myself past my fear and into the light.

Today as a member of a women's dance group, I perform all over town, bringing joy to senior audiences. And, yes, there I am in the front row shaking my tambourine in time to "The Maple Leaf Rag." Who'd have ever thought!

My Spiritual Practice for Today

What is the inner cry of my soul? What is my inner voice saying about my fear, my shame? Today I will pause to listen to the whispering voice of courage within me.

May 28

What, Me Worry? (Pat)

"What, me worry?" is the famous line of *Mad Magazine's* iconic character, Alfred E. Neuman. Trauma engenders high levels of fear in survivors. For some survivors this leads to becoming chronic worriers. You constantly and compulsively focus on what could go wrong. Your mind projects nervously into the future, scanning the horizon for the next perceived threat, the next shoe to drop.

This is a form of mind control. Your mind is attempting to protect you from being surprised and caught off-guard—as you were in your trauma—by pretending to control or prevent potential events by obsessing about them. Unfortunately, this doesn't work and, in fact, makes matters worse. It creates a constant level of stress and anxiety. It keeps you in a future you are projecting from your past, crippling your ability to be in the present and enjoy the moment. Worry is damaging to your body, your mind, your heart, and your spirit.

Have you ever experienced moments when the worrier part of you is silent? When through meditation, a moment of love, or even through medication, your mind is calm, peaceful, and present to now? What happens to your worries and fears then? If they have temporarily disappeared, how real are they?

It's estimated that 90 percent of fears are delusions, constructions of our minds manufactured out of usually flimsy evidence. Obviously there are some truly fearful situations, but most of your fears are unreal, illusion, chimera of your amygdala (the fear center of your brain).

What is more real than most of your fears is peace, trust, love, and the power of your soul to guide you, ground you, and keep you safe. It is possible for you to live without worry and fear. Who lives without fear? The spiritually enlightened, those who have had near-death experiences, mystics, and any spiritual seeker who has looked deeply into the profound spiritual realities hidden beneath the surface appearances of their life.

You too can experience periods of freedom from your worries. Perhaps you already have. Trust these gifts from your soul more than your fears.

My Spiritual Practice for Today

Act today as if most of your fears are not real. Let your soul be in charge, not your mind. Simply notice how your life is different without worry.

May 29

Soul Bird (Pat)

A tiny bird with a big, clear-noted voice sings to me daily from her perch atop the large storm-battered cedar tree in our front yard that Sue and I call Great-Grandfather. She sings in every season, in any weather good or bad. I have rarely gotten more than a glimpse of her, perched high and hidden in the green folds of the cedar.

I call her my soul bird because she is mysterious and elusive, yet always there, singing to me. Her song is always the same: a melody of three even notes, so very clear and pure, then a rising tone, followed by a sustained trilling belted out with all her might as the finale. If I am outside very long, she may sing this to me dozens of times, no matter what personal emotional or spiritual weather I am experiencing.

I called her my soul bird when I realized I heard a soul libretto to each musical phrase, each a brief message from my soul. This is what I hear in the five sections of her song:

"Fear not".
"You are loved."
"All is well."
"Live gratefully."
The final high trilling section is a wordless exaltation of joy and praise in being alive.

This is what I hear each day from my soul bird. My soul and my God know that I need to hear these. This song from high atop Great-Grandfather reminds me of what I need to live centered and gracefully, no matter the challenges of the day or the particular season of my life.

Sometimes I don't hear my soul bird's song. I am too preoccupied with my self or with my latest anxiety du jour. Other times it takes me a while to be mindful enough to hear my soul bird's song. Other times, the most graced moments, I go out the front door eagerly expectant to hear her song and be soothed by her melodious proclamation. Then I am lifted up with her to the high branches of Great-Grandfather, and together we sing and fly.

SOUL LIGHT FOR THE DARK NIGHT

My Spiritual Practice for Today

How does your soul sing to you? What is her melody? What are her lyrics? What is her daily message to you?

May 30

The Wilderness of Fear (Vicki)

The wilderness of fear is a good metaphor for how I felt when I was so angry. When I walked away from an abusive relationship that had gone on too long, I was angry, and I felt shamed and lost in an emotional wilderness. I'd never been an angry person, and I generally loved everyone I met, always thinking the best of people before rushing to judge anyone. And I had never really felt rejection from anyone.

Because I decided to walk away from my abuser, I was described as psychologically damaged because I was receiving counseling. And this was made known publicly in the small town where I lived. This brought out an anger I had not felt before. I was deeply saddened. My reputation had been judged harshly by people who had known me my entire life. For the first time in my life, I felt rage. So often the survivors of abuse are criticized, called overly dramatic, called liars. It is the perpetrator's attempt to save face amid his own failure.

By processing this anger with my counselor, I was able to come out of it thanks to her assurance that I was very healthy psychologically. She helped me to understand the truth of who I was and that I had the strength and stamina to stand in my own truth and authenticity. My circle of friends also stood with me in love and support.

Loving support is there for each of us in our walk toward healthy living. Creating a circle of family and friends who know your struggle brings them into your circle of healing.

I was able to let go of the deeply held anger and hurt, and heal because I could for the first time in a long time accept that I was strong and living an authentic life based in the truth of who I was and because I was surrounded by my circle of support. This was a milestone in my healing process.

My Spiritual Practice for Today

Today I will reflect on my anger toward those who have hurt me. I will include in my reflection how I can take care of myself amid the anger. I will be aware of the strength that resides in me. I will find healthy ways to deal with my anger.

May 31

Today I Reclaim the Sacredness
of the Temple of my True Self (Sue)

On this day, with holy anger I shout to the heavens:

I am God's precious child and a magnificent person of value. I am not bad, wrong, dirty, or defective. Rather, what you, the abuser, did to me was wrong and sick.

I am innocent. The abuse was not my fault. You, the abuser, are responsible for what you did to me and for the painful wounds and suffering the abuse has caused me. You took advantage of my vulnerability, my innocence, and my trust to overpower me and exploit me. I now reclaim my personal power to take charge of my body, my heart, my mind, my soul.

You made me feel worthless, desecrated, of no value. With my holy anger and God's, I drive you out of the holy temple of my soul and reclaim the sacredness and eternal and ultimate value of who I am and was created to be. I reclaim the holy temple of God that I am in my True Self, the sanctuary of my soul.

My Spiritual Practice for Today

Write a letter to your abuser or to the abuse or trauma itself expressing your holy anger. Tell your abuser that you are taking back the sacredness of your True Self that was stolen from you. Then imagine yourself as a temple or a church or some other sacred space, cleansed and free and filled with a sacred light. Notice how that feels, and let it soak into your body and consciousness.

June 1

The Mountain Meditation: Forgiveness (Sue & Pat)

My Spiritual Practice for Today

We invite you to do the forgiveness version of the Mountain Meditation. Do this only if you are ready to enter into the pathway of forgiveness. Wherever you are in the forgiveness process is just fine and is where you need to be for now. Again, find a comfortable sitting position. As you read, pause, close your eyes, and imagine the scenes described.

Picture yourself on a beautiful beach. See the waves, the sand, the brilliant color, and the vastness of the ocean. Feel the sun and the wind on your skin. Hear the crash and whoosh of the surf. Turn around now, and face away from the sea. Looking down, you see a backpack. Place in it your anger and whatever readiness to forgive you possess at this point in your healing. Notice how it feels to carry this load.

In front of you is a beautiful forest. Envision yourself walking along a trail into the forest. Appreciate the coolness and the shaded light. You reach the edge of the forest and see an open meadow filled with colorful wildflowers. The trail leads you through the meadow to a clear, flowing stream with a bridge across the dancing water. Stop for a moment to enjoy the light sparkling on the water.

Now look up from the bridge and see a shining mountain before you. Following the trail, you ascend the mountain. You arrive at your sacred boulder. You take off your backpack and unload your anger.

Your spirit friend sits down with you. Your guide draws your attention to a figure off in the distance who is on a separate trail ascending the mountain. It is your abuser. Do not be afraid. You are safe. Your abuser's path is different than yours. Your abuser climbs to a rock below you, again at a safe distance, on the other side of a deep chasm. Your abuser cannot see you.

Be aware of what you feel as you behold your abuser. How does the spiritual being look upon your abuser? If you are ready, express whatever forgiveness you can to your abuser. Feel your spiritual companion encouraging you as you do this.

When your time on the mountaintop is complete, leave behind any anger you are ready to relinquish. Your abuser descends by the separate path, and you do not see him again. Return down the mountain, through the forest, to the beach. Record and reflect in your journal.

June 2

Ruminate Only on Rumi (Pat)

Rumi, the great Sufi mystic and poet of the thirteenth century, writes, "Everything that is beautiful and fair and lovely is made for the eye of one who sees." What do you see? What does your mind focus on?

If you are like many survivors, you probably ruminate on what you perceive to be wrong in your life and in the world. Your whole mental focus may be all the doom and gloom in your past or present. Your mind goes over the same negative obsessions and worries, like a dog that has only one bone to gnaw. The worry part of me is an expert at this. When it's in control, I obsess over the perceived danger—often delusional—until it is my only focus, and my stress cortisol levels go sky high. I become blind to everything beautiful, fair, and lovely, and everything that is hopeful.

The soul invites you and I to ruminate only on what is beautiful and lovely, uplifting, and soul nurturing. Ruminate only on Rumi and on the life-giving wisdom of all the great spiritual teachers. Train yourself to ask, "What's right?" rather than always asking, "What's wrong?" As Rumi suggests, become one who sees the life-affirming truths right before your eyes, and make those your obsession. This doesn't mean you ignore real problems. You face them and address them as needed; you simply return your focus then to the soul beautiful.

Most of our minds are like typical TV news broadcasts. The first 27 minutes are focused on the woes of the world; "if it bleeds, it leads" is the media motto. Only the last 3 minutes are about the good news of an uplifting human-interest story. Which part makes you feel inspired and hopeful? What if you flipped the sequence and the time allotment and spent 27 minutes focused on your good news, all that is beautiful and noble, before addressing your problems for the last 3 minutes? Rumi would smile.

My Spiritual Practice for Today

Observe what your mind focuses on. Is it mostly bad news? You are your mind's director. You can choose what personal news leads. Consciously redirect your mind to your good news and the beautiful and lovely all around you. Reading an uplifting spiritual quote each day will help you do this.

June 3

Shattered Soul? (Pat & Sue)

Your soul, the essential core of who you are, is untouchable. It cannot be shattered, damaged, weakened, or altered—even by trauma or abuse. In your soul you remain your true and essential self, no matter what is done to you or what you experience. Your sacred worth and eternal value abide despite all that life may throw at you. Your ineradicable soul's capacity to move you beyond yourself and the limits of your ego remains within you. You may be hurt and significantly affected by abuse or trauma, yet you have not been metaphysically damaged or diminished. Your soul endures.

However, trauma can alter and sometimes almost sever your connection with your soul. Trauma can obscure your vision of your soul's inner light. It can block your ability to hear its whispers of wisdom and guidance. It can prevent you from knowing the truth of who you are and from seeing your innate value and worth. Trauma can trap your soul like a caged bird and confine or even block its ability to set you free and lead you to the divine. This has been called *soul murder*. Again, your soul cannot truly be killed, but your connection with your soul can be murdered or at least significantly wounded by trauma and abuse.

It might best be expressed this way: The divine spark, the inner light of your soul, cannot be extinguished, but its light can be obscured from your vision. Even when we use language such as *soul wounds* or *soul murder* to describe your experience of spiritual darkness, we hold the absolute belief that nothing, including trauma, can actually damage your soul or dim its radiant, powerful light.

It may feel as if your trauma has shattered your soul, and yet it is not so. Your soul is shatterproof—and so essentially are you! A central goal of your healing is for you to rediscover your untouched and unbroken wholeness of spirit.

My Spiritual Practice for Today

How have you felt spiritually shattered? How has your relationship with your soul been disrupted by trauma? Reflect on the spiritual truth that your soul, your essential identity, shines brightly, wholly undiminished within you.

June 4

The Fire Blazing Within (Vicki)

I wish I could give you a taste of the burning fire of
love. There is a fire blazing inside of me. If I cry about
it, or if I don't, the fire is at work night and day.
–Rumi

There is a fire in the heart of every human being. It blazes whether we are reeling in pain or consumed by joy. It is the same fire that allows human beings to be so astoundingly resilient in the midst of great hardship. This resilience can be seen around the globe in the suffering of the poor, in those caught up in the crossfire of war, and in the competition of rampant capitalism that doesn't care about who gets hurt in the middle.

Rose Mapendo is a human rights activist from the Congo. Despite the most unspeakable violence perpetrated against her and her family, Rose's fire caused her to walk out of a death camp and start her own foundation to help other refugees. Rose and her family of seven were caught up in a civil war and imprisoned in a death camp. Rose witnessed the torture and murder of her husband, then found out she was pregnant with twins. With her body emaciated from starvation, she gave birth to twin boys who survived because she named the boys after the two men who tortured and murdered her husband. Her captors were so humbled by this action they gave Rose and her children food and drink. Several months later they were rescued by UN aid workers and immigrated to the United States. Today Rose lives in Phoenix with her family and runs her New Horizons Foundation to help other refugees from the Congo.

Do we have such a fire burning in us? I believe we do and that we would do anything to survive. Thankfully most of us will not have to face such overwhelming odds. Can we rest in the confidence that we have this same kind of fire burning within us and have the power inside to re-create our lives just as Rose Mapendo did?

My Spiritual Practice for Today

Today I want to find deep within me the blazing fire that will give me the courage to confront and challenge all that keeps from becoming my True Self. I want to heal all that is keeping me from living my life fully.

June 5

The Hugging Prayer (Sue)

(Adapted from an article by Sister Jose Hobday, a Native American Franciscan sister)

In life and along your healing journey, you will have times when you will feel the need to cry, but there will be no one available to hold and comfort you. There will also be times when others—or even you—may not understand why you are crying. This prayer is for those times. It is a simple, yet powerful and tactile prayer.

It goes like this. If you feel the need to be comforted, wrap your arms around yourself in a tight hug. Put your arms all the way around yourself, cuddling your body the way you would hold a child. After you have a good hold of yourself, close your eyes and begin to rock yourself as you would a hurting child. Imagine that God is rocking you, holding you through your own arms. Or imagine a soul friend or some other spiritual being or someone loving and close to you holding you.

As you do this, remember that you are God's little girl or boy—no matter your current age—and that God and your soul understand why you are crying, even if no one else does. Realize too that God holds you close the same way that you are holding yourself because God loves you more than you can imagine. Feel God holding you like a mother holds a child to calm and console. Keep holding and rocking yourself as long as you need, and be comforted.

My Spiritual Practice for Today

Do the Hugging Prayer at least three times today, allowing yourself to fully absorb the consolation, love, and healing. Put this in your healing toolbox to be used whenever you are in sorrow or simply when you need a hug and no one else is available.

June 6

Jumping Off a Cliff, Part 1 (Pat)

A few years ago, I jumped off a 100-foot cliff into a rocky gorge and lived to tell the tale. The jump was the highlight of a weekend of professional training for Sue and me and seven other therapists at the Ranch, an in-patient treatment program outside of Nashville, Tennessee. It was a part of a therapeutic ropes course using ropes, zip lines, and the jump.

The cliff was actually a pre-Civil War dam that towered above the gorge. The therapeutic process was to be fitted with a rope and harness manned by a staff member who would control my fall and landing. Then I had to scale a very steep ladder up the face of the dam. I was already in trouble because I have a strong fear of heights. I summoned my courage and forced myself up the ladder. Then I had to walk along a narrow ledge to where another staff member was waiting. I had a death grip on the low wall above the ledge as I talked to the facilitator.

He asked me what I was holding onto in my life and what I wanted to let go of. We prayed a prayer of letting go, and then he said to jump when I was ready. I was terrified and frozen above the 100-foot precipice. Everything in me screamed, "Hold on for dear life! Don't let go of the wall!" After an eternity passed, something moved within me to allow me to relax my grip, and I jumped, pushing out into the open void.

The fear totally left. I was flying and I was exhilarated. I flew for several seconds, and as I flew, a spontaneous and joyous laughter erupted from deep within. I felt the rope gently catch me midair. As I walked back up the hill to rejoin Sue and the group, I continued to laugh and felt great peace and a soul-deep joy. The idea of the jump was to give me an experiential feeling of letting go and making a leap, literally, of faith—and it worked!

My Spiritual Practice for Today

Do not try this at home! However, use my experience to reflect on letting go and surrender in your life. What are your fears? What do you hold onto that holds you back from "flying" in your life? What has been it like for you when you have made a leap of faith?

June 7

Jumping Off a Cliff, Part 2 (Pat)

Every significant decision requires a leap of faith. Even if you go through an exhaustive preparation for the decision, looking at every angle and planning for every possibility, at some point you have to make the decision and leap into an unknown future. You cannot see into the future from the vantage point of the present, no matter how hard you work a decision.

After my jump, I realized that my real fear was not about the height. It was about leaping into the unknown and my pattern of deliberating forever before finalizing a decision. Just as I held tightly onto the wall, I hold onto the process of examining all of the potential factors and fearfully resist letting go and making the decision. For example, I once took seven years to make a major life-transition decision. I mulled over all that was involved until my brain hurt and my soul began to rebel. When Sue and I traveled to Southern Africa, I spent months studying and preparing for all the god-awful ways to die in Africa, from lions to hippos to crocodiles to tsetse flies. None of it happened.

Perhaps you can relate. Your own trauma may stop you from making important decisions. You may hold onto the status quo for dear life, resisting the necessary leap into the future. You may fret over every threatening possibility and become frozen by fear. However, what I have learned in my own healing journey is that it is safe to jump, to make that leap of faith. I learned this by making the leap and then experiencing that the decision usually works out, often better than I expected.

Even more important, I experienced that I was given all the resources that I needed for the future, no matter the outcome. I was not abandoned if the decision didn't play out as I hoped. I was taken care of; I was caught and gently let down to solid ground. If a professional worrier like me can learn to leap, you can too.

My Spiritual Practice for Today

Look at your own pattern of making decisions. How does your trauma fear affect you in your process? Take a test leap today and risk making a small decision. Notice how it feels and what resources your soul gives you as you experience the outcome.

June 8

Jumping Off a Cliff, Part 3 (Pat)

Another lesson from the cliff experience came from watching a fellow therapist go through her process of jumping. Jane was in her late 30s, a very skilled and experienced psychotherapist. We watched her from the side of the gorge. She effortlessly climbed the steep ladder, having no difficulty with the height as I had. She walked confidently along the ledge to the facilitator. It was there that she froze. She and the facilitator talked intensely, just outside our hearing. We could tell that the cliff had brought up a very difficult issue for her.

After a long emotional discussion and a couple of aborted attempts to jump, Jane walked off the dam and came to talk to the group. She shared that her block was her inability to trust that the staff member would catch her. Her personal history was that she had never experienced anyone being there for her. She had always been the strong one who cared for others. When she had struggled in life, no one had been there to catch her and help her land safely. She had become totally self-reliant and a competent self-sufficient woman. She couldn't jump because her emotional belief was that no one would catch her, including God.

Perhaps, you can identify with Jane's fear. Perhaps like many survivors, no one was there for you; no one caught you after your trauma. This makes it difficult for you to let go, to make a leap of faith and trust that someone, including your soul or God, will catch you. This can impair your ability to take the risks required for major decisions. You can't believe it will work out and anyone will support you.

After the group listened to Jane and expressed our support, she was able to climb back up and jump. We cheered for her as she unroped. She glowed with a sheen of new confidence. She had finally been caught.

My Spiritual Practice for Today

Do you identify with Jane's struggle? Was no one there for you? Is there a leap of faith that you need to make? Push past your fear by imagining someone or your soul or God catching you when you leap. Practice jumping by taking small risks today and seeing how they feel.

June 9

This Dark Night Will Pass (Vicki)

This night will pass
Then we have work to do…
Everything has to do
With loving and not loving
–Rumi

Indeed this dark night will pass if we allow our deepest feelings of grief to surface so they can be healed. To allow deep pain to continue to swirl like a gyroscope within us is to allow disease to go unhealed in our body. Just as a medical condition is diagnosed and treated, so must we give equal attention to the pain of grief. There is no prescription for grief. It requires the hard work of bringing up from deep within what needs to be healed. Some live their entire lives without doing this, and they are held hostage by their inability to move forward. Mark Nepo in *The Book of Awakening* writes, "There is no freedom until we dance the ghosts from the chambers of our wounds, until we pile our wounds like stones at the mouth of our own quarries."

I had not grieved the loss of my sister, Becca, who was killed in an auto accident when she was 5 and I was 8. I had held twenty-seven years of unresolved grief when I first began talking about her death with my therapist. I was also caught up in an abusive relationship with a priest that had gone on for seventeen years. Initially, working with my therapist, I did not understand that I had not grieved the loss of Becca or what I had lost in my formative years because of the abuse by a Catholic priest.

It was time to pile the stones at the mouth of the quarry as Mark Nepo writes. It was time to let love bring up what needed to be grieved and healed. I wanted to love myself enough to heal the deep grief I held for the loss of Becca. I wanted to grieve the loss I experienced from the abusive relationship. I wanted to become whole; I wanted to become my True Self.

My Spiritual Practice for Today

It is time to consider my own grief and unhealed wounds. What are my issues of grief today? What steps can I take to begin to heal those things I still grieve? Today I want to move toward healing.

June 10

Pat's Breast Cancer (Sue)

A lump! Breast cancer? My husband, my Pat, who had always been 100 percent healthy? Total shock! Numb! Disbelief! After a mammogram and a biopsy, it was breast cancer.

"Peace be with you." "Fear not, I am with you." Oh my, I could not even think of those soothing words.

I drew from the well of wisdom that my work and my life had given me. One of my sayings to clients is, "It's what's so, and so what!" Time to face it and focus on what's next. Breathe and breathe again. Pray and pray some more.

Next step, a mastectomy. More bad news: four lymph nodes cancerous; Pat's cancer is stage III, requiring intensive treatment. Also, there's a bleed in his chest. A second surgery. The post-op healing is long and painful. Twice daily bandage changes. Watch that drain! Seven months, two rounds of intensive chemotherapy, followed by radiation every day for five weeks.

Pat became so sick and weak. Seeing Pat suffer was excruciatingly painful. Like a mother, you don't want your child to hurt. Well, I didn't want my Pat, my best friend, lover, and life partner to hurt—or die.

At the Infusion Center, I'd visit with other patients, young and old, and their families. So many people in pain, suffering. Somehow that strengthened me. I was not alone.

Pat and I would return home from chemo wiped out. Time to rest and watch funny old movies and TV. One moment at a time! When emotions would well up inside of Pat, I'd sit next to him on the couch and we'd cry, talk, share our fears, and even sneak in a laugh or two. As we tell our clients, "Tears are holy water; bless yourself with them."

Our children and grandchildren, friends, and neighbors were awesome. We were surrounded by love: visits, meals, Sunday drives for Pat, two late-night trips to the ER, one over dark back roads during the great flood of 2016. Our neighbor, Liddia, age 6, assisted her daddy putting out our trash at 7 a.m. twice a week, rain, snow, or shine.

Sometimes I think that I didn't know what love was until I made this journey with Pat. "Love is patient, love is kind…"

My Spiritual Practice for Today

Every moment, even the most painful ones, contains seeds of grace and spiritual learning. What have those moments been for you? What grace did you receive? What learning was opened for you?

June 11

La Dolce (Pat)

"La dolce far niente" is an Italian saying that means, "The sweetness of doing nothing." This is a puzzling statement for most people in our culture. How could doing nothing be sweet? There are strong social messages to be always doing something productive. Our value is often measured by what we do. When we meet someone new, one of the first questions is "What do you do?" and rarely, "Tell me about yourself."

We have become Human Doers instead of Human Beings. The fine, and spiritually necessary, art of just being has been largely lost. Really "chillin'," simply enjoying being with family and friends, listening to music, or hanging with your soul in quiet and solitude is little valued. We are driven to always be accomplishing something, and even feel guilty when we are not. The ancient and beautiful custom of Sabbath—a time-out for rest and reflection, for worship and prayer, and for long, slow meals with our families—has largely been lost.

Our bodies, our minds, our families, and our souls need this time of doing nothing. It is difficult to learn to listen to our souls and our deeper feelings and needs if we are constantly busy and striving.

This is especially challenging for many survivors. The memory of your trauma can impel you to always stay hyperactive and distracted so you do not feel your pain. You may believe that you have to always be accomplishing something to prove your worth and counter your shame. You might unconsciously keep your life noisy and overly full, streaming this, googling that, chasing the latest meme or Facebook or Instagram post. This deprives you of your own inner richness.

It is spiritually vital that you learn to simply be, to develop the art of doing nothing and consciously set aside time for Sabbath moments. Yes, you will feel some more pain, but you will be able to access your deeper mind, become aware of your intuitions, and hear the quiet voice of your soul. You will be renewed and refreshed body, mind, and spirit.

My Spiritual Practice for Today

Set aside some precious time of doing nothing productive or goal oriented. Be aware of any fear or resistance. Honor your feelings, and yet push through them. Allow yourself to feel the sweetness and body and soul refreshment of doing nothing.

June 12

Everyday Moments (Pat)

Your soul can provide the spiritual vision to enable you to see that despite the apparent darkness of trauma, the light of love—whether we name it God or a force of the universe—still shines forth. Love is working against the darkness of these events to restore life, to bring healing, to give meaning and purpose to the seemingly senseless, to restore hope.

Days after the horrific story broke about three women in Cleveland who were abducted and held as sexual slaves for 10 years, my soul helped me to see an example of the triumph of love right before me. I was walking into my second-floor office with a client when I happened to glance out my window to the sidewalk leading from the office building next door. The elderly psychiatrist who practices there was slowly walking backward down the sidewalk guiding his patient, who was paralyzed on his left side and was struggling to make the short walk to his car. The patient's daughter was steadying her father from behind. The psychiatrist and the daughter patiently and gently helped the man into the car. They hugged and parted, and the psychiatrist returned to his office. My client and I stood there in awe-filled silence and then began our session. This scene has been repeated every week for the past year below my office window. The doctor and the daughter's kindness and love and the man's courage and determination touch and inspire me each time.

These moments are all around us every day, millions of times a day. They are rarely reported in the media; and yet they are much more common than the moments of trauma, darkness, or evil. They are so common that we fail to see them. Our sight is blinded by the glare of coverage of the dramatic tragedies. We have to learn to see with the eyes of our soul to become conscious of these small miracles of kindness that surround us everyday. So when the next traumatic news story assaults your mind and spirit, remember to look around you for the many manifestations of love and kindness that are in your midst.

My Spiritual Practice for Today

Let your soul open your eyes to the everyday miraculous moments of love that you encounter this day.

June 13

Uncomfortable Truths (Vicki)

Empower me
to exercise the authority of honesty,
and be a participant
in the difficult ordinariness of now.
Ted Loder, *Wrestling the Light*

The declaration "Uncomfortable truths are still unassailably true" came from a note sent by my friend Kathleen. While it was in reference to the lack of leadership in the hierarchy of the Catholic Church concerning the sex abuse crisis, the statement led me to pause and reflect.

I was facing the uncomfortable truth that a Catholic priest had taken control of my life. I could not own this truth. I was so young when the emotional abuse began. When the sexual advances began, I felt special. I was unaware that he was emotionally manipulating me to see him as superior. In my naiveté I succumbed to his control and for years could find no way out.

Healing takes time. It may seem like an eternity before there is any sign of hope or light. It took a long time for me to discover my power. You have to be the champion of your own cause and be willing to engage the difficult challenges you face in the healing journey. You must accept that your uncomfortable truths are still unassailably true.

My Spiritual Practice for Today

Today I will take a long loving look at myself to discover any truth that I have buried deep in the secrecy of my heart. Naming this truth will be my first step toward healing.

June 14

The Power of Surrender (Pat)

I'm still not sure what happened. I only know that it may have saved my life. I'll tell the story and let you decide.

Sue and I were on vacation in the Turks and Caicos Islands. One afternoon I decided to go for a quick sail on a small boat while Sue was getting a massage. The sail started out beautifully. The wind was strong and steady. The sun sparkled on the brilliant blue water, which was calmed by a reef about 4 miles out from the beach. I went on a long, fast reach at an angle away from the beach. It was exhilarating.

When I saw that I had gotten pretty far, I decided to turn around (the sailing term is "come about") and head back. Only I couldn't. The sailboat would not come about. So I went farther on the same tack and tried to come about. The same result. I tried over and over with no success. I used every trick I knew as an experienced sailor. Nothing worked. I was starting to get worried. Then it got worse.

On one of my attempts to come about, the boat got stuck directly into the wind, and I couldn't steer it either way. The wind was pushing me backwards toward the reef. The sound of the breakers on the reef was growing louder. Beyond the reef was the open Atlantic. Next stop, Africa. If I didn't get control soon, either the breakers would overturn me, or I would be swept out to sea. I was now at my wits end and really scared.

I turned to prayer: "Lord, I am in real trouble. Everything I have tried isn't working. I put myself in your hands and surrender myself and this situation to you." I let go of the tiller and the sail and just sat there. I began to feel at peace with whatever was about to happen. Then an amazing thing occurred.

After a seeming eternity, the boat slowly swung around on its own. I grabbed the mainsheet and tiller and sailed directly back to the beach where Sue was waiting for me.

So what happened? Was there some sort of divine intervention in answer to my prayer? Or did my letting go of the boat's controls allow it to just naturally right itself? Either way, it would not have happened if I had not let go and surrendered.

My Spiritual Practice for Today

Think of times in your life when you tried to steer your life in a certain direction and were unable to. Could you let go and surrender control? How did that feel? What was the outcome?

June 15

Water Meditation (Pat)

Water will level with you more than most things will. Water can speak to your soul like few other natural elements can.

There is much that water teaches. It teaches and demonstrates (water practices what it preaches) living with fluidity versus the rigidity that fear and shame impose on you. Water flows around, over, or under obstacles in its path, tirelessly seeking a way through.

So much in life is flowing, like time, blood, light, and love. Learning to live fluidly and flow around the boulders in your life—learning to live like water—is transforming.

Speaking of transformation, water is the champ. It transforms from a solid (ice) to a fluid to a vapor or a gas. Water shows us what we are capable of doing. It is a shape-shifter like us. We can transition from the solidity of our bodies to the fluidity of our minds to the vaporous mists of our soul and Spirit and back again. For an element so changeable, water has great power. And of course, it is the necessary ingredient of all life.

Water is used in the rituals of many spiritual traditions. It is a universal sign of refreshment, cleansing, and living in flow. Water is used to bless your self. In baptism you are spiritually cleansed and renewed. You also symbolically drown or die as you go into the baptismal waters and rise up to a new life and new community. Water can represent dying to or drowning your ego, your false self, and being reborn into your True Self.

There is an energy being in or around water that is enlivening. Perhaps it is because your body is made up of so much water (about 60 percent). Maybe the water outside somehow speaks to and communes with your water inside.

My Spiritual Practice for Today

Find a way to spend some time around a natural body of water today. Stroll along a beach, a stream, or the shore of a lake. If that's not possible, use your bathtub or shower (which is where I get many of my writing inspirations) or even a bowl of water. Center your meditation on water. Be aware of the life-giving energy you receive being around water. Reflect too on what it is teaching you. At the end of your meditation, bless yourself with the water.

June 16

Make it Personal (Pat & Sue)

Through a balanced program of prayer and meditation,
we develop an authentic and personal relationship with
our God and invite God into every area of our lives.
–The Spiritual Laundry List

Your ultimate soul friend is God. The ultimate purpose of all prayer and meditation, all religion and spirituality, is to draw you into a close and intimate friend relationship with your Higher Power.

Think of prayer as having coffee with your best friend. It is a time to talk and listen, share your feelings and the events of your life, and nurture and enjoy the bond that you have with your friend. Prayer is not an empty ritual to be rattled off out of some sense of obligation or guilt. It is a means of drawing closer and inviting God into every area of your life, as you would a friend. In other words, it's hanging out with your best friend and lover, God.

Rumi, the Sufi mystic from the thirteenth century, writes: "Your task is not to seek for love, but merely to seek and find all the barriers within yourself that you have built against it." Survivors, because of the spiritual wounds from trauma, often have internal barriers to love, including God's love. Those barriers make it difficult to make it personal with God.

One path of healing is to identify your barriers and systematically use your soul courage to dismantle them. Another way is, through a program of regular prayer and meditation, to let the love and friendship of God seek and find you. Spend enough time with your friend and gradually the barriers will melt away and a personal, intimate, and deeply enjoyable relationship will emerge. You will never be alone again. Remember the old saying, "It's good to have friends in high places!"

My Spiritual Practice for Today

Make a plan to regularly spend quality time with your Higher Power through a consistent program of prayer and meditation. Treasure and protect this time. See it as a precious opportunity to grow and nurture the most personal of friendships.

June 17

Father's Day (Sue)

On this day, I'm having a flood of memories of my dad: the good, the bad, and the ugly. Mercifully, time passes, wounds heal, and the goodness of the loving times now outweighs the sadness, the pain, and the sorrow. Then there is a flood of memories of another life: my children's dad, the goodness, the not so good, and the neglect (all from my experience and perspective).

Time—and consciously working to be free—does heal. The importance of memory and loss is to remember, mourn the loss of what could've been better, and forgive what it was. Holding on only weighs me down and burdens me. It's difficult to smile when you are gritting your teeth. Breathe in God's love; breathe out God's love. Focus on what is and what I am grateful for. Oh my, that will take all day!

Think about your own father. How do you feel about him today? What are your memories like? Can you rejoice and be grateful for the best of him and for what you received from him? Do you have a mixture of joy, sadness, anger, and grief? Whatever you feel, embrace it, and know that it is all right and a part of your healing. If there are painful or abusive memories, are you in a place to forgive? Can you see the good in your dad behind the negative and hurtful? Can you see him in the circle of value, as a child of God, a person of infinite value and worth? Can you see that, like yourself, he is, or was, on his own journey, in most cases doing the best he could with the tools he had?

My Spiritual Practice for Today

Reflect on your dad in your life. Recall your memories with him. Pray for him. Let your soul lead your prayer to whatever kind of prayer is best for you now: giving thanks for him; a prayer of joy, sadness, or even anger; or a prayer of forgiveness and reconciliation.

June 18

Toward Intimacy (Vicki)

It's taken more than half my life to understand the meaning of true intimacy. For years I understood intimacy only in sexual terms in an abusive relationship. As I have matured spiritually (an ongoing journey), I have come to understand intimacy in a more comprehensive, life-sustaining way. I count among my most precious gifts the gift of intimacy that I share and receive among soul friends and confidants. This gift of intimacy is the freedom to speak, from the core of my being, my joys and sorrows, my accomplishments and failures. I recognize this as a gift.

While doing outreach with the homeless in Los Angeles, I learned that a single loving action shared with a stranger can be as intimate and transforming as that received from a trusted friend. The depth of our intimacy with those around us is a reflection of the depth of our relationship with the God of our understanding. Intimacy with another human being on any level, be it a brief encounter with a homeless person or a lifelong relationship, is an encounter with the divine presence inherent in each human being.

Mother Teresa taught the greatest poverty in the world today is the poverty of despair and loneliness, the poverty of not being loved, of not having an intimate loving relationship with another. When I reflect on the richness of my life in terms of the love and affirmation I receive, I know I have been transformed out of the darkness of suffering and into the light of love. When we are caught up in the negative cycle of abuse, we cannot see the love that surrounds us. I am thankful that my family and friends did not give up on loving me through it all. When I acknowledged my anger and grief and could begin to forgive my abuser, I was able to truly believe in that life-sustaining love. This confidence buoyed me in my continued journey to the wholeness I was seeking.

My Spiritual Practice for Today

Love is all around me today, and I want to be aware of how it lifts me like a buoy in the sea and holds me securely.

June 19

Fear Not (Pat)

One of the most frequent phrases in the Jewish-Christian scriptures is: "Fear not, for I am with you." These are God's words to particular individuals or, in other cases, universally to everyone.

Notice carefully what is said and promised. You are invited to have no fear about whatever you are facing. This is not based on God intervening and stopping the threatening event. It is simply because God is and will be with you, and so you are not alone.

There is no promise that bad things will never happen to you. The promise is faithful presence. The promise is that you will never be alone with whatever may occur. It is always more traumatic to face a threatening event alone. The fear is magnified. However, if you feel that someone is by your side supporting you, it is much less intimidating and easier to find the courage required. Fear diminishes, and you feel more empowered when you have an army of at least two to go into battle.

It is often difficult for survivors to trust that that their Higher Power is with them and that they are not alone. Difficult spiritual questions, like "Where was God when I was abused" and "Why didn't God stop or prevent my trauma?" can undermine your belief in God's promise of presence. And yet as you grow spiritually and begin to experience God's loving omnipresence, the words of this promise will come alive for you and lessen your fear.

As you learn to listen to the whispering of your soul, you will sense the Presence within and around you more and more. Presence can also come through people in your life. Your soul friends will always accompany you. Your sisters and brothers in the #MeToo movement invite you to join the swelling chorus of voices breaking the silence and speaking up for all survivors. There is a "cloud of witnesses" that surrounds and embraces you. Another way to say the scripture then is: "Do not be afraid, for you are never truly alone."

My Spiritual Practice for Today

Reflect on the promise made in this phrase. Focus today on all the ways that you are accompanied and not alone. Consciously sense the Presence with you during all the events of your day.

June 20

Let the Milk of Loving Flow (Vicki)

Cry out! Don't be stolid and silent with your pain.
Lament! And let the milk of loving flow through you.
–Rumi

Family dynamics can sometimes keep us stuck in emotional chaos. The intense grief my family experienced upon the death of my sister, Becca, at age 5 was not something I was aware of growing up. My parents hid so much from us. It was the only way they knew how to cope. It wasn't to hurt us. It was to protect us. Only in retrospect could we all figure out why our grief was held so tightly for so many years. What we know about dealing with grief today simply wasn't available in 1963. Today we can put the pieces together.

When I was in counseling, I invited my family to attend a family counseling session so we could talk about the accident and the loss of Becca. My three siblings and my mother came. We were on pins and needles because none of us had ever mentioned Becca's name in front of Mom. As the counselor began the conversation, we each shared our memories from the time of the accident. Each of us shared different recollections of the accident. After some time, the counselor stopped us and pointed out that after talking about Becca for half an hour, our mother had not fallen apart. For twenty-seven years we did not speak Becca's name. The silence was finally released, and no one had fallen apart.

We hold onto the unknown for so long and don't realize the toll it takes. Rumi says, "Cry out! Don't be stolid and silent with your pain. Lament!" If we knew then what we know now. "Let the milk of loving flow through you." We lamented at that counseling session. We spoke Becca's name as if we were crying out. For the first time we could break the silence and release the collective family pain that had been held captive for all those years. We could, for the first time, grieve as a family. What a healthy thing to do! We are still talking about dear Becca. She holds a sacred place in our family history.

My Spiritual Practice for Today

Today I will reflect on the role grief plays in my life. I will think of the unresolved grief that I may still be holding deep within my soul.

June 21

Hating Yourself (Sue)

If you hate yourself, you obviously haven't yet met yourself. You certainly have not met your soul or come to know your True Self. If you had really been introduced to yourself, you would know who you are: God's precious child, a magnificent person of infinite value, and you would believe that you are loved and lovable with many amazing gifts and nobody to be hated—especially by your self.

Abuse and trauma leave you with the feeling and belief that you are unlovable and worthy of hate. You have been taught to hate your personal characteristics. You were led to believe that you are at fault somehow for your abuse and have learned to blame the victim—yourself. Whatever real mistakes you have made in your life you see as evidence confirming that you are hateable. You punish and sabotage yourself in various self-destructive ways. You are guilty of a hate crime, and you are its target.

Living in your soul's circle of value brings freedom from this vicious cycle of self-hate and invites you to meet your self, your True Self, perhaps for the first time. Your soul tells you that your value and worth are not defined by what was done to you. You are not your story of abuse and trauma. You are not your mistakes. You are so much more than either. Your infinite value just is. It is simply so. You are God's precious child. How can you hate any child, including the child that you are? Your soul invites you to meet the priceless and beloved child within you—and stop hating.

My Spiritual Practice for Today

Be aware as you go through the day of any self-hating thoughts or actions that you habitually fall into. Question each of them. Respond to each with your soul's message: "You are God's precious child, a magnificent person of infinite value; no one (including yourself) should hate this child who is you."

June 22

Immortal Diamond (Pat)

Throughout history the human species has displayed an intuitive understanding that there is something within us that transcends the physical, external, observable world around us. We are more than our body—glorious as it is—and the rest of the material world. Whether this understanding is expressed religiously in the great spiritual traditions and belief systems of East and West, or through art, myth, literature, dance, music, theater, or through the pursuit of scientific truth and the origins of the universe, we humans generally feel that there is something more about us than the material and tangible. That which is transcendent within us is named many things in many different spiritual traditions: our inner spark of the divine, our Christ or our Buddha nature, our inner essence and freedom, our wisdom box, the life breath or life force that animates us, the energy of the universe, our True Self. The spiritual writer Richard Rohr calls the soul an "immortal diamond." In this book, we will call this transcendence soul.

This immortal diamond is an ineffable, essential, eternal core of light, love, and energy that is most truly and essentially who we are. Your soul is not only your True Self; it is also the life force within you that seeks to move you beyond the limitations of your mind, your ego, and your life circumstances.

Your soul is in itself untouchable. Like a hard and brilliant diamond, it cannot be broken, damaged, weakened, or altered—even by trauma or abuse. In your soul, you remain your true and essential self, no matter what is done to you or what you experience. Your sacred worth and eternal value abides despite all that life may throw at you. Your soul's power to move you beyond yourself and the limits of life remains within you. You may be hurt psychologically and even spiritually by abuse or trauma, yet you have not been metaphysically damaged or diminished.

The eternal diamond of who you truly are, your soul, endures, shines, glows, and sparkles against whatever darkness you may have experienced.

My Spiritual Practice for Today

Spend the day reflecting upon and imagining the immortal diamond that resides within you. This is who you are, a brilliant spark of the divine fire. Just as your body is literally composed of star stuff, your soul, your True Self, is made of God stuff.

June 23

Receptivity to Healing (Vicki)

Intuition cannot be produced. It has to be allowed to happen. But that is just what the rational mind cannot endure. It wants to control everything. It is not prepared to be silent, to be still, to allow things to happen. Of course, there is a passivity of inertia, but this is an "active passivity." It is what the Chinese call wu wei, action in in-action. It is a state of receptivity.
–Bede Griffiths

They are seemingly contradictory words, "active passivity." For so long, I actively resisted reaching out for help in the most confusing of times. Holding onto a deep, dark secret that felt impervious to any other person. The resistance to allowing anyone to break through was like armor. I would tell myself, "You can figure this out on your own." How wrong I was!

A spiritual director I was seeing at the time will never know that she was a catalyst for active passivity. She had no idea that her mere suggestion that I seek help for whatever was troubling me was the seed that allowed me to reach out for help. She was acting in my in-action. Her mere suggestion compelled me to act.   When the student is ready, the teacher appears.

My intuition that something was terribly wrong was real even though I did not understand it completely. I was resolute in my need to control the information I would disclose, to whom it would be disclosed, and when. Telling my story to that first trusted friend allowed me to enter into a state of receptivity to the compassionate response of others. Over time this happened with friends and family. Each of us can recount our own story of truth unfolding and bearing witness to the way it moved our healing forward.

My Spiritual Practice for Today

My deeply held intuition drives my desire for healing. I want to trust that my intuition knows what is best for me. I want to move from within that trusted intuition and not from the false self that wants to control everything. I want to be free to do what is best for me.

June 24

Poor Me, No _____ (Pat)

The story goes in my family that when I was very young, I would hold up my empty cup and in a pitiful little voice tell everyone within hearing, "Poor Pat, no milk!" Unfortunately, this became somewhat of a life mantra: "Poor me, no _____ (fill in the blank)." Mercifully, I am mostly free of this life theme now. Yet for many years in my self-pity pot moments, this mantra led me to concentrate on what I thought I lacked, rather than to see what I had.

Trauma and abuse cause lasting and painful losses of many kinds. These are real and need to be grieved as part of your healing. However, for some survivors this can develop into a primary focus on what was lost or taken away, and an inability to see what is still there and can be restored. "Poor me" can become your theme song and prevent you from seeing what is within you and around you that are gifts and blessings. The losses should never be denied, yet they do not have to obscure the good you have done and the good you have been graced with. You can learn to write a new mantra: "Blessed _____ (your name), look at what I have been given _____ (fill in the blank)."

My Spiritual Practice for Today

Today identify your own personal self-pity mantra, and then see how it affects you and how often you replay it in your mind during the day. Notice how the self-pity song makes you feel. Rewrite it toward the positive in the form of an affirmation that highlights your blessings. Repeat this affirmative mantra at least once an hour for the whole day. Notice how you feel differently saying the affirmation to yourself.

June 25

Writing a New Personal Creed (Pat)

The experience of abuse or trauma and the questions that it produces about suffering, evil, and providence can shake you to the very foundation of your being. It brings into question many of the beliefs and assumptions that were the spiritual bedrock of your life. Spiritual healing must then also involve a reconstruction of that fractured foundation and the discovery of new truths to live by. In a sense, you are being challenged to write a new personal creed for yourself, discarding the old understandings that no longer fit for you and incorporating the new beliefs that you discover in your spiritual healing journey. The exercise below is a good vehicle for doing this. Your soul will be your guide.

My Spiritual Practice for Today

Divide a large piece of paper in half lengthwise.

On one side of the paper, write "What I Now Believe."

On the other side, write "What I No Longer Believe."

Reflect and pray, then list things on both sides. You do not have to list strictly religious things. Let your soul guide you however she wants to.

List the things that you now value and those that no longer fit for you.

Now look at each item on your list and be aware of the feelings that surface. Perhaps there is anger, rage, sadness, loss, hopefulness, encouragement, or surprise. These are the seeds of your spiritual healing and growth and the start of a new personal creed to build upon and live by.

Finally, when you are ready, take what you have listed on the "Now Believe" side and write them as a personal creed. You can do this by simply filling in the blank, "I believe in _____." Do this over and over until your creed is complete. Post it on your refrigerator or on the wall of your prayer or meditation room.

June 26

Love Brings Up Anything Unlike Itself (Pat & Sue)

L ove brings up anything unlike itself for the purpose of healing. This is
a universal spiritual principle that we have seen in our own lives and
over and over in the healing journeys of survivors. Love—especially God's
love—brings to the surface and into the light anything that is not love for the
purpose of healing—never for the purpose of inflicting more pain or shame.
This is because anything that remains hidden creates more pain and shame.
Eckhart Tolle, paraphrasing St. Paul in *The Power of Now*, expresses this same
principle: "Everything is shown up by being exposed to the light, and whatever
is exposed to the light itself becomes light."

Survivors experience this principle when they break through their fear
and shame and tell their story to a trusted soul friend. This brings your story
into the light for your healing. The principle applies also whenever a painful
memory or emotion erupts into your awareness. This emergence is for your
healing, not to punish or oppress you, as it may seem at first.

When any of us is challenged to face something in ourselves that is unlike
love, it is not to shame or condemn. Rather, love's goal is to invite us to be
further transformed into love and light. These processes may begin with pain,
like childbirth, but this principle assures us that the purpose is loving and will
in time bring forth new life in us.

Remember this if you are experiencing emotional or spiritual pain from
your abuse or trauma. Hold onto its hope. The time of pain will move to a
time of restoration and new freedom. Even though it may not feel like love
when you are suffering, it is truly love at work in your healing.

My Spiritual Practice for Today

Often it is only when we look back that we can see love at work. Think of
a time in your life, especially some phase of your healing journey, when you
emerged from a period of emotional or spiritual pain to a new place of freedom, joy, light, or deeper connection. See now how love was acting for your
healing. Anchor this awareness deep in your heart and soul. Savor it and save
it for whatever comes forth next in your healing path.

June 27

A Gratitude a Day (Pat & Sue)

To coin a new version of an old saying, "A gratitude a day keeps the therapist away!" Research has shown that a daily expression of thankfulness for something in your life helps to prevent depression. And there are no side effects or fees! Gratitude lifts your spirits by opening your eyes to what is good and loving in your life. Gratitude turns your focus from obsessing and depressing about what is wrong and turns it toward seeing and appreciating what is right about yourself and your life. Daily gratefulness is transformative. You are now seeing what your soul sees. You are seeing with spiritual 20/20 vision.

Gratitude, though, can be difficult for survivors. Your trauma or abuse may have darkened or altered your spiritual vision so your focus is mainly on what was done to you or what feels damaged in you. It is important to face those wounds, and yet you can also learn to see what is positive in your life and in yourself and be grateful.

My Spiritual Practice for Today

Develop a gratitude list. Check it daily and choose at least one thing each day you are grateful for and give thanks for it in a prayer of gratitude. In time, notice how it changes what you focus your mind and heart on and how it lifts your spirit.

June 28

The Key to Our Sanctuary (Vicki)

Remember, the entrance door to the sanctuary is inside you.
–Rumi

The image of a door speaks to openness, entry into, access to something deeper. The poet Rumi reminds us here of the beautiful sanctuary that is within each human being. We can think of the door to the heart, which opens to love and acceptance.

Some years ago I was sitting with a dying man named Jack; he had been abandoned by his family because he was gay. When they found out he was HIV positive, they scorned him further. He was now dying from an AIDS-related cancer. Jack had only a few friends by his side to sit with him as he lay dying. In an intimate conversation about his life, only days before he passed, he realized the true gift of his life. Listening to him talk about the love he held for his family, I reminded him of that gift of love that he carried. He had forgiven his family for abandoning him, and that forgiveness allowed him to see his life as radiant beauty and to be in touch with his inner sanctuary. Amazingly, some members of his family arrived just hours before he died, and despite his weakened state, I could see the joy in his heart. It was a beautiful moment to see him transformed, and this allowed him to die in peace.

Helen Keller once wrote, "The world is full of suffering. It is also full of the overcoming of it." In every life there is suffering, and in each life we can overcome suffering. Becoming attuned to our inner sanctuary can provide us the strength we need to weather life's battering. The stories of those who have overcome suffering are signs of wisdom for us. They are lighthouses of hope that show us how all manner of struggle can be overcome. We may have to dig deeply to be attuned to our inner sanctuary; however, trust that it is within you and believe in its power to hold you in its care.

My Spiritual Practice for Today

Believing that my inner sanctuary is the place of soul strength within me is my greatest treasure. Today I choose to find ways to overcome the suffering I am enduring. I will work toward healing my painful past so I can look forward to a new life filled with hope and peace.

June 29

Burning Bushes (Pat)

Burning bushes are everywhere. Perhaps Moses simply woke up one day with spiritual 20/20 vision to be able to see the burning bushes that were always there, all around him in the desert and in his people. Divine fire, light, and presence shine forth in so many places in our lives, if we only have the eyes to see them.

Burning bushes are the smile on the child's face alive to the wonders of the world. They are the fire and ecstasy in your lover's eyes or in the afterglow of making love, lying enraptured in each other's arms. Bushes are burning when you notice the smiling faces of a field of wild white daisies shining in the light of a sun-drenched day. Or when you pause to see the ancient, shimmering light of an improbably distant star born many millions of years ago gleaming in the night sky. They appear within you in the moment in meditation that you are totally present and mindful, and perhaps carried away to another spiritual dimension of oneness with all that is. Or when you see and feel what is graced in your life, and you are overwhelmed with gratefulness.

We can all be Moses standing in awe before the divine spark and fire that reveals itself all around and within us. Your soul has the ever-present capacity to open your eyes to see what is always there, yet seemingly hidden and disguised. Trauma and tragedy can dim your sight and make you believe that the fire, the light, and the presence are not there, and that all is cold and dark and empty. Yet you are walking by burning bushes each day that are blazing forth for your attention. If you can pause, be present, look, and see with the eyes of your soul, a bush in your own front yard will burn just for you.

My Spiritual Practice for Today

Pray for the gift of 20/20 soul eyes. Be open in each moment today to slow down and behold with awe all of the burning bushes in your life.

June 30

Love and Suffering (Pat)

The Franciscan spiritual writer Richard Rohr says, "Love and suffering are the main portals that open up the mind space and the heart space, breaking us into breadth, depth, and communion" (*The Naked Now*). More than anything else in life, these two vital life experiences open us to profound personal change and life-altering grace.

It is easy to see how love can be so life changing and life enhancing. The transformational power of suffering is not so obviously seen or desired. In fact, because we want to avoid pain, we look away from it. Yet embedded in every experience of suffering, including your abuse, is a seed of transformation and new life. Pain is certainly not redemptive in itself. It is our response to suffering that makes it redemptive. It requires that we tap into the resilience of our soul, into our inner resources of soul, faith, and spirit. This allows us to spring back into our original shape, into our wholeness of mind and spirit, and grow stronger and even more resilient.

You can see this soul resilience in many survivors. You see it in people's capacity to transform what originally stressed and stretched them out of shape into something that actually reshapes them into a stronger and more vibrant expression of their soul. You witness this when you see people discover the surprising spiritual gifts and opportunities hidden in the heart of their traumatic experiences. You can observe it when survivors manage to find deep spiritual meaning and purpose in their suffering. It is evident when you behold the miracle of individuals or whole groups resurrecting a new life mission or ministry from the ashes of some life disaster or challenge.

Each of you possesses this same well of soul resilience deep within you waiting to be tapped.

My Spiritual Practice for Today

Write down your trauma losses on the left side of a piece of paper, and then write what gifts have or might emerge from them on the right side opposite each loss. Ask your soul to help you to uncover the spiritual gifts that have come from your trauma suffering. What does your soul reveal to you?

July 1

The Mountain Meditation: Transformation (Sue & Pat)

My Spiritual Practice for Today

We invite you to do the transformation version of the Mountain Meditation. To enter into this meditation, find a comfortable sitting position. As you read, pause, close your eyes, and imagine the scenes described.

Picture yourself on a beautiful beach. See the waves, the sand, the brilliant color, and the vastness of the ocean. Feel the sun and the wind on your skin. Hear the crash and whoosh of the surf. Turn around now, and face away from the sea. This time bring nothing in your backpack. Notice how it feels to carry such a light load.

In front of you is a beautiful forest. See yourself walking along a trail into the forest. Appreciate the coolness and the shaded light. You reach the edge of the forest and see an open meadow filled with multicolored wildflowers. The trail leads you through the meadow to a clear, flowing stream with a bridge across the dancing water. Stop for a moment to enjoy the light sparkling on the water.

Now look up from the bridge and see a shining mountain before you. Following the trail, you ascend the mountain. You climb above the timberline through the clouds to the top of the peak. Look around you at the glory of creation. Then you notice a large boulder to sit on and rest.

From the other side of the peak, your spiritual guide comes and sits down with you on the boulder. You can discuss whatever you want. Be sure to ask your guide for a new life mission and purpose that arises in some way from your transformed trauma and your healing journey.

After you have received your life mission, embrace it, and put it in your backpack to bring it down the mountain to the outside world. Notice how light and energizing this new mission feels as you carry it on your back.

When you are ready to leave, thank your guide. Slowly hike back down the mountain, over the bridge, through the meadow, through the forest, to the beach, and to the edge of the vast ocean. Open your eyes. Record and reflect in your journal.

July 2

Random Acts of Transformation (Pat)

A recent study showed that two-thirds of cancers are caused by "random, unpredictable DNA copying mistakes" made by our cells as they grow and divide, resulting in mutations that can turn into cancer.

As a survivor of male breast cancer, I find this research strangely reassuring. When I was diagnosed, I searched for a cause or blame for my cancer. I couldn't find any. I have never smoked. I have taken reasonably good care of myself. There is no family history of breast cancer. The only risk factor I had was that I had never been pregnant! So when I read this study, a surprising peace came over me. It was not my fault or my genes' fault. It was not even God's fault. It was simply a naturally occurring random act of my cells, which on some unknown day made a mistake.

What isn't random is the transformation my cancer experience wrought in me. God and my soul employed my cancer and treatment to teach and change me in ways I could never have predicted. I learned how much I was loved by family and friends whose love and prayers carried me through a very rough year. Beforehand I had often taken a lot for granted. Now I have a more grateful spirit. I treasure each moment and am more mindful of the daily beauty of my life. In short, I was mutated by love.

Survivors often seek to find a reason or explanation for their trauma. Although this is understandable and can at times yield some insight, it may also lead to self-blame and shame. It might help you to view your trauma as a random act. You did not cause it. There is nothing wrong about you that invited it. You are an innocent victim. If you were abused, you did nothing to cause your perpetrator to hurt you. You are a random and blameless victim of their sickness. However, there will be nothing random about the transformation that is offered through your suffering. Your soul, your God, did not want you to suffer, and yet they can use it for your ultimate good. You too will be mutated by love.

My Spiritual Practice for Today

Consider the idea that your trauma was random. How does that change things for you? Reflect also on how you are being healed and transformed.

July 3

The Gem of Every Possibility (Vicki)

"We are kept from the experience of Spirit because our inner world is cluttered with past traumas ... As we begin to clear away this clutter, the energy of divine light and love begins to flow through our being."
–Thomas Keating

Making the journey toward our True Selves is finding our way home, home to ourselves and to whom we were meant to become. There is a precious gem inside all of us that holds every possibility that our lives can become. Yet from the moment of our birth, it seems every attempt is made to stifle that True Self. There comes a time in every life when we have to stop and take stock of where we are and how we got here. We must look at what has been lost or what has thwarted us from living the life we wanted to live.

Having a family and raising my own children were always my dream. I wanted to fall in love and create my own family dynamic with all the love in my heart. That dream was interrupted. Although it took some time to dissect what had occurred, once I understood what happened and could make sense of it, I had to take the steps to create a new dream, a new hope. I can't say that this is what God wanted for my life. I simply don't know that. What I do know is that I feel a grace has been given to me, the grace to live the life I have been given and to make the most of it. Gifts and losses can blend together to make a rich life of understanding and love.

Each of us can experience this if we walk the path of love that heals everything. If we can believe that a different life can be lived and that it too can be fulfilling, we can move forward with a sense of hope and live a new life in service to the world.

My Spiritual Practice for Today

Today I want to consider how my gifts and losses can work together to create a new life lived in love. Reflecting on these two seeming opposites could bring me new clarity in my journey.

July 4

Freedom For (Pat)

When I was in seminary, a group of us students believed that our academic freedom was being suppressed by the school's administration. In reaction, we decided to protest by doing three days of prayer and fasting. To end our fast, we invited one of our scripture professors to address us.

I will never forget his words to us. We expected him to say something that would support our cause for freedom and galvanize our protest to some further action. Instead, he brought us up short and challenged us to look beyond our narrow self-interests. He said in biblical spirituality, freedom is not primarily freedom *from* something; rather, freedom is *for* something beyond the individual self. Freedom means being liberated from some oppression; however, it is for something beyond you as well. You are freed so you can more effectively and selflessly give, serve, and love. This, he reminded us, is the ultimate spiritual purpose of freedom.

On the Fourth of July, Americans celebrate our independence and the inalienable rights and liberties we are all guaranteed. We tend to think in terms of individual freedoms and what we have been freed from. We often neglect to reflect on what we are being freed for. Our freedom cannot just be about building our own lives and pursuing our own happiness. The deeper call is to use our freedom for building a better society and world, and for becoming responsible to help release others from whatever oppresses them.

Hopefully, as a survivor, you are freer from the oppression of the wounds that your abuse has inflicted upon you. What is your freedom and healing for? It is no doubt meant to be a gift for you so you can live more abundantly and freely in the light and love of your soul. However, your soul seeks to bring forth a further, even higher purpose for you. Your freedom is for your own sake, yet not for your sake alone. It is also for the healing, freedom, and love of all those in your world.

My Spiritual Practice for Today

This holiday is a good day to explore what your healing and freedom from trauma is ultimately for. As you experience liberation from the tyranny of your past, what is your soul calling you to do with your newly gained freedoms?

July 5

Tundra Flowers (Sue)

Breathe in God's love. Breathe out God's love. Allow your breath to quiet you. Listen to the first part of the Serenity Prayer: "God grant me the serenity to accept the things I cannot change."

While on a family vacation in Rocky Mountain National Park, I learned a valuable lesson and a new meaning for this powerful, liberating prayer. We had hiked to the high mountain tundra region above the tree line. Beautiful vistas, cool, pure air, brilliant blue Colorado sky, and awesome billowy white clouds dancing across the mountaintops.

As we hiked, I noticed small wooden signs, "Please do NOT pick the flowers." Another sign informed that "Here in the tundra, alpine flowers grow very slowly due to the harsh conditions. Some are a century old."

As I stood there taking in the beauty of the alpine meadow, I noticed my precious 2-year-old daughter standing close to me wearing a beautiful smile from ear to ear, delight dancing in her eyes. One hand was behind her back. Then her little hand came forward, and she presented me with a tiny, colorful bouquet of tundra flowers. Maybe five hundred years' worth!

"The courage to change the things I can; and the wisdom to know the difference." I was faced with a quick and difficult choice. Do I correct and discipline my little girl, or do I accept her innocent gift? What would those who were watching think?

I chose to surrender what I couldn't change—she had already picked the flowers—and have the courage to change my initial reaction, which was to play to the crowd and correct her. Choosing love over rules, I squatted down to her height, received the loving gift, and gave her a big hug. I looked up to see all my fellow tourists smiling warmly.

It's amazing to me that this sacred moment happened forty-nine years ago. To this day it remains fresh in my mind. God gifted me with the grace to accept with love the gift of tundra flowers. For this I remain most grateful.

My Spiritual Practice for Today

Pray the Serenity Prayer today. See what wisdom and grace you are given in surrendering to the unchangeable, and having the courage to change what you can. Discover, most of all that, the secret wisdom of the Serenity Prayer is love.

July 6

Your Call (Pat)

There is a spiritual call embedded in the heart of your healing journey. A call is an invitation, a passion, a choice, and a commitment all rolled into one. This call from your soul invites you to discover a new purpose for your life, which will use the spiritual gifts your soul has given you in your healing journey for service or ministry to others.

Many spiritual traditions teach that you are made for a life mission and purpose unique to you. Once you have experienced a spiritual transformation and rebirth, you are commissioned to go out and share what has been given to you. Jesus sends his disciples to go forth and spread the good news of his teaching and kingdom. The disciples of Buddha felt a call to carry his message of enlightenment and freedom from suffering to much of Asia. The last step of the twelve steps of Alcoholics Anonymous reads, "Having had a spiritual awakening as the result of these steps, we tried to carry this message to alcoholics, and practice these principles in all of our affairs." Recovery from addiction is not just for the benefit of the individual addict, but involves a call, and is not complete without a mission to share what has been given.

The call is your experience of hearing some life mission deep within you and reshaping your life to serve your new purpose. Your call, as a survivor, arises in part from your trauma or abuse. Your soul has transformed your wounds into spiritual gifts that have been given to you for the purpose of sharing them with others. What is your call? What is your mission to share and serve? The service or ministry that comes forth from your call as a survivor can be small, medium, or large. The size or the prominence of your mission does not matter. Your soul and your God want to play you and your life, including your trauma, like a harp to bring beautiful and healing music to the world.

My Spiritual Practice for Today

What is the unique and beautiful music that you are called to play with your life as a healing survivor? What mission or new purpose is your soul calling you to?

July 7

The Fear of Death (Pat)

*Listen, O drop give yourself up without regret, and in exchange gain the
Ocean. Listen O drop, bestow upon yourself this honor,
and in the arms of the Sea be secure.*

–Rumi

Sometimes at funerals I tell the fable of the little wave.

One day a beautiful wave was swiftly moving through the ocean. It had
traveled thousands of miles. It was ebullient with the joy of lifting its sparkling head proudly into the bright sun. Toward the end of the day, the little
wave saw that it was approaching a high cliff on the shoreline ahead. With
horror it beheld the sight of wave after wave crashing against the rocks and
disappearing.

The little wave cried aloud, "Save me! I'm going to die!"

One of his friends, the wave just before him, replied, "Look again. Look
behind you. We do not die. When we strike the shore, we are just changed and
reflected back as a new wave rejoining the great ocean. Our life is changed,
not ended."

It is said that facing your own mortality is essential for spiritual maturity. Accepting your inevitable death helps you more deeply appreciate each
moment of your life in the present. Paradoxically, the realization that you will
stop breathing some day makes you more grateful for each breath now.

It is not only your final dying that you are invited to accept, but also how
you die or can choose to die each day. You die a little each time you let of go
of your ego and choose to surrender your way to the way of your soul. You
die to your little self every time you sacrifice your own wishes for the benefit
of someone you love. Each of these small deaths prepares you for the big one.
Dying regularly to your ego, and experiencing how this enlarges your spirit,
prepares you to face your final day with serenity, especially if you realize that
your dying gains you the ocean of love.

Whatever you believe about the afterlife, consider Rumi's drop and the
fable's little wave and the great ocean to which they are united.

My Spiritual Practice for Today

Reflect on your feelings about your death. Consider too how you can practice for your death by the small deaths you choose when you die to your ego now.

July 8

That Deep Intimate Place (Vicki)

Perhaps everything that frightens us is, in is deepest essence, something helpless that wants our love. So you mustn't be frightened, if a sadness rises in front of you, larger than any you have ever seen; if an anxiety moves over your hands and over everything you do. You must realize that something is happening to you, that life has not forgotten you, that it holds you in its hand and will not let you fall.
–Rainer Maria Rilke

Can we imagine ourselves being open to access the most hidden and intimate places in our soul? What would we find there? I believe we'll find everything we need to know about ourselves if we can be open enough to access this hidden place.

Nothing opens us up like the death of a loved one. When my was father dying, I remember feeling the world going on around me while I sat by his bedside waiting for his imminent death. After the funeral, I felt I was still standing at the graveside with his casket. I remember having to travel to California to give a retreat just weeks after his passing. That morning I stood before the mirror weeping and feeling as though I had nothing to give. How could I stand before this group and share any thoughts when I couldn't stop weeping? Yet they were waiting for me. I had opened access to the most intimate place in my heart in that moment.

I was able to move forward when I asked the women if they would pray with me so I could speak, despite the deep grief I felt. By acknowledging the deep feelings I was having, they were able to enter into their experience of grief and stand with me. It turned out to be a day filled with intimate sharing. Something indeed was happening to us; life had not forgotten us, and none of us fell. When we share our grief, we ensure we will not fall. I was able to share that I felt helpless and needed their love. By honestly sharing my intimate feelings, I was able to receive their support. It was a beautiful day.

My Spiritual Practice for Today

Today I want to reflect on what I hold in that deep and intimate place within my soul. I want to access that place so I can release what is held so tightly there.

July 9

Your Personal Lie and Your Eternal Truth (Pat and Sue)

We all have one, a personal lie that we tell ourselves that is severely self-damaging and self-limiting. Your personal lie is a core negative emotional belief of which you are only vaguely aware. Yet it is very powerful. It filters and distorts everything you perceive about yourself and your life. It is a deeply entrenched delusion that creates the searing and disabling feeling of shame. Toxic shame is always a lie. The belief that triggers shame is always false. The difficulty is that your personal lie feels true, and the shame seems to validate its truth.

Survivors' personal lies usually arise from trauma. If your trauma involved abuse, your abuser likely created your personal lie. You were told that you are bad, defective, and deserving of abuse. Your personal lie develops into a statement like: "I am worthless, and no one who really knows me can love me." One client, who was sexually abused by a family member, believed, "I am evil and dangerous." She lived in constant fear of hurting those she loved, including her husband and children.

You are not who your personal lie says you are. You are rather the eternal truth that your soul quietly whispers to you. Your eternal truth is always positive, self-loving, and liberating. Your eternal truth is unique to you. It is often the opposite of your personal lie. Your soul works to contradict and eventually delete this toxic distortion. Your eternal truth might be, "I am loved for who I am, simply because I am." Or, "I am able to be kind and loving with everyone in my life." Listen to your soul. Your eternal truth will set you free.

My Spiritual Practice for Today

Identify your most damaging emotional belief, the one that causes you the most shame. Name it as your personal lie. Reflect on how it hurts you. Then create a statement that refutes your lie. This is your eternal truth. Repeat it frequently to yourself throughout the day.

July 10

Tough Spiritual Questions (Pat)

Abuse and trauma raise difficult and legitimate spiritual questions that can shake your faith and spirituality. Where was God when you needed protection from the abuse? Why didn't God stop the abuse from happening to me? If God is love, how could he allow such an unloving act?

This is the God problem for many victims of trauma. You will need real soul courage to face the spiritual questions that trauma can provoke. These questions can shake your faith to the core. They can be obstacles to rediscovering a relationship with God. It is important to face your questions head on at some point, even though they plunge you deep into the heart of the mystery of suffering and the mystery of God.

Explore your questions with your pastor, spiritual director, or soul friend. Pose these questions to your soul, to God, and listen. All spiritual traditions attempt to give some answer to the question of suffering. Explore these traditions and their answers. There may not be one entirely satisfying answer. If you continue to search, you will eventually find an understanding of your tough spiritual questions that will yield peace and bring you closer to God.

In my own search for answers, a few truths have become certainties to me. God does not want abuse to happen—ever. It is never God's will. God wants peace and wholeness for you. Most importantly, God is intimately present to you as you suffer. Though you may not feel God's presence, God is right beside you when abuse or other oppression is done to you. God is weeping with you at your pain, seething with divine anger at the injustice, grieving with you at the damage the abuse is causing, and suffering along with you in every way.

My Spiritual Practice for Today

What are your own tough spiritual questions about your trauma? How do they affect you? Pose these questions to your soul or to God and begin to listen.

July 11

Blessing Bits (Sue)

Blessing bits are the small everyday graces that greet us each day. They are the modest beauty spots that daily appear before our eyes. They are the little acts of kindness and love that we receive and give in our ordinary interactions. Blessing bits are events like a momentary sense of peace and presence, winter light glimpsed on the white bark of a sycamore, or the unexpected smile of the checkout person at the grocery store.

We often miss the blessing bits in our lives because they are so small and because we are too often looking only for the big-bang blessing: the spectacular beauty, the extraordinary event, or the passionate love. These are wonderful, and yet, if that is what we always yearn for, we will be blind to the bitty blessings all around us.

Survivors are especially vulnerable to this selective vision. Because you have endured trauma, paradoxically, you may tend to look for only the extreme events, good and bad. You may even become addicted to the adrenaline rush of frequent highs and lows, and seek excessive drama in your life. One antidote to this is waking up and opening your eyes to the blessings bits you are given daily. Let go of seeking the special, the extraordinary, and be open to the small joys you are graced with in each present moment.

My Spiritual Practice for Today

Look for all of the blessing bits that come your way today. Feel the soul satisfaction each one offers you.

July 12

The Power of Your Story (Pat)

We are all storytellers. We all compose, edit, and tell a story about our lives. You have a running narrative in the back of your mind that expresses who you believe you are, how life events fit into your personal story, and what these events mean in your ongoing tale. You are the novelist, screenwriter, director, and star of your own life novel or movie! Your personal narrative profoundly shapes how you see yourself and your life. It becomes the lens through which you interpret everything that happens. Your story creates many of your feelings, beliefs, and choices for your life. For instance, if you tell yourself the story that you are worthless, helpless, and at the mercy of others, you will create a life that reflects such a narrative. If you write a self-story of triumph and transcendence over great obstacles, you will experience and accomplish such victory in life.

Abuse powerfully shapes a survivor's personal story. As a survivor, fear and shame from abuse or trauma can heavily color and define your story. However, remember that you, not your abuse or your abuser, are the author and director of your own story. You, with your soul, are in charge of writing and even rewriting your life script. No one else can do that for you. At some point in your healing journey, you will need to tell your story of abuse or trauma. This is an act of courage that will help you break free from the secrecy, shame, and fear that surround your abuse. Just telling the story is liberating and healing.

If you have not yet shared your story with someone you can trust, such as a therapist, pastor, or spiritual director, it is vital that you do so. When you do this, remember that you are in charge of your own story and can write it and rewrite it with new meaning and understanding as your healing unfolds.

My Spiritual Practice for Today

Reflect on the story that you tell yourself about your life, including your abuse or trauma. How does the way you tell it affect your image of yourself and your view of your life? Can you begin to see new ways to see and rewrite your story, ways that reflect new perspectives and new strengths?

July 13

Seeking Alternative Ways of Healing (Vicki)

In the name of the air,
The breeze,
And the wind,
May our souls
Stay in rhythm
With Eternal
Breath
–John O'Donohue
Bless the Space Between Us

During the years I was in counseling, I sought out a variety of alternative healing methods beginning with massage. Then I tried the Japanese healing art of reiki, a process of connecting with the chakra energy in nineteen areas of the body. I found this to be the deepest form of meditation and prayer I had encountered. It felt like a healing balm, and I came to believe in its transforming power.

Experiencing biofeedback also taught me to breathe deeply as a means of restoring health. I learned how important breathing is to health and discovered that most days I took very shallow breaths that rarely filled my lungs with healing oxygen. The rhythm of our body and soul depends on the healing exchange of oxygen.

My new understanding about breathing led me to connect more deeply with my body as a temple, as the container for my soul. And as I reflected on this container, I realized how deeply expansive every person's soul is. Rather than think of the soul as fitting within the container of the body, I came to understand the soul as having no limits to its capacity to love, to hold my own pain, and indeed to hold the pain of the world. This awareness felt like a new sense of freedom. When I didn't know where to hold something that was painful, I trusted the soul's capacity to hold the tension. Richard Rohr teaches how important it is for us to hold the tension of those things we can't resolve. There is so much in life for which we cannot find answers. The soul's capacity to hold the tensions of the world is there for us.

My Spiritual Practice for Today

Today I want to think of alternative healing modalities that might be helpful in my own journey. I will begin the practice of breathing deeply as a means of restoring my body with life-giving oxygen.

July 14

A Fish in an Ocean of Love (Sue)

A great Brazilian spiritual leader, Dom Helder Camara, once said that the universe is an ocean of divine love energy, and we are all fish swimming in that love. The water of love is so clear and we are so immersed in it, that, like fish in the sea, we cannot see what we are swimming in. We sometimes sense its movements, its tidal pull, the waves and ripples, perhaps a glimpse of love as it moves us along the reefs and beaches of our lives. Yet we are so in it that, as a fish is one with the ocean, we cannot perceive what we exist in, what surrounds, buoys, holds, and nourishes us. We look for love in so many ways, and sometimes find it and sometimes not, but mostly we are looking for little ponds when we are really great fish immersed in the Great Ocean.

Survivors understandably tend to only see the sharks and the barracudas, the tsunamis and the undersea volcanoes. Trauma has narrowed your vision to scan mainly for the dangers. It may have triggered a macular degeneration of your spiritual sight, a disease where you can see the periphery of things, but have lost the central vision of the core of things. You see mainly pain and threat, and struggle to see the love you are swimming in all of the time. You can, however, heal your vision and retrain your eye to see the love that is manifested in your life in so many ways, small, large, and even infinite.

My Spiritual Practice for Today

In your meditation image yourself as a fish (or a snorkeler) swimming in a warm ocean. Feel yourself buoyed and surrounded by the water of this sea, immersed in its energy. You cannot see the water, but you feel it as it gently rocks you in its waves. Imagine this as divine love. Then remember the times in your life when you have felt loved or when you have felt and given love to someone else. This, magnified infinitely, is the ocean universe of love that you are swimming in daily, which surrounds and embraces you always. Enjoy your swim. When you come out of the water, be watchful all day for signs of love all around you.

July 15

Awe for the Universe (Pat)

For some people, modern science threatens to take away their sense of the awe and sacredness of nature. It has done the opposite for me. The unfolding of a new cosmology of the origins of our universe in the Big Bang theory, the amazing, life-affirming story of evolution, the possibility of multiple universes, the intricacies and even bizarreness of quantum theories of energy and matter at the hidden center of Nature—all of these infuse nature with an even more profound awe, mystery, and sacredness. How could all that we see and experience in our vast universe have been born of one unimaginably dense singularity of energy and matter at the Big Bang! If that does not inspire awe, what could?

Although we may not yet have fully articulated God's role in the new cosmic story, it has deepened my awe for the mystery of God both revealed and hidden in nature. After reading some of the new cosmology or some of the more bizarre aspects of quantum physics, I have sometimes thought that God is even greater—the other word that comes to mind is weirder—than we could have ever imagined.

The biologist J.B.S. Haldane said, "The universe is not only queerer than we suppose; it is queerer than we can suppose." With all the respect due God, nature seems to reveal a God, a transcendent and incarnate creative intelligence, who is greater, weirder, and queerer than our poor minds can comprehend—a God utterly beyond us, and yet ever immanently present to us.

As we further probe the mystery of God and creation in the light of modern science, I have settled for myself on this image: Nature is God's great work of art; evolution, the Big Bang, and all the complexities of science are God's most unusual and most creative palette and brush. What a terrible beauty to behold.

My Spiritual Practice for Today

Go for a walk during the day. Observe the vibrancy of light and life all around you. Consider the scientific stories of the origins of all that you see. Take a walk after dark. Pause to look up at the night sky. Ponder the vastness of the universe, trillions of stars, billions of galaxies. Sense the creative intelligence behind and within it all—and within you.

July 16

Being G.L.A.D. (Pat)

G.L.A.D. stands for Grateful, Learned, Accomplished, and Delighted. It is a spiritual practice that works powerfully to create gratefulness, bring life lessons to your awareness, provide a sense of accomplishment, and cultivate greater delight and joy in you. It is a simple practice of daily, weekly, or periodically pausing—usually at the end of the day—to reflect on these four attributes in your life and writing them down to make them more real for you. You simply fill in the blank to each of these statements:

I am Grateful for _____

I Learned _____

I Accomplished _____

I Delighted in _____

Deepening your gratefulness, discovering delight, realizing what you can learn about life and yourself, and staying conscious about what you are regularly accomplishing—even when you don't think you are—are powerfully healing spiritual experiences for survivors. Having been through trauma and all of its aftereffects, you may find it difficult to be grateful, delight and joy may be elusive, and your low self-worth may convince you that you are not capable of learning or accomplishing much. The G.L.A.D. meditation can be a powerful tool to change that for you. So give it a try for a time. You will be G.L.A.D. you did.

My Spiritual Practice for Today

Incorporate the G.L.A.D. reflection into your daily schedule today and the rest of the week. Notice how you feel differently and what your soul teaches you about yourself and your life. Consider making the practice a regular part of your prayer and meditation.

July 17

The Terror of Unconditional Love (Sue)

To be loved with unconditional love sounds wonderful. To be fully accepted for who you are, and just as you, would seem to be a real Nirvana experience, a touch of heaven on Earth. Who wouldn't welcome it and embrace it?

Trust me, it's easier said than done! In fact, it can be terrifying! In the past, if someone saw into the inner core of my real self, it would "scare me spitless." Because of my abuse, "to be seen was to be hurt." If I sensed someone noticing me, I would summon all of my defense mechanisms to hide and keep that person at bay. I though that if they saw me as I am—oh my, the fear that would flood me! Trusting was excruciating. I was constantly testing the water. "Was it safe and deep enough to swim in?"

In my relationship with my best friend, my husband, Pat, I have opened myself gradually to unconditional love. When we first met, it would take me six months to let Pat know I had felt hurt or upset about something. Oh, the pain and anguish of keeping it inside, so fearful to share! Then, by the grace of God, I'd muster up courage to be congruent and would open myself to moments of unconditional love with Pat. I felt safe, intimate, peaceful— and amazed. Each time I spoke up, sharing my truth, and it was received with love, my safety increased, and the freedom to be myself expanded into the relationship. It is a whole new world, living in unconditional love and in the truth of who I am in God's eyes.

Giving unconditional love to another was much easier than receiving it. I have been blessed for the most part with 20/20 spiritual vision. Being able to see the essence of the individual as God sees: a loving being who has amazing potential. But to receive unconditional love, that's been a whole different story. In order to receive, I have had to practice what I teach my clients: to remind myself over and over that I am loved unconditionally by God; that I'm worthy of love; that I'm human with strengths and weaknesses; and that I am God's magnificent child. Besides allowing love from others, I have learned to give that unconditional love to myself.

My Spiritual Practice for Today

Reflect today on Sue's experience and how it relates to your own.

July 18

Safely Channeling Anger (Vicki)

Anger simply wasn't expressed in my family dynamic. That's not to say that it didn't happen; my parents just made sure we never heard it from them. There were the usual bursts of anger at my siblings and me for the ornery things we did to each other. I remember well into my counseling being asked how I expressed anger. Was I angry at my perpetrator? I remember answering, yes, of course! I was angry for sure, but I didn't know how to express it. In therapy sessions I was given a whiffle ball bat and told to beat a pillow as a means of safely expressing my anger. This actually became a solid practice that helped me to express my anger.

Mark Twain wrote, "Anger is an acid that can do more harm to the vessel in which it is stored than to anything on which it is poured." I knew anger was causing the clenched fists, the grinding of my teeth, and my inability to sleep. Finding ways to express holy anger without hurting anyone is healthy for the soul, I found out.

I continued to use that whiffle ball bat on my bed at home on those days when I felt overwhelmed and frustrated. Anger needs an outlet, so finding a nonthreatening way to get it out of our system is a healthy activity.

To finally understand the power of anger as a block to my emotional healing helped the feeling of bitterness to subside. Maya Angelou wrote, "Bitterness is like cancer. It eats upon the host. But anger is like fire. It burns it all clean."

My Spiritual Practice for Today

Today I will reevaluate how I express anger. I will be conscious of finding ways to relieve my anger in nonviolent ways that do not threaten or hurt the people around me. I will recognize that my anger has the potential to hurt others if not channeled properly. I will work toward letting the bitterness subside.

July 19

Happiness Happens (Pat)

At the risk of sounding heretically un-American, there is one phrase from the Declaration of Independence that sounds admirable and true, yet in practice causes much suffering and depression. Proclaiming our "inalienable rights" the Declaration states: "…among which are the preservation of life, liberty, and the pursuit of happiness." There is, of course, no difficulty with the rights to preservation of life and liberty. And we most certainly have the right to *be* happy. It is the *pursuit* of happiness that can get us into trouble and undermine our ability to experience happiness. It can even sabotage your healing journey.

Pursuing happiness by doing this or that, or purchasing just the right product, or achieving some certain success, or finding the right person sets you up to frenetically chase happiness and expect it only when you have gained these things. This makes you unhappier and makes the happiness you do achieve more fragile and fleeting. Survivors can even think that happiness can only come to them when certain healing milestones are achieved.

The truth is happiness cannot be pursued. The reality is happiness happens. It happens when you let go of its pursuit and let it find you. Happiness is an inside job and is not dependent on anything outside ourselves. It is the fruit of learning to love yourself and others. It comes as a byproduct of accepting who you are and embracing your infinite value. It happens when you are present in the moment.

When you listen to your soul, open to her peace. It arises when you let in love. Stop pursuing and chasing happiness. Let go and let it happen. And when it does, enjoy it fully and gratefully. That is certainly your inalienable right.

My Spiritual Practice for Today

Reflect on all of the ways you pursue happiness and examine whether they truly bring you happiness. Are you ready to let go of any of these pursuits or expectations about happiness? Also, think back through your life about moments of happiness that spontaneously came to you. Rest in these memories for a time and re-enjoy them. From what interior experiences did they arise? Be open this day to all the ways that happiness happens to you now.

July 20

Today I Will Fast from Should (Pat)

As we said previously, "should" may be the most destructive word in the English language. It is the word of shame. Shame is one of the most damaging and debilitating effects of abuse and trauma. Shame is the entrenched emotional belief that you are bad, defective, worthless, ugly, unlovable, or even evil. Shame blocks you from knowing and experiencing the infinite value of your True Self. It can cloud or obscure your connection with your own soul. Shame can distort or even destroy your relationship with your Higher Power.

The word "should" arises from shame and helps to maintain shame. It is most often a word of self-judgment and toxic self-criticism. Eliminating "should" from your vocabulary can help emancipate you from the power and slavery of shame. "Should" is not in your soul's vocabulary. Your soul knows that shame is a lie and knows who you truly are in your beauty, glory, and inexpressible magnificence.

My Spiritual Practice for Today

Carefully observe your thoughts and speech today. Notice how often you use the word "should" or "should not." Be aware of how it makes you feel, especially about yourself. Does it provoke shame in you? Fast from "should" by stopping yourself every time you are tempted to use it. Substitute another word that is healing, freeing, or at least less shaming, like "I can," "I may," "I choose," and "I choose not to." Notice how you feel different. How does it change your feelings and beliefs about yourself?

July 21

Fear is (Mostly) Useless (Pat)

The natural purpose of fear is to activate us to resist, run, or be still—fight, flight, or freeze—in the face of true danger. The difficulty for survivors is that this natural response has been hijacked and amplified by the experience of trauma. Little dangers look like major threats. Situations of no danger appear to be menacing. Fear floods your mind, preventing you from seeing the circumstances clearly and blocking your inner voice, which is trying to guide you and keep you safe. When you need to respond and assert yourself, fear freezes you, and you cannot act. Your thoughts are dominated by constant worry, which is the mind's fruitless attempt to control the uncontrollable: the future.

What is needed is trust. Trust is the ultimate source of safety and is the answer to fear run amok. Abuse and trauma often destroy the capacity to trust. Your abuser likely took advantage of your trust, leaving you to doubt your perception of what and who is safe. But trust can be restored. You can learn to listen to your inner voice, your intuition, and your soul, and believe in them again. You can grow in trusting your Higher Power. All of this shrinks the power of fear and allows you to put it back in its natural place. Healing your essential ability to trust empowers you to act from the courage of your soul. It enables you to see things clearly and to move through and past fear. The result is that fear, especially false and useless fear, does not paralyze you or rob you of your power.

My Spiritual Practice for Today

All day listen to your inner voice and choose to trust it. Ask it: Is this situation safe? Is that person trustworthy? Which of your anxieties and worries are unfounded and magnified by your traumatic fear? Which fears can you now let go of? Your ability to trust will gradually be restored by listening carefully to the quiet, wise, and peaceful voice of intuition, soul, and spirit deep within you.

July 22

Moving Beyond Stinkin' Thinkin'! (Vicki)

Down below the stirring waves of indifference and dissimilarities,
there lies a deep sea of humanity that unites us all.
–From a Japanese English teacher, unknown

Henri Nouwen said, "What is most personal is most universal." This thought draws me to an understanding of every human heart to be equally as fragile as the next. We are all wounded healers, broken in some way by our broken family dynamic or some unusual tragedy that has brought a dark cloud over our lives. So how do we respond to this human experience of brokenness? We see it all around us, one story more heartbreaking than the next. The human will to survive the most insurmountable life experiences tells me that all of us have that capability. We may not think we do, but there lies a deep sea of humanity that unites us all. We are one in more ways than we can fathom.

How does that bring me strength and courage to move forward? Once I began to change the negative thinking I continually processed in my mind, once I understood "stinkin' thinkin'" as AA teaches, I could begin to motivate myself away from the negative and focus on the endless possibilities that life can give. Moving our attitudes away from the person we were to the person we want to become is the shift that can happen on the journey if we can allow it to come forth.

Letting go of the brainwashed understanding I had of myself, someone else's vision of me, was difficult but necessary. My life wasn't about me; it was about someone else, and I had to take back my life in order to make it my own. I needed to find my own humanity before I could know I was part of a larger community of humans seeking truth.

My Spiritual Practice for Today

Today I want to take courageous steps to understand my own True Self. I want to close the blinds that keep me from seeing my True Self. I will begin to take steps toward changing my thinking from the negative to the potential goodness that life offers.

July 23

Fear Creates Exactly What You Fear (Pat & Sue)

Over many years of working with people, we have come to the realization that it is a spiritual principle that if you allow yourself to be controlled by fear, you will inevitably create exactly what you fear. For instance, if you fear abandonment, you will act in ways and make choices in relationships that will eventually invite people to abandon you. If you fear failure and are consumed with this fear, you will create the very failure you fear.

Abuse and trauma understandably engender a great deal of fear in survivors. What you experienced was indeed frightening and threatening. Who or what you thought was safe became your source of harm. It is difficult, then, not to be controlled by fear and adopt a defensive view of life and see the world as a fundamentally dangerous neighborhood to live in.

However, fear and the life of your soul are antithetical to each other. Your soul desires freedom, openness, space, exploration, growth, connection, oneness, transcendence, and love. Fear is fearful of all of these and tries to block or restrict you from seeking them. Fear says, "Danger, danger everywhere," and preaches, "Safety, safety, first and above all." Soul whispers, "Trust, grow, be open, risk, let go, explore."

Your soul says to you the words of Julian of Norwich, the 15th-century English mystic: "All shall be well, and all shall be well, and all manner of thing shall be well." Your soul is not saying ignore all fear and make yourself vulnerable to danger or abuse. It is inviting you to soften your tight grip on fear and no longer be controlled by it. Your soul wants to free you from the further suffering that is the fate of fear unbridled.

My Spiritual Practice for Today

Today look at the role of fear in your life and any ways in which you are controlled by fear. Look particularly at how your fears may be reproducing what you most fear. Then quiet your mind in meditation and hear your soul speak these words: "All is well, and all shall be well, and all manner of thing shall be well." Repeat this throughout the day as your mantra for the day. Reflect on what this means for your healing journey and in your life today.

July 24

Doubt (Pat)

Doubt is not the enemy of faith or the spiritual life. In fact, doubt is part of the journey and helps guide your spiritual search. Survivors often experience doubt seared into them by the spiritual trauma of their abuse in the form of difficult yet legitimate spiritual questions that shake the foundations of their faith and spirituality. Why did this happen to me? Where was God when I needed help and protection from the abuse? Why didn't God stop the abuse? If God is loving, how could he allow such an unloving act that has caused me so much pain? What kind of world, what sort of universe is this that such suffering and abuse exists? It is important to face your questions head on at some point, even though they create doubt and plunge you deep into the heart of the mystery of suffering.

Bring your doubts to your trusted pastor, spiritual director, soul friend, or other spiritual guide. In prayer express your doubts also to your soul, to God, and listen. All spiritual traditions attempt to give some answer to the question of suffering, including that caused by fellow human beings. Explore these traditions and their answers. There may not be one entirely satisfying answer (which is one of the themes of the Book of Job). If you continue to search, you will eventually find an understanding of your spiritual questions about your abuse that will yield peace and bring you even closer to God.

Spiritual healing requires a courageous period of doubt and posing the hard questions. In time, this will lead to the discovery of new truths to live by. In a sense, you are being challenged to write a new personal creed for yourself, discarding the old understandings that no longer fit for you and incorporating the new beliefs that you discover in your spiritual healing journey. Your questions and your soul will be your guide.

My Spiritual Practice for Today

In your journal, write down the main spiritual questions arising from your trauma. Ask your soul or the Spirit to begin to give you new understandings about these questions. Listen as deeply as you can in prayer and meditation, periodically checking back on these questions until you receive new insight.

July 25

"It's Not Your Fault!" (Pat)

This is the famous pivotal line from the powerful movie *Good Will Hunting*. Robin Williams, playing the psychotherapist Sean Maguire, speaks these liberating words to Will Hunting, played by Matt Damon, a brilliant, angry, and hurting young man who was abused as a child by his father. Sean keeps repeating, "It's not your fault!" to Will. Will keeps replying, "I know," but Sean realizes that Will doesn't yet truly know that the abuse wasn't his fault. Sean continues to say the line until Will gets angry and says, "Don't f--- with me! Not you, Sean." Sean says it again with both great tenderness and force. The words break through to Will, and he sobs and embraces Sean. This is the breakthrough for Will that frees him from his false guilt and unlocks his brilliant gifts and allows him to love.

Survivors of childhood abuse almost always feel that the abuse was their fault. Your abuser may have said or implied that it was your fault. Even when this is not said, children will automatically assume guilt and responsibility for their abuse because of the way a child's brain is wired. It is crucial to hear this message: Child abuse is never the fault of the child. Some adults experiencing adult trauma can also plunge into self-blame and guilt, even when there is no shred of truth to this. Such groundless and irrational guilt is a huge burden for you and a potential block to spiritual well-being and growth.

It is vital to hear your soul saying to you over and over again, "It's not your fault!" until it sinks in and you accept and embrace it. This truth will certainly set you free.

My Spiritual Practice for Today

Watch the "It's not your fault" scene from *Good Will Hunting* on YouTube. All day long hear your soul repeating those words to you. Join your soul and say it to yourself as your mantra today: "It's not your fault!"

July 26

Tapping into a Universal Love (Vicki)

A universal love is not only psychologically possible,
it is the only complete and final way in which we are able to love.
–Pierre Teilhard de Chardin

There is more to the word "love" than the first understanding we were given. There is a deeper love than the love that we are bombarded with each day as it is overromanticized. There is a universal love that comes from the Creator of the universe, a universal love that loved us into being because of the potential that every human being is endowed with. We are called to this greater love, the love that envelops the world, in fact, the entire universe.

There is an image of a human being sitting cross-legged on a mountaintop holding a large globe in his or her lap, embracing it with an all-consuming love. This is the love that is there for all of us. It is the love that breathed life into us; it gathered up the stardust and created us into the unique beings we are, to love and serve.

This is the love that holds us up. This is the love that carries us when we do not feel we can carry ourselves. For some it is Jesus or God or Buddha or Muhammad or Gaia. It doesn't matter who our God is; it matters that we lean into and upon something much greater than our own life. This is the love that speaks volumes to us about painful issues of abandonment and abuse. It is the love from which we draw our strength in times of great need. It is the love that calls us forth to heal that which is broken so we can give it away to others.

Hildegard of Bingen writes from the 10th century: "O Beloved, your way of knowing is amazing! The way you recognize every creature even before it appears. The way you gaze into the face of a human being and see all your works gazing back at you. O' what a miracle to be awake inside your breathing."

My Spiritual Practice for Today

Today I want to sit in silence and allow the cosmic love that created me to surround and envelop me in its loving kindness for the purpose of healing.

July 27

God's Anger at Abuse (Pat)

In the Gospel of Mark, we see Jesus clearly angry with those who have profaned the sanctity of the temple. He uses his anger to cleanse the temple and drive out those who were abusing its sacredness—and not in a timid or mild way! Imagine the chaotic scene. Jesus has just come from the countryside into Jerusalem. He enters the temple area, crowded with people and bustling with activity, and sees that its sacredness has been defiled by commercialism. Filled with *just anger*, he gets physical. He overturns tables and stalls, scattering money, doves, and buyers and sellers alike. He then launches into a strong and spirited teaching, accusing those he has driven off of profaning the sacred temple, turning "the house of prayer" into "a den of thieves." No meek and mild Jesus here! Here is a man filled with just anger and indignation. This is holy anger.

Trauma and abuse, and how it has harmed you, angers God. In and through God's anger, and in and through your own anger, God wants to restore your sacredness taken from you by abuse. Your own just and holy anger is a part of this spiritual process of cleansing and restoring the sacred temple that is you. Joining your anger to God's anger at the abuse is a vital part of your healing.

For the survivor, at first this can be very difficult, scary, even terrorizing. Your anger feels so strong, even destructive. You have witnessed or been victimized by the destructive power of anger. You have buried, repressed, and hidden your anger for years. Your anger has been directed mainly at yourself. Or you have let your anger flare out toward others in hurtful ways. You have been blocked from tapping into the potential healing in anger and from joining with God's anger. Your anger's voice is also the voice of God crying out against injustice and the profaning of your sacred temple. When you tap into your anger, you begin to reclaim the sacredness of your personal temple, body, mind, and soul.

My Spiritual Practice for Today

Reflect on God's anger not at you, but at your abuse and abuser. How does that change how you feel about your own anger? Can you see its holy power?

July 28

Imago Dei (Pat)

Because God is within you in the light of your soul, God was abused when you were abused. Part of God's abuse is that God's image often gets distorted and deformed by the abuse. The victim's picture of God often is damaged, and as a result, the potential for a healing and meaningful relationship with God is inhibited or blocked. Sometimes this damage to the victim's image of and relationship with God is caused by clerical sexual abuse or religious abuse. For survivors of any type of abuse or trauma, trust is destroyed, shame and fear are injected, and abandonment and rejection are experienced. This gets projected onto God. You come to believe that God has shamed, abandoned, and rejected you as well. It becomes difficult to trust God, to believe God is with you, loves you, and wants to draw close to you to comfort you and heal your pain.

Richard Rohr writes, "Your image of God creates you. You become the God you worship." Your image of God shapes how you see yourself and your world. The first step in resolving the problem is to identify who God is for you. What is your image of God? What adjectives would best describe your God? What parts of this picture have been shaped by your trauma or abuse? Does your perception of God facilitate a relationship? When you go to God in prayer, meditation, or worship, do you feel loved and comforted, or do you feel shame, fear, distance, or rejection? Whose face do you have on God? Is it the God of your faith, or is it the face of your abuser?

As you clarify your image and see its connection to your abuse, you will make room to rediscover and experience a new Imago Dei, a "God of your understanding," not the false god of your abuse.

My Spiritual Practice for Today

Reflect today on the questions above and become aware of how you perceive God and how that relates to your abuse or trauma. Begin to seek a new understanding and image of God that helps rather than hinders your healing. Who can God become for you?

July 29

Forgiveness Is a Spiritual Revolution (Sue)

Forgiveness for so great a harm as abuse both requires and creates a spiritual revolution in the forgiver. Forgiveness needs the grace of a complete turnaround, an overthrowing of what your ego, your lower self, wants when you have been abused. In turn, the choice of forgiveness turns you away from your old self and lifts you up into your higher self. This is the spiritual revolution that your soul desires for you in calling you to forgiveness. This requires a profound paradigm shift, a transformational change of your mind, heart, and spirit concerning your abuse, your abuser, and yourself. This opens up new consciousness, awareness, and healing.

One of the most powerful paradigm shifts in forgiveness is seeing your abuser in a new light, illuminated by your soul. This is a shift from viewing your abuser as evil or monstrous to seeing them as wounded, sick, and often addicted. They are wounded as you are wounded. Their wounding of you arose from their own wounds. This is the tragic cycle of abuse. It is one of the main lessons Pat and I learned as we moved from working primarily with survivors to also counseling perpetrators. Listening to the stories of abusers and seeing how their abusive behavior often began in their own childhood abuse put them in a whole different light for us.

The spiritual revolution of forgiveness challenges you to move from the us-versus-them paradigm to seeing your abuser as a fellow sufferer, caught with you in the vicious cycle of abuse. You are not enemies. You are brothers and sisters struggling with the same great burden and wound of abuse. This paradigm has the potential to open your eyes to a whole new vision of your abuse and your abuser. It opens your heart to forgiveness and much more. This is a revolution of Spirit.

My Spiritual Practice for Today

Ask for the grace today to see your abuser in a new light, to see beneath what he or she did to you to the pain and woundedness that spawned their abuse of you. This is not to excuse anything. It is for you to move further in your healing and open your heart to the forgiveness that sets you free.

July 30

Overcoming Fear: Just Do It (Vicki)

Surely there is more meaning to Nike's advertisement, Just Do It! Those three words pack a powerful message about rising above the challenges of life. When we apply it to the Pathway of Courage, it takes on a meaning that is broad and deep. Some things simply must be done; waiting won't make it easier.

When we realize we are stuck in an emotional stagnation, we know we need to act. Some of us remain stagnant for a long time until some experience propels us to act. How long do we want to delay our ability to live fully? The challenge of acting is within our power, so why do we wait?

Life is filled with opportunities and eagerly awaits the use of our gifts and talents. Let us embrace the healing journey with the excitement and expectation of a great adventure. Yes, there will be issues of anger, grief, sadness, and the need to forgive. None of these are insurmountable. Releasing all of these long-held issues in your soul will be tantamount to releasing a huge boulder you have been carrying for too long. Embrace the journey, no matter how fearful it feels. Waiting won't make it easier. You are only delaying your development and the use of your gifts in the world. Think of the opportunities you are missing because you are stuck and fearful. Just do it!

During a particularly difficult time of my healing process, I received a telegram from Mother Teresa of Calcutta asking me to assume the role of USA National Link (Chair) for her lay association, the Co-Workers. I was filled with fear, didn't think I had the stamina to do it. My decision to just do it saved my life. It took me away from my abuser and showed me a big world that needed the gifts I could share. I continued my counseling and became a new person.

My Spiritual Practice for Today

Today I will take one step in overcoming my fear. I will say to myself, Just Do It!

July 31

Now Here This! (Pat)

What some call our "monkey mind" often jumps about, back and forth, between the past and the future, regretting and replaying this and worrying and fretting about that. We find it difficult to be in the present moment. We all struggle with this.

It is especially difficult for survivors. Trauma creates anxiety about the present and the future. Your mind may be hypervigilant, scanning your surroundings, hyperalert for impending threats. You obsess about the past and its painful memories, gnawing on the old bone of what happened years ago. You may suffer from dissociation, that experience of being numb or disconnected from your emotions or your physical environment. All of this makes it difficult to be present to the present, to be here now.

Your soul invites you to experience the peace and serenity of living each moment in the present, free of your traumatic past and liberated from your projections of a catastrophic future. This is a vital spiritual skill that many spiritual writers speak of as key to living in peace and living from soul. Here are a few ways to do it.

Whenever you catch your monkey mind in the past or fast-forwarding to the future, use this phrase as a command to your mind to stop, be still, be present: "NOW HERE this!" Be in this now, be here in this present moment and place. Then employ a mindfulness tool to still your mind into awareness of now. Focus your attention on your breathing, breathing deeply and slowly in and out to the count of seven, repeating as needed. Or repeat a short prayer as you breathe, focusing your mind on the words of the prayer.

You can also simply look intently at something beautiful and natural like a flower or the light on the leaves of a tree.

Whenever your mind monkey tries to pull you into past or future thoughts, gently and without judgment return your focus to your centering tool. Feel and absorb the peace of the now like a sponge.

My Spiritual Practice for Today

Watch your mind today. When it pulls you into future fear thoughts or past shame-and-blame thoughts, order it to stop with the command above and employ a centering tool to gently return yourself to the present.

August 1

The Mountain Meditation: You (Sue & Pat)

My Spiritual Practice for Today

We invite you to do the Mountain Meditation again. This time the theme is you. Bring to the mountain anything you have learned in the last month, any questions you have, or any need for healing that you are experiencing. Let your soul and the Spirit guide you. To enter into this meditation, find a comfortable sitting position. As you read, pause, close your eyes, and imagine the scenes described.

Picture yourself on a beautiful beach. See the waves, the sand, the brilliant color, and the vastness of the ocean. Feel the sun and the wind on your skin. Hear the crash and whoosh of the surf. Turn around now, and face away from the sea. This time pack your backpack with any questions, lessons, or needs you have experienced in the last month. Notice how it feels to carry this.

In front of you is a beautiful forest. See yourself walking along a trail into the forest. Appreciate the coolness and the shaded light. You reach the edge of the forest and see an open meadow filled with multicolored wildflowers. The trail leads you through the meadow to a clear, flowing stream with a bridge across the dancing water. Stop for a moment to enjoy the light sparkling on the water.

Now look up from the bridge and see a shining mountain before you. Following the trail, you ascend the mountain. You climb above the timberline through the clouds to the top of the peak. Look around you at the glory of creation. Then you notice a large boulder to sit on and rest.

From the other side of the peak, your spiritual guide comes and sits down with you on the boulder. You can discuss whatever you want. Unpack your backpack and lay its contents out before your spirit guide. Listen for what is said to you about what you have brought. If you receive anything, embrace it and put it in your backpack to bring it down the mountain to the outside world.

When you are ready to leave, thank your Higher Power. Slowly hike back down the mountain, over the bridge, through the meadow, through the forest, to the beach, and to the edge of the vast ocean. Open your eyes. Record and reflect in your journal.

August 2

The Gift of Resilience (Vicki)

How challenging it is to look at our seemingly small lives and think of them as a work of art. And yet, we know our lives are a work of art brought forth from a divine Creator who wants only for us to live fully, to appreciate the beauty within and around us. We were loved into being with a vision of largess, with a heart and soul expansive enough to embrace the world.

In 1991 I was experiencing the most painful part of my journey. The struggle was just so difficult. It seemed as though so much was converging that year in my counseling and with changes I needed to make in my life. I was still in the grip of fear and shame. I was doing everything I could do to keep my head above water. Then one day, out of the blue, a Western Union message came from Mother Teresa appointing me the head of her lay association in the United States, the Co-Workers of Mother Teresa, who supported the work of the sisters around the world. Each country had a national link. She was asking me to step into that role. I had been active with them since 1984; however, I never imagined she would invite me to lead it.

Feeling overwhelmed with my life and now this? It was a moment of sorrow and joy! And then the truth rose up in me and said, "Who could say no to Mother Teresa?" Of course, I said *yes*! It became the passion and the light that pulled me from the darkness. It sparked the human resilience in me that said, "Go out of yourself and serve, and there you will find the true value of your life." In that moment I became strong enough to say yes to Mother, to let go of what was holding me down, and to enter into a work that would be my salvation. And it hasn't stopped.

What are you passionate about? It doesn't have to be an invitation from Mother Teresa. We are all called to different passions.

My Spiritual Practice for Today

I want to find my passion for living. I want to discern where my gifts can best serve others. This week I will begin to make a list of those things that bring me joy and fulfill a passion.

August 3

Our Inherent Ability to Transform (Vicki)

Evolutionary theologian Ilia Delio, OSF, speaks of the human capacity to heal one's self. Nature has its own inherent capacity to heal itself. The challenge we face as human beings is to unblock the energy fields that naturally produce healing. They can be blocks such as trauma, abuse, the sudden loss of a loved one, or a chronic or terminal illness. Nature is constantly re-creating itself, and this natural capacity includes human beings. I'm not excluding the need for modern medicine. However, look at the Iraq and Afghanistan war veterans who have returned home with lost limbs from injuries sustained in those wars and how they have re-created themselves with prosthetics and now compete athletically. They have overcome their obstacles with an unstoppable self-determination. To be sure, they also suffer deep emotional wounds that require healing. They have reached deep into themselves to re-create their lives to be of service to others again.

Ilia Delio writes:

> The openness of nature to creativity means that no aspect of nature can be constrained by form or boundaries. Given a sufficient amount of time and the right conditions, created entities will transcend their limits, especially if the limits constrain rather than liberate the element/subject. Transcendence means to go beyond the boundaries of self-existence. In a sense, transcendence complements creativity because the movement beyond self means enhancing the capacity for new relationships and thus for new things to happen.

We have the ability to transform our brokenness into something life giving! We are the things of nature, and we can evolve into more than we ever dreamed possible. The journey of the soul is never ending. The layers of resilience, the compound interest of all our lived experiences bring us to a degree of relatedness that puts us in touch with our authentic selves. Isn't this what we all seek?

Let us rejoice in the awareness of ourselves and our life experiences, regardless of how painful, because we play an important part in the healing of the world.

My Spiritual Practice for Today

I want to believe that my life experience has value and that it can inform the future of my life. I want to transform my pain into a life-giving awareness that, no matter what befalls me, I have the strength and capacity to overcome it all. I believe that my life has purpose in this universe.

August 4

Forgiveness Is Power (Pat)

Forgiveness can feel threatening. It can feel as if you are making yourself vulnerable to be abused once again. Forgiveness does involve eventually letting go of your anger at the abuser. This holy anger helped you to feel empowered, free of shame and self-blame, and the temple of yourself sacred. So it may now appear to be insane and unsafe to let it go and forgive.

Forgiveness is scary business, yet it is necessary business if you are to fully heal your heart, your mind, your soul, even your body. You cannot be fully free from your abuse unless you are open to forgiving. Forgiveness does not mean you are going soft and weak, relinquishing your hard-won personal power. It does not mean you will allow abuse back into your life. In fact, through forgiveness your soul empowers you for final victory over your abuse. Forgiveness both comes from personal power and bestows and develops even greater personal power. As Mahatma Gandhi said, "The weak can never forgive. Forgiveness is the attribute of the strong."

It is important here to say clearly what forgiveness is not. Forgiveness of your abuser does not in any way excuse what was done to you. Forgiveness is not denial. Forgiveness is not forgetting. You will never forget what was done to you. Nor should you. Forgiveness allows you to hold the memories of your abuse in your mind, heart, and soul, and yet be free to love, heal, and not be controlled by your painful memories.

Forgiveness does not necessarily mean a restoration of your relationship with your abuser. Forgiveness and reconciliation with your offender are two different and distinct spiritual acts. You can forgive, and yet keep distant from your abuser, or never have a relationship at all. For many survivors, this is the only sane and safe choice. A relationship with your abuser might be too toxic or even spiritually, emotionally, or physically dangerous. Your soul invites you to forgive, and yet also implores you to stand strong against any potential abuse in your life. Forgiveness is power.

My Spiritual Practice for Today

Check to see where you are in the forgiveness process. Do you have any fear that forgiveness would make you weak or vulnerable? Reflect on Gandhi's quote, and list the ways forgiveness would make you stronger.

August 5

Original Innocence (Pat & Sue)

A newborn baby is the picture of innocence. They are so fresh and brand-new in the world. You sense that the baby comes from good, comes from love, and has the original blessing of goodness in every cell. This is original innocence. We are all born with it. You were born with it.

Many survivors, especially victims of sexual abuse or sexual assault, feel that they lost their innocence. You may feel that way too. Your trauma may have left you feeling strong guilt about what happened. Your trauma may have left you feeling dirty and permanently stained. Some survivors talk about taking multiple baths and showers in a vain attempt to wash away the awful feeling of being soiled and impure. You feel you have been robbed of your innocence. No amount of washing or cleansing or making yourself perfect restores your sense of innocence.

Mercifully, your soul has been holding your original innocence for you. The innocence that you were born with never left you. Abuse only makes it feel that way. Your soul says to you, "You are innocent. You are not and never were guilty. You are not dirty or soiled. You never were unclean. Goodness still abides in every cell in your body, in every particle of your being."

Your True Self is pure and infinitely good. You are invited by your soul to rediscover and reclaim your original innocence and know in your bones that no person or event can take it from you.

My Spiritual Practice for Today

Find a picture of yourself as a baby or a young child. Make it the focus of your meditation. Gaze at yourself and feel the goodness and innocence that you see in your beautiful young self. Breathe in the feeling of innocence from your picture and know that it is still within you. Breathe out any feeling of being dirty or impure and let it go. Again, breathe in innocence, breathe out guilt. Keep repeating periodically through the day.

August 6

This New Spirit Gradually Forming (Vicki)

Only God could say what this new spirit gradually forming within you will be...accept the anxiety of feeling yourself in suspense and incomplete.
–Pierre Teilhard de Chardin

These words from de Chardin speak of the ongoing journey through life. We are all incomplete and will be until the day we die. There is no achieving perfection; there is only the striving to become more of who we are called to become. I was able to let go of that need for perfection a long time ago. Yet there is still a deep desire to know and understand life. There is a certain suspense to it because we simply don't know what is next for us. Some of it we can control, but most is a random experience that leaves us wondering what is next. Will I have cancer? Will I be involved in an accident and left handicapped? Will a loved one suffer any of these fates needing my care and attention? So many troubles could befall us.

Much like what Richard Rohr teaches about holding the tension, de Chardin is telling us to accept the anxiety of feeling yourself in suspense and incomplete. Be happy with who you are at any given moment in life, knowing that you are an unfinished product still on a journey to wholeness. Trust that as you grow you will gain the wisdom and fortitude to walk through any challenges.

A journey to wholeness is filled with myriad opportunities. What keeps us stuck and unable to pursue those opportunities for healing? Life presents all kinds of obstacles that make us want to curl up in the fetal position in the corner of our bedroom and stay there. What can we do to pull ourselves out of that false sense of security and come out into the light? Healing happens in the light, not in the dark. Healing begins after we have shared our story with one person. Healing begins when we can accept the anxiety of feeling in suspense, yet seek the help we need to move our lives forward. Healing begins when we take that first step toward being authentic.

My Spiritual Practice for Today

Today I will work toward stepping out of the dark. I will reach out to one person to share my story. I will become more aware of how I can hold the tension and accept the anxiety of not knowing all the answers.

August 7

Lake Michigan (Vicki)

Looking out my window at Lake Michigan in Wisconsin, I am aware of how many times a day the color of the water changes into multiple colors of blue. Sometimes it looks as though the lake is striped! When I'm on the shores of one of our Great Lakes, I often feel like I'm at the ocean because their shores are so distant.

I'm remembering all the times throughout the last twenty-five years when I have sat by water or in nature to reflect. I've written hundreds of pages! There is no silence like the silence found in nature. It is the most healing of all environments. Being in a place with no distractions opens the heart to understand more deeply, to forgive, to accept. It has even bolstered my courage. A great softness comes over me when I step away from the busyness of work and caregiving. It's a profound and humbling experience.

Once I spent many days in a hermitage in Missouri. I was invited to write the full story of my abuse for publication in the book *Broken Trust* by Patrick and Sue Lauber-Fleming. They are trusted friends. Without hesitation, but with a little trepidation, I said yes. It would be the first time I put my entire story on paper.

I asked for a month-long sabbatical to do this. I wanted to pray and prepare myself to do this well and gain the courage to release the story. I also knew it would be the first time my family and close friends would understand the entire story. To be sure, it was cathartic. Some aspects of the story are so intimate and personal, yet they are integral to explaining the abuse. I kept reminding myself that the telling of my story would help others articulate their own stories and help them know they are not alone. Telling my story in writing was also an opportunity for me to stand in my own truth.

Embracing our own story, having the courage to tell others, and moving forward to the full potential of our lives is a journey for every human being.

"The acceptance of all that God has given us and the willingness to let it go—to give it back to him at a moment's notice—that's true human freedom." –Thomas Keating

My Spiritual Practice for Today

Today think about spending time in nature, whether it is at a local park or refuge or a hermitage in the woods. Begin thinking about writing your story and what that would mean for those who love you.

August 8

Double Rainbow (Pat & Sue)

It happened many years ago, and yet our memory of that day is as bright and vivid as the rainbow we beheld. We were driving west through the eastern Utah desert on our way to a professional conference in Salt Lake City. The skies had been alternately sunny and blue, and dark and ominous as afternoon thunderstorms built up their giant cloud castles.

As we rounded a curve, there before us was a huge, brilliant double rainbow, both multicolored arcs spanning the sky with the darkest black cloud as its backdrop. We immediately pulled to the shoulder and wordlessly got out of the car. Holding each other tightly, we stood in silent awe for what felt like an eternity. Time stopped. Boundaries and limits melted away. We both felt at one with the earth, the sky, the brilliant light, the incredible rainbow, with Spirit, and with each other.

It was a most sacred moment for us. It deepened our bond of friendship at a time when we had been struggling. We felt as one. The double rainbow healed some wounds and drew us close to each other in natural awe and wonder. That double rainbow moment also helped us define the healing work with survivors that we would develop together.

Since then the double rainbow has been a symbol for us of our call and commitment to integrate spirituality with the best of psychology in order to provide the deepest healing possible. A double rainbow is one light refracted into two rainbows, mirror images of each other, the second often a bit fainter than the first. This is the relationship of psychology and spirituality in our healing work; a holistic, dual vision seeing and interweaving both the psychological and the spiritual. Both rainbows are needed for full healing.

The double rainbow moment also became one of the wellsprings of our call to heal. We felt called to bring hope and light to all those whose lives had become darkened by storms and trauma. Sometime later we wrote this line in a poem: "And we will make of our love, a bright, impossible noonday rainbow."

My Spiritual Practice for Today

Think back to an experience of awe and oneness that you have been gifted with. How did it shape, change, and direct you?

August 9

Do Look Back! (Pat)

The common injunction "Don't look back" is often illustrated with the dramatic biblical story of Lot's wife who froze into a pillar of salt when she did just that. Despite this ominous warning, sometimes it is vital for you to risk the salt and look back. At times, looking back is the only way you can realize how your soul and your God are acting in your life in the present.

When you are highly stressed by life's pressures or when the darkness of your trauma feels like it is enveloping you, you may wonder where God is and why he seems to have abandoned you. You may find it difficult to imagine that your soul is at work on your behalf. You probably feel all alone and bereft of any solace and support. You look for what your soul or your God is doing to help, and you don't see anything.

At such dark and lonely times, sometimes the best remedy is to look back and remember a time when you see God's presence and your soul's consolation. This can help you to trust that God must be at work now. Looking back to what may be called your soul history and applying it to your present can be hugely relieving. A personal example: When I was going through my cancer treatments, there were times that I could not see God at work and a few times I felt abandoned and vulnerable. Looking back now more than two years later, I can see that God was surrounding me with incredible love. I can also see how my soul was guiding and directing me to get the healing I needed.

Perhaps you cannot see clearly what is being done for you in the present. Yet extrapolating from your past soul history into your present will reassure you. Your eyes will open to see what your soul and God are doing on your behalf even in the most difficult of times.

My Spiritual Practice for Today

Begin to compile your soul history by recalling times when, in retrospect, you can see how God was with you or your soul was helping and consoling you. Hold this in your heart and memory for the times it feels as if God is gone and your soul has left you.

August 10

Live the Questions Now (Vicki)

Be patient toward all that is unsolved in your heart and try to love the questions themselves like locked rooms and like books that are written in a very foreign tongue. Do not now seek the answers, which cannot be given you because you would not be able to live them. And the point is, to live everything. Live the questions now. Perhaps you will find them gradually, without noticing it, and live along some distant day into the answer.
–Rainer Maria Rilke

We walk through different phases of life without the answers to the questions that most puzzle us. Sometimes they are simple questions, like which school should I attend, should I go back to grad school? Sometimes they are more serious questions, like should I seek help from a professional?

Rainer Maria Rilke, a famous German writer, says how important it is for us to live into the questions about our own lives. We may not be ready to handle the truth of who we are. We may not have the maturity to understand all the complexities of life. We have to live into the questions, continue living our daily life while we are waiting for the answers to emerge from deep within us. We may not find the answers to some questions until much later in life.

I remember how I struggled with answers about the death of my sister, Becca. However, I didn't struggle until I was in my 30s. From age 8 there were many unanswered questions that I wished I could ask. The older I became, the more questions I had. Opening up the mystery of the accident and what it meant for my family emerged in my early 30s and continued for another ten years.

Today I know everything I can know about that horrible day. Today I know who my mother is: a woman of incredible strength and resilience. She has made her children the focus of her entire life, despite the suffering she endured at the loss of her daughter. She is a heroic woman in my life today.

My Spiritual Practice for Today

Today I will begin to let go of my anxiety over having all the answers so quickly. I will begin to think about growing into the questions. I can begin to understand the importance of holding the tension until the answers can emerge.

August 11

Backstory (Pat & Sue)

Everyone has a backstory. Everyone has a his-tory or a her-story. Everyone who has lived more than a day has experienced a combination of events and circumstances that has shaped them and influenced their actions and made them who they are.

You cannot truly know or understand anyone else unless you know their backstory. If you are tempted to judge someone for how they are now or for their current or past actions, remember there is a story behind what you see. Once you know someone's story, you find it much harder to judge them. Knowing the story brings understanding and often compassion, even for people who repel you or have hurt you. Even your abuser has a backstory that is behind the abusive behaviors. Most abusers have some kind of abuse and trauma in their own history. No one's story is an excuse. And yet knowing anyone's story can bring you to a place of understanding and aid you in your own self-healing forgiveness process.

Another way to look at this is to reflect on your own experience of being judged. Many people in your life probably do not know your story. They may not know about your trauma, and so may not understand how that trauma has shaped your life. They look at you now and see certain externals, some actions or characteristics, and not understand them. Perhaps they even judge you for them. You know how this feels. When you have shared your story with someone you trust, you have probably experienced their deepened understanding and empathy.

Another way of saying all of this is the proverb, "Never criticize a man until you have walked a mile in his moccasins." However, it is our experience that if you walked that mile and you have heard the other's story, you would not criticize at all.

My Spiritual Practice for Today

Wherever you go today, look closely at the people you encounter and try to imagine a story for them. What have they been through, both good and bad? What is happening in their lives now that you don't see? Particularly do this with people whom you find difficult, irritating, or obnoxious. Notice how your feelings shift when you ask, "What's their story?"

August 12

To Find Our Joie de Vivre (Vicki)

Sometimes the most important thing in a whole day
is the rest we take between two deep breaths or the
turning inwards in prayer for five short minutes.
–Etty Hillesum

Time seems to stand still when you are deep into grief and searching for answers. So many questions, with no immediate answers, leave you feeling emotionally destitute. Those stubborn questions that will not be answered until you have walked the journey. You know the old saying, "We make the path by walking." The questions can't be answered until we embark on the walk. Left foot, right foot is another way to look at the steps we need to take to regain the *joie de vivre* that we lost because of the abuse and trauma we experienced. That light in our soul, which has grown dim, can be rekindled again if we have the courage to take the journey.

The movie *The Way* is a great example. Martin Sheen plays a bereaved father who seeks to know his son after a tragic accident took his life while walking the Camino de Santiago, an ancient pilgrimage route across Spain. For years pilgrims have made that long journey on foot. To know his son, Sheen embarks on this pilgrimage hoping to experience what his son was seeking. He was able to come to terms with the loss of his son at the end of the journey and realize the true gift his son was to him.

In the midst of my counseling years, I experienced a pilgrimage of sorts. I called it my Vision Quest. I traveled alone for seven weeks to many states in the West, visiting friends along the way, spending extended time in nature, thinking, regaining my sense of self. It was a sacred time that I used to cleanse my body, mind, and spirit. Traveling the Oregon and California coast with its rugged landscape was transforming. Being alone and not having a schedule to maintain provided the freedom to renew myself.

My Spiritual Practice for Today

Today I will resolve to give myself five minutes to just sit quietly and breathe deeply, knowing that each breath I take is providing me everything I need to take the next step in my healing journey. I will practice left foot, right foot.

August 13

Horror Vacui (Pat)

Horror Vacui is a Latin term meaning "fear of empty space." Many survivors suffer from this fear. It is most often seen in a fear of being alone. If you struggle with this, you avoid quiet moments alone and feel compelled to fill your time with noise and activity. You do this because you fear painful emotions and memories will come to the surface. You do not want to be alone because your shame has convinced you that you are not a good or enjoyable person to hang out with. "Who would want to hang with me? Certainly not me!" might be your refrain.

Sadly, this horror of solitude is robbing you of experiences that are healing and crucial to deepening your relationship with your True Self and your God. It is in moments of quiet aloneness that you can best hear the small, still voice of your soul whispering to you. It is solitary quietude that allows your intuition and wisdom to bubble up from your center and guide you. When no one is available, learning to turn to soothing solitude can be a valuable weapon to fight off the feelings of abandonment and despair. In moments of aloneness, you learn to befriend yourself once again, or for the first time.

If you spend quality alone time with yourself, you will gradually discover that you are quite enjoyable and amazing to be with. At first you may feel uncomfortable, and difficult emotions will probably surface. If you continue to create moments of solitude, you will eventually find it so healing that you will seek it out and will miss it when it's not possible for you. You will discover that the empty space that you feared is actually full of spiritual energy and grace, deep peace and consolation, and profound inspiration and creativity. You will find that the space is not empty. It is filled to the brim with you, your True Self, your soul, and your God. Nice company to hang with!

My Spiritual Practice for Today

Set aside some quiet time to be alone with yourself. If painful memories or feelings arise, don't flee into busyness. Breathe through them and move your body. Center yourself and sense the solitude and your soul embracing you.

August 14

Gratefully Recovering (Pat)

It can be startling and puzzling when you attend an AA meeting and hear some of the more veteran recovering alcoholics introduce themselves as "gratefully recovering alcoholics." They are saying not only that they are grateful to their Higher Power for their sobriety, but also for being alcoholics in the first place! Their spiritual program in AA has brought them to see that their alcoholism, despite all the pain and damage it caused in their lives, was ultimately a gift. They are grateful for what they have learned and for who they have become, especially spiritually, as a result of being alcoholics and traveling the road of recovery. The once shameful, destructive, and debilitating disease of alcoholism has been transformed into a blessing for them. This can become true for you as well in regard to your trauma.

Understandably, it takes a tremendous leap of faith to accept that your painful experience of abuse may in the end be a gift. Yet in the lives of many of our clients, we have found it to be so. Your abuse is not only a wound to be healed, but, through the inner work of your soul, it is also a gift to be opened. In fact, your abuse wound can become the center and core of your spiritual transformation and soul strength. It can ultimately be experienced as blessing!

This is in no way to say that it was a good thing that you were abused. It was not. It is not to say, either, that your soul or God wanted you to suffer abuse in some sort of twisted plan to punish or improve you. They did not. It is to declare from our experience that your soul and your God can bring forth goodness, grace, and life-giving psychological and spiritual blessings even from such an unwanted and devastating curse as trauma and abuse.

My Spiritual Practice for Today

Meditate on the phrase "gratefully recovering." What does it mean to you in your recovery from trauma? What blessings or spiritual gifts have you received from your journey as a survivor? What inner wisdom, strength, creativity, or deeper awareness have you been given along the way?

August 15

Today I Will Find God Within (Sue)

People seek to find God in many places: religion, Holy Scriptures, prayer and meditation, nature, art and music, other people, to name only some of the pathways to God. All of these can be excellent ways to discover your Higher Power. However, all of these can mislead you to only seek God outside and beyond yourself. Even the term "Higher Power" can divert your search to something "higher" and outside of yourself, and away from what can be the most powerful and liberating place to find God: deep within yourself, in the depths of your soul where the divine spark of your True Self dwells and meets the Divine Being that you have been seeking.

To discover the holy and divine light within is particularly surprising for survivors. It is also freeing and healing for survivors. Abuse or trauma often involves an unwanted intrusion into the sacred temple of your unique being, leaving you with the sense of your innate and ultimate value being taken from you or forever profaned. It may have left you feeling cut off from access to your soul and given you a belief that its light has been darkened or dimmed. Yet your light, your divine spark, can never be dimmed or lost. Seeking God within you, and realizing your divinity, can open up your spiritual vision to see that light once again.

An inner Higher Power dwells within you in light, divine energy and mystery beyond your mind's comprehension. For a time, stop seeking God beyond you and look within. You will be delighted and surprised beyond measure about what you discover.

My Spiritual Practice for Today

Today I will look deep within myself through prayer and meditation. I will look for the light of my soul. I will open myself to experience the subtle energies of my spirit. I will listen to the quiet whispers of divine wisdom voiced by my soul. Centering on my breathing in meditation, I accept it as the breath of my Creator. I embrace the divinity, the Christ or the Buddha, within me.

August 16

My Forgiveness (Pat)

Eva Kor is a survivor of the horrors of Auschwitz. She was a child who, with her twin sister, endured monstrous medical experimentation at the hands of the infamous Dr. Josef Mengele. In a May 2015 NPR radio interview about her meeting and forgiving a guard at Auschwitz, she said:

> My forgiveness has nothing to do with the perpetrator, has nothing to do with any religion. It is my act of self-healing, self-liberation, and self-empowerment. I had no power over my life up to the time that I discovered I could forgive. When a victim chooses to forgive, they take the power back from their tormentors. But it is their choice to make.

Many survivors struggle with the choice to forgive. Forgiveness can feel wrong and unnatural after the great harm you have suffered. Your instinct may be to strike back, get even, or wish that your perpetrator suffer as much as you have. Forgiveness can feel threatening. It can make you feel you are weakening yourself by letting go of your anger, making yourself vulnerable to more abuse.

However, forgiveness is actually an act of self-soul empowerment. You take back your power from your abuser, cutting the final ties to your abuser that your anger maintains. Anger is a holy, necessary, and empowering phase of your healing journey. However, anger held too long actually imprisons you. You stay tied to your abuser with the chains of anger, carrying your abuser around with you every day. Forgiveness cuts those chains and breaks the trauma bond with your abuser for all time.

My Spiritual Practice for Today

Reflect on what you feel about forgiving your abuser. Is it time for you to begin the forgiveness process, or do you still need your anger for your healing? There is no right or wrong answer. Your forgiveness will come when you are ready. Be patient and gentle with yourself, and simply notice where you are now with the choice to forgive.

August 17

Holding the Secret (Vicki)

In my workplace, two doors led into my office. Both doors were closed as I covertly dialed the number of the therapist who was recommended to me. To my dismay, no one answered, so I left a number and waited several pensive and fearful hours for a return call. This was the first hurdle to climb, and it was the seminal moment that began the journey of healing. The mere suggestion from a trusted friend that I needed professional help was all I required to take that first step.

After a full year of counseling sessions, it was only by letter that I could come clean and break the silence about a secret abusive emotional and sexual relationship with a priest that had imprisoned me for fourteen years. The fear of telling that secret was monumental. The level of stress I lived with in holding the secret had begun to chip away at my soul. I believed it was mostly my fault. I believed I was the one who initiated it. I believed I was at an impasse, although I didn't really realize what that entailed, and it seemed only despair loomed ahead.

Years later I now know how important that first step was for the healing of my heart. I learned a depth of knowledge in the counseling process that I would never have learned otherwise. A wise and trusted therapist can be the tipping point to make sense of the chaos that abuse brings into one's life. Finally I could begin to make sense out of what had transpired in my life. Only someone outside of that experience could lead me to understand why it had happened to me. Having been led to believe the abuse was my fault, I would spend months unraveling the circumstances that led me to this time of questioning.

My therapist said over and over to me, "Love brings up anything unlike itself for the purpose of healing." It was something that Virginia Satir had taught her. The fear had to be confronted if I was to ever to begin a process of healing. I finally understood what she was talking about.

My Spiritual Practice for Today

Today I want to find the courage that is needed to truly understand my story and the circumstances that have caused me to question why my life feels so out of control. Give me the courage I need to explore my life and to ask the difficult questions.

August 18

Garbage In, Garbage Out (Pat & Sue)

"Garbage in, garbage out" is a phrase from the world of computer software developers. It means that if you start the development process by entering invalid, incorrect, or useless data, what you will get in the end is questionable or unworkable computer programs. Bad input will result in bad output. Garbage in, garbage out.

We can apply this saying to our minds. If we feed our minds a lot of negativity, we will have a lot of negativity come out of our minds and enter our speech and actions. This is particularly true when the Internet and 24/7 news coverage barrages us with tragic and catastrophic news stories, disturbing images, a tsunami of online porn, and many other assaults to our senses, mind, and soul. All of this depressing material flowing in can lead to a flash flood of negativity pouring out.

All of us to be aware of this issue, and it is particularly acute for survivors. Over the years of doing therapy with survivors, we have noticed a surprising pattern. Some survivors avoid negative visual and mental stimulation relevant to their trauma. However, some survivors seek it out and almost obsessively overwhelm themselves with images and stories in TV, movies, and social media that are similar to their trauma story. In doing so, they often retraumatize themselves. This is an attempt to master what happened to them, but it backfires. All that ingested garbage results in depression, shame, rage, and despair.

There are two important lessons here. First, it is vital for you to screen and monitor what you let into your senses and mind. You may need to avoid some input entirely. We limit young children's screen time. Perhaps you need to do that for yourself. Secondly, it is crucial that you feed your mind with images and stories of human kindness, love, positive creativity, Spirit, and hope. The spiritual answer to "garbage in, garbage out" is *soul food in, soul delight out!*

My Spiritual Practice for Today

Look carefully at what you are feeding your mind on a daily basis. How much of it is retraumatizing and depressive? How much of it is uplifting soul food? What changes do you need to make from what you see?

August 19

Update Your Personal Creed (Pat)

The experience of abuse or trauma and the questions that it produces can shake you to the very foundation of your being. It brings into question many of the beliefs and assumptions that were the spiritual bedrock of your life. It can lead you to ask such questions as "Why didn't God stop the abuse?" "Why is such suffering allowed to happen when God is supposed to be loving and merciful?" "Who or what then is my Higher Power?" The abuse itself can create spiritual beliefs that your healing reveals as untrue.

Spiritual healing must then also involve a reconstruction of your fractured spiritual foundation and the discovery of new truths to live by. In a sense, you are being challenged to write a new personal creed for yourself, discarding the old understandings that no longer fit for you and incorporating the new beliefs that you discover in your spiritual healing journey. Your soul will be your guide.

My Spiritual Practice for Today

On June 25, we invited you to write your own personal creed. Today, look at what you wrote then. See if it still fits for you or if you want to make any changes. Keep doing this periodically through the year until you have a solid sense of what you now believe.

August 20

Your Spiritual GPS (Pat & Sue)

Your smartphone provides an excellent image for what it means to live in the Circle of Value. Its map app, which can help you navigate anyplace in the world, employs a GPS function that tells you exactly where you are on the planet and from your location gives you directions to wherever you want to go.

Open your map app now and look at it. The icon for your current location is a blue point of light with a blue circle of light pulsing and radiating out from it to the surrounding real estate you happen to be in. Theoretically, you can never be lost because you always know where you are.

The point of light is your soul. The pulsating light emanating from the point is your own circle of God's love and value that always surrounds you. Living in the circle of value, you can never truly get lost because the GPS of your soul will always tell you where—and more importantly, who and whose—you are. You only have to hit the search button for your soul to activate your inner point of light and your circle of value. You will find your way, then, in each moment. This is what centering prayer and meditation and other spiritual practices can do for you. They are your "search buttons" to reconnect you with your soul and your infinite value in the center of your sacred inner circle so you can always be guided on your journey.

My Spiritual Practice for Today

Any time you feel lost today—not knowing what to do about a problem, who to turn to for help, or which direction to go in a situation—stop, hit the search button for your soul, and spend a moment in centering prayer or meditation. Listen to the inner voice of your True Self. You will often receive directions. You will certainly be given peace and know who and where you are.

August 21

I Can See Clearly (Vicki)

The problem is not that our vision has grown too small,
but that we are using too little of ourselves to see.
–Cynthia Bourgeault, *A Wisdom Way of Knowing*

What happens in our lives that reduces our ability to see clearly who we are? When we come into this world as a child, we see so clearly and so innocently the world around us. Everything is exciting and new, ready to be explored and appreciated. Even though we don't understand everything, we are delighted to see and learn. And then we grow out of that age of innocence and begin to realize that life is filled not only with joy but disappointment and hurt. Sometimes the hurt is beyond imagination, beyond reason, beyond any moral compass. Our vision becomes more like a tunnel, and we begin to see life though a narrower lens. We forget how broad our original vision was. We came into this world equipped with a broad vision, a deep love, a desire to grow. And then.

The work of growing into who we were created to become is the work of a lifetime. We can choose to remain closed and living our lives with a small vision, or we can embark on the work of a lifetime so our vision can expand to truly see the beauty, grace, and opportunity to serve in this grand world we were born into.

What do we have to do in order to use our full potential to see and understand why we are here and what our work is while here? Whatever your pain and suffering has been, there is a place within you that cannot be defiled. Our work is to heal that suffering so you can truly know the place that cannot be defiled. There you will be able to see clearly who you are to become.

In his book, *To Bless the Space Between Us,* John O'Donohue writes, "For everything under the sun there is a time. This is the season of your awkward harvesting, when pain takes you where you would rather not go…Now the act of seeing begins your work of mourning."

My Spiritual Practice for Today

Today I want to see more clearly. Today I will begin to reflect on my ability to truly see what needs to be healed in my life. I choose today to seek a clear and expansive vision for a lifetime.

August 22

Forgiveness Breaks the Cycle of Abuse (Pat)

By forgiving your abuser, you cut the Gordian knot that binds you to the abuse and your abuser. In doing so, you break the cycle of abuse for yourself and your family. You can end it now with you so it is not passed on to the next generation.

Richard Rohr writes, "Pain that is not transformed is transmitted." The pain you do not transform, you will unwittingly, unconsciously pass on to your children, your life partner, your friends, and even to your spiritual community. How you transmit your pain will differ from how other survivors transmit theirs, but sadly, unless you heal and release your pain, you will somehow convey it to those you love. The cycle of abuse will keep going round and round. Hurting people hurt. Wounded people wound. The cycle can stop with you. You can choose to stop this destructive wheel from turning in your world. Forgiveness is one of the most powerful tools you can use to achieve this freedom.

If your pain has also been projected onto God, forgiveness is also a potent process you can use to transform your relationship with your Higher Power. Some survivors find it necessary and liberating to include forgiving God in their forgiveness process. You may have felt abandoned and rejected by God because of your trauma. You might struggle with the central questions: "Where was God when the abuse happened? Why didn't God stop the abuse and protect me better?" If these have become major blocks in your spiritual growth and healing, you may want to work on forgiving God. You may think it is silly, disrespectful, or even grandly presumptuous to forgive the Creator of the universe; it is really a mark of deep respect and reverence.

With trauma the old saying holds: "The buck stops with you." You can keep from paying forward the pain by forgiving. You can pay and pray forward love instead, including paying your love forward to God.

My Spiritual Practice for Today

Reflect on ways that you might be transmitting your pain. If you are, use this awareness to motivate yourself to begin or continue your forgiveness process. See too if you need to include God in your forgiveness.

SOUL LIGHT FOR THE DARK NIGHT

August 23

Suffering (Pat & Sue)

How can we find the words to describe to you, or have the nerve to say to you, that the undeserved experience of your suffering can ultimately have great spiritual value, meaning, and purpose? Yet it can. Although suffering in itself is in no way good nor desired by your soul or your God, it can be turned to your spiritual benefit. This is the mystery of all suffering. It is painful, and the correct spiritual response is to end and heal it. Yet it can be transformative.

Suffering is difficult to make sense of. All spiritual traditions address the question of suffering. Although many provide partial answers, none of them provide a completely satisfying answer. We wish there were a grand unified theory of suffering that would put all the pieces of this mystery together. This has eluded humanity, and we suspect it always will. In the biblical Jewish tradition, suffering is portrayed as a purifying, refining force that shapes spiritual character and draws the sufferer closer to God. In Christianity, Jesus's suffering on the cross, leading to his resurrection, is the means and the prototype for transforming suffering and brokenness into new wholeness and freedom. The Buddha sought enlightenment, surrendering ego and attachment, in order to break the cycle of human suffering.

These insights, along with our own experience, have led us to some partial answers about the meaning of trauma suffering. It is important to say again that suffering is not good in itself, nor does your soul or God sadistically want you to suffer to make you better. They desperately long for your healing. Yet God and your soul can use your suffering to shape you into a new creation, stronger precisely because of your suffering. This is the paradox and mystery of suffering. Your suffering can become a gift, a sacred wound. Your very brokenness becomes the road to wholeness. This gives your suffering its spiritual meaning and purpose, even though the trauma that caused your suffering was unjust, undeserved, and unwanted by you, your soul, and your God.

My Spiritual Practice for Today

In your meditation simply sit with the words above. Do not seek any grand understanding. Just be present to the great mystery of suffering. Be open to whatever you hear in your spirit about what you have suffered.

August 24

Spiritual Resilience (Pat)

Research recently has focused on the capacity we possess, even as young children, to regenerate, bounce back, and even grow emotionally and spiritually from adversity. Resilience is the name that researchers have given for this psycho-spiritual capability. The word "resilience" comes from the two Latin words: "re-" meaning "back," and "salire" meaning "to jump, or leap." So "resilience" literally means to jump or leap back. It is the ability to spring back like a stretched rubber band to your original shape after you have been stretched, stressed, or even temporarily deformed by challenging events in your life. Resilience is one of the key psycho-spiritual strengths for your life journey.

Four main attributes make you resilient: an ability to form supportive relationships; the capacity to construct essentially positive meanings or personal narratives for life events—even traumatic events—that create understanding of these events; the capability to maintain a sense of identity and coherent sense of self following trauma; and the resourcefulness to problem solve and hope in response to stressful life events.

Resilience comes more naturally to some, and yet can be developed by everyone. It is a birthright of the human spirit and a soul capacity in all of us, empowering us to transcend and transform even our darkest moments. We all have the soul force within us to spring back to form when life tries to stretch us too far. We all possess this inner spiritual resilience, a life spring of soul and relationship that we can tap to carry us through our traumas and trials. It requires that you delve deep into your inner resources of soul, faith, and Spirit, allowing you to spring back into wholeness of body, mind, and spirit, and grow stronger and even more resilient.

My Spiritual Practice for Today

First affirm yourself for the resilience that you already possess. You have survived and perhaps even grown stronger because of what you have suffered. Look at your strengths as a survivor and acknowledge yourself for each of them. Then look at the four attributes that create resilience. Pick one that you think you could improve on and choose one course of action that would create more resilience in that area. Start on it today.

August 25

The Salmon's Story (Pat & Sue)

The lifecycle of the salmon provides a dramatic story of the journey and travails of returning to the source. This story parallels your soul's own process of drawing you home to your source.

Every salmon is born with an instinct to swim away from its home pool and stream to wander the oceans of the world and grow in strength and size. Every salmon is also born with an even more powerful instinct to eventually find its way back to its source stream and home pool where it was spawned. To return requires much effort, many hurdles, and significant challenges, what we might even describe as suffering. In the end, the return to the source and the creation of new life necessitates the death of the salmon in order for it to pass on life to the next generation.

So it is with the suffering you've experienced as a result of your trauma or abuse. Transformation requires a difficult, sometimes painful journey with many challenges and much swimming against the current. It involves dying to your old ways of thinking, feeling, and responding to your abuse. It challenges you to let go of ego and let your soul and your God be in charge in the midst of your dark night. Your suffering can, though, like the salmon, give birth to wondrous new life in you. Your suffering will pull you deeply inward into a profoundly more intimate relationship with your source.

My Spiritual Practice for Today

How did your trauma hurt your relationship with your Higher Power? How are you now being invited to heal and return to a deeper connection with your source? What will you need to let go of to allow this homecoming to happen?

August 26

Hard-Won Wisdom (Vicki)

I may be changed by what happens to me, but I won't be reduced.
–Maya Angelou

Why are we so in tune with our inferior self and so much less aware of our innate goodness? Sure, life can beat us down, people can be cruel and abusive, and this can suppress our inner goodness. We often grow into adulthood with a damaged self-esteem. In the first half of life, we seem to push through life and ignore the deeply held pain. In the second half of life, we realize that if we want the life we imagine for ourselves, we have to heal the pain that has been held captive.

When I first began counseling, I could not own my own goodness. I knew I was doing good things but couldn't admit I was a good person, that I had gifts to share. I couldn't see my own beauty. I would shy away from any talk of my own goodness.

We are all walking wounded people. We don't have to look far to find someone whose wounds are deeper and more painful than our own. We don't have to stay there. There is help. There are people who can help us sort out our lives to awaken us to what is real. We can move toward authentic living. People who have gone through their own healing often become wounded healers, offering great insight for those just beginning.

Parker Palmer shares, "The inner life of any great thing will be incomprehensible to me until I develop and deepen an inner life of my own." To develop your inner life is to be in touch with who you are. Every spiritual tradition calls us to be in touch with our inner life, to nurture it, and care for it so we can each grow into loving service to the world around us. There is no other purpose for the interior life but to love the Creator of all things, love others and every created thing.

And finally, the wisdom of Pierre Teilhard de Chardin reminds us: "We are one, you and I. Together we suffer, together exist and forever will recreate each other." And into the world we go, sharing our own hard-won wisdom.

My Spiritual Practice for Today

Today I will reflect on the times in my life when my true goodness was stifled, when my genuinely held self-esteem was attacked.

August 27

God Is Not Absent from Our Suffering (Vicki)

It's cliché to say, "God never promised us a rose garden." God never promised us that life would be easy. Many find it hard to believe that God is not with us through our sadness and Whatever our Higher Power, the reality is that no one is going to save us from suffering. However, I believe God's grace is there for us to find wisdom in our suffering, and we can let that wisdom guide us to a new place of being.

Having gone through a very difficult process with the diocese where I live, I lost any sense of trust I had in the Church as an institution. Its actions led me away from the Church for a time. Even today I'm tentative with my commitment to it. However, my faith in the God of my understanding did not waiver. I held on to the merciful God I loved throughout my journey. I grew spiritually throughout the counseling process and found a wealth of teachers who would continue to form my spirituality into the future. I never blamed God for what happened. I placed the blame where it belonged: with the abuser and with the Church for its many failings in dealing with the issue of sexual abuse.

God is not absent from our suffering, nor did God cause our suffering. God is within our suffering, for God knows that in the depths of our suffering we will learn and grow and become more simply because of our suffering. Today after all these years, I can truly say that I have learned more from this process of healing than I could have with a doctorate in any other subject. Today my relationship is with a universal and dynamic divine energy that speaks to a Cosmic Christ as well as an incarnate Jesus who came to show us how to live and how to love. This is the God I have grown into through the dark night of my soul.

My Spiritual Practice for Today

Reflect on where you are with your understanding of God. How has your relationship been forged through your own suffering?

August 28

Thinking Makes It So (Pat)

Hamlet tells us: "There is nothing either good or bad but thinking makes it so." Your thoughts have great power. How you think about something, including traumatic events, will largely determine how they will affect you and how you will respond to them. Researchers have determined that 90 percent to 95 percent of your happiness is created by how you think of your life and yourself. Only 5 percent to 10 percent of happiness is caused by the events or circumstances of your life. If it is true that "we are what we eat," it is even more true that we are what we think.

Even something as innately negative and painful as abuse and trauma can be mitigated, and even transformed, by how we choose to think about these events. If you have been taught to think about your trauma from a perspective of shame and fear, then you will become a prisoner of these thought patterns, and your mind will tend to obsess over these thoughts, increasing their power and your pain. If, however, you can see your trauma in a different light and find reasons for hope, love, worth, and healing, your thoughts can set you free.

Your thoughts, especially inspired and guided by the leading of your soul, have an extraordinary power for transformation and freedom. You cannot rewrite the past or make all of your trauma pain go away, yet you can reshape the way you think about the past, and in doing so shape your present and future. You were a victim of what was done to you. However, you do not have to be a victim of how you think about your abuse. You can choose to change any negative thoughts about yourself and what you suffered. Realizing your power to think in a new way is a graced moment of redemption. Your mind carries within it the seeds of goodness, love, truth, and beauty. To nourish and grow those seeds is to partake in divinity.

My Spiritual Practice for Today

Are the thoughts you have about yourself and your story mainly negative? Pick one negative thought and notice how often you think it during the day. Create a positive answer to that thought and repeat it to yourself each time you have the negative thought.

August 29

The Keel of Your Boat (Pat & Sue)

An image that captures the nature of our soul comes from sailing. If you go to a lake or the ocean, you will see sailboats catching the wind with their sails and being steered by the sailor at the tiller or wheel operating the rudder of the boat, the combination that supplies power, movement, and direction. What you do not see, because it is hidden underneath the boat in the water, is the keel (or, as it is sometimes called, the center board). It is the keel that makes the rudder, the sails, and the sailor work. Without the keel, the sailboat will be somewhat steerable, but susceptible to drifting off course, or even being driven sideways by the wind. Turning or tacking is difficult and sloppy. Most disastrously, without the keel, the sailboat can be easily capsized by a gust of wind.

Your soul is the keel of your being. You cannot see it, and yet it is vital that it is lowered into the waters of your life and that you stay connected to it. Without that relationship, you will tend to drift through your life. You will find it difficult to tack and turn when your life requires a course correction. You will sometimes be blown sideways or even backward away from your goals and life direction. When the great gusts of crisis bear down on you, you will roll and perhaps even capsize. Your soul-keel provides the spiritual pivot and weight to help you safely navigate through your life, even through the storms.

My Spiritual Practice for Today

How connected do you feel to your soul? When life's storms blow into your life, do you seek her solace and strength? When you are unsure where to steer the boat of yourself, do you turn inside for direction? Today take one action that connects you more deeply to your soul and holds you steadier in the waves and currents of your life.

August 30

God is in the Cracks! (Vicki)

If we could only see that God is in the cracks of our spiritual lives,
we would already be healed.
−Ilia Delio

Author and speaker Richard Rohr has long been one of my master teachers. Today our societies are polarized by ideologies that portray life as black or white with no gray area to be considered. Society puts people into boxes or categories that do not allow for a deeper understanding of the human person.

One important teaching I learned from Richard was the spirituality of both/and. We are never just about one thought or one way of living. We are all both/and. The priest who abused me was both a visionary and a bully. He could be kind to the elderly and a bully to those who worked for him. He could at once be compassionate and understanding as a priest and yet also punitive to those who questioned his authority. We each have a combination of endearing qualities and negative attributes.

It took me years of maturation to accept that the man who had hurt me so deeply could also be thought of as a person whom someone else loved dearly. Or to confess that he had done good things for me. Thankfully I found God in the cracks in my spiritual life. When I examined those cracks to find out why they were there, I was led to an even deeper understanding in the crevices below the surface.

One of the hardest things to forgive was the characterization of me as being "psychologically imbalanced." Those were the words circulated about me in the small town where I grew up. It has taken years to let go of that. It was another example of the perpetrator blaming the victim. In his bullying mentality, this gave him the upper hand and diverted attention away from his own failings. If we could only know that God is in the cracks of our lives, we would already be healed.

My Spiritual Practice for Today

Today I will think about the cracks in my spiritual life and reflect on their importance and the energy I've expended to keep them concealed. I will seek to find God there and envision healing from those cracks.

August 31

The Mystical Pull of the Hawk (Sue)

An experience:

I glimpsed you soaring,
high distant speck in the sky.
You were almost touching
the loftiest of clouds.
Though far above,
I thrilled to feel your magnetic pull.

What is it about you?
Your freedom to be?
Your majesty as you inscribe
tight circles in the uplifting wind?
No road map for you,
as your trust and courage
allow the winds to take you.

My Spiritual Practice for Today

Use the image above as the focus of your meditation today. Can you see your-self as the hawk soaring among the clouds? In your healing journey, when do you feel pulled upward and out of yourself and your earth-bound fears to soar with your soul? Tap into your courage and trust today—even if you do not easily feel it—and allow the winds of the Spirit to guide you through your day rather than follow a set plan or road map for today. See the hawk in your mind's eye and let yourself soar and be led by the *ruach*/wind of the Spirit blowing gently, or even vigorously, within you.

September 1

The Mountain Meditation: You (Sue & Pat)

My Spiritual Practice for Today

We invite you to do the Mountain Meditation again. This time the theme is you. Bring to the mountain anything you have learned in the last month, any questions you have, or any need for healing that you are experiencing. Let your soul and the Spirit guide you. To enter into this meditation, find a comfortable sitting position. As you read, pause, close your eyes, and imagine the scenes described.

Picture yourself on a beautiful beach. See the waves, the sand, the brilliant color, and the vastness of the ocean. Feel the sun and the wind on your skin. Hear the crash and whoosh of the surf. Turn around now, and face away from the sea. This time pack your backpack with any questions, lessons, or needs you have experienced in the last month. Notice how it feels to carry this.

In front of you is a beautiful forest. See yourself walking along a trail into the forest. Appreciate the coolness and the shaded light. You reach the edge of the forest and see an open meadow filled with multicolored wildflowers. The trail leads you through the meadow to a clear, flowing stream with a bridge across the dancing water. Stop for a moment to enjoy the light sparkling on the water.

Now look up from the bridge and see a shining mountain before you. Following the trail, you ascend the mountain. You climb through the clouds, above the timberline through the clouds to the top of the peak. Look around you at the glory of creation. Then you notice a large boulder to sit on and rest.

From the other side of the peak, your spiritual guide comes and sits down with you on the boulder. You can discuss whatever you want. Unpack your backpack and lay its contents out before your spirit guide. Listen for what is said to you about what you have brought. If you receive anything, embrace it, and put it in your backpack to bring it down the mountain to the outside world.

When you are ready to leave, thank your Higher Power. Slowly hike back down the mountain, over the bridge, through the meadow, through the forest, to the beach, and to the edge of the vast ocean. and open your eyes. Record and reflect in your journal.

September 2

WOOP! (Pat)

You have heard the sayings "Follow your passion!" and "Live your dream!" These are inspiring injunctions. However, they frequently lead to a frustrating path to nowhere. It is not as easy as advertised.

Many people experience that dreaming and trying to make your dream come true through passion and willpower is not successful. Survivors have an additional obstacle. Because of the pain, fear, and shame that trauma has engendered in you, you may believe that you are not allowed to dream or that you are not worthy to have your dream fulfilled. Your dreams and your inner dream-maker may have died with the trauma—or at least so it feels. This is no way to live. Everyone needs a dream, small, medium, or incredible.

WOOP may be your answer. It is a process of goal or dream fulfillment developed by Professor Gabriele Oettingen of New York University and proven highly practical and successful by twenty years of testing. WOOP stands for: W – Wish, O – Outcome, O – Obstacle, P – Plan.

The process is to first identify your goal, wish, or dream. Flesh it out with as much detail and color as you can. Then summon from your soul the courage to affirm to yourself that you are worthy of whatever dream you might wish. Tell yourself that it is safe and possible for you to create a dream for your life.

Then focus on the outcome you desire. What would your dream look like? What form will it take? How will it change and reshape your life? Visualize the outcome your dream would create.

Then identify the potential obstacles, realizing that there are always obstacles; that's just the way it is. Many people skip this step, and it is here that many dreams die.

Finally, develop as detailed and practical a plan as you can to overcome the obstacles and achieve your dream. Then put your plan into action.

With this process you can WOOP your fear. You can WOOP your shame. And you can WOOP your fondest dream into shape and into reality.

My Spiritual Practice for Today

Apply the WOOP process to a goal or dream you have. Take one small step along the path of the plan you develop.

September 3

It's What's So... (Sue)

A personal proverb that I tell my clients, and sometimes myself, is, "It's what's so, and so what!" When I say this to my clients, it sometimes sounds a bit harsh. I don't mean it to be. I say it to jolt my client into a freer, healthier perspective about their pain or stressful situation.

The proverb means that you can accept the reality of your situation with peace and aplomb, and don't get pulled into unnecessary drama about it. The situation is simply what is so, and so what; you don't have to let it define you or pull you down. You are so much more than the situation or your history. So accept it, deal with it, and move on.

I use this saying with myself when I am confronted with some dilemma or painful experience that I am allowing to control me. I shrug my shoulders and say, "Oh well. It's what's so, and so what! No drama, please. I'll find a way to handle this and be okay."

As your healing progresses, you will be able to say the same thing about your trauma: "It's what so that I was abused, and so what." It isn't who you are. You are not a trauma. You are a magnificent person of infinite value living a divine life in a human body. This does not mean you should not be compassionate with yourself. It's about putting your trauma in a new and spiritual perspective. It's declaring that your trauma doesn't define or control you. It's about rejecting the role of victim and accessing your power to live large and proud versus small and victimy. This phrase is wonderful for preventing pity parties.

So the next time you are tempted to get out the violin and serve yourself pity pies, remember my saying, take a deep breath, and declare to yourself, "It's just what's so, and in this moment so what." You will feel the same freedom and power that this has given my clients and me.

My Spiritual Practice for Today

Apply the saying to a situation you are struggling with now. Repeat it like a mantra until you feel its hold on you loosening. Or if you feel ready, use the saying with your trauma itself.

September 4

It's No Longer About Me (Vicki)

Dare to declare who you are. It is not far from the shores of silence to the boundaries of speech. The path is not long, but the way is deep. You must not only walk there, you must be prepared to leap.
–Hildegard of Bingen

In the beginning of any healing journey, we can find ourselves so self-focused that we become blind to others' needs. The egoic mind is more concerned about how we feel than how others feel. And that's the ego's job—to protect our sense of vulnerability, to prop us up so we don't feel the pain.

Any healing process worth its weight helps us define our life circumstances, understand why they happened, and then begin to take steps to heal whatever needs to be healed. Working with a skilled therapist breaks down the fear we have of speaking the truth about our life. What happened in our childhood, adolescence, or young adulthood that is keeping us from living from a generative spirit? What is it that is keeping us from actualizing our true gifts?

Richard Rohr, OFM, reminds us that our lives are not about us. We are about life. We are to be about others. We are to give our lives away to the ones we love. We are called to live life to the fullest.

My Spiritual Practice for Today

Today, as I continue to move through the healing process, I want to begin thinking about the ways I can live more fully. Once I have addressed the many issues that need healing, I want to live a fuller life without fear, without hesitation. I have gifts, and I want to share them.

September 5

It's What We Leave Behind (Vicki)

*Plunge into matter. Plunge into God. By means of all created
things, without exception, the divine assails us, penetrates
us, and molds us. We imagine it as distant and inaccessible,
whereas in fact, we live steeped in its burning layers.*
–Pierre Teilhard de Chardin

This thought has compelled me to go forward into life. To leave the past behind me and walk confidently toward a clear vision. Words and phrases like "plunge into God" or "God luring us forward" speak such power. It's a power that I can feel, not like a tether pulling, but an energy moving. To have walked through a time of intense healing and then over time allowing all of it to take root in life is the gift of time and endurance. After a 1,600-mile trek across the Australian Desert with three camels and her dog, Robyn Davidson said in the film *Tracks*, "After all it's not what we carry, it's what we leave behind."

Wanderlust for new places and people has enriched my life. I have felt assailed by the Divine, penetrated by its power, and molded into a spirit of confidence and trust. All of life is an energy of burning layers that cause us to be present to those in our midst and to all that is happening around us. Each layer that burns away brings us to a more authentic self.

To have the courage to embrace life with all of its subtle nuances is the gift that came out of the struggle. Abuse is one part of the struggle, and the transformation is born out of hope. We must keep hope alive amid the struggle. To see a glimmer of hope on the horizon is all we need on the journey. Can we trust that glimmer of hope, knowing we already have within us what is needed?

My Spiritual Practice for Today

At whatever stage of life's journey I find myself, I will recognize the healing I have accomplished and what I have left behind, and be jubilant about my progress toward a new life.

September 6

Worry (Pat)

Worry is a paradox. Worrying goes like this. If you are anxious, your mind starts to focus on specific things to be anxious about. Worry about this. Worry about that. Your thoughts speed up, and you go over and over the same things, or you discover new items to worry about. Your mind is actually trying to calm you down by giving you a feeling of control and preparing you for what bad things it is thinking might happen. Except that it doesn't work. It backfires. The more you worry, the more anxious you get. Your brain projects all sorts of scary events for your future, and they begin to feel more real and more likely to occur. You feel more agitated, emotionally vulnerable, and spiritually weakened. What started as your mind's effort to worry you into feeling safe actually leaves you more out of control and feeling decidedly unsafe.

Survivors are particularly prone to worry. Your trauma was very hurtful, scary, and often unexpected. So your mind, with the best of intentions, creates worries to protect you by alerting you to all the potential dangers so you will not be caught off guard or unprepared ever again. This is where you may not be able to trust your mind, and you need to trust something else instead. But what?

The answer will be different for each survivor. For some of you, the solution may be your growing ability to trust your own intuition and inner strength to face and handle whatever comes. For others it will involve practices like meditation and mindfulness that still your mind and open you to the quiet, guiding voice of your soul. Still others will find the peace and freedom from worry in trusting your Higher Power and surrendering your worries to God. Do whatever works for you because worry doesn't work at all.

My Spiritual Practice for Today

Notice today how much you worry and what you worry about. Notice what you feel after a good session of worry. Better or worse? Safer or more vulnerable and anxious? Thank your mind for trying to protect you by turning on the worry machine in your brain, and then say "no thanks" to the worry. Practice letting go of your worries, packing them into a bundle, and putting them in a worry box (virtual or actual). Either place it out of sight or set the box in your meditation place, entrusting your worries to your soul or to God.

September 7

A Tweet from Your Soul (Sue)

Remember you are stardust, divine spark, of infinite value. Never alone, always loved. So no worries, no shame. Be peacemaker.

@yoursoul.div

#TrueSelf

#BelovedChildoftheUniverse

#NeverForgetWhoYouAre

My Spiritual Practice for Today

R ead and absorb this tweet from your soul over and over today, and bask in its meaning for you. When you are ready, tweet a message back to your soul about whatever you are feeling (in 140 or 280 characters or less, of course).

September 8

A Long Standing Grief (Vicki)

Becca was only 5. Two teenagers ran a stop sign on a country road and hit our car broadside. The car rolled and rolled into a newly harvested cornfield in late September. We were all thrown from the car. The car rolled on top of Becca and crushed her little body. My two brothers, my mother, and I were scattered about the field. My eldest brother, age 9, was never unconscious and has a clear memory of the accident scene. I can recount this story only because of his memory.

In 1963, people who experienced trauma didn't have counselors to see. Nothing was available for my mother. The loss of Becca was an unspeakable grief in our family. Mom's sisters quickly went into our home and removed everything that belonged to Becca, save her lunchbox. That's just what they did then. It's horrifying to me now to think that when Mom came home two weeks later after an extended hospital stay, she couldn't even pick up a piece of Becca's clothing to smell her sweet scent. To add to this family trauma, I grew up thinking that my parents would have been happier if I had died and Becca had lived. They certainly didn't seem happy that my brothers and I had survived. Our grandmothers reminded us frequently, "Don't talk about Becca, it will upset your mother!" So we didn't speak Becca's name in our family for twenty-seven years.

Grief is a necessary part of living. No one can escape the scope of its pain. My traumatic story of grief is just one of millions of stories of grief in the world. I cherish this story. It's how I remain united with Becca and keep her memory alive in our family. How does your story of grief fit into the grand story of your life?

My Spiritual Practice for Today

I accept that grief is a part of every human story. I give thanks that those who have graced my life were a gift given to me to help me fulfill my own life story. I want to transform my grief into something life giving for myself and others. I want to live my life fully and honor those who have gone before me.

September 9

All Shall Be Well (Vicki)

Sometimes I think about the massive amount of unhealed wounds in the world, and it makes me wonder how people can actually live: The horrific abuse of women in Asia and Africa and here in the United States. Mothers who watch their children starve to death for lack of food and medicine. So many refugees from war and human trafficking. It's enough to overwhelm any of us. So many do not have access to healing services or any semblance of medical care. They either find a way within themselves to come to terms with their pain and loss, or they wander around as broken human beings.

We give into a passive sense of inevitability, and our ability to figure things out is eliminated. Some things are so difficult to find a way to heal. We all need help. We all need direction of some kind. We all want to live with hope.

When I meditate, I often hold the world in my lap and just imagine the large swirling blue ball. I wrap my arms around it and pray for peace and safety for every family. I pray that we may all know the peace that holds families together and allows the world to be whole.

We are called to find a way to commit to the mystery of life. How do we come to a place where we can be at peace with mystery, with the unknown? The only way I have found is through silent meditation. In silent meditation, I can metaphorically hold the spinning ball called Earth in my lap, envelop it in my thoughts and prayers, and then trust that all will be well.

St. Julian of Norwich (1342–1416) wrote a lovely prayer that said, "All shall be well, and all shall be well, all manner of things shall be well." I believe she was reminding us how important it is to embrace mystery and trust in the slow work of God.

My Spiritual Practice for Today

Today as I sit in silence and reflect, I want to practice trusting in the slow work of God in my life. I want to believe that all shall be well.

September 10

An Awakening at Windridge Solitude (Vicki)

There is a hermitage I visit as frequently as I can to write and to just be silent. It's restorative, and the silence of this sacred ground is permeated with the sounds and scenes of nature in the lovely rolling hills of Missouri. Once during a visit, as evening approached and the moon began to rise, I was awestruck at the size of the moon on the horizon and the massive iridescent moonbeam that it laid upon the ground. I followed it to the pond with a friend and sat and watched it rise high in the sky. That evening stands out today as one of the most significant unions with nature that I have experienced. I could see in the moonbeam what I could not see in the darkness. I could see all of the life that was dancing joyfully beneath the surface because of the narrow beam of light that painted a strip across the pond.

I began tossing bites of fish food into the moonbeam, and catfish and bass popped up to grab a morsel for their evening supper. The dragonflies were dancing like fairies performing a ballet just for me. The power of the light exposing the hidden dynamism in the pond spoke to me.

I thought about all the hours I hid in the dark, afraid that some light might illuminate my deeply held pain and sorrow before I was ready to release it. I held onto that darkness almost as a source of comfort from being exposed. However, remaining in that darkness, necessary as it was for a time, could not be the place that I would live out the remainder of my life. Once I realized that the light could free me from the darkness, I could emerge into my own moonbeam and remain there. It was there that the healing began and moved forward.

My Spiritual Practice for Today

Where is the light in my journey? Today I want to begin thinking about how the marvels in nature can be a source of metaphorical light for my healing journey. I want to think about creating opportunities for such an experience with nature.

September 11

9/11 (Pat & Sue)

$9/11$ is a day of remembrance, a day to remember the victims and courageous first responders who died in the horrific terrorist attacks on September 11, 2001. It is also a day to recall that they were victims of religion-inspired hate. The terrorists believed that they were performing a holy act pleasing to God.

This is blasphemy. Nothing that creates hate has God's approbation or is in any way religious. As we have said, abuse of any person is an abuse of God. Any violence based on hate is violence toward God. This is especially true when the perpetrators of hate justify their violence by claiming that their actions have divine approval. This is sacrilege. "If anyone says, 'I love God,' and hates his brother (or sister), he is a liar." (1 John 4:20)

This is a day to hold in our hearts the victims of 9/11 and all victims of religion-inspired hate. It is also a time to examine our own hearts to ensure that we are not misusing our faith to justify hating any person or group. For, "God is love and he who abides in love, abides in God, and God in him." (1 John 4:16)

God is love—and only love.

My Spiritual Practice for Today

Remember and reflect on the losses and lessons of this day in history.

September 12

Who Am I without My Worry? (Pat)

It feels fairly weird to live with much less worry. Wonderful, but weird. During my treatment for breast cancer, the worrying part of me that had been under pretty good control went wildly out of control. I was consumed with worry. Since the treatment is over and was successful, I have lost my tumor and most of my worrywart. I now have much less fear than before my diagnosis. This is beautiful, yet feels strange. It feels like some part of me is missing and that I have lost a key part of my motivational package. I don't feel as driven. Tasks seem less urgent. There is much less, "If I don't do this, then _____" or "If this happens, then _____, so I'd better hurry and do this_____. " Sometimes I'm not sure what to think about this profound shift. It feels much better, but disconcerting at the same time.

I even wonder if I care as much about people, what they are feeling and thinking, what they need, and how they are doing. Was part of my motive for being caring caused by anxiety about what they thought of me or whether they would remain my friends or client? It vaguely feels like something is missing and an old, but troublesome friend has gone away. What will fill worry's place in my head and in my personality?

What does this say about me—or all of us—if anxiety, worry, or some other dysfunctional part of us was a prime mover for choices and actions? And what does it mean if it is now gone?

Toward the end of your healing process, you may have questions like this. It may feel vaguely threatening and odd to experience your trauma symptoms abating or even disappearing. Be not afraid. You will find new meanings and motivations for your life as you relinquish the trauma chains that weighed you down. What is growing in me is that I am learning to more deeply trust and to be motivated by love, not by worry and fear.

My Spiritual Practice for Today

Reflect today on what wounds and symptoms are being healed in you. How does that feel? Does something feel like it is missing? Are you ready to say "goodbye" and "thank you for your service" to your "old friend" and discover you will be just fine without her?

September 13

What Is Most Personal Is Most Universal (Vicki)

During one of my darkest times, I met a very sick homeless woman while volunteering in inner city Los Angeles. Marguerite was a crack addict and a sex worker, and she was seriously ill, lying on a filthy mattress next to a vacant motel in ruins. She had only the clothes on her back. She lived in this burned-out hotel with a community of homeless men and women. Meeting Marguerite and providing care while she was ill was a wakeup call for me to realize how insignificant my story was compared to hers. Seeing this profound suffering told me it was time I stopped feeling sorry for myself and started living a life for others. It was a transformational moment. I was staying with a group of religious brothers, and that night in their prayer space I wept for both of us.

Henri Nouwen writes, "We like to make a distinction between our private lives and public lives and say, 'Whatever I do in my private life is nobody else's business.' But anyone trying to live a spiritual life will soon discover that the most personal is the most universal, the most hidden is the most public, and the most solitary is the most communal. What we live in the most intimate places of our beings is not just for us but for all people. That is why our inner lives are lives for others. That is why our solitude is a gift to our community, and that is why our most secret thoughts affect our common life. The most inner light is a light for the world. Let's not have 'double lives,' let us allow what we live in private to be known in public."

Someone once said, "The way we do anything is the way we do everything." Let this be the truth we are known for, not the secrets we bury so deeply.

My Spiritual Practice for Today

Finding my true self so I may live an authentic life will be my quest. I want my private life and my public life to be consistently true to one another. My story is the story of all humanity yearning for truth and reconciliation.

September 14

Freedom in Forgiveness (Vicki)

John O'Donohue writes in *Eternal Echoes*: "Forgiveness is one of the really difficult things in life. The logic of receiving hurt seems to run in the direction of never forgetting either the hurt or the hurter. When you forgive, some deeper, divine generosity takes over. When you can forgive, then you are free. When you cannot forgive, you are a prisoner of the hurt done to you. If you are really disappointed in someone and you become embittered, you become incarcerated inside that feeling. Only the grace of forgiveness can break the straight logic of hurt and embitterment."

The need to forgive those who have harmed us calls for us to realize the other has a story too, even those who have hurt us the most. Although I do not know my abuser's full story, I know he was a broken man; he never transformed a deep loss he experienced early in his life. Once again I'm reminded of Richard Rohr's message; if we do not transform our pain, all we are left to do is transmit it to others.

I did not understand this until well into my counseling. I see where this applies to so many situations, particularly to the issue of healing from emotional and sexual abuse.

For years, all I could do was feel hateful toward my abuser. I had to be right about all that was wrong with him. Then, as my healing progressed, I began to understand his brokenness, and I began to soften. The anger and hatred began to fade. It took a very long time for the anger toward him to decrease. However, with time, I could see my attitude change. In the end I could honestly forgive him.

My Spiritual Practice for Today

On this day, I want to take a long, loving look at what is real in my story of abuse. I want to take time to reflect on what I know about my perpetrator. What was his or her story that could have led them to abuse me? How can I feel more empathy and compassion when I consider the Two Hands of Nonviolence?

September 15

Perfection (Pat & Sue)

We have come to believe that God's love is conditional and
that we have God's acceptance only if we are perfect.
–The Spiritual Laundry List

It is said, "The perfect is the enemy of the good." It could also be said that the perfect is the enemy of your soul. Many survivors' reaction to the shame that was dumped on them is to drive themselves to be perfect. If you have been told you are super-bad, maybe you can make yourself super-good, and then you will be loved.

This shame-driven attempt to achieve perfection is not only impossible, it is extremely stressful and spiritually toxic. If you feel you have to be perfect to be loved, even by God, then you will wait your whole life for that conditioned love to happen. You strive for perfection and always feel that you are still unacceptable and unloved. You work so hard to "earn your salvation," and yet you are not working hard enough. You believe that God's love is conditional and you have to figure out what those conditions are. Except you will never figure them out and never live up to them for the simple spiritual fact that there are no conditions to God's love.

Infinite love is unconditional love. The truth is that you are enough already. You are acceptable and accepted just as you are now. You are loved simply for being you. Stop working so hard to earn love. Let go of the impossible task of becoming perfect. Relax and receive the gift of love that is given without a price tag. Bask in the warmth and light of the infinite love offered you without conditions. Certainly, live to be your best self—and yet know you are already loved.

My Spiritual Practice for Today

Look inside for any tendency toward perfectionism. How has that affected you? Are you ready to let go of perfectionism? Then close your eyes and imagine that a beautifully wrapped gift box has been placed before you. It is a surprise. You didn't buy it or order it from Amazon. When you open the box, infinite love flows out as a warm light that enters and surrounds you. Simply receive it and feel it as deeply as you can.

September 16

An Empty Cup (Pat)

A saying recently seen on a church signboard: "You can't pour from an empty cup; take care of yourself first." This is a wonderful reminder for survivors of abuse and trauma.

Survivors find it difficult to focus on and choose self-care. They often become overly focused on caring for others and in the process neglect themselves. Jesus meant the same thing when he said in the second part of the Great Commandment (this is also in Jewish scripture and literature, and in other great spiritual writings), "Love your neighbor *as* yourself." He is saying that you need to love yourself at least as much as you love others. Then that self-loving frees and empowers you to love others. You must first fill your own cup with self-love, self-nurturing, and self care. Then you have something to pour out in loving and caring for others.

Survivors are deaf to the second part of the commandment. They often pour themselves out for the other when they feel totally empty and have neglected to pour anything into themselves. This is part of the abuse and trauma wound. You may feel that you don't deserve to love yourself, to feel good, or to have joy, fun, and pleasure in your life. Fear and shame may have led you to be so focused on placating and taking care of others' needs that you have little time or energy for yourself.

It's a good time to ask yourself a few questions: How well do you love yourself? How well do you care for yourself physically, emotionally, mentally, socially, and spiritually? Do you have a regular schedule of self-nurturing, self-enhancing activities? Do you frequently put others first and yourself second, third, fourth, etc.? How often do you refill your own cup? What's blocking you from doing so?

My Spiritual Practice for Today

Create a pie chart. Put inside each slice a category of self-care: for example, physical care, your eating habits, medical, social, environmental (your physical space), spiritual, etc. Then rate yourself 1 to 10 on how well your care for yourself in that category. Reflect on what this reveals and choose at least one, but no more than three, actions you will commit to doing to better fill your own cup.

September 17

The Fog of Unknowing (Vicki)

There is a blindness that we must break through to begin to see more clearly that which needs to be healed. I remember that fog of unknowing! Nothing felt right, everything felt out of sync, I was going through the motions. I had become a workaholic. I was directing a big project at the time that required my full attention, but I knew I was spiraling downward. I was enmeshed in the control of an abusive man, a Catholic priest. Because I had been groomed from childhood to meet all of his demands, I wanted to make him proud of me. I was still in that childish framework of keeping him happy. In the midst of it all, I knew I had to make a change, but how? It would require a big dose of courage!

It was the mere suggestion by a friend to call a counselor that began to lighten the fog that had kept me from seeing what needed to happen. It's ironic how one simple suggestion can be the catalyst for change, but it was. I had been brainwashed into believing that I would be nothing without him. Yet I knew I was doing great work in spite of him. His control and oppression of me was taking a toll. I knew it was time to confront this secret I had been holding onto for so long.

Little did I realize that this one step would bring about tremendous courage to face hardship, forgiveness, understanding, grief, and an amazing transformation of life. We all must find a way to summon up the courage we need. It may just save us and the world. "To forgive is to set a prisoner free and discover that the prisoner was you." (Unknown)

My Spiritual Practice for Today

Today it is time to reach out to a close friend or loved one for help. Today is the first day of my new life, a life that will be filled with a new understanding of myself and a discovery of my True Self.

September 18

Who You Gonna Call? (Vicki)

The famous mantra of the movie Ghostbusters, "Who you gonna call?" comes to mind when I think of the first people I reached out to in my healing journey. It was a huge struggle to tell a close friend that I was being manipulated and used by a Catholic priest and that the abuse had been going on for quite some time. I asked her to meet me at a park bench by a small pond in the town where we lived. It felt like a clandestine meeting. We had never met there, so she knew something was up. Breaking that long-held and intimate secret felt like confessing to a murder, but it was my own murder I was confessing. I had lost my sense of self because I had allowed someone else to take control of my life. It was a huge admission.

John O'Donohue writes in his signature book, *Anam Cara: A Book of Celtic Wisdom*, "In everyone's life, there is a great need for an *anam cara*, a soul friend. In this love you are understood as you are without mask or pretension…you can be as you really are. Love allows understanding to dawn, and understanding is precious…When you really feel understood, you feel free to release yourself into the trust and shelter of the other person's soul."

I chose two trusted friends at the time. They understood completely without judgment. They understood my fear. They understood how much I needed their support and love as I walked this gauntlet. Telling my friends allowed me to begin to tell my family and other close friends. It began to liberate me from the fear of holding that interminable secret. I continued trusting and creating a circle of sacred trust that could hold this pain and this story with me.

This circle of friends has followed me through every aspect of this healing. My heart is filled with gratitude when I think of all the friends who have supported me.

My Spiritual Practice for Today

Creating a sacred circle of trust beginning with one family member or friend is the first step in beginning to share long-held secrets. Today I will begin thinking of who that trusted person is in my life. I will envision the strength I will have when I tell her or him my story and ask for their support.

September 19

A Surprise Calling (Sue)

God has used my own healing journey to be an instrument of healing for my clients. I am awed and grateful for this, but I was not surprised by it. I sensed God would use my own abuse. What is happening now, and for the last fifteen years, has come as a great surprise, even a shock to me. Let me tell you the story of how this happened.

One day an invitation came to Pat and me to work with priest perpetrators of sexual abuse. My goodness, our bodies speak loudly. My stomach was churning, my heart burning, my body tight, my head spinning. Every cell in my body resisted the idea of working with abusers! All the fear and anger that I had ever experienced about my own abuse and the abuse of hundreds of clients surfaced and said *"No way!"* I feared that I would hate these men—I mean 100 percent hate them! Yet part of me knew this was a great opportunity to put into practice what I believed about the healing power of forgiveness. I began to perceive a real spiritual call.

After much prayer and anguish, I heard the call to walk the walk of what I believe in: *unconditional love.* I was being called to use sacred listening and hear the sacred and tragic stories of these men. I heard of their horrendous abuse as children. I walked with them as they felt the shame of their horrific actions. I wept with them as they expressed their pain from harming their victims, their priesthood, and their church. I helped them discover goodness in themselves and embrace the truth of who they are in God's eyes.

I have grown to truly love these men. I 100 percent hate their crimes and the horrific trauma they have inflicted on their victims. At the same time, witnessing their commitment to their recovery and their dedication to pray each day for their victims, I am able to see each one with 20/20 spiritual vision. This vision allows me to say without reservation or embarrassment that I really do love each and every one of them unconditionally as God's precious child. I am still surprised and humbled.

My Spiritual Practice for Today

Reflect on my story and notice what you feel. Every emotion is understandable and okay.

September 20

Letting Go (Pat)

Fear makes living from your soul very difficult. Your soul invites you to experience the peace and serenity of living each moment in the present—a key spiritual tool and experience. This requires letting go of the past and the future. Fear from your abuse makes this challenging, constantly drawing you back to live in the pain of your abusive or traumatic past, leaving you chronically anxious or even terrified of your projections of a catastrophic future.

Your soul invites you to learn to let go of past and future, to accept powerlessness over what you cannot control, and to be in the present moment. The soul sickness of chronic abuse-based fear blocks this spiritual surrender. Fear drives you to hold on for dear life, to grasp, to control even the uncontrollable. While understandable because of the abuse, this gives you a false sense of security at a high cost. There is no peace, no serenity in tightly holding on; in truth, it simply makes you more frightened and insecure. Fearful clinging begets more fear in a vicious circle. Soul-centered surrender yields serenity and peace, even if it initially feels threatening.

My Spiritual Practice for Today

You can experience this difference physically with a brief exercise. Hold a small object in one of your hands. Squeeze it tightly with all of your might. Keep trying to hold it tighter. Do this for about 3 minutes. Then notice what your body feels. Feel the tension, tightness, and perhaps even pain in your muscles all the way up your arm and into your shoulder or beyond. If you keep doing this, your muscles will fairly soon begin to lose their strength. Now slowly, gently relax your grip on the object, eventually letting it go and dropping it. Notice how your body feels now. That is the difference between the spiritual effect of fear and soulful surrender. Repeat this several times during the day, especially absorbing the feeling of letting go. You can link this with centered breathing to be present in each moment of your day.

September 21

Our Courage Can Inspire Others (Vicki)

Once while on a mission trip to Mexico, our group reached out to help a community of women and their children. The women had resorted to prostitution as a means of supporting their children. They lived in tiny adobe dwellings along a busy intercontinental highway that went from Canada down into Central America, so their customers were frequent. Our group wanted to help them develop a cottage industry so they might have an alternative to the dangerous work they were doing. We purchased sewing machines and began to teach them to sew. Each year we would return, and slowly they began sewing and selling their products.

In the middle of the afternoon, we gathered in a nearby chapel and each of us were invited to share a personal struggle. We hoped that by sharing our personal stories and issues that needed healing, they might feel called to do the same. When my turn came, I shared that I had been abused by a man who was greatly trusted by my family and for a long time the light in my soul burned dimly; however, once I had the courage to share my story, I began to heal and the light in my soul began to shine more brightly. A woman sitting next to me threw her arms around me and began to weep. And although no words were spoken, her tears spoke volumes about her own journey and pain.

Sometimes the courage to tell our stories not only helps us, it helps those around us. It helps others understand who we are and that perhaps they are not alone. Telling our story opens wide the gates to healing for us and for those who love us. We all have a story to share, and it is in the courageous telling of it that we begin to heal. The light in our spirit can grow dim because of long-harbored pain and suffering. Once we find the courage to express our experience, the opportunity for healing and grace can wash over us like a flood. When we can transform our own pain, we no longer need to transmit it to others.

My Spiritual Practice for Today

In this moment, may I find the courage to tell my sacred story to a trusted friend who will hold it with me. I will look forward to the freedom I will feel when I take this step.

SOUL LIGHT FOR THE DARK NIGHT

September 22

Loving Acts of Kindness Come Back to Us (Vicki)

A friend of Mohandas Gandhi once asked him if his service to the people of the small village where he lived in India was being done for purely humanitarian reasons. Gandhi responded, "Not at all. I am here to serve no one else but myself, to find my own self-realization through service to my friends who live here." His point, of course, is that while we are serving others, we are also nourishing ourselves through acts of loving kindness. When we attend to ourselves with compassion and mercy, healing progresses. When we serve others with an open and generous heart, it all comes back to us.

In my own experience this rings true. I remember the day I walked away from a ministry of seventeen years and felt lost without a clue about my future. I flew to Los Angeles to spend time with friends who served the poor daily on the streets of L.A. I immersed myself into this giving away of myself, and the gifts I received in return were immeasurable. I felt such healing in my soul. Even today, the encounters with the poor on the streets and the conversations we shared hold great memories for me. More than anything, my experience with those who had nothing reminded me that the difficult time I was having wasn't so bad after all. It was a reminder for me to stop whining and take responsibility for my own life and realize what a blessed life I enjoyed.

It's all about perspective. We can sit and wallow in our grief for a time, and then we have to stand up and do what is required to heal our life and move forward. However difficult this may be, it is up to us to do the work required to heal our issues. Every human being has been given the innate ability to re-create themselves. Where will you begin?

My Spiritual Practice for Today

Today I will pick up the phone and find a therapist I can see. I will begin my healing journey with this one phone call. I can summon up the courage to take the first step.

September 23

Burning the Grump (Pat & Sue)

Several years ago, we traveled to the beautiful Colorado mountain community of Crested Butte in the autumn to experience the spectacular beauty of the aspen trees turning gold on the mountainsides. The town was having its fall festival, which included an annual ritual, apparently derived from an old Slavic tradition, called "burning the Grump." This involved building a large bonfire in the center of the town with Mount Crested Butte as the backdrop. When the bonfire was lit and burning fiercely, the scarecrow-like figure of the Grump was thrown on the fire to be burned up. The Grump represented all of our losses, sorrows, resentments, grudges, conflicts, and regrets of the past year. Its burning symbolized the choice to let go of all of these so we could start fresh for a new year.

As the Grump smoldered, everyone in the circle around the fire was invited to throw onto the pyre any object that would more personally symbolize the "grump" of each individual. There was, at first, relative silence as we all threw our symbols into the fire, the main sound the crackling of the flames. Then a great cheer went up as we watched our grumps being consumed and destroyed by the great fire.

At some point in your healing process, it will be time for you to "burn the grump," to express, finish, and let go of whatever holds you back. Burning your grump will lighten your spirit and probably make you less "grumpy"!

My Spiritual Practice for Today

What is your "grump"? What negativity is holding you back from moving on? Are you ready to let it go and throw it on the bonfire of universal love? When you are ready, devise a personal ritual of burning your grump. You can do this alone or with a group of soul friends. Write your grumps on pieces of paper, and put them into a small fire that you (safely) have kindled. Let your grump go as you watch it being consumed by the flames.

September 24

You Are Not A Donkey! (Pat)

There is a story of a father and a mother who brought their young daughter to a holy monk who lived as a hermit in the desert. When the monk answered the knock at the door of his hut, the parents said to him: "We are sorry to disturb your solitude, but an evil wizard has cast a spell on our daughter and changed her into a donkey, as you can plainly see. We humbly ask that you pray over her and free her from the wizard's curse."

The monk looked at the three of them silently for a few minutes, invited them in, and then asked the little girl if she was hungry. The girl said yes, so the monk prepared her some food and talked to her quietly and gently while she ate. The parents were touched deeply by the monk's obvious love for their daughter, and as they watched, their eyes were opened, and they could see that their daughter was not a donkey, but was herself.

Suddenly they realized that the wizard's spell had been cast on them, making them believe that their daughter was other than she always was. They left grateful to the monk, as was the little girl for it is difficult to live in a home where everyone thinks you are a donkey!

Abuse and trauma can be like the wizard's spell. It can make you see yourself as something other than you are. You may think you are donkey, an ass, defective, bad, less than others, etc. None of these are true. They are from the "evil" spell of shame that abuse casts on survivors. Thinking that you are a "donkey" is painful and devastating. What a huge freedom when you discover that the spell was never true and was only a distortion of sight. What bliss when you see that you have always been the daughter or son of your Higher Power that you were meant to be. Sometimes your eyes will be opened by the love and affirmation of someone else, sometimes from learning to be gentle with yourself. Your soul and your God always see you as you are: a magnificent person of infinite value. Never ever a donkey!

My Spiritual Practice for Today

Reflect on any ways in which abuse or trauma has distorted your vision of yourself. Ask a soul friend, your soul, or your God to break the spell of shame and tell you who you truly are. Be gentle with yourself.

September 25

Love Speaks in the Silence of the Heart (Vicki)

Plunge into God. By means of all created things, without exception, the
divine assails us, penetrates us and molds us. We imagine it as distant
and inaccessible, whereas in fact, we live steeped in its burning layers.
–Pierre Teilhard de Chardin

As I write this reflection, I'm sitting in a sweet little hermitage in the middle of a forest in rural Missouri. Windridge Solitude is a place I have spent many hours reflecting, praying, and writing. Places of retreat offer opportunities for silence, something that is sorely needed in this busy, technology-dependent society.

Silence is needed in our healing journey too. Mother Teresa of Calcutta said, "God speaks in the silence of the heart." I never forgot the wisdom of this.. Mother made time for silence and prayer so she could hear the voice of God guiding her as she and her community cared for millions of people around the world.

The silence of nature allows us to be present to the moment, to be quiet long enough to hear what our soul is longing for us to know about who we are. Do you know the feeling of silence? There is almost a ringing in the ears when first we turn off the music and noise of our lives. It takes time for that ringing to subside, but then the silence falls over us like a warm blanket. As Teilhard de Chardin says above, "the divine assails us, penetrates us and molds us."

First, we have to be silent to hear the divine and open our minds and our hearts to be taken over by that silence that is love. Love speaks in the silence of the heart. Plunging into God is plunging into silence. Sitting in silence, journaling in silence can bring up what needs to be healed. Allowing ourselves time to be silent can allow those things we have held secret in our hearts for so long the time to come forth.

My Spiritual Practice for Today

Practice being silent for a few minutes each day. Start with 3 minutes, then 5, then 10 with the goal of reaching 20 minutes each day. Keep a journal and write down your thoughts and feelings from being silent.

September 26

iGod (Pat)

The iPhone has been in our midst for over a decade. It now feels like an essential part of our lives. More than just a useful device, it has become a pocket god, a sleek metal, glass, silicon, and rare earth idol that—let's be honest with ourselves—we worship. The average American looks at their smartphone forty-six times a day. How many times a day do you check in with your God or your soul? Thirty-three percent of Americans check their phone in the middle of the night; 12 percent while showering; 9 percent checked their phone during sex! The smartphone has become a new idol, an electronic graven image that we are now often addicted to (every addiction is a form of idolatry). One especially concerning spiritual side effect of this addiction is the invasion and pre-emption of our moments of solitude.

We are being robbed by this false god of our quiet moments with ourselves and with our souls. In the past, if we had some empty time, we might daydream, fantasize, or creatively tap into our imagination. We might even enter into a few moments of prayer and mindfully be present in the moment with ourselves or with our friend or our beloved. We might feel some deep emotion or stirring of our soul. The Spirit might whisper something deep inside, and we were quiet enough to hear it.

Now we tend to reach into our pocket and take out the iGod and start to worship in a numbing liturgy of googling, texting, tweeting, gaming, Facebooking, or other rituals of our new iReligion. Although all of us are vulnerable to this idolatry, survivors may be especially at risk because of the natural desire to escape the inner emotional pain and shame that so many of you carry.

The escape that your electronics seem to offer can be very alluring. Do your best to resist, and put no false gods before your God. Leave the smartphone in your pocket or purse. Treasure and protect your quiet times. Make soul space to hear the deep whispers within, even in moments of pain.

My Spiritual Practice for Today

Notice today your relationship with your smartphone or other device. Do you use them excessively to fill your quiet times? Can you freely choose to not check your device and instead listen and be mindfully present? Could you go 24 hours without?

September 27

New Life (Vicki)

Even though I thought I was prepared for my father's passing on to new life after nine long years with Alzheimer's disease, when the time came, I found myself asking him to wait. As sick as he was, something in my heart still didn't want him to leave. I wouldn't be able to squeeze his hand or feel his warmth if he left.

As I waited and watched his labored breaths, I began to let go of my ownership. As I bore witness to the changes in his body in those last hours, I knew he was beginning a rebirthing process into new life. It is a struggle to be born. It is a struggle to die; however, the final letting go brings peace. I like that metaphor of rebirth, and I wanted to celebrate his rebirth into the next life.

Moments after my father died, I bathed his emaciated body. As I quietly bathed him with my mom and sister watching, I thanked God for the gift of his unconditional love. When I worked with Mother Teresa's sisters in India, we would often find someone who had been left to die on the streets. We would gently pick them up and place them in the ambulance. Returning to the home for the dying, we would bathe their emaciated bodies and care for them until they passed away. Now I was seeing the poor in their distressing disguise once again. I had never imagined that vision would come back to me with my own father. Indeed, I was bathing the sacred, and it was that living spirit in him that loved and nurtured me.

I am thankful for all who walked with me, including my father. As we move toward transformation, we must be reborn into who we are called to be. So many people helped usher me into new life. I finally knew I had a life to live and a new passion to give my life away in service to others.

I am most grateful to my father for his love and concern for me. He never doubted my story. And that meant the world to me.

My Spiritual Practice for Today

As I think about my life today, to whom am I most grateful for their love and support in my journey? How can I thank them for their nurturing love?

September 28

Today I See My Suffering in a New Light (Sue)

Love and suffering are the primary gateways to transformation of our minds, hearts, and spirits. More than anything else, these two vital life experiences break us open to profound personal change and life-altering grace. It is easy to see how love—loving and being loved—can be life changing and life enhancing. The transformational power of suffering is not so obviously seen or desired. In fact, because our instinct is to avoid pain, we tend to look away from it.

Yet embedded in every experience of suffering, including your abuse, is a seed of transformation and new life. There are graces and gifts, unpolished diamonds and other gems, hidden in the soil of the pain, suffering, and wounds you endured because of your abuse. They can be discovered, unearthed, polished, used, and displayed in ways that you could not have imagined earlier in your healing journey.

My Spiritual Practice for Today

Reflect on these questions of transformation today: What are the gems, the gifts of spirit and character, that are hidden in your experience of abuse? Who are you now—that you could not have been otherwise— precisely because of your abuse? What inner wisdom, strength, creativity, or new life purpose has come from your trauma? What is your soul bringing forth from the depths of your suffering and woundedness that can awaken new light and life in your spirit? Where will this transformation lead you on your spiritual journey?

September 29

What to Do in the Darkness (Vicki)

What to Do in the Darkness

Go slowly
Consent to it
But don't wallow in it
Know it as a place of germination
And growth
Remember the light
Take an outstretched hand if you find one
Exercise unused senses
Find the path by walking it
Practice trust
Watch for dawn.
–Marilyn McEntyre, *Weavings*

If only I could have read this poem at the beginning of my journey toward healing. What wisdom and hopefulness is found in these simple words. Go slowly, consent to it, don't wallow in it, trust the place of germination, remember there is light, take the outstretched hand, awaken your senses, walk the path, practice trust, and watch for the rising dawn. I call it the wisdom of retrospect—if we knew then what we know now. But then again, having all that knowledge without the experience of it would not have allowed it to travel deeply within us. You make the path by walking it means just that. Unless we do our own emotional work, we cannot come to the truth of who we are or find answers to the questions of our lives.

I often refer to my healing journey. What I really mean is my entire adult life. This work isn't just for a few counseling sessions. It is embarking on a lifetime of reflection, to heal what must be healed and to grow into a new human being ever willing to serve and be present to the beauty of this life with all its joy and sorrow. Being attentive to this journey gives us the strength and wisdom to endure what life has in store for us. It is in this that we can truly find the joy of living, the joy of our creation, the joy of loving and being loved.

My Spiritual Practice for Today

Today I want to reflect on this poem and renew my commitment to my personal healing journey. I want to discover the joy of living, but first I must make the path by walking it and doing my personal healing work.

September 30

Imagination and Possibility (Vicki)

I first became aware that I was on a spiritual quest in 1991 when I took a seven-week sabbatical from work and drove nearly 10,000 miles to many destinations west of Illinois through Western states that held grand landscapes. It was a vision quest to just be with myself and think. The journey included connecting with new and old friends, spending time in the mountains and at the sea, and volunteering in a home for people living with AIDS in San Francisco. Driving down Highway 1 through Oregon and California was a highlight of natural beauty. I allowed my imagination to ponder all of life's possibilities amid this inspiring landscape. I was never really alone on that journey because my active imagination kept me company.

John Donahue, a Celtic writer and philosopher, writes, "Each person is always on the threshold between their inner world and their outer world, between light and darkness, between known and unknown, between question and quest, between fact and possibility. This threshold runs through every experience we have, and our only real guide to this world is the imagination."

It seems we are always betwixt and between, leveraging this and that. I think it boils down to weighing our options and finding what fits for us. My therapist taught me to ask the question, "How does that fit for you?" How does this new understanding of this abusive relationship fit for you? How does this decision you have made to move away from your abuser fit for you? How does your decision to leave his employment after seventeen years fit for you? How does being free of this abusive person in your life fit for you?

My goodness, it feels wonderful! I finally have my life back, and my imagination is on overload! There are so many possibilities in life. Now my challenge is, how do I choose among all these possibilities? And life begins anew!

My Spiritual Practice for Today

On this day, I wish to begin thinking about all of the possibilities that life has in store for me! I trust that my life has purpose and that if I envision positive thoughts about my life, they will come true for me. I will take a first small step in creating a new possibility.

October 1

The Mountain Meditation: You (Sue & Pat)

My Spiritual Practice for Today

We invite you to do the Mountain Meditation again. This time the theme is you. Bring to the mountain anything you have learned in the last month, any questions you have, or any need for healing that you are experiencing. Let your soul and the Spirit guide you. To enter into this meditation, find a comfortable sitting position. As you read, pause, close your eyes, and imagine the scenes described.

Picture yourself on a beautiful beach. See the waves, the sand, the brilliant color, and the vastness of the ocean. Feel the sun and the wind on your skin. Hear the crash and whoosh of the surf. Turn around now, and face away from the sea. This time pack your backpack with any questions, lessons, or needs you have experienced in the last month. Notice how it feels to carry this.

In front of you is a beautiful forest. See yourself walking along a trail into the forest. Appreciate the coolness and the shaded light. You reach the edge of the forest and see an open meadow filled with multicolored wildflowers. The trail leads you through the meadow to a clear, flowing stream with a bridge across the dancing water. Stop for a moment to enjoy the light sparkling on the water.

Now look up from the bridge and see a shining mountain before you. Following the trail, you ascend the mountain. You climb through the clouds, above the timberline through the clouds to the top of the peak. Look around you at the glory of creation. Then you notice a large boulder to sit on and rest.

From the other side of the peak, your spiritual guide comes and sits down with you on the boulder. You can discuss whatever you want. Unpack your backpack and lay its contents out before your spirit guide. Listen for what is said to you about what you have brought. If you receive anything, embrace it and put it in your backpack to bring it down the mountain to the outside world.

When you are ready to leave, thank your Higher Power. Slowly hike back down the mountain, over the bridge, through the meadow, through the forest, to the beach, and to the edge of the vast ocean. Open your eyes. Record and reflect in your journal.

October 2

Into Crystal Clearness (Vicki)

Silence is a great help to a seeker after truth. In the attitude of silence the soul finds the path in a clearer light and what is elusive and deceptive resolves itself into a crystal clearness. Our life is a long and arduous quest after Truth, and the soul requires inward restfulness to attain its full height.
–Mahatma Gandhi

Isn't it truth that we seek when we begin walking toward a psychologically healthy life? We desire to understand why things happened to us. We want answers, or we want someone held accountable, but often there are no clear answers as to why life turned out the way it did for us. We can draw near to the truth, but there will always be an element of mystery to the story. We seek that crystal clearness that Gandhi speaks of above.

How do we move forward when we have tried to piece together the questions and answers and yet there is still a sense of loss? The wisdom of Gandhi reminds us that silence is a great help to a seeker of truth. Perhaps the truth we seek is much bigger than who is to be held accountable for hurting us. Perhaps the spiritual truth that we seek can overcome the mystery and the unresolved parts of our lives. If we can commit ourselves to the practice of silent meditation, our soul can find a way toward that crystal clearness. Once we find that sense of peacefulness that can come with the practice of silent meditation, our expansive soul can hold the unresolved questions and over time they will be held there without disrupting our search for a real truth.

The Course in Miracles teaches:

"Here is a silence into which the world can not intrude.

There is an ancient peace you carry in your heart and have not lost. There is a sense of holiness in you the thought of sin has never touched. All this today you will remember."

My Spiritual Practice for Today

Today, in my practice of silent meditation, I want to reflect on the greater truth that I seek. Today I want to move toward allowing the silence to lead me to that greater truth that resides within me.

October 3

Hijacked by Fear (Pat)

Your brain is the most amazing and complex phenomenon that we know of in the universe. It is very powerful and more resilient and flexible than you may realize. It is also surprisingly vulnerable to being hijacked, taken over and controlled by various chemicals and processes, like addiction, depression, or other brain illnesses. Fear, or extreme anxiety, is one of the most potent hijackers of your brain. Shame is the other. When anxiety is in control of your mind, you can be convinced that your fears are real and imminently dangerous, even when the fears are not a threat. This is particularly true of PTSD fears and flashbacks. They feel so real that you react to them as if you are in an imminent danger right now.

A few months after I finished my treatments for breast cancer and my physical and mental systems had stabilized, my grandson, Kevin, asked me what I had learned from my traumatic experience. I instantly replied, "I learned that 90 percent of our fears are not real." My own brain had been temporarily hijacked by fear related to my cancer treatment. Some of what I feared had some reality to it, although almost none of it came to be. This is what traumatic fear can do to your brain.

After you have suffered a trauma, especially if it occurs in your childhood, the fear center of your brain, the amygdala, can become too powerful and control your brain at times. This will lead to a distortion of reality. Normal anxiety becomes F.E.A.R.: False Evidence Appearing Real.

What is reality? It is in part a construction that you create in your brain, and when your brain is hijacked, even small or remote dangers can appear huge and monstrous. All this says that your fears are mostly unreal. They are illusions, mutations of your amygdala.

What is real is peace, trust, and love. Who lives without fear? The spiritually enlightened, those who have had near-death experiences, mystics, and anyone who has experienced that we are always—no matter what else is happening—surrounded and held by love.

My Spiritual Practice for Today

List your main fears. Then consider that 90 percent of them are likely not real, or at least are highly magnified and exaggerated. Cross off 90 percent of your fears, and see what you feel.

October 4

Forgiveness Is for You (Sue)

Many survivors are reluctant to forgive because they think forgiveness is for the person who hurt them. You understandably resist the idea of granting such a gift to your perpetrator after everything they did to you. In addition, some abusive acts feel as if they are unforgivable. This is why it is vital to realize that forgiveness is for you. Forgiveness is primarily and first for the forgiver. Forgiveness is only secondarily for the one who offended you.

The purpose of forgiveness is to set *your* soul free, to let it fly and soar. Chronic anger and bitterness can ground your soul with heaviness and block your soul from fully expressing its love, its peace, and its desire for mercy. The beatitude "blessed are the merciful, for they shall receive mercy" reminds us of the circle of forgiveness. When you show mercy, you receive mercy. You are blessed in turn with a merciful and loving heart for others and for yourself.

Remember the AA maxim: "Holding onto resentments is like swallowing the poison pill you intended for the one who hurt you." Don't forget that holy anger is just and right and necessary for a time to heal your shame and empower your spirit. Yet held too long, anger turns into resentment and bitterness that poisons you. Eventually you hurt not your offender but yourself. Bitterness is like a cancer that invades your soul. If it is allowed to metastasize, you suffer, not your abuser.

Research has shown that chronic anger contributes to the development of a variety of physical and mental conditions. Other research has demonstrated a link between forgiveness and improved physical and emotional health, including a boost to your immune system. When you do not forgive, the person who pays the greater price is you, not your abuser. When you do forgive, the person who receives the greatest gift is you.

My Spiritual Practice for Today

Meditate on your anger and discern if it is turning into bitterness or a desire for vengeance. If you are not ready to forgive, affirm yourself. You will know when the time is right for you. If it is time, write a forgiveness letter (that you will not send) to your abuser. When it is finished, share the letter with a soul friend.

October 5

Engaging Impasse: How to Move Forward (Vicki)

The Spanish mystic St. John of the Cross (1542–1591) coined the phrase "dark night of the soul." The imagery of a dark night speaks to our inability to see clearly and climb out of deep sadness because of overwhelming circumstances. A breakdown in communication, our inability to fix a situation despite our best efforts, dwindling of hope, disillusionment, and feeling obsessed with the problem all speak to a personal *dark night*.

This describes my emotional health at the time. The thought of communicating the details of the abuse seemed impossible. The fear of being judged about something so intimate was a colossal and oppressive barrier to every endeavor of my life. It invaded my family life, my work life, and my social life. I felt powerless to change the circumstances of my life, and I was beleaguered by my own inability to create change. Hope was not something I reflected on during this painful process of self-disclosure.

How could I find the courage to engage such impasses when all of my best efforts felt like hitting a brick wall? Meditation and processing my experience guided me through the questions and powerlessness. Sitting in silence gave me time to embrace the questions I had no answers for and hold them until there was clarity. Centering prayer guided me to a peaceful acceptance of the questions.

A time arises when the tension of unanswerable questions has to be held. What to do next? Will this sadness ever end? These questions held me captive for a time. Only in retrospect was I able to see how important it was to just hold the questions until their answers emerged. Venerable Pema Chodon shares her wisdom"

> To stay with that shakiness—to stay with a broken heart, with a rumbling stomach, with the feeling of hopelessness and wanting to get revenge—that is the path of true awakening. Sticking with that uncertainty, getting the knack of relaxing in the midst of chaos, learning not to panic—this is the spiritual path.

> (*When Things Fall Apart*)

My Spiritual Practice for Today

Allowing answers to my questions to emerge will take time. Today I will begin practicing quiet, meditative exercises that will silence my questions long enough to allow the answers to emerge.

October 6

Engaging Impasse with Contemplative Sitting (Vicki)

At a point, it felt like I had hit a brick wall. It did not feel like I could move forward, but I didn't want to go backward. Thanks to a good therapist, I was encouraged to stay the course and was constantly reminded of the progress I was making. Still, I had that overriding fear of being stuck again. One night while in a group therapy session, all I did was sit silently and weep. That's how deeply it hurt and how horribly stuck I felt. It felt like I was being emotionally tortured.

Several years later, I learned a valuable lesson about "engaging impasse" from the Institute for Communal and Contemplative Dialogue (ICCD.org). Engaging impasse is a process that guided me to the understanding that when we feel like we have hit that proverbial brick wall, we are to bring it to contemplative prayer or meditation. I knew centering prayer and believed that God speaks in the silence of the heart. Engaging impasse brought me to a deeper understanding of the contemplative and communal aspect of dealing with societal and personal impasse.

Today I'm grateful to be part of a global solidarity of people who bring impasse to contemplation. Through the international work I have done, women often open up to me about their own stories of abuse and trauma. It can be overwhelming to hear their stories. While there may be little I can do to change their circumstances, I know there are millions around the world who use meditation as a means to heal the world. ICCD provides this global network of people who sit in contemplation to bring spiritual power to such societal issues that have no quick answers or solutions. In contemplation, the divine energy takes hold of these issues with us. And it can take hold of our own personal issues to help us carry and hold the tension.

My Spiritual Practice for Today

Today I will explore the meaning of contemplation and meditation as a way of helping me to partner with others who are practicing engaging impasse.

October 7

Soul Shadows (Pat & Sue)

Have you ever seen the wind? Probably not since you cannot directly see the wind itself. You see its presence and effects in the bending limbs of the trees, the scattering leaves in the fall, its touch on your face when it playfully tousles your hair, or the stinging bite of a frigid, snow-laden gust of wind in winter.

You cannot see the wind when you are sailing either, even though you are dependent on it for propelling you through the water. You see the sail filling with an invisible force and feel the boat speeding up and heeling over. When we sailed, we learned to watch the surface of the water for the ripples caused by gusts of wind that were approaching us and about to hit our sails. We called these ripples "wind shadows." They are visible signs of the invisible approaching wind.

As with the wind, so it is with your soul. You cannot perceive it directly, but you can learn to see its presence and action in the "soul shadows" all around you. You can see your soul's shadow in ripples of peace arising from deep inside, at times of unexpected insight and spontaneous intuition and moments of creativity and inspiration. You can see soul shadows in the sparkle in the eyes of an excited child or in the soft, warm light emanating from the eyes of your beloved as you are held in their gaze. You can sense your soul's presence in moments of great love expressed or received and in the divine ecstasy of loving sex or intimate prayer.

The Hebrew word *ruach* means both wind and Spirit. It is the breath of God that dispenses the life force. It is the invisible force of your soul that cannot be seen, but yet can be felt and experienced. You can develop spiritual 20/20 vision that sees your soul's shadows within and all around you. The invisible energy and love of your soul will become subtlety visible and tangible. You will perceive the ripples of your soul as it blows toward you over the waters of your life.

My Spiritual Practice for Today

Simply be mindful and aware of the soul shadows that appear during your day. See and marvel at how your soul is alive and active within you and in your life.

October 8

The Entangled Bank of Wolf Creek (Vicki)

Studying the new universe story includes reflecting on theories of evolution. One profound learning is that the evolution of human beings is like an entangled riverbank. When I was a child, we played along Wolf Creek, which meandered between the corn and soybean fields in central Illinois. It was just a short bike ride from our house. We would catch fish, snakes, and crawdads. It was a child's playground. We appreciated it in every season. The banks of Wolf Creek were an entangled web of tree roots and vines where all kinds of creatures lived.

As I've been studying evolution and learning how profound its teachings are in human development, I have come to understand that our lives are much like the riverbanks that evolve with every season. They are complex systems that we often take for granted. We are born with such innocence and complexity. God created us in the stardust, an intricate combination of billions of years of evolving toward our current existence. We continue to evolve in subtle and not so subtle ways. Our very DNA is made from the same protons and neutrons found in stardust. And when we die, we return to stardust, which then creates new life again; we truly are ashes to ashes, dust to dust. Everything I've learned about the theory of evolution points to human beings as the ultimate culmination of life on Earth. The God who created this universe also created us. We are the only species that reflects on itself and is in awe of all of creation that surrounds it.

How does this knowledge fit into our own transformation? If we can look at the trauma we have suffered as a small part of the expansiveness of our lives and this blue ball that revolves around the sun, perhaps we can understand being transformed as essential to our continuously evolving lives. Does everything happen for a reason? Perhaps it happens so we can learn the next step in our own evolutionary process. Here is hope!

My Spiritual Practice for Today

Knowing my place in the vastness of the universe, I can see that my suffering can lead me to a deeper understanding of my life and purpose. Today I will think about my own story as part of my evolution as a human being. I want to unblock the flow of energy that is my life.

October 9

What's Going Right? (Pat & Sue)

Many of our counseling clients come to us to tell us what's wrong with them or their life. Of course we listen to this and take their concerns seriously and work with them to address their problems. However, sometimes we turn the tables and ask them what's right with them and their life. What's going well for them? What gifts and strengths do they have? What are they proud of and what makes them happy? Some clients are perplexed by this, and yet most are able to name at least a few things that are right with them.

Starting with the question "What's right?" is the better place to start the healing process. You start from a position of strength rather than from perceived defect or weakness. Then you are better equipped to deal with the real problems you face.

We find the question "What's wrong?" so negative and debilitating that we have banned it from our own communication in our relationship. When we observe something troubling the other, we ask instead, "What's happening?" or "What are you feeling in this moment?" or "How can I be of help to you?"

Focusing on what's right empowers you and feeds the grace of gratitude. And, in turn, cultivating a grateful heart and spirit opens your eyes to better see what is indeed right about you and what is positive about your situation.

So the next time you notice that you are obsessing about everything that's wrong, shift your perspective and raise your mood by asking yourself: "Hey you, what's going right in this moment? What's right with you? What can you be grateful for here?"

My Spiritual Practice for Today

All day long keep repeating the question, "What's going right?" Use it like a mantra. Notice how it changes how you feel about your day and about yourself.

October 10

Being Human Requires Everything (Vicki)

I was privileged to hear Chris and Phileena Heuretz share stories from their twenty years of outreach in some of the poorest and violent places on earth. Feeling a deep call to make a difference in the world, they set out for Kolkata and immersed themselves in the lives of women forced into prostitution; they went to Sierra Leone in West Africa in the aftermath of a civil war and met with refugees and survivors of unspeakable acts of cruelty. After twenty years of experiencing the trauma of the world, they were depleted. They felt empty. They began to understand the need to integrate contemplation into their desire to serve, and it has transformed them and their work.

Contemplation was key to my healing. The practice of sitting in silence is a way to get in touch with our deepest thoughts and hopes, as well as unite with our Higher Power. Contemplation allows for union with the universal divine energy who animates everything, especially our healing. Contemplation allowed me to unite my struggle with the human struggle in the world. It allowed me to move outside of myself and to think of others who were also suffering. Having been to Kolkata and experienced firsthand the poorest of the poor, I could relate deeply to this despair.

Our effort to heal our own trauma is an effort to heal the world. I was always touched by Mother Teresa's words, "I just focus on picking up the one in front of me. If I looked at the magnitude of need, I would give up."

Healing requires everything from us. It requires our full attention to move through the pain, the guilt, and the shame with an eye to becoming whole again. Integrating contemplation into our healing process allows us to think about how our lives will be fulfilled in service to the world. A million stories a day are shared about the suffering in the world. And a million stories a day are shared about those who have overcome incredible obstacles to move their lives forward. One soul at a time. Yours included!

My Spiritual Practice for Today

Today I want to begin thinking of my healing journey as an opportunity to be in solidarity with the suffering of the world. I want to take small steps in uniting my struggle with others around the world.

October 11

Humpty Dumpty (Pat)

> The nursery rhyme goes like this:
> *Humpty Dumpty sat on a wall,*
> *Humpty Dumpty had a great fall.*
> *All the king's horses and all the king's men*
> *Couldn't put Humpty together again.*

You are not Humpty Dumpty! Like Humpty, as a survivor of trauma or abuse, you have had a great fall. You may feel broken into pieces by your trauma.

However, you are not like Humpty Dumpty in any other way. You are not a fragile egg. You have strength and resilience beyond what you may realize. You are stronger than you know. You possess inner resources that will heal the cracks and weld all the pieces into a new wholeness. Your soul is at work within you to ensure this. You can access great inner resources such as meditation and prayer, mindfulness, courage, determination, creative imagination, faith, and many others. You also have the ability to reach out to external resources for your healing: counseling, spiritual guidance or mentoring, support groups, yoga and other physio-spiritual disciplines, and soul friends who will love you back to wholeness.

If you listen well, soul and Spirit will guide you in your healing quest. You will be led to create whatever mix of inner and outer resources that best fits your unique person and needs. There might be some scars left where the breaks occurred. However, you will be stronger than before at those broken places, just like a bone that is broken regrows stronger at the point of fracture.

You are not Humpty Dumpty. You have had a great and fracturing fall. And yet you *will* be put back together again, unbroken, whole, and stronger than ever. There was no hope for poor Humpty. There is every hope for you.

My Spiritual Practice for Today

Focus today on your strengths and resources for healing. What are your top three inner resources? What are your top three external resources? Pick one from each list and make a plan for how you will use that resource to further your healing today.

October 12

Who Am I without My Wounds? (Pat)

For some survivors in the healing journey, it can be challenging and even threatening when their trauma wounds are healing. You have become so identified with these wounds that it feels like an essential part of you is being lost, even though you are glad to see it go. You may even ask, "Who am I without my wounds?" For instance, if the fear that was engendered by your trauma has made you a chronic worrier, it may feel strange and even dangerous to let go of that part of you and learn to live in trust without worry. It feels like something is missing and that you have lost a key part of what makes you you. Or you are losing the part of you that has protected you. This can make it difficult to allow this part of you to be healed and transformed. If you remain without worry—or anger or some other wound—what will take its place? And what does it mean if it is now gone?

Your soul has the answer. Many people who have had a profound spiritual experience report that all of their anger and fear has been removed. They experience instead an abiding and indomitable peace that enables them to see themselves and the world in a different way. They move through their world with a new confidence and trust. They no longer need their anger. They see that their fears have mostly been an illusion. They find that their inner worrier has been calmed and is no longer necessary.

Whether or not you have experienced such a powerful revelation, your soul reminds you that it is safe and liberating to allow parts of you to be profoundly changed or even replaced. Your soul's truth is that your healed and transformed self is your True Self, and living from your True Self is the safest and most powerful way to be in the universe.

My Spiritual Practice for Today

Imagine today what your life would be like without the worry or anger part of you. What would your God and your soul give you to replace it? What would it be like to live wholly from this graced new self?

October 13

At Peace with the Questions (Vicki)

On a journey to India at age 24, amid my own personal "cloud of unknowing," I had too many unanswered questions and felt the need to step away. Actually, I felt desperate. In the midst of an abusive and secret relationship, I wanted to go as far away as possible. I thought by immersing myself into something selfless, I could find the answers to the questions stirring. It was a courageous first journey to another country. Upon landing in New Delhi, it seemed I had landed on another planet. Fearfully I found my way around this country alone, willing myself to see and experience all that makes India such an intriguing culture.

The kindness of strangers, who quickly became trusted friends, gave me hope and comfort. Each day I worked with Mother Teresa's Missionary of Charity Sisters, bathing and caring for the dying who were brought in from the streets, left to die like animals. We cared for orphans left at their doorsteps or found amid a pile of garbage. We changed the bandages of those living with leprosy. All of this brought me to my knees in gratitude for my own life and blessings.

A little boy named Dubuk suffering with tuberculosis of the bone stole my heart during our daily visits in a mission hospital where I stayed. Opportunities to go outside of ourselves to be present to others, when we ourselves are hurting, open new pathways to healing our own soul. We don't have to go to India to find this. We just have to have the courage to put ourselves aside to allow that healing portal to be opened. Once it is opened, it will seek its own experiences that will bring healing to your soul. "The most divine knowledge of God is that which is known by not knowing." (St. Denis) Being at peace with unanswered questions, that cloud of unknowing, is a place of deep growth and often the precursor to change.

My Spiritual Practice for Today

Finding a way to open your heart to others amid your own struggles is challenging. Today can you see the possibilities for this to be another way forward in healing your own pain?

October 14

You Can't Make Me! (Sue)

Remember this defiant statement from your own childhood, or perhaps from your own children? Unfortunately, it is not always true, as you experienced in your abuse. Someone else with enough power over you can force and manipulate you to do something you desperately do not want to do. This is especially true when you were a vulnerable child. It's still true to some extent for us as adults. Try telling your boss, "You can't make me."

However, there is one thing no one can ever make you do: change your inner emotions. No one can make you feel anything. You are in charge of your own emotions. You determine what your emotional response is. It may not feel like that sometimes, especially for trauma survivors, yet what is true is that you make your emotions yourself by your thoughts, perceptions, and beliefs. They're all yours and belong to no one else. You own them. You create them. And you can change them by changing how you perceive and think about any event. No one can make you feel anything unless you let them—and you don't ever have to let them.

Some wisdom from Facebook: "Inner peace begins the moment you choose not to allow another person or event to control your emotions." Inner peace and personal power. This will come when you realize you have the ability to stop anyone from making you feel anything you don't want to feel. Everyone has this ability, and it is our birthright as human beings. You get to choose.

You might have to grow and strengthen in this ability and consciously work to choose your emotional reactions. It will take some awareness and practice, but this work will yield great peace for you. Whether it's to your spouse, your partner, your friend, your enemy, your boss, or even surprisingly to God, you will be able to say or think with perfect confidence, "You can't make me" feel any different than I want.

My Spiritual Practice for Today

How often do you let other people determine your emotions? How does that feel? Now think of a time when you didn't let someone else change your feelings. Build on that feeling today to consciously be in charge of your emotions as you go through your day.

October 15

We Become What We Think (Pat)

Buddha said, "We are shaped by our thoughts; we become what we think. When the mind is pure, joy follows like a shadow that never leaves." Buddha discovered through his enlightenment 2,500 years ago what modern psychology has only recently realized: Our thoughts and perceptions of ourselves and our life do indeed create who we are in the world. It's possibly true that "We are what we eat," and it is certainly true that we are what we think.

Buddha's whole mission was to discover how to be free of suffering and how to free others. In his enlightenment it was revealed to him that most human suffering comes from your mind, especially those negative thoughts that you are attached to. His spiritual practices and teachings all strive to purify your mind of the thoughts that create your suffering and teach you to access a "pristine mind" that resides deep within your soul and is focused on this present moment. Then joy and peace enter, no matter what else is happening in your life.

Buddha's message is liberating for survivors. If you stay in the thought that you are a victim and define yourself by your trauma, you will be a victim. If you know you are not your trauma, you will transcend your trauma and lessen your suffering. It's as simple as that.

However, it usually is not so simple or easy to change your thoughts. As Buddha realized, we all become attached to our concepts and emotional beliefs, even if they cause great suffering. Also, some survivors were repeatedly told that you are a worthless piece of junk. These embedded beliefs are especially difficult to break free from. It helps to realize that thoughts are just that—thoughts. They are not reality, and particularly not deep spiritual reality. Your thoughts are not you. Your trauma is not you. Your True Self, who you really are, is so much more.

My Spiritual Practice for Today

During meditation today be aware of the thoughts that cause you suffering. When they enter into your mind, image them as ephemeral clouds just moving through your mind. Don't judge them or attach to them. Refocus on your centering breath or prayer, and calmly watch as the thought clouds blow by. Keep coming back to your peaceful center.

October 16

Spend to Pretend (Pat)

Money may not seem like a spiritual issue, and yet our relationship with money, how we use it, and what meaning we place on it are spiritual questions.

How does this relate to survivors of trauma? Some survivors develop an unhealthy relationship with their money in part caused by their trauma. For some there is a profound fear of scarcity. They believe that there is never enough, that the bottom is about to drop out. They are fearful of spending on themselves; they hoard money or material things. Others have a compulsion to spend and spend to pretend that everything is all right and that they feel much better about themselves than they actually do. For survivors—and many other people as well—money can be used to pretend that all is well even when it is not.

Money can be a spiritual good or asset depending on how you use it. It can be an expression of love, of empowering, of self-care. Studies show that it is never really a source of happiness. Having enough money to cover the basics and provide basic economic security can make you feel more secure and thereby contribute to happiness, but the research shows that any further money beyond that does not add to happiness at all. Happiness comes from inside, from a serene and loving heart, from rich relationships, from providing service and giving and receiving love, and from a serene and regular connection with your soul. Once you have this, you can discover for yourself how money fits in to express your heart and soul. You can't spend to pretend. You can spend to love and create.

My Spiritual Practice for Today

Reflect today on your relationship with money. How does the way you view and use money show what it means to you? Do you live in great fear of scarcity? Do you spend to pretend in some fashion? Does your use of money reflect your spiritual values?

October 17

Vulnerability Leads to Understanding (Vicki)

Every spiritual tradition points to weakness and vulnerability as the starting point of growing into understanding about ourselves. Clearly, the journey of healing I began brought me to my knees, literally. It was not until I could see the impact of the abuse I endured, the reality of what I suffered, that I began to see the possibilities of a different life. For so long, we hold onto the chaos we have become accustomed to living. We do not realize how unbalanced our lives are until a singular moment wakes us up to the reality of what we are living.

A friend's suggestion that I should seek a counselor was all it took for me to understand my problems were deeper than I imagined. Because I trusted that friend's opinion, I was able to make that first phone call to a therapist. Perhaps we can all look at the sequence of things that happened that allowed us to take that first step. Those are sacred moments that lead us to understanding.

Life becomes clear to us in retrospect, doesn't it? In the midst of suffering, most often we cannot see the larger picture, but weeks or months or perhaps years later, we can look back and see the significant growth that came from enduring the suffering. Once we know that growth and grace come out of suffering, we are more able to endure it with wisdom and acceptance. When my father was dying, I remember telling myself, "I know I can get through this." It's too bad that we only gain such wisdom from living through episodes of grief and sadness.

Paula D'Arcy once said that, "God comes to us disguised as our life." She also says, "This is it!" This moment, this day, no matter what we are going through, is it. Because life and suffering are inevitable, perhaps today it is just our turn.

My Spiritual Practice for Today

I will welcome moments of vulnerability as pathways to growth and understanding. I will choose to see vulnerable moments as gifts that open my soul to a deeper awareness of who I am.

October 18

We Are One (Vicki)

In one atom are found all the elements of the earth;
In one motion of the mind are found all the motions of existence;
In one drop of water are found all the secrets of the endless oceans;
In one aspect of you are found all the aspects of life.
–Kahlil Gibran

Discovering the science and spirituality of oneness has been an immeasurable gift. Walking through my own self-discovery, I came to understand that my story was the story of every other woman who was suffering. I came to believe in that oneness and global solidarity. In my work with Theresians International, I have spent time with women on every continent who have shared their own stories of abuse and trauma. So often they are without access to counseling services and have found in their communities of women a place to share their vulnerabilities and woundedness. They are embraced and held sacred by that group. I feel at one with my friends around the world who are working through their own issues as best they can.

I think of the many hurting people in the world: Refugees fleeing war-torn countries trying to find a better life. Those who perished when their boats capsized in the Mediterranean Sea. How do they find a way to heal their grief, their fear of being another casualty?

We are one; we are brought into this world by a benevolent God; we are made of stardust, and we return to the universe as stardust. Ashes to ashes, dust to dust. Can we think of ourselves as being part of this incredible universe created by God? Can we think of ourselves as brothers and sisters sharing a common humanity? Can we think of our pain as the universal pain of humanity? Can we open our hearts to accept this global solidarity with our brothers and sisters and know that we are one in our suffering and in our healing?

We can transform our personal struggle into something life giving that can make a difference in the world. Our every act of healing is a step toward healing the world.

My Spiritual Practice for Today

Today I will think of my own struggle in life as part of the global struggle of humanity. I will think of my healing journey as a way to bring healing to the world.

October 19

Words Can Kill (Pat & Sue)

Jesus said, "You have heard the commandment imposed on your forefathers, 'You shall not commit murder; every murderer shall be liable to judgment.' What I say to you is: 'Everyone who grows angry with his brother shall be liable to judgment; any man who uses abusive language toward his brother shall be answerable to the Sanhedrin, and if he holds him in contempt, he risks the fires of Gehenna.'"

You have heard the nursery rhyme, "Sticks and stones may break my bones, but words can never hurt me." Well, it's wrong. Words can kill. Sometimes literally, and most often they break and kill the victim's spirit. This has been called "soul murder." Abusive words have a way of worming into your brain and embedding themselves there. Like a nasty parasite, they grow and sicken you. They help to create the inner critical voice that can dominate your thinking and cripple your emotions. The abusive words gain great power over you. You feel that they must be true. Someone else's shaming words become your own destructive words to yourself. They may even feel like "God's truth" about you. This can lead you to believe that you are judged, condemned, and rejected by God.

Your soul implores you to reject the words of your abuse and emerge from their power. Examine the contents of your critical inner voice for the words that come from your abuser. You will see that these messages are abusive and they are lies. No word from your soul or your God is going to be critical or shaming. Challenging, sometimes, but never critical or judgmental. These abusive messages are not the voice of God or soul. They are not even your voice. It is the insidious voice of your abuser.

It's time to kick the abusive words and the abusive voice out of your brain. Time's up for the words that kill! Time's up for soul murderers!

My Spiritual Practice for Today

Make a list of the top 10 critical messages in your mind. Identify whose words they are. Then create an affirming statement from your soul or God's truth to counter these lies and write it opposite the critical words. Pick one affirming statement at a time and repeat it to yourself until it soaks in.

October 20

The Still Waters Within (Pat)

The Christian spiritual writer Beatrice Bruteau provides a beautiful image for a type of prayer derived from Hinduism. You can also use this prayer, from her book *Radical Optimism*, as a visual meditation in itself:

The Hindus say that if you look at your mind and emotions as if at the surface of a lake, you will see your agitation as rough waves. But if you continue just to look at them and notice that you who are looking are not the agitated waves, then gradually those waves will subside. They will damp down, smooth out, and after a while the surface of the lake will be calm. Once the water is calm, it also becomes transparent. Then you can look down through it, clear to the bottom. When our mind becomes clear and transparent, we can perceive what lies at its bottom, its foundation: It is the stillness of your soul, the peace of God, the divine eternity.

You can use this visual meditation in regard to any troubling thoughts about your abuse or trauma that cloud your mind. You can see any negative thoughts or your soul wounds themselves as the "agitated waves." However, you are not the waves. You are not your negative thoughts. You are not your soul wounds. The waves of your wounds—painful as they are—are just temporary agitations on the surface of your great depth of soul.

Visualize these waves gradually subsiding and a great calm settling over the water. See, then, into the depth of who you are and into the depths of God's presence within you to the divine peace and serenity that is available to you in any moment. Although this may be difficult at first, with practice you will be able to go to a place within yourself where the waters of your soul are always still and calm.

My Spiritual Practice for Today

Take some time to visualize this meditation, perhaps doing it twice today, in the morning and just before you go to sleep. Reflect on your experience of this meditation in your journal. You will find it helpful to return to this visual meditation at other times on your healing journey.

October 21

Defying Gravity (Sue)

My heart thrilled with awe and pride as I watched my granddaughter, Erin, dancing in her high school play, *The Wiz*. She was dancing in midair held up by a guide wire 20 feet above the stage. So fluid, graceful, and free that she looked like she was truly flying. She was defying gravity. It reminded me of another time at the beach when Erin spontaneously leapt high into the air, struck a dance pose at the peak of her leap, and seemed to hang there an impossibly long time. Defying gravity.

These memories of Erin's dancing are a powerful visual for me representing the power within us survivors to defy the strong gravitational pull of our trauma. Trauma can feel like the gravity of an immense black hole that pulls you down into depression and despair and will never let you out. Trauma can make you believe that you cannot break free of the downward force of shame and negativity.

Erin's dance also brought to mind the powerful song, "Defying Gravity" from *Wicked*. Elphaba sings: "It's time to try defying gravity. I think I'll try defying gravity. I'm defying gravity, and you can't pull me down...I'm through accepting limits 'cuz someone says they're so. Some things I cannot change, but 'til I try, I'll never know...I'm flying high, defying gravity."

You can learn to defy gravity in your own personal dance of life. The key is that in every moment, you have a choice to change your thoughts about your trauma and your life and your negative beliefs about yourself. You do not have to accept the burdens and limitations others—especially your abuser—have placed on you. It will take some time and work, but you can do it! With the help of your soul, you can learn to fly and be free of the gravitational pull of your trauma. As Elphaba sings as she soars above the stage, "Everyone deserves to fly!"

My Spiritual Practice for Today

Think of one negative thought or belief that weighs you down and keeps your spirit grounded. Create an affirmation that counters and transcends that thought. Close your eyes and imagine how you will fly free as you believe the affirmation more and more.

October 22

Healing Our Lives so We Can Give It Away (Vicki)

Some years ago while doing mission work in the north delta of Mississippi (a very poor area of the United States), a group of students and I had just finished putting a new roof on the home of a poor woman. We had spent three days working and sweating on this roof in mid-July, and we loved getting to know Miss Lizzy. Each day, with love, she would bring out ice-cold lemonade for us. She was grateful she would not have to strategically place buckets throughout her humble home to catch the water when it rained.

When we had finished, we carried our ladders and tools several blocks to another project. I remember walking down the middle of the street carrying a ladder and feeling the pure goodness of life. I was aware of everything around me. It brought tears to my eyes then and still does when I think about it. I was rejoicing in being alive and celebrating the gift of love and relationship. All was right with the world at that moment. And I rejoiced in the relationship I had developed with Miss Lizzy. I was aware at that moment of the richness of my life. I visit that time and place often in my mind, and it still brings tears of joy. It is among my most sacred memories of celebrating life and love. Understanding the fullness of life's simple joys and living in the now always reaps abundant, cherished memories.

This was several years after I had worked my way through therapy after being abused by a Catholic priest. There was pure joy in my heart that day. I knew who I was. I loved what I was doing. I felt the presence of the sacred all around me, from the birds singing to the newly roofed house that wouldn't leak to the heat of Mississippi in July. In that moment, I knew I was exactly where I was supposed to be, doing what I was supposed to do. If we don't transform our pain and trauma into something life giving, all we are left to do is transmit it to others.

My Spiritual Practice for the Day

Today I want to find something meaningful and life giving that allows me to give back to the world, simply because I am grateful for my healing journey. I am whole, and I can give my life away because I know who I am.

October 23

Other-Phobia Leads to Other-Cide (Pat)

Other-phobia is the tendency of individuals or groups to fear and then criticize, ostracize, negate, abuse, and see as inferior any individual or group who appears to be different or other than them. This leads to various forms of "killing" the other verbally, socially, emotionally, sexually, spiritually, even physically—their otherness and supposed inferiority being the justification.

Other-phobia and other-cide demean such differences as appearance; racial, ethnic, or other backgrounds; gender; sexual orientation; religion; class; financial status; and social status. This leads the other-phobic person to objectify and dehumanize whoever is considered other and therefore unworthy of equal care and love. This has been called soul murder. It is the underlying source and justification of abuse and even terrorism.

Other-phobia is based in hidden feelings of low self-esteem and shame, which is paradoxically manifested in believing one's self or group to be superior and entitled above whoever is considered to be other and inferior. This leads to a compulsion to define one's self or one's group as against anyone different from you and your group.

Even survivors can fall into this trap. You have been the victim of other-cide, the victim of soul murder by your abuser. You have been objectified and dehumanized. Yet your own fear, shame, and anger can lead you to judge, marginalize, negate, or reject individuals or groups in your world. The abused can become the abuser, which is what drives the circle of abuse.

My Spiritual Practice for Today

Think about those who are "other" in your life, who are different than you or your group, especially those you tend to judge. Look for what you have in common with them. Reflect on the shared humanity and the essential oneness of us all. Imagine being them. Walk for a time in their shoes. Engender empathy for them. With spiritual 20/20 vision, see the gift and value of otherness and the divine glory of diversity of all creation. See each as a unique, valued, and indispensable manifestation of the divine, just as you are.

October 24

A Long, Loving Look at What is Real (Vicki)

Nancy Sylvester, IHM, coined the title of this reflection in her work with the Institute for Communal and Contemplative Dialogue (ICCD.org). When we engage the impasses in life, we take a long, loving look at what is real. We're being honest with ourselves. Honesty is the key to moving forward from any event that causes us to feel stuck. How did things happen? How do I piece together this puzzle to make sense of it?

I didn't understand how to do this when I entered my years of counseling. I took it one day at a time. That's why it took me a year to admit that I was being abused by a Catholic priest. I didn't even trust my counselor. And I couldn't speak the words; I had to write it in a letter so I wasn't there to see her expression. She expected this; she was just waiting for me to have the courage to speak it. A long, loving look at what is real takes tremendous courage. Once I opened the vault that held this secret, I began to feel more authentic. The more authentic I felt, the more real and healthy I felt. It became the guiding light for me.

When I was 24, I felt compelled to travel to Kolkata to work with Mother Teresa and her religious sisters. I was so taken by Mother's desire to pick up just that one who was dying on the street. She knew she couldn't save them all; there were just too many forgotten human beings to rescue. It was always just that one whom she could take home and provide a dignified way for them to die or to recover and continue life.

The abuse was ongoing at home, and I felt that if I could just get away from it for a time, I could discover how to stop it. Mother Teresa taught me how important it was to integrate faith and action. Now I had to return home and bring this understanding into my life. I had to find a way to pry myself away from the abuse. The seed planted during that time in Kolkata was the initial seed that would give me the courage to find help.

My Spiritual Practice for Today

To have the courage to take a long, loving look at what is real is what I want. I want to be real and not continue feeling numbed by my secrets.

October 25

Now (Pat & Sue)

We often employ the metaphor of a journey, a spiritual pilgrimage, to describe the spiritual healing process. It is a powerful image. Healing is a journey. Life itself is a pilgrimage of soul. Yet this metaphor has limitations. It implies that there is a journey's end, a destination, and that once you are there, when your healing is finished, you have arrived and need to travel no more. The imagery of journey also tends to focus awareness on a past that you have come from and a future you are heading toward. This can distract you from the spiritual power of simply being mindful in each sacred moment of your life.

In fact, the journey of spiritual healing and transformation has no end. You will never cease to travel its roads and its pathways. The destination is an ever deepening dance and union with your soul and with God. There is no past or future on this trip. Every journey of the soul, every life, is a series of nows strung together like a string of "pearls of great price," one sacred, precious, eternal moment after another.

The challenge is being fully alive and fully present to each moment of your life and to the blessings of that moment. This is the actual destination of your journey. Yet it is not a destination at all. It is a movement, a dance with your soul and with God. It is a dance ever unfolding from one eternal now to the next. You have not arrived. You never can arrive. You are ever arriving and dancing in this moment now.

My Spiritual Practice for Today

Be mindful today of the pearl you are given in each moment. When your mind wants to obsess about the past or worry about the future, bring it back to the present. Focus your attention on the blessing of that moment: the color or smell of a flower, the smile of a child, the light on a tree, the love you feel for someone special in your life, or even simply your breath flowing in and out. Then dance inside with the joy of your soul. Stop several times today, breathe, and be alive to the now.

October 26

The Sacred Healing Power of Nature (Pat)

Nature can be an extraordinary place of healing and sacred experiences for survivors. It certainly has been for me. Sometimes my nature experiences have been solitary times of reverie, and sometimes they have been shared with Sue in moments of soul-bonding creation awe together. Some of these experiences have involved a felt sense of the presence of Spirit in creation, divine energy, and grace immanent in the beauty of a natural setting. Other times, nature has been a sacramental sign revealing some meaning that I had been seeking or that I unexpectedly received.

A few examples of these nature/Spirit moments: Sue and I being swept up together in mutual awe beneath a huge, brilliant double rainbow in the desert of Utah; the soul fire that kindled within me, and lifted me someplace far beyond myself, while sitting around steaming hot rocks in a sweat lodge on a frigid winter night; meditating on a rock beside a mountain stream, becoming one for a time with its energy and purity; hiking through the woods without a single care on a warm spring day at a monastery in Missouri, completely caught up in the burgeoning life around me, oblivious to the life decisions and worries that I had come to resolve—this peace being the answer I was seeking.

Many of these sacred, healing experiences have happened in spectacular natural settings. However, nature also catches me by surprise in the ordinary natural settings of everyday life. I call these backyard epiphanies. Many of these unexpected spiritual episodes literally happen in the back yard of our house. They come when I am mindful of a plant, a flower, a tree, or a certain intensity of light gleaming on these. I am then temporarily without thought, carried away, lost in the moment. Dramatic natural settings have drawn me into great mountaintop spiritual experiences, but I have learned that all that is required is natural beauty, small or large, solitude, silence, and an openness to be in the present and to see what nature puts before me.

My Spiritual Practice for Today

How does nature speak to you? How is it healing for you? Spend some time outdoors today focusing on the beauty that surrounds you. Be present and mindful, and let nature bring her healing to you.

October 27

Resting in the Inexplicable Future (Vicki)

Why do you stay in prison, when the door is wide open?
–Rumi

It may seem like this healing journey is taking a lifetime. I refer to my years of counseling as the hardcore time of transformation. The time after is when I began to rest in what the future held. We get trapped in the seemingly inescapable time of seeking answers to questions, asking why, and lamenting about never being able to move forward.

The Middle Eastern Sufi master Rumi says, "Let yourself be silently drawn by the strange pull of what you really love. It will not lead you astray." The divine Spirit of every faith tradition is constantly luring us forward, just as the black holes of the universe continue to expand ever deeper into this expansive universe. I like to think of this as my understanding of God calling me forward, always inviting me to expand my thinking and awareness of the love that awaits and is around me. We simply have to say yes. I often think of a lover calling me to draw nearer, to be close, to be known, to be open to receiving an embrace. This is the allure of God's life and energy. Love is the ultimate allure of God, and we are constantly being called to know it.

Paula D'Arcy's thought that God comes to you disguised as your life fits beautifully. Everything around us is exactly what it is supposed to be. It is up to us to find the significance. Only today can I look at my experience and say with confidence, I learned a tremendous lesson about life from my abuser. He taught me inexplicable lessons I might not have learned from any other teacher. Today I can say I am grateful. I wish today that he were alive so I could tell him what I learned. This kind of forgiveness, which has entailed years of struggle, is the most liberating experience of love. It is the closest we draw to the Great Spirit within us. It was love luring me to itself throughout all these years.

My Spiritual Practice for Today

Today I will trust that everything I am experiencing in my healing journey is God luring me to draw near so I can experience universal love. I will not remain imprisoned with my secrets.

October 28

On the Death of a Survivor (Sue)

Catherine was one of my most memorable clients. She endured one of the worse cases of childhood trauma I had ever experienced, suffering horrible abuse from the age of 2 well into her adulthood. She lived with a wounded body, a tortured mind, and a trampled soul.

And yet she was caring, kind, gentle, fun, and musical. She became a Catholic sister who loved children and loved to sing to them, accompanying herself on guitar at the preschool she ran and taught in. She was loved by the children because of her gentleness and childlike spirit. The wounded little girl within her could become one with the little children as she sang and played with them. She worked hard to help all the children to believe in themselves, to feel their worth, value, and giftedness. That was her own greatest struggle, to believe and feel this about herself. She wanted each child in her care to know God's love for them, each child cherished by God.

As I ponder Catherine's death and celebrate her life, I am filled with both sadness and awe. Sad because she often could not see and feel the great truth of who she was, despite the trauma of abuse; awe and joy because Catherine was able to transform her struggle and pain into something life giving for her children. I honor Catherine's life and the gift she was to so many children. How blessed they were to have experienced her teaching. I strongly believe they are better human beings because of Catherine in their young lives.

Celebrate Sr. Catherine with me and reflect on your own recovery journey. How fully have you been able to believe in your own magnificence and ultimate value in God? How have you transformed your own pain into something life giving and transformational for others? What have you passed on about what you have learned, especially to the generations behind you?

My Spiritual Practice for Today

Listen to your soul speak to you today about the call to transform your suffering into something healing and liberating for others. As Catherine did, give the gift you have been given. Pay it forward, up and down, and all around you.

October 29

Can We Imagine a Different Life for Ourselves? (Vicki)

*Each person is always on the threshold between their inner world
and their outer world, between light and darkness, between known
and unknown, between question and quest, between fact and
possibility. This threshold runs through every experience that we
have, and our only real guide to this world is the imagination.*
–John O'Donohue, *Anam Cara*

The survivor's soul calls for deep reflection on the damage that has been caused from abuse and trauma. To bring our lives toward a healthy balance, it is vital to take stock of what happened, why it happened, and how you can move forward from being a victim to being a survivor. As Donohue writes, we all live the tension of being at the threshold of inner and outer reality. How we create a healthy balance of the inner and outer leads us toward the soul of a survivor.

It felt like I was living a lie. My inner emotions were tangled up with a million questions of why and how. How will I ever get to the other side of this chaos? Yes, my outer world appeared that all was well. I made sure no one knew about the abuse I experienced, not even my closest friends. My favorite aunt sent me a quilted message once that said, "Remain calm and unruffled on the surface, but paddle like the devil underneath." I was proud to say at times that this was my mantra. Yet it allowed me to hide the deepest pain I had ever experienced. In the end I knew it was not authentically me. The tension between the inward and outward was destructive; it kept me trapped in a cycle of inner chaos.

Speaking my truth, finally, allowed me to begin the process of healing. The gift of a good therapist is to point us toward possibilities that can lead us toward healing. The work is ours to do. No one can do it for us

My Spiritual Practice for Today

My deepest longing is to move from victim to survivor. Today I know that I can take another step toward understanding my experience more clearly and trust that it was not my fault. Today I want my inner and outer reality to be more complementary rather than contentious.

October 30

The Purpose-Driven Survivor (Pat)

Hopefully, in your healing journey you have experienced significant healing and freedom from the effects of your abuse. What is this healing and freedom for? What is the larger purpose of your healing path? It is no doubt meant to be a gift for you to live more abundantly and freely.

However, your soul seeks to bring forth an even higher purpose for you. Your soul has been working in you to transubstantiate the oppression and darkness of your abuse into something life and light giving. This is for your own sake, yet not for your sake alone. It is also for the healing and enlightenment of all those in your world. Your soul then is creating, and inviting you to discover, a new and transcendent purpose for living as a healing survivor.

Another way to say this is that a spiritual call is embedded in the heart of your healing journey. A call is an invitation, a passion, a choice, and a commitment all rolled into one. This call from your soul invites you to discover a new purpose for your life, which will use your new spiritual gifts for service or ministry to others. Many spiritual traditions teach that we are made for a life mission and purpose unique to each of us. The call is our experience of hearing that mission deep within us and reordering our lives to serve that mission.

All spiritual calls are shaped in some way by our life experiences. Your call, as a survivor, arises in part from your traumatic experience. Amazingly, your wounds can become gifts of healing for others who will be sent into your life. The size or scope of your mission does not matter. All of it is significant. Your soul and your God want to play you and your life—even your experience of trauma or abuse—like a flute or a harp to bring beautiful and healing music to the world. This is the mission of a purpose-driven survivor.

My Spiritual Practice for Today

What is your call? What is the larger purpose of your healing? What might your mission be? Listen to your soul in meditation, and you will hear.

October 31

Halloween (Pat and Sue)

The original name for Halloween was All Hallows Eve, or the evening before All Saints Day. All Saints Day is a Christian celebration of the unnamed and unsung saints in history who do not receive official sainthood. It recognizes that there are many saints all around us, people in our lives and in our communities who courageously—not perfectly—live their spirituality to the fullest.

This original meaning of Halloween has been mostly lost in the secular, nonspiritual way that we celebrate this feast today. It is still a wonderful celebration of fantasy and fun for children—not to mention the opportunity to snag lots of candy. It has also become a commercialized excuse for another party, a party that is strangely focused on the ghoulish, the bloody, and the demented.

Perhaps in one sense it is good to face your ghosts, goblins, and demons and dress them up and make them look exaggerated or ridiculous. This can help you master your darkest fears and so can be healthy for survivors. You can look the dark and scary straight in the eye and know that you and your soul are more powerful than any of your darkness.

However, returning to some of the original meaning and spirit of All Hallows Eve is of the most spiritual benefit for you today. You can focus on the saints in your life who have been your soul friends in your healing journey. You can look for spiritual heroes in your community or in the media.

It is just as important that you realize that you have sainthood within you as well. Remember "God dwells within you as you." You are a sacred vessel of divinity. All of us are saints in training. All of us are saints in some way. You are a saint simply for having the courage to survive your trauma and for working so hard to transcend and transform your suffering. Enjoy your saint day.

My Spiritual Practice for Today

Reflect on the saints in your life and express a prayer of gratitude for each of them. Also meditate on the sanctity that is within you.

November 1

The Mountain Meditation: You (Sue & Pat)

My Spiritual Practice for Today

We invite you to do the Mountain Meditation again. This time the theme is you. Bring to the mountain anything you have learned in the last month, any questions you have, or any need for healing that you are experiencing. Let your soul and the Spirit guide you. To enter into this meditation, find a comfortable sitting position. As you read, pause, close your eyes, and imagine the scenes described.

Picture yourself on a beautiful beach. See the waves, the sand, the brilliant color, and the vastness of the ocean. Feel the sun and the wind on your skin. Hear the crash and whoosh of the surf. Turn around now, and face away from the sea. This time pack your backpack with any questions, lessons, or needs you have experienced in the last month. Notice how it feels to carry this.

In front of you is a beautiful forest. See yourself walking along a trail into the forest. Appreciate the coolness and the shaded light. You reach the edge of the forest and see an open meadow filled with multicolored wildflowers. The trail leads you through the meadow to a clear, flowing stream with a bridge across the dancing water. Stop for a moment to enjoy the light sparkling on the water.

Now look up from the bridge and see a shining mountain before you. Following the trail, you ascend the mountain. You climb through the clouds, above the timberline through the clouds to the top of the peak. Look around you at the glory of creation. Then you notice a large boulder to sit on and rest.

From the other side of the peak, your spiritual guide comes and sits down with you on the boulder. You can discuss whatever you want. Unpack your backpack and lay its contents out before your spirit guide. Listen for what is said to you about what you have brought. If you receive anything, embrace it and put it in your backpack to bring it down the mountain to the outside world.

When you are ready to leave, thank your Higher Power. Slowly hike back down the mountain, over the bridge, through the meadow, through the forest, to the beach, and to the edge of the vast ocean. Open your eyes. Record and reflect in your journal.

November 2

This Is Your Life! This Is It! (Vicki)

Like the moon
come out from behind
the clouds, and Shine!
–Buddha

I once heard a phrase that referred to personal struggle as an unwanted grace. Today I can look at my experience of abuse as an unwanted grace. It is both/and. The abusive relationship was, of course, unwanted. However, when I look at the grace that has come into my life as a result of that experience, I am humbled. Never in a hundred years could I have imagined what has come in to my life because of the course of healing it pointed me toward. It makes no sense to wonder what my life would have been if it had not happened. We live the life that is given to us.

Richard Rohr's teaching of non-dualistic thinking challenges us to move into a contemplative way of thinking and living, a practice that encourages us to stop being the judge and jury of every situation and person. It is a way of looking at the world as both/and. My abuser both used and manipulated me, and he taught me many things. He was both a visionary and a compassionate man, and he had serious abusive tendencies. It was only after several years of counseling that I could begin to see his failures as well as his goodness. He inspired a missionary heart in me at an early age, which led me to seek out Mother Teresa. He gave me professional opportunities in leadership that I would not have found at such an early age.

We can wish that we could learn life's lessons along an easier path that doesn't carry such trauma. Life doesn't work that way. Life happens to all of us in myriad ways, and we have a choice to try to understand why it happened and find a way to work through it. Paula D'Arcy, a marvelous spiritual writer and friend, has a wonderful saying: "This is your life, this is the life you have been given, this is it!"

My Spiritual Practice for Today

Look at your experience of abuse or trauma and then reflect on what you have learned about yourself in the midst of your healing process. What are the both/and aspects of your story? Can you find parallels?

November 3

The Preciousness of Every Life (Sue)

For many months a mother is bonding and anticipating the birth of her baby. Talking to the baby. Feeling the baby swim from side to side as she places her hands on her tummy. How thrilling it is! Deep connections are being made. Dreams of a new life and all the surprises and joys to come.

Billy, my second full-term baby who lived 90 minutes, was a real trooper. He was born on a very cold Arkansas Thanksgiving morning in an antique Army ambulance, 40 minutes from the hospital. It was like he wanted to be born in a hurry. There was no stopping his coming. He was determined to experience a wee bit of life on this side. He was beautiful and amazing, despite his condition (his organs were visible through his thin, translucent skin; he was jaundiced yellow and blue at the same time). Such a cutie! His swift arrival in that ambulance allowed time for an even deeper connection with him. Time to hold and cuddle him before the angels came for him. For this I am grateful.

In a moment life is snuffed out. In the blink of an eye life totally changes. Dreams are dashed. Grief sets in. "Well-meaners" try to reassure: There'll be a next time; you didn't know this child; you are so blessed to have the family you have now. Some people acted as if Billy had never lived and died, and subtlety implied I should act that way too.

Bottom line, your baby has died. Your loss is great, and the sorrow is deep, and the pain is real. The pain of loss requires time to weep, to feel, to be angry, to want to be alone or share your grief with a soul friend.

Words are not needed at times. Gentleness, patience, love of self, love of who or what you have lost, this is what is required. Length of time does not define a relationship; intimacy does. I was deeply bonded to Billy, and I still am. Length of life and life events do not define life's value. Billy and his brief life will always be so precious to me.

My Spiritual Practice for Today

Who or what have you lost that is precious to you? How can you honor that preciousness in your sacred grief?

November 4

Into a Great Blossoming (Vicki)

All of us have icons of courage we have identified in our lives. Perhaps we carry images of those heroic people in our heart to help inform our own lives. It is easy to look outside of ourselves and acknowledge the heroic actions of others. It is much more difficult to see the small courageous steps that we take. Often we don't realize the struggles they endured in their own lifetime.

Mother Teresa of Calcutta was that courageous figure for me. The example of her life, her commitment to saving just that one who was dying on the streets of Calcutta, was archetypal for me. And I came to understand that I was one who needed to be saved too. Perhaps that's why I went to India all those years ago, to be rescued.

The poet Rumi reminds us: "I will soothe you and heal you, I will bring you roses, I too have been covered with thorns." My journey to India didn't rescue me immediately, but it was a life-changing experience that allowed me to see the world with new eyes. Sometimes we have to let ourselves be drawn by what we really love. It can lead us to new discoveries about ourselves that lead to new possibilities for healing.

My Spiritual Practice for Today

Today I will reflect on those who are walking with me in my journey to healing, and I will be grateful for their loving presence in my life.

November 5

Your Default Emotion (Pat)

Survivors tend to have what is called a default emotion or mood. This is a core emotion that you often fall back to, particularly when you are stressed and even when your life events are quite positive.

The three core default emotions are sadness, anger, and fear, or an alternating combination of the three. These are feeling states that your trauma has created in you and that your mind will pull you back into no matter what is happening. For instance, the joy that you feel at the birth of your child or grandchild may be tinged with a deep sadness lingering from your own childhood. Or when your spouse or partner beautifully expresses love for you, you find it difficult to receive it and rejoice in it because of the anger you feel about being denied love in the past. Or you are burdened by chronic worry and fear even though your life is now safe and secure. These feeling states linger below the surface of your usual awareness and lurk in the background of every life scene, darkening your mood and muting the joy and happiness you seek.

Your soul ardently desires to free you from these negative emotional states. Your soul can help you click into the Settings section of your brain and reset the default emotions from sadness to joy, from anger to acceptance, from fear to trust and peace. Wouldn't it be marvelous if your first response to various life situations would be joy and gratefulness, acceptance and serenity, peace and ultimate security? Unfortunately, unlike our smartphones and computers, it is not so easy and quick to change these default settings.

Led by your soul, you can change them if you devote enough focus and time to this healing process. It requires that you notice the default emotion when it arises and then ask yourself what emotional response your soul desires for you. Over time the defaults will be reset, and these core emotions will increasingly be lifted away.

My Spiritual Practice for Today

Your task today is to identify your primary default emotion, reflect on it, and see if it actually connects with the present. Then ask what feeling response your soul invites you to instead, and choose to embrace and feel it.

November 6

Untether Yourself from the World (Vicki)

There should be at least a room, or some corner where no one
will find you and disturb you or notice you. You should be able to
untether yourself from the world and set yourself free, loosening
all the fine strings and strands of tension that bind you,
by sight, by sound, by thought, to the presence of others.
–Thomas Merton, *Seeds of Contemplation*

Sometimes it may seem counterproductive to isolate ourselves from people. Yet we know how important it is to find time for silence, the kind of silence that envelops you into nothingness. I like the word "untether" that Merton uses. We have to take that step to untether ourselves from all that keeps us from entering into silence. The healing process relies on your ability to create that healing quiet for yourself. Imagine visiting your therapist every two weeks and then going about your busy life as if you have nothing to reflect on. It seems contrary to the calling of the deep that was elicited from your time in counseling. This is the work of our lives. To ignore deep calling on deep is to stymie your healing process.

Over the course of my years in counseling, I would take a few days here and there to get away, and I would be in relative silence. I would always have some music with me in case I couldn't handle the silence, but it was always quiet, reflective music. What I have found, though, is that the more time I have given to silence, the more easily I can immerse myself into it. Once I made the commitment to do an eight-day silent retreat. When I arrived with my luggage and a large bag of books to read, Sr. Macrina Wiedekehr, OSB, who was to be my spiritual director, greeted me at the door and said, "Oh, I see you've brought your bag of longing!" It took me two days to get over myself and truly enter into the silence. At the end of the eight days, I didn't want to leave.

Let's loosen all the fine strings and strands that keep us tethered to meaningless busyness and be in touch with who we really are and with those who surround us.

My Spiritual Practice for Today

Today I will begin to create a space where I can sit in silence.

November 7

My Brave Little Chickadee (Pat)

Just now, as I was sitting at our kitchen table writing a meditation, I saw out of the corner of my eye all the birds at our feeder frantically flying away in a panic. I stood up to scan our little woods to look for the cause of the panic. Ah! There he is, a large, beautiful tan-and-white bird hawk perched in a tree above the feeder. Then I spotted two chickadees perched nearby on the bare inner branches of a lilac bush. These tiny birds were the only ones who didn't flee. Chickadees are charming little creatures with a black-and-white face, a white-and-tan breast, and a jaunty little black cap on their head. Very cute little birds, and yet very bold and courageous.

The hawk flew from perch to perch trying to get an angle on them. The chickadees continued to twitter as if nothing was wrong and almost seemed to tempt him to try to catch them. The hawk finally gave up and flew away. The two chickadees flew back to the feeder—the first to do so—and resumed their breakfast. I have seen this before. They are the only birds that will stay at the feeder while I fill it. They are the first to come back even when I stand nearby to watch them. They seem to have little or no fear despite their size.

My brave little chickadees remind me that no matter how small you are, physically or socially, no matter how small you feel, you can learn to be courageous and bold. Size does not matter. Heart, soul, and spirit do matter, and they are the source of your courage.

I think we all have a chickadee soul. Your soul may seem small and faint at times. The divine spark may look like only a tiny pilot light. The birds of prey in your life might look awfully large and powerful. Yet your soul is powerful and courageous, and when you tap into it, you become a brave little chickadee as well. You can stand against the bird hawks around you and continue to courageously sing your song.

My Spiritual Practice for Today

How has your trauma made you feel small? What is one thing you can do today to enlarge your spirit and discover your courage?

November 8

Yes, But (Sue)

But, along with *should,* is one of the most negative and dangerous words in the English language. *But* always negates the positive meaning of the previous statement. If you are saying or thinking a positive *yes* statement and you follow it with a big *but,* you have negated and blocked the positive energy and power of your *yes.* For instance, if you say to yourself, "I am a gifted and talented person, *but* I have many made many mistakes in my life," you have cancelled your positive affirmation and any good feeling that was coming from it. Say that sentence to yourself and notice how you feel. *But* is a small, short word and yet a powerfully limiting and even destructive word. It infiltrates many people's speech and thought processes. It de-energizes any positive statement you say or think about yourself and your life.

Making *yes, and* statements or thoughts builds positivity and allows you to be *both* affirming a*nd* truthful about yourself. Say to yourself, "Yes, I am talented and gifted, *and* I have made many mistakes in my life." Can you feel the difference? The *and* affirms both statements, allowing you to feel good about yourself and acknowledge something that you struggle with. *And* is affirming and liberating. *But* is negating and pulls you down.

So the healing challenge is for you to eliminate *but* from your vocabulary, even from your thoughts, and consciously substitute it with the empowering word *and.* Over time you will notice the difference. It might be subtle, or it might be very strong. In time you will feel more positive about yourself and your life, you will possess more energy and motivation, and you will be less burdened by your human imperfections and weaknesses.

My Spiritual Practice for Today

Notice how often you say or think *yes, but* throughout the day. Become aware of what this does to you. Consciously substitute the *but* with *and,* and make it a *yes, and* statement. Notice what you feel after the change.

November 10

A Time of Complexity (Vicki)

The silence and emptiness of contemplative stillness spring
from an intentional opening to Holy Mystery, an active
attentiveness to deeper inner movements and other levels of
perception. Darkness is then perceived as transformative.
–Pat Farley, OSF, *Transformational Leadership*

We are living in a time of great complexity. At times it seems as if war is being raged all around us. Often we feel helpless to create the kind of change that alleviates the suffering we see daily in the news. Whether it is Iraq, Afghanistan, Syria, or North Africa or even in our own hearts. What happens to us when we are suffering our own pain in the midst of so much global suffering around us? I've always thought that my suffering was not the same kind of suffering—perhaps less than others who have been uprooted from their homes, fleeing for their lives. The complexities can be mind-boggling.

However, pain is pain. We simply cannot compare what we are going through with anyone else. In order to heal our darkness, we must remain focused on our personal journey while at the same time remaining aware of what is going on around us. Often we can take courage from the suffering of others. How they respond can be a light for us to continue walking through life's difficulties. We can walk in solidarity with the human family.

Every spiritual teacher of every tradition would tell us that silence and contemplation can be the doorway to uncovering our own darkness. Bringing light into the darkness of our unresolved issues is the key to healing and moving forward. It takes time and discipline to build a life around the practice of silent meditation. This silence coupled with psychotherapy can be the key to unlocking your pain, releasing it, and allowing you to live the full life you deserve. It can be what allows you to be present and helpful in a hurting world. And when your true passion in life is uncovered, your possibilities are endless.

My Spiritual Practice for Today

Today I will begin to learn about meditation and consider making it a daily discipline. With intention, I will work toward integrating my counseling work with meditation to more easily bring forth the light of my soul.

November 11

Affirmation Sandwiches (Pat & Sue)

Affirmation sandwiches are tasty and nutritious little communication meals for yourself and your loved ones. They are like relationship tapas. Words have power, and good communication is essential for healthy relationships. An affirmation sandwich is an effective and positive tool for expressing love and positive feelings, even when you need to express a concern, a challenge, a request, or a need.

Putting together an affirmation sandwich goes something like this. Let's say that you felt hurt by something your spouse or friend said. The first slice of bread is an affirmation: "I love you, and..." Then you put in the meat and cheese of your feeling or concern: "I felt hurt when I heard you say_____" Over that you place the second piece of affirmation bread: "And I love you." (Or "I feel so loved when you are gentle with me.") You can fit any content into this recipe. It makes your concern much easier for the other to hear. It creates a space of emotional safety and positivity for both of you.

You can feed yourself affirmation sandwiches as well. When you have a critique of yourself, put it between two pieces of self-affirmation before you swallow it. For instance, "I am a loving and kind person, and yesterday I really hurt my best friend, and I am a good friend and I love myself." Try this and feel the difference from just slamming yourself for what you did.

It is crucial that affirmation sandwiches only be used, whether with yourself or someone else, with sincerity and positive intention. Don't use it to sneak in a harsh zinger under the cover of nice-sounding words. Start making affirmation sandwiches today, and see how they feed your heart and soul, and the heart and soul of your relationships.

My Spiritual Practice for Today

Cook up two affirmation sandwiches today: one for someone special in your life; one for you. See how they feel. Observe how they turn out. Be patient with yourself. This is gourmet communication and takes time and practice to perfect it.

November 12

To Walk a Mile with Sorrow (Vicki)

I walked a mile with Pleasure
She chattered all the way;
But left me none the wiser
For all she had to say.

I walked a mile with Sorrow
And ne'er a word said she;
But oh, the things I learned from her
When Sorrow walked with me.
–Robert Browning Hamilton

Walking through a process of healing the soul from deep inner pain can be enough to derail any person. I've heard stories of horrific abuse overcome by courageous men and women. It is possible to overcome. It is possible to prevail. It is possible to create a new life that is richer because of the sorrow that has been healed.

No one can convince you of that in advance of your healing journey. You find out by taking the baby steps toward healing. Hopefully by reading and listening to the struggles and sorrow of others and how they have overcome their pain, you will be able to do it too. Let their courage steel you as you embrace your own journey.

I've written often about silence in these reflections. My experiences of profound silence have brought insight, understanding, and acceptance. The five pathways to healing the spirit, which are key, have been my constant companions and framework on this journey. Telling my story, facing the anger, feeling the grief, forging a path toward forgiveness, and embracing transformation continue to be my path for living as a survivor of abuse. "Oh the things I leaned from her, when sorrow walked with me."

I was aware of the slow opening of my heart through each pathway. The pathways aren't sequential. After all these years, I still struggle to tell my story publicly. Grief continues to rise up and close my heart. As the patriarchy of the Church continues to fumble the sex abuse crisis, anger sometimes consumes me. I call myself back to the deeper understanding of forgiveness, and I'm reminded that my transformation continues day by day. The five pathways we have coined in our book, *Shattered Soul,* continue to be a life-giving resource to many, and I'm grateful.

My Spiritual Practice for Today

Today I will consider the five pathways to healing as a framework for my healing journey, and I will think of quiet places that will heal my sorrow.

November 13

Star Stuff, God Stuff (Pat)

Did you know that you are literally made of stardust? It's true. All the ingredients that make up your body were originally formed in the great, creative fires of the stars over billions of years. This star stuff was created and floated around in space for billenniums, and then uniquely coalesced one fine day into you. You are the only person who came together in quite the same way in the whole universe. In the entire enormity of cosmological time, you are the only one who became you. When your stardust was mixed together in the unique formula that is you, when you were complete, the recipe was thrown away! When the shame from your trauma is trying to make you feel small, worthless, and defective, remember what you are made of.

Remember too that you are also made of God stuff. Your soul, which breathes life into you, is your God stuff. This personal divine energy permeates you with the fire, light, and wisdom of Spirit. It is the divine spark that illuminates and kindles every aspect of your being. It is that which is transcendent within you and is named many things in different spiritual traditions: your divine inner spark, your Christ or your Buddha nature, your inner essence, the life breath or force that animates you, the energy of the universe, your True Self. Your soul is the indwelling of the divine within you.

If you are star stuff and you are God stuff, how can you believe you are bad stuff, no matter what was done to you, no matter what mistakes you may have made? Your divine spark, the inner light of your soul, cannot be extinguished, or even dimmed, by anyone or anything. So when your trauma shame is pulling you down and trying to make you feel unworthy, remember what you are made of and who you are. You are star stuff. You are God stuff.

My Spiritual Practice for Today

Tonight look at all the parts of your body and marvel at its amazing construction. Go outside and look up at the stars. Realize your body is made of stuff from these stars. Then close your eyes and image a warm, brilliant white light at your center. This is your God stuff, your soul. Consider what it means that this is who you are.

November 14

Your Tears Are A Blessing (Sue)

You probably do not usually think of grief and sorrow as a blessing. These emotional states are painful, and we normally attempt to avoid and anesthetize their pain at all costs. Yet there are indeed blessings hidden in the sorrow of grief.

Tears are holy water. They bless and cleanse the eyes of your soul and allow you to see the losses from your abuse or trauma in new and more spiritual ways. This is why allowing yourself to descend for a time into the sadness and suffering of grief and mourning is a necessary, although painful pathway to healing your spirit, broken and wounded by abuse or trauma.

Sacred grief quiets your spirit, and pulls you inward for a time so you can own and feel what you have lost. It allows you to sort out in your soul what these losses mean, renew and reorient your shaken and broken spirit, and eventually re-energize yourself to reinvest in your life in a new and more deeply soul-directed way.

Grief is your soul's way of calling you inward to a personal spiritual retreat. This is a time to slow down and reflect, to mourn, and yet also begin to see new possibilities for your life. Your soul will guide you. How will you respond to her call?

My Spiritual Practice for Today

Write your own "broken-heart prayer" expressing your sorrow, sadness, and grief about your abuse. Name the losses you have experienced because of your trauma, what was taken from you, or what did not happen because of what was done to you. Address your prayer to God or your soul, and in some small ritual, lay it before your God as if on an altar. Give yourself time and space to feel and mourn your losses. You are worth it.

November 15

A Place of Vulnerability (Vicki)

Love is a place of vulnerability. Yet we were created to love one another. Many obstacles interfere with our ability to love others or receive love. Our love for our children that first moment they are conceived and then are placed in our loving arms to gaze upon—no other human love compares. The love of a mother is for a lifetime, and it brings with it such vulnerability. When we open ourselves to love, we also open ourselves to suffering. Life brings many challenges that break open the heart in sorrow and pain as well as joy.

We are called to love despite that call to vulnerability. Author Brene Brown calls it wholehearted living. We are worthy of being loved deeply, not because of what we do but because of who we are. We come to a place where we accept who we are as being enough. We don't have to pretend to be something we cannot be.

Learning to love deeply is the path of healing. When we decide to open up our lives, as dysfunctional as they can be, and talk about what is working and what is not working, we are opening ourselves to a universal love. Love is the only true path to healing ourselves and the world. After all, isn't love the root of all that makes life worth living?

My Spiritual Practice for Today

Today I want to consider how I can learn to love myself. I want to begin to consider the universal healing power of love in my life. I want to uncover it and begin to live it.

November 16

Even the Moon Has a Dark Side (Pat)

Picture a full moon on a clear night. The moon, reflecting light from the sun, beautifully lights up the night. Moonlight has a special character of peace, serenity, and romance that we celebrate in our songs. We tend to forget, though, that the moon has a dark side, a side always in shadow and never seen.

We are all like the moon. We all can shine brilliantly and yet have a dark side. The dark side is the part of you that you are embarrassed or even ashamed of. So you hide this part from other people, and even from yourself, and try to bury it deep in shadow. The difficulty is this gives the dark part of you even more power, sometimes diminishing your light.

I experienced this myself. I thought of myself as a kind, understanding, and gentle man. What I was ignoring, though, was a shadow side of me that could be sarcastic, judgmental, and even mean. I kept this mostly hidden and under control. Periodically, however, this part of me would erupt. I would then lash out and hurt people, especially Sue, whom I love with all my being. It was very painful for me to hurt Sue, but I didn't want to face that I was capable of this.

Sue helped me to see my dark side. She lovingly and yet strongly challenged my behaviors. Bringing it into the light, I began to accept and understand it and grew less ashamed of it. I even named it "Muammar Gaddafi," after the nasty dictator of Libya (naming a part of yourself makes it more real and personal). Facing and even embracing Muammar gradually tamed him. He is not entirely gone, yet he acts up much less frequently.

The same process can work for you. You can bring into the light the part of you that acts up sometimes. Naming and befriending this part will help you tame it as well. The key thing is to let go of the shame you may have about your shadow. So remember, even the glorious moon has a dark side.

My Spiritual Practice for Today

Look deep within to see your dark side. Describe it with whatever adjectives fit. Perhaps come up with a name for it. Realize that we all have such a shadow and begin to accept yours.

November 17

Forgiving Too Fast (Sue)

Forgiveness, as powerfully healing as it is, is a daunting and difficult spiritual task. It is a process that must ripen in soul time, in the fullness of God's time. Forgiveness is a process that unfolds in you. It is not usually a single, one-time choice to forgive. Its timing, duration, and progression are different for each survivor. Give yourself whatever time and space you need to forgive.

It is, in fact, vital to walk through forgiveness slowly. Quick forgiveness is usually false forgiveness. What you forgive prematurely or too freely, or under guilt or compulsion, does not stay forgiven. To genuinely forgive, you need first to have thoroughly tapped into your holy anger and have found your voice to tell your story and speak out in some way against the injustice done to you.

Sometimes forgiveness is like peeling the layers of an onion: Each time you choose to forgive and surrender your anger, another layer is revealed for the next step in your forgiveness journey. So be gentle and patient with yourself. Do not heap guilt on yourself about wherever you happen to be in the forgiveness process or about how much time it takes you. Forgiveness is not meant to be another "should" to berate yourself with. Your soul is eternal and eternally patient with you.

Ultimately, forgiveness is a matter of grace. Forgiveness for such awful trauma and harm may be beyond your capacity to choose and give by your power alone. Yet grace from God and your soul is there for the asking. All that is required of you to begin is to ask for the grace to forgive and to be willing to receive it. Or, if even that is too daunting, it is enough, as it is sometimes said, "to be willing, to be willing, to be willing…" to begin to forgive.

My Spiritual Practice for Today

Are you willing to be willing… to ask for the grace to forgive? What do you need from your soul or God to move the process of forgiveness along? What is the next step for you?

November 18

The Distressing Disguise (Vicki)

We are so inclined to cover up our poverty and ignore it that we often miss the opportunity to discover God, who dwells in it. Let's dare to see our poverty as the land where our treasure is hidden.
–Henri Nouwen

I've been drawn for many years to finding ways to serve the poorest. It started by helping low-income families in my home community, and it continued into thirty years of leading high school and college students on mission trips to some of the poorest areas of our country. In the midst of these years, it also led me to work with Mother Teresa who taught me very early that it is Christ whom we serve in the distressing disguise of the poorest of the poor. Christian Gospels tell us in Matthew 26:11, "The poor you will always have with you." Today I know the poor have so much more to teach us than we could imagine.

The abuse perpetrated against us is our poverty, emotional instability is our poverty, shame is our poverty, and a lack of self-confidence is our poverty. We are the distressing disguise of the poor at the moment when we feel hopeless, forgotten, and victimized. The good news is that the hidden treasure that will allow us to move out of pain is the Spirit that lives within us. It is the living God who lifts an emaciated woman from the side of the road in Calcutta, and it is the living God who lifts each of us up and out of our cries of desperation and sadness.

It is ours to say yes to how that help is going to come to us. When we begin to look into our lives, we can begin to see the hidden treasure, the Spirit that animates us and the soul who wants wholeness for us. The soul's desire for wholeness is greater than our worst trauma and sadness. The challenge for every human spirit is to find ways to heal from the wounds that are sure to befall us. It will always require one giant step, and once that first step is taken, we are on the path to becoming our True Self.

My Spiritual Practice for Today

Reflect on your own poverty today. Can you name it? Are you actively working to heal your deepest hurts? Where are you on your journey of healing?

November 19

90 Percent Delusion (Pat)

About six months after my treatment for breast cancer ended, I was riding a golf cart with my grandson Kevin, a very spiritual and deep young man. Between holes, Kevin asked a penetrating question, "So what did you learn from your cancer experience last year?" My immediate answer was, "I learned that 90 percent of our fears are delusions."

During my nine months of chemo and radiation, I had developed many fears. By the end of treatment, they had grown into a full-blown anxiety disorder with some aspects of PTSD. The combined trauma of chemo, radiation, and medications had left my brain racing with constant anxiety. There was reality to some of it: The cancer could kill me, the treatments themselves had severe side effects, and my future was uncertain. But after my mind calmed down, I realized that these real fears were only about 10 percent of my anxieties. The remaining 90 percent of the fears were false or greatly exaggerated and had been concocted by my brain. In short, 90 percent of my fears were delusional.

One day after my treatments were over, I went for a meditative walk in the woods on a cool September morning. I was able to be present to the natural beauty surrounding me in a way I couldn't in the previous twelve months. It suddenly hit me that all of the fearful thoughts had disappeared entirely. I was stunned, grateful, and curious. If they could simply disappear, how real had my fears been? They felt real. But I became aware that most of them were artificial constructs of my brain and were as wispy as the billowy white clouds above me that day.

What does this mean for survivors? Trauma creates great fear. There is real fear in the trauma experience itself. However, its aftermath may leave you with a brain that creates fears that are unreal. Your brain does this to protect you from future trauma, but it can overdo it. So it's worth asking yourself what percent of your fears are real and which are perhaps delusional. Your soul will help guide you in this self-exploration.

My Spiritual Practice for Today

Examine your fears today. Listen to the calm, quiet voice of your soul. Which of your fears might be a fabrication of your brain? Are you ready to surrender them and let them go?

November 20

Who Are You Anyway? (Pat)

The search to discover who you are is a lifelong quest. Recently a client in his 80s started his session with the statement: "I'm gradually getting to know this new person in my life, my new aging self."

Throughout our life we are challenged to seek a deeper understanding and acceptance of our personal identity and our place in the world. Trauma complicates this search. So it's important to say first of all who you are not. You are not your trauma. You are not Mr., Mrs., or Ms. Abuse. You are not PTSD or your depression or your trauma-induced addiction. There are phenomenon that describe parts of you, and yet do not capture the whole breadth and depth of you. You are not your small ego. You are not your genetic makeup. You are not your history. You are not a bag of chemicals or the sum of your neurons' electrical connections.

Who you are is so much greater. Like light you are both particle and wave, sometimes acting like earthbound mass, sometimes like pure, pulsing spiritual energy. You are an immortal diamond, a spark of the divine, a chip off the old God block. You are a beloved son or daughter of God and the universe. You are a splendid blend of the spiritual quantum energy of life force manifesting itself in the unique quirky quarks that are you. You are unbound, unlimited spirit soaring to the farthest reaches of the universe, and you are flesh and blood, heartbeat and neuronal flash rooted in Mother Earth. You are soul light manifesting as a particular personality and a physical body. You are brother or sister to every human, to all other creatures, and to Nature herself. You are one with all, and at the same time you are your own individual, glorious self. There is no one else like you, nor will there ever be.

In the end, who you are is indescribable. Like God, you are an ever-unfolding mystery. Your life quest, like my elderly client, is to always probe deeper into that magnificent mystery of your True Self.

My Spiritual Practice for Today

Make your own list of who you truly are. Choose one description and make that your mantra for today: for example, "I am a beloved son or daughter."

November 21

Climbing Our Own Mt. Everest (Vicki)

Every life is full of emotional struggle and daily challenges. It took time to learn that difficult things do not have to be the only focus. With time we can learn that the difficulties become the fabric of the whole of our life. When we can grasp the grace and learning that come from struggle, we can begin to see life as more gift than suffering. Life will always promise us hardships. The challenge then becomes learning how to embrace it. Our egoistic mind will constantly want to draw us back into victimhood. It will want us to dwell there. We are made for so much more. We are filled with so much potential to shine and to become all that God has called us to become.

At a most difficult time in my journey of healing, I felt trapped and victimized. I couldn't see a light at the end of the tunnel yet. Yes, I dwelled there for a time. During that time, though, I was inching forward in my healing journey. I hadn't yet reached the tipping point where I could see it all coming together. It takes tremendous courage to take each step. Moments of clarity kept moving me forward toward more clarity. And then there is a *eureka* moment when an overwhelming feeling of clear vision arrives. It's at this time that we can begin to see the whole of our lives.

We can liken it to climbing Mt. Everest. First, create a base camp. Then the arduous climb begins, which can have difficulties along the way. After a herculean effort, it leads to the majestic vision of the Himalayan Mountains.

Early in my counseling, I was browsing in a Buddhist-leaning bookstore in Chicago when I came across a book about trekking the Himalayas. I'm not a mountain climber, but I purchased this book because it reminded me that I was in the process of climbing my own metaphorical Mt. Everest. I still have that book and take it off the shelf occasionally to remind myself that I can see the whole landscape now.

My Spiritual Practice for Today

Take some time to reflect on the larger fabric of your life. Where are you on your climb? Base camp, midway, or closing in on the peak?

November 22

Thanksgiving (Pat & Sue)

Thanksgiving is transformative. No, we don't mean the tryptophan-induced torpor of your turkey dinner! The act of giving thanks itself can powerfully transform your core life perspective and raise your spirits as well.

It is no accident that giving thanks is part of the spirituality of every culture and religion around the world. We often prescribe a gratitude list, choosing one thing to be grateful for each day, for counseling clients who are feeling depressed or hopeless. Research has shown that a daily dose of gratitude is a very powerful antidepressant—with no negative side effects. Gratitude can open your eyes to the gifts and blessings that are within you and around you all the time, even though you may have become blinded to them.

Transformation is the fifth Pathway of Healing. Part of the transformation is developing the capacity to daily give thanks despite what has happened to you. This can be difficult for survivors who are burdened with the heavy pain of their trauma. Yet each act of thanksgiving says to yourself and to the world that you are not a victim. You are more than your abuse. Abuse does not define you. You and your own personal world are still gifted and blessed.

So enjoy your turkey and stuffing this year. Don't hold back. Enjoy and celebrate. Give thanks. And on the day after—yes, Black Friday—start a diet of gratitude, a daily helping of giving thanks for all that you have been given, despite what you have suffered. This diet will work better than most to bring real transformation to you.

Happy and blessed Thanksgiving to each of you from Sue, Pat, and Vicki! Among the many things that we are grateful for is you, our readers, and for all survivors of abuse and trauma who are on their pathway to healing and who are breaking the vicious cycle of abuse.

My Spiritual Practice for Today

Be especially aware today of all the ways you have been blessed and gifted, and simply be thankful. Start your gratitude diet tomorrow morning.

November 23

Creating Rituals (Pat)

Rituals are powerful ways to symbolically express spiritual meaning or experience. They can involve the sacred rituals of various religions, or they could be your own personally created rituals. Either can initiate powerful experiences of healing that touch your body, your mind, and your soul.

Let me give examples of two rituals created by my survivor clients. Beth is a survivor of extensive sexual, physical, and verbal abuse. She is very spiritual, and yet had a lot of anger at God for her abuse. To express her intense anger, she bought a set of cheap china dishes, placed them in a cloth bag, and took them and a hammer to a private Catholic chapel. After a few moments of prayer alone before the tabernacle, Beth asked God to understand and accept what she was about to do and then laid the bag of china on the floor in front of the tabernacle. Breaking the chapel's silence, she took the hammer and shattered the china into tiny pieces to express her profound anger at the Lord. Beth later described to me the immense relief she felt afterward. She still had some bones to pick with God, but now she felt more at peace.

My second client, Kate, devised a ritual to help her grieve the losses caused by her trauma. She declared a period of mourning. She hung black cloth around the mirrors in her apartment. She wore her favorite little black dress on more occasions. She wrote down all of her losses on pieces of paper and put them in an ornate box that she placed on the mantle. She made time to feel her sadness and loss. When she sensed that she had grieved enough, she took down the black cloth and put away the dress. She invited a group of friends to join her around an outdoor fire pit into which she dumped the papers. As she watched the papers burn and the fire and smoke lift into the sky, she prayed and put the losses in God's hands. She felt lightness and great peace.

My Spiritual Practice for Today

Reflect on whether you need a ritual for holy anger, for forgiveness, for transformation, or for some other part of your recovery. If you do, create a ritual and set a time and place to do it.

November 24

Ever-Flowing Source of Holiness (Vicki)

Embrace the present moment as an ever-flowing source of holiness.
–Jean Pierre de Caussade

The phone call came early in the afternoon while at I was at work. My mother had been living with a chronic and serious illness for many years, and yet it was still such a shock to get the call that she had passed. Driving to her home about eight miles away, I thought, "Well, this dreaded moment is here." I knew that I loved her and she loved me. I kept reminding myself of this and that she was finally able to let go of her long suffering.

My mother dedicated her entire life to her five children. She loved us unconditionally; it wasn't until she passed that I realized how precious a gift this was to us. Imagine having one person devote her entire life to you. Somehow I knew this on a deeper level than ever before. It was an "ever-flowing source of holiness" for each of us. This has become a profound thought for me since she passed.

What other ways can we feel this "ever-flowing source of holiness?" Often our closest relationships are not always about unconditional love. Sometimes they may be the cause of our need for healing. It's important that we identify other sources of holistic well-being and love that are present to us. How do we heal a broken heart or a disappointment from someone who should have had our best interest at heart but didn't?

In my story, our parish priest crossed some serious boundaries and not only abused me but also left my parents and siblings feeling betrayed. Someone whom they had trusted for thirty years broke a sacred trust in a heinous way. The heart holds such great capacity for love. Our soul is capable of holding all the pain of life; its capacity is limitless. It will hold it until we set it free. And set it free we must, or we can be held hostage to it throughout our entire life.

My Spiritual Practice for Today

Is there an ever-flowing source of love in my life? Today I shall reflect on the strength that comes from this love.

November 25

Dogs and the Love of God (Pat & Sue)

Our granddog, Maisie, is a cute, 12-pound blond dachshund whose short legs become a blur when she runs. Maisie has some curious habits in her interactions with us. She obviously craves attention and affection, and yet she runs away whenever we try to put her on our laps. In human terms this is called an approach/avoidance pattern of relationships: "Come close, stay away; pick me up, I'm running away." After playing this game a while, Maisie allows us to put her on our laps. You often see this pattern with dogs that have been abused. With Maisie, who is well loved, it seems more a matter of temperament.

Another dog we know, Pollette, displayed this pattern very dramatically. She showed up on a client's property very wary and afraid of people. You could not get close to her except when she came for her food. She would not come in the house and slept outside in even the most brutal weather. She had obviously been badly abused. Our client, who understands trauma too well, patiently set out to woo Pollette to come close and heal her fear. It took four years of slow and patient love and kindness, and finally Pollette allowed herself to be held and petted, and now she lives snug and warm in the client's house.

Human survivors can act similarly. You may be fearful of allowing anyone to get close while at the same time desperately craving intimacy. You may play come close/stay away games in your relationships. You might avoid people as much as Pollette and become estranged and alone. These are deep wounds from your abuse, yet healable and redeemable.

Like our client with Pollette, your God wants to patiently woo and love you from your fear to closeness and intimacy. It may be through a friend or lover, or even a pet. Or it may come from a personal relationship with God in which God patiently loves and invites you closer. God loves you more abundantly than you can imagine and invites you in from the rain and cold into her (or his) house, all cuddled up on her lap.

My Spiritual Practice for Today

Reflect on your patterns in relationships, including your relationship with God. If you are fearful and distant, can you let God's love draw you a little closer? Image yourself crawling up onto the lap of God.

November 26

Divine Discontent (Pat)

Everybody passionately seeks to be well adjusted.
But there are some things in our world
to which men of good will must be maladjusted.
–Martin Luther King Jr.

As a survivor, you want healing and wholeness, and to feel content with yourself and your life. You yearn to be "normal" (whatever that is) and "well adjusted" like everyone else. Yet because of your trauma, you find it difficult to see life in quite the same way as others do. You may experience a deep discontent about life as it is.

Martin Luther King suggests that this may be a good thing. He is saying that it is spiritually healthy to be "maladjusted" and malcontented about things that are unjust, things that cry out to be changed. You can call this a divine discontent that your soul feels about what is not right in the world. So not only is it healthy to be discontent, but it can also be a spiritual call. You certainly need to stay aware that what was done to you was not right. You are also called to have a divine discontent about abuse and injustice experienced by others and about the conditions that create these.

Even after you have experienced much healing, even after you have achieved substantial forgiveness and peace, your soul will invite you to retain a divine disquiet about things in your world that are unjust and wrong, particularly where abuse remains in your life. Your divine discontent can be the driving energy to transform your trauma into action to change your life and help others change their lives as well. So heal, be happy, and yet about some things, stay discontent.

My Spiritual Practice for Today

What divine discontent are you experiencing? What does your soul not want you to be happy and quiet about? Is there any action your discontent is prompting you to take?

November 27

Let the Tears Flow (Vicki)

The loud voice is famous to silence,
which knew it would inherit the earth
before anybody said so.
The cat sleeping on the fence is famous to the birds
watching him from the birdhouse.
The tear is famous, briefly, to the cheek.
–Naomi Shihab Nye,

In her poem "Famous," Naomi Shihab Nye reflects on knowing. As water runs quickly through a riverbed, it is only known briefly to the bottom and the sides of the riverbed as it makes its way toward another reservoir. We don't think of tears after they have stopped flowing. They appear because of joy or pain, and as quickly as they come, they dry up and are gone. We either remain broken or the tears lead us to a new understanding, a clearer picture of what brought the tears, what made them dry up, or perhaps how long they will continue flowing. A tear is like a waterfall releasing the power of all that is pushing it down the river.

To be sure, we must let tears flow. Letting go and allowing the flood of tears will help wash away the heartbreak, the pain, the feeling of abandonment. We must find a way to set the tears free, to let go of the shame of crying. They are a flushing of sorts, a detoxification from pain and heartache. Tears are a healthy reminder of the true nature of human compassion and understanding.

How often we have experienced those who could not allow themselves to cry. Their emotions are held so they simply cannot weep. Certainly many young boys have been taught they should not cry, that true men don't show their emotions. We know now how important it is to express inner pain and turmoil in whatever way fits. Remember that release is key to letting go of long- held pain and trauma.

My Spiritual Practice for Today

Can you embrace your tears and trust they will lead you to a new understanding? Can you dwell in the relief that comes after a good cry? Can you accept that tears are a normal response to the healing process?

November 28

The Universe is Ablaze (Pat)

The world is charged with the grandeur of God. It will flame
out, like shining form shook foil; it gathers to greatness, like the
ooze of oil crushed... And for all this, nature is never spent;
There lives the deepest freshness deep down things...
Because the Holy Ghost over the bent
World broods with warm breast,
and with ah! bright wings
–Gerald Manley Hopkins, 1844–1889

The universe is ablaze with the fiery grandeur of God, the poet writes. Then why don't we see it? Have our eyes been so dimmed by our increasing distance from nature as we live our modern, heavily urban and suburban lives? Have we rationalized away the mystery and mysticism of creation with modern science? Do we live at such a fast pace that we don't slow down enough to perceive the grandeur of God in the myriad shapes and colors of orchids or the sharp-edged winter light on the trunks of a white oak? Are we too distracted to hear the song of the cardinal's special spring song?

Native American spirituality has a keen sense of the aliveness of Spirit in Nature. For them, Spirit is present in all creation and in all creatures. They live closer to Nature with a deeper awareness and respect for the rhythms of the created world. They know and sense the energy of Spirit within and behind all that we observe in the material world. This led them to live in greater harmony with their natural environment.

This is something you can recover. You can learn to look deeper and see divine energy burning all around you. You can more closely notice the passing of the seasons. You can watch for the phases of the moon. You can track the planets and stars as they whirl above your head. Spending time around water, especially water on the move, will soothe your stress and enliven your spirit. Watch and listen to the birds. Marvel at your neighborhood squirrels. Seek out natural light and color. Be on the prowl for surprising scents. Then you will be rewarded with the soul refreshment of Nature where "lives the deepest freshness deep down things."

My Spiritual Practice for Today

Be aware and mindful of the natural world around you today.

November 29

Life is Great (Sue)

"Life is great. Change is constant. And Love flows from heart to heart."

This has been my life motto and mantra for many years. It helps me stay conscious of the essential truths of my life in the joyful times and in the sad and challenging times. It's my GPS guiding me through the ups and downs of each day. I'd like to share what each part means to me.

"Life is great." No matter what is happening in my life and in the world, an abundance of goodness is always available to me. I want to stay aware of this abundance, enjoy it, and be ever so grateful for it. The abundance for me includes so many wonderful events and celebrations: grandchildren's soccer, baseball, basketball, volleyball, water polo, dance, and theater; birthdays, anniversaries, funerals, neighborhood eclipse parties, and fire pit gatherings; vacations, day trips, candlelight dinners; sunrises, sunsets, rainbows, spectacular storms, beautiful snows. The abundance is too much to count. Meanwhile, my body is aging, hurting, and presenting challenges; and the world seems about to fall apart some days. And life is still so incredibly great.

"Change is constant." Life equals change. Every second the cells in our bodies change. Nature is constantly evolving and remaking herself. Our human environments are always in flux. Children grow up, family moves away; our local, national, and world communities swirl with ever-churning change. Change is a challenge. We want things to stay the same, and they never will. Accepting this gives me great peace. I may not like the change, and I can be at peace with it. One of the most painful days of my life was when I graduated from high school. I had experienced four marvelous years of friends, cheerleading, band, and dances. Then poof, it was all gone! I had to accept that this part of my life was complete, and life moved on.

"Love flows from heart to heart." Love is the life force of the universe, the energy of my soul and my God ever-flowing from person to person. Love is my true GPS, my guardian angel. Love matters more than anything. Especially when I'm struggling, I look for love flowing all around me. I pray to be love, to be its channel, and to be its wellspring. As St. Paul says, if I am without love, I am nothing at all.

My Spiritual Practice for Today

Meditate on how my motto speaks to you.

November 30

The Geography of Destiny (Vicki)

Many different strands of your past experience begin to weave together until gradually the new direction announces itself. Its voice is sure with the inevitability of the truth. When your life-decisions emerge in this way from the matrix of your experience, they warrant your trust and commitment. When you can choose in this way, you move gracefully within the deeper rhythm of your soul.
–John O'Donohue

Have you ever stopped to take a serious look at the weaving of your life? We take for granted the life experiences we have endured and fail to see the interconnection between the seasons of life. What in your childhood led you to think a certain way or behave a certain way? What brought you great joy and confidence? What in your childhood has caused you to distrust people? In your adolescent years, was there a person who made you feel uncomfortable? Was there someone who caused great emotional distress? Can you stop and assess who you are and how you have arrived at this moment?

There is a pattern and story to every life. And lots of things can happen to disrupt our healthy emotional development. Who among us has not lived through some kind of disruption? The point is to look at what that issue is and then begin to understand how to move beyond it. As John O'Donohue says, the goal is to "move gracefully within the deeper rhythm of your soul." What is the rhythm of your soul? Can you feel a rhythm? Is there a sense of peacefulness in your soul, or do you feel chaos?

My therapist and Richard Rohr taught me to trust my lived experience. They challenged me to let go of my self-doubt and to realize that my unique life, with its myriad experiences, are honest and authentic and have meaning. Can you trust that what you feel about how your life has unfolded, no matter what you lived through, is authentically your story and it is very real? Can you share that story with confidence to a trusted friend? Can you stand in your truth with confidence? Every life has its own intrinsic value. It is for us to discover and truly own that gift.

My Spiritual Practice for Today

What is your life worth? Everything! Find some time to map out your life and identify the intersections of grace that have brought you to today.

December 1

The Mountain Meditation: You (Sue & Pat)

My Spiritual Practice for Today

We invite you to do the Mountain Meditation again. This time the theme is you. Bring to the mountain anything you have learned in the last month, any questions you have, or any need for healing that you are experiencing. Let your soul and the Spirit guide you. To enter into this meditation, find a comfortable sitting position. As you read, pause, close your eyes, and imagine the scenes described.

Picture yourself on a beautiful beach. See the waves, the sand, the brilliant color, and the vastness of the ocean. Feel the sun and the wind on your skin. Hear the crash and whoosh of the surf. Turn around now, and face away from the sea. This time pack your backpack with any questions, lessons, or needs that have experienced in the last month. Notice how it feels to carry this.

In front of you is a beautiful forest. See yourself walking along a trail into the forest. Appreciate the coolness and the shaded light. You reach the edge of the forest and see an open meadow filled with multicolored wildflowers. The trail leads you through the meadow to a clear, flowing stream with a bridge across the dancing water. Stop for a moment to enjoy the light sparkling on the water.

Now look up from the bridge and see a shining mountain before you. Following the trail, you ascend the mountain. You climb through the clouds, above the timberline through the clouds to the top of the peak. Look around you at the glory of creation. Then you notice a large boulder to sit on and rest.

From the other side of the peak, your spiritual guide comes and sits down with you on the boulder. You can discuss whatever you want. Unpack your backpack and lay its contents out before your spirit guide. Listen for what is said to you about what you have brought. If you receive anything, embrace it and put it in your backpack to bring it down the mountain to the outside world.

When you are ready to leave, thank your Higher Power. Slowly hike back down the mountain, over the bridge, through the meadow, through the forest, to the beach, and to the edge of the vast ocean. Open your eyes. Record and reflect in your journal.

December 2

Dung Happens! (Pat)

Nature does not waste anything. Everything gets recycled for a new purpose beyond itself. All matter gets recycled into some new matter, some new life or energy. This is the great circle of life. Dung is transformed into fertilizer. A wounded or dying tree provides housing for owls and woodpeckers, and eventually food for insects and the earth into which it finally falls.

As I mentioned in an earlier meditation, one of my favorite nature metaphors for transformation involves a certain species of palm tree in Africa. It produces a large nut, a seed that can only sprout into new life and produce a new tree if it is eaten by an elephant. It must pass through the elephant's digestive system to be activated and then is ejected onto the ground with the elephant's copious and smelly excrement. This provides an excellent fertilized start for the new tree that sprouts from the nut.

There is a seed of new life in your traumatic experience. Even the dung of your trauma and abuse, transformed in the digestive process of your healing journey, can become fertilizer to grow something new and life giving for you.

To paraphrase the bumper sticker, Dung Happens! Dung—in the form of your trauma—has happened to you. That is, well, shitty. You did not deserve it, and neither you nor your soul nor God wanted it for you. And yet it happened. (By the way, remember that just because dung happened to you doesn't make you dung).

Nature teaches us that nothing is wasted, not even the suffering that came from your trauma. Like the palm nut passing through the elephant, your personal dung can become fertilizer for you that can generate new life within you. Something will grow, blossom, and bear fruit from the pile of dung you are now sitting in. Right now it may be smelly and disgusting. Trust that your soul, however, is at work in you and at work in your dung transforming it into a resilient and strong new tree that will bear much fruit in your life.

My Spiritual Practice for Today

Reflect on nature's circle of life, on the process of transformation and renewal. Can you see or imagine how the dung of your suffering will be recycled into something powerful and hopeful for you?

December 3

The Joy of Soul Sex (Pat & Sue)

One of our clients once said, "Sometimes sex with my wife is orange juice sex, and sometimes it is cathedral sex." What he meant was that sometimes their sex was like the daily glass of orange juice that provided the ongoing daily vitamins and minerals of connection that help sustain a loving relationship. Cathedral sex was when their sexual relationship brought both of them to a deep intimacy with each other and beyond themselves to an intimate connection with a Higher Being. This sex is like praying in a Gothic cathedral that lifts up your heart and soul to the heavens. Such sex is soul sex, sex that comes from the soul's holy longing for God and joins with your body's sexual energy to engender ecstatic passion. It is when you are on fire with love and the divine spark, and enter into deep intimacy with God in your profound closeness with your partner. Soul sex is a passionate soul-to-soul connection that invites Spirit to enter and bless your loving intimacy. It is a prayer with your bodies, hearts, and souls that graces each other and the world with divine love and new life.

The spiritual writer Ronald Rolheiser states, "Sex is the most powerful of fires, the best of all fires, and the most dangerous of all fires, and the fire which, ultimately, lies at the base of everything, including the spiritual life." Because of its power, sexuality is not always easy to channel into life-giving ways. Consequently, we all make mistakes with sex. For some survivors, your sexuality may have been misused and wounded by abuse. Or you may have been raised with shame messages about your body and your sexuality. Perhaps this created an alienation from your own body and its desires and energies.

Befriending your sexuality is a part of your healing journey. Healing involves becoming aware that your body is your sacred temple and your sexuality is holy and beloved to your soul. Healing also is to realize that the capacity for soul sex is a birthright of each person. Your soul desires to draw you closer and lift you up higher.

My Spiritual Practice for Today

Reflect on your feelings about your body and your sexuality. Can you begin to see and embrace their sacredness and beauty?

December 4

Move Toward the Light   (Vicki)

It is you who decides what you think, say, and do. You can think yourself into a depression, you can talk yourself into low self-esteem, you can act in a self-rejecting way. But you always have a choice to think, speak, and act in the name of God and so move towards the Light, the Truth, and the Life.
–Henri Nouwen, The Inner Voice of Love

This reflection by Henri Nouwen reminds me of a time when I couldn't begin to believe this. In fact, I didn't think anyone could talk me out of the low self-esteem I lived with for several years. It was of my own making because I was holding on to the shame of being abused by a priest for whom I continued to work. The future seemed dark because I had no freedom to think of being or doing anything else.

When we find ourselves in such a controlling and abusive relationship, it takes untold courage to step out of the cycle of abuse to look objectively at how your life has been manipulated. This is seen in domestic violence scenarios. Women are often left without support, and often it seems no one can convince them to leave because of their insecurities. They've been convinced they are nothing without their spouse or boss or, in my case, my pastor. Hopefully, someone outside of the situation can speak truth to the power that controls another person.

If you are reading this meditation and find yourself in an abusive situation, remember the words of Henri Nouwen above. You always have a choice to think, speak, and act so you can move toward the light, the truth, and the life.

May you find strength among your family and friends who can embolden you to seek freedom from any kind of bondage in which you find yourself. For that is what emotional, physical, and sexual abuse is. May your way toward wholeness and confidence lead you to a life fully and completely as *you* envision. This is your life to live. It belongs to no one else.

My Spiritual Practice for Today

Today I will reflect on my life and think of how I can reach out to my family and friends for support. I will take time to envision a new life for myself. I will pray about moving toward light and truth.

December 5

Happy Be-Day! (Pat)

The Italians have a wonderful saying: "*La dolce far niente;*" "the sweetness of doing nothing." This is a challenging concept for many survivors and many Americans. As a result of your trauma, and especially if shame has arisen from it, you likely feel you should be constantly doing something to justify your existence and create and prove your self-worth. You may have become perfectionistic or addicted to work. The word "should" likely rules your life: you *should* be doing this or pursuing that, you *should* be accomplishing whatever would make you valuable. Again, all of this stems from the trauma-based compulsion to overcome the feeling and belief that you are nothing, of no worth, or even that you are bad or nearly evil.

If you do, do, do…then you may have made something of yourself. Except that this never works. It simply creates a deep sense of emptiness and an even more manic drive to do more and more to prove and manufacture your value.

You are not a human do-ing. You are a human be-ing. Your worth and value abide in you, just because you are, because of your be-ing. There is a delightful sweetness in accepting this and giving up the constant striving. Then you are able to rest in the truth of your value, just because you are, simply because you live and breathe. Then you can take time out to just be, to have recreational times when you have no goals, nothing to do, nothing to prove. Perhaps you will want to be with another or be with the beauty of nature or be in meditation.

Without purpose or frenetic design, you revel in the joy of be-ing. This is the meaning of making "holy the Sabbath," resting and being present to yourself, others, and your God. Any day can be a Sabbath. Declare a Sabbath day soon and enjoy "*la dolce far niente.*"

My Spiritual Practice for Today

Today simply be! Or choose a day this week that will be your Sabbath so you can gift yourself with just be-ing for a day.

December 6

The Power of No (Sue)

It often seems to me that survivors have had the word "no" stripped from their vocabulary. Your trauma was in some fashion forced on many of you. Your "no" to what was being done to you was not respected and was overpowered by your abuser or your situation. For some this takes away the power to say no in future situations. You may find it difficult to say "no" or "stop it" when your personal space and boundaries are being invaded. You may also struggle with saying no to others' requests, demands, or needs that don't work for you or that require you to sacrifice your own needs. This can set you up for a spectacular case of codependency.

"No" is such a powerful and positive word. It enables you to set limits and boundaries in your life that protect you and keep others from entering your personal space without your permission. "Yes" is a powerful word too, though only if it is freely chosen and not coerced by force, intimidation, or guilt.

Regaining the word "no" in your vocabulary is vital for you to regain your personal power. My mentor, Virginia Satir, taught me a wonderful tool to restore the power of no. She called it the "Yes, No Medallion." Imagine that deep inside you is a shiny medallion. On one side it reads, "Thank you for noticing me...And the answer is *no*... that does not fit for me." The other side reads, "Thank you for noticing me...And the answer is *yes*...that does fit for me." The medallion reminds you that you have the right and the soul-inspired power to say no.

The more you practice your no, the easier and more natural it will become. No, yes, stop, go, red light, green light, the choice is yours.

My Spiritual Practice for Today

Close your eyes and imagine the Yes, No Medallion within you. Imagine using it in response to some recent requests where you said yes when you really wanted to answer no. See yourself consulting your medallion; if the answer is truly no, see yourself saying no to the other person. Practice this in your mind several times, and then use the medallion in at least one situation today.

December 7

A Repository for Tears (Vicki)

In the lyrics to Carrie Newcomer's song "Geodes" from her CD *Geography of Light*, she beautifully shares her thoughts on the ancient and unique geodes found in her beloved Indiana. She sings that they throw them in their gardens; they're as common as the rain, like corn silk in July.

> *Some say geodes are made from pockets of tears,*
> *Trapped away in small places for years upon years.*
> *Pressed down and transformed, 'til the true self was born,*
> *and the whole world moved on like the last notes of a song,*
> *a love letter sent without return address.*

Listening to Carrie's song over time, I began to think about a historical repository of tears shed throughout the life of the world. I hadn't thought our tears might have a life after they are shed. We all shed buckets of tears throughout life—happy tears, sad tears, angry tears. They act as a release of tension, a bubbling up of joy at a piece of music that touches us, a burst of anger over something we have no control over, or an outlet for deep grief. Tears flow as the body responds to internal and external events. Pressure cookers release steam systematically so the pot doesn't explode. Perhaps that is what our soul is designed to do with tears.

What if we thought of tears as a cleansing wash for our soul? It wouldn't matter what kind of tears we cried. Perhaps they are a wash and rinse for the soul; perhaps they bring to the surface long-stuffed tension and anxiety as we try to show the world that we are okay.

When was your last good cry? When have you had a good cleansing sob?

My Spiritual Practice for Today

Moving forward I will accept my tears as a way of releasing long-held hurts or trauma. Tears can be a friend to console my soul and bring clarity.

December 8

Your Mission Statement (Pat)

My Spiritual Practice for Today

Write your personal mission statement. Your mission is what you will do to live your purpose. A mission statement is an expression of the purpose, passion, vision, and commitment that has grown in you as a result of your healing experience on this journey. It is the distillation and crystallization of all that you have learned and been given along the way into a short statement of how you are going to live your emerging life purpose. The mission statement includes a concise formulation of your life purpose and a brief description of your life mission. Think of this as a press release or a spiritual tweet to the world and to yourself about how you intend to live your life now and in the future from your new sense of purpose.

Below is a process for creating your mission statement. Go to a safe and sacred place, either your inner sanctum or the sacred physical space where you go to meet your soul. Reflect on your passage through these meditations and listen to your soul speaking to you about what has become most important to you now:

> *What essential values have surfaced?*
> *What have you become passionate about in regard to your life?*
> *What vision do you now see for your life?*
> *What have you been given that you want to share?*
> *How would you share it?*
> *Who do you want to gift with the gift that you have been given?*
> *What actions can you take to live this vision and be of service?*

From your reflections and your dialogue with your soul, write a mission statement by completing the following:

> *My purpose as a survivor at this time in my life is...*
> *To fulfill this purpose, the mission that I accept and commit to is...*

December 9

The Butterfly Effect (Pat)

The butterfly effect is a scientific concept that is a part of what is called chaos theory. The butterfly effect states that even a small event like the flap of a butterfly's wings in China can change the dynamics of the weather and influence the formation of a thunderstorm or tornado several weeks later in Oklahoma. This is not just a wonderful metaphor; it is a scientific fact. Small inputs or changes at the start of a dynamic system, such as weather, can result in large differences later on and produce a significantly different outcome.

These tiny butterflies are more powerful that we knew. So are you. The butterfly effect means that every time you flap the wings of your spirit, you change the world. Each time you take even a small step of healing or experience a little more freedom from the effects of your trauma, this ripples into the world and alters it.

Just as there is a physical ecosystem impacted by the butterfly's wings, there is also a spiritual ecosystem. The spiritual energy field is highly dynamic and sensitive to each and every one of your victories over trauma. For instance, when you free yourself from fear and take even a small courageous step, your change ripples through your family system and transforms it, making your environment a little freer. Healing your shame and loving yourself better will influence how your children and grandchildren feel about themselves. This will change their present and enhance their future.

Your butterfly wing flap will alter the whole spiritual ecosystem of the world, even beyond your family to your community, your church, your workplace, and even your nation and the whole planet. Flap, little butterfly, flap!

My Spiritual Practice for Today

Reflect on the butterfly effect in your healing journey. Can you accept the power and influence of the changes that you make? Be in awe of how your soul uses your healing to transform the world.

December 10

Acting as If (Pat & Sue)

A powerful spiritual weapon in the war against shame is the powerful tool of *acting as if*. Millions of people, especially in twelve-step recovery programs, can testify to its power. It is not just a Pollyanna approach, not just the power of positive thinking. It is based in the proven principle, based in modern brain science, that if you think and act as if something is true for long enough, whether you feel it in your emotions at first or not, it will eventually become real to you. A good example is smiling. We not only smile when we are happy, we are happy when we smile. Choosing to smile, even when we feel down or sad, physiologically lifts our mood. Smiling makes us happy.

"Acting as if" against shame simply involves the courageous decision to believe what your soul and your God say is the magnificent truth about you and to practice that belief on a daily basis. Ignore what your mind and your emotions—so brainwashed by your abuse and abuser—scream at you.

Choose to live from the soul. Believe that you are a magnificent person of value. Act on this truth, relate from it, choose from it, pray from it, love from it, sleep in it, breathe and eat from it. Regularly and mischievously smile as if only you know the magnificent secret of who you truly are. Wholeheartedly act as if it is true, and eventually your feelings will follow. You will know in your head and feel in your heart that your soul speaks the truth: You are a magnificent person of infinite and inestimable value.

My Spiritual Practice for Today

All day long act as if you believe and feel your magnificence, value, and worth. Also smile as often as you can today, as if all is well and joyful for you. Act grateful for all that you experience today. Notice how all this shifts your mood and perspective.

December 11

Shame Quadruples (Pat & Sue)

We tell our clients that shame at least quadruples whatever emotional pain or stress you are experiencing. If you are in a difficult situation and in a great deal of pain, especially if the level of your pain seems bigger than the situation, it is always helpful to ask yourself if your shame has been stirred up. You may be in what we call a shame storm. A shame storm worsens any situation and greatly magnifies the pain. A fairly accurate indicator of the presence of shame is if you feel badly about yourself in the situation. Identifying that you are in the midst of a shame storm can often help you see your situation in a clearer perspective and help you lessen the emotional pain involved.

Shame is, of course, the emotional belief that you are essentially defective, bad, and worthless. It is a false belief about yourself that is caused by your trauma. Most survivors have some level of shame and are prone to shame storms when under stress. Shame is a very sticky substance. It adheres to you tightly and is difficult to remove. It helps to realize that all shame is a lie. None of it is ever true. The difficulty—and this is what makes shame so sticky—is that it feels like it is true. It feels real that you are somehow rotten to your core. Because it feels true, your mind searches for proof to confirm the lie. It invariably finds something that would seem to verify your shame. Except that your mind is in a shame storm that distorts your perception and deludes you into believing a lie by presenting you with false evidence for your shame. This is when you have to distrust your mind and trust your soul.

Your True Self knows the truth about your infinite value and worth. In a shame storm, listen only to your soul.

My Spiritual Practice for Today

If you are in a stressful situation, ask yourself if shame is multiplying your pain. If there is shame, identify the central lie underlying the shame. Ask your soul for the truth.

December 12

Scars (Pat)

The other day I decided to count my scars: three on my face and one on my chest. First is the scar above my right eye where I was hit by a bottle that I tried to take away from a teenage boy who was trying to hit another boy. The second scar is on the right side of my nose, the result of an infection that I incurred while working as a hospital chaplain. Number three has a less heroic story. It's a scar on my right cheek that happened while horsing around on a wet pool deck. My fourth scar is the best one, or at least the largest one. It is my mastectomy scar from my breast cancer surgery in 2015.

I used to worry a lot about how my scars looked to others. I eventually realized that no one else even noticed or cared but me. I now accept my scars as simply part of my life story and even as badges of courage. They are reminders of what I have survived and transcended. My scartography is simply the map of my life. My facial scars have blended into my face and are hardly noticeable. The scar on my cheek even turned into a dimple. I consider my mastectomy scar a badge of honor that marks that I am a cancer survivor. These scars have become a part of me, and yet do not define or limit me. I wear them with pride.

Trauma leaves emotional and spiritual scars that are not usually visible, and yet equally painful to bear. Some of them will heal fairly well and will blend into the rest of your beautiful self and will be hardly noticed. Others will never fully heal and will at least occasionally be painful, as my mastectomy scar is for me. No matter what though, your scars do not define you. You do not need to be embarrassed by them. They are a part of you and your story. Your scars are a reminder that you are a survivor. They are badges of courage and honor. Wear them with quiet pride in what you have overcome. Your soul will transform your scars into blessings and even into extraordinary beauty.

My Spiritual Practice for Today

Count your trauma scars. How have they been transformed, or how can they be transformed, into badges of honor for you as a survivor?

December 13

Flow, Flow, Flow Your Boat (Pat)

While watching the 2018 Winter Olympics from South Korea, I noticed a male coach for one of the downhill skiers knitting while standing beside his skier at the starting gate. At first I thought this was weird. Then I realized that the coach was using the knitting to stay centered in the stressful moments before his skier zoomed down the slope. He was entering into flow.

Flow is the mental and physical state in which a person performing an activity is fully immersed in a feeling of energized focus and full involvement and enjoyment. Flow is such complete absorption in an activity that you lose your sense of time and space. You are carried away from your normal stresses and anxieties to a different zone of consciousness. It yields great peace and a deep sense of satisfaction, competency, and confidence.

I experience flow in a variety of ways: when I'm writing, counseling, or making love; oftentimes while hiking, skiing, or sailing; even sometimes when I'm doing yard work. I love these moments of healthy escape and total absorption doing something I love. They are a marvelous timeout from stress, worry, or even time itself. They are body, mind, and soul nurturing.

Cultivating flow in your life can be a valuable tool for survivors. Going into flow can give relief from intrusive thoughts and emotional pain. You can learn to get so absorbed in some activity that you will be mercifully oblivious to your trauma and its aftereffects and become focused on what you are doing in a merger of action and awareness. You will temporarily forget yourself and all your troubles. Your soul loves these moments and invites you to discover them for yourself. It doesn't matter what activities you choose as long as they fully engage your attention or are a little challenging and give you a sense of competency and accomplishment. So start knitting, cooking, running, or whatever you choose to do, and learn to "flow, flow, flow your boat, gently down the stream, merrily, merrily…"

My Spiritual Practice for Today

Do you experience any moments of flow now? How can you incorporate more flow into your life? What activities can you engage in that allow you to be totally absorbed and centered?

December 14

You Are What You Let Inside (Vicki)

One of my favorite aspects of the spiritual life is the daily unfolding of grace. To wake up each morning with a feeling of gratitude and the expectation of a day filled with all possibilities. Saying a resounding yes to each day and all that might unfold.

We are made to be happy. The universe wants us to be happy. God has made us to love one another and be happy. Life happens though, doesn't it? And so often our days can be filled with nightmare stories that bring us to our knees. One important thing to remember when we are in the midst of chaos and dysfunction is that God is with us. It's not just a cliché to make us feel better. God's presence in our lives is where our strength lies. It doesn't matter what religion you are; the God of your understanding is the God that is walking through the aches and pains with you.

Having seen for myself the resilience of human beings to overcome the most unimaginable crisis, how could we doubt that we have the capacity to do the same? God's grace is there for all of us. Our attitude about change is key to understanding the inherent human capacity to overcome anything.

We are what we let inside. What we allow to influence our behavior is key to progressing in the healing journey. If we continue to entertain negative thinking, allow negative people to corrupt us, or resign ourselves to the idea that nothing will change, then we become our own worst enemies.

What are you letting inside today that is going to fill you with joy, with goodness, with affirmation that you are worth becoming all that God has called you to become?

My Spiritual Practice for Today

Take time to realize what you are allowing to influence your life. Is it life giving? Is it helping you to become your True Self?

December 15

Ego (Pat)

Acounseling client's first words to me recently were, "I just realized that our worst burden in life is our ego." I was struck by his words, particularly because he is a trauma survivor and currently lives in a challenging situation. We explored his statement together, unpacking its wisdom. We talked about ego as the ultimate source of dread and fear, no matter what trauma you have endured.

Ego in itself is not bad. Its purpose is to give you a sense of identity in the world and to protect you. However, a life based mainly on ego is a life precariously founded on the constant need to build yourself up by pretending you are superior, unique, and special. No wonder ego generates so much insecurity and fear. Ego is defining yourself by what you do and what you have rather by who you are in your True Self. Ego then is your false self or, better, your little self. It's been rightly said that an ego trip is a trip to nowhere. The greatest test of the spiritual life is to learn to shed the burden of ego and live in selflessness.

This can be very confusing to survivors. You have worked hard to build your self-image. So to be told to let go of ego sounds like the opposite of healing. However, it is the heart of healing and the truest way to discover your True Self.

You are not what you do or what you have. You are not what others think of you. You are not separate from others; you are not separate from Spirit. You are so much more than ego tries to tell you. Learning to let go of ego's hold on you is a lifelong process.

To overcome ego, you can: let go of your need to win or be right; surrender your need to be superior; let go of your need to possess more; quit measuring yourself by your achievements; stop being concerned about what others think about you. Life with less ego is life without fear. It is living in the lightness of being and experiencing a new freedom and serenity.

My Spiritual Practice for Today

Consider how much you live from ego and how much from your soul. Choose one way you can surrender some part of your ego today.

December 16

Beauty and Trauma Together (Sue)

Sometimes trauma and beauty, loss and joy, sacrifice and love are all woven together in a beautiful tapestry. This has been true for me in my experience of adopting two wonderful daughters. From the beginning of the adoption process, I was aware of the birth mother's trauma. She chose to gift her child with life in an act of great love. Then after carrying her baby for nine months, she chose to let her baby go so the baby could have a better life than the mother was able to give her at that time. An act of love that involved oceans of pain, loss, and oftentimes shame. After bonding with her baby for nine months, the mother chose the trauma of separation in an act of sacrifice and love for her precious little one. Such an admirable and courageous journey. Such pain and love all wrapped up together in a bundle of joy.

I have been the receiver of this gift twice. This has been a great joy each time, and continues to be so as I watch my two adopted daughters—as well as my three older children—grow into wonderful adults with children of their own. Yet I never forget the trauma and pain, the sacrifice and love, of my daughters' birth moms. It reminds me that great love and great joy can be born of terrible trauma. It seems strange, and yet it is so.

Today some birth moms and dads reconnect with their child later in life. This happened with my youngest daughter, who sought out her birth mother and in the process of connecting to her also discovered her birth father. She now has a strong relationship with them as well as their two subsequent children. Such a joyful gift for all of us. I am so grateful and blessed. And I am still aware of the pain, sacrifice, and love that brought me all of this joy.

My Spiritual Practice for Today

What possible love, joy, or new life is intertwined with your trauma? Without denying the pain, can you see any blessings or grace that can arise from your experience?

December 17

Perennial Wisdom (Pat & Sue)

Underneath the differences in world religions lies a unifying foundation of core beliefs and principles called the perennial wisdom. This is summarized from the writing of Aldous Huxley, a British philosopher (1894–1963), and the Christian mystic Meister Eckhart (1260–1328). There are five core principles of the Perennial Wisdom:

- There exists a Godhead, or Ground of Being, that is an unmanifested being behind and in all that is manifested in the universe.
- The Ground of Being is both transcendent and immanent; this means that God is both beyond us and within us and in all of Creation; God is Higher Power and God is Emmanuel (the Hebrew word meaning "God with us").
- All humans can grow to know, love, and be identified with the Ground of Being.
- To achieve a unitive, loving relationship with God, the Ground, is the final end and purpose for all human beings.
- There is a Word, a Dharma, a Tao, or a Way that can be learned and followed to fully live the first four principles and achieve serenity and enlightenment.

Many survivors struggle with religion and faith because of what they have experienced and because of all of the spiritual questions that trauma raises. You may no longer know what to believe. A part of your healing pilgrimage is to reconstruct for yourself a belief system and reimage a "God of your understanding."

These perennial principles can provide a new foundation of core beliefs to rebuild and personalize your faith. It is also encouraging to realize that all religion and spirituality share a core unity despite all of the differences and distressing conflicts.

My Spiritual Practice for Today

Reflect on these principles. What do they mean to you? Can you accept them as the central beliefs of your faith and spirituality?

December 18

A Larger Reframing of Life (Vicki)

It takes time to heal and gather our life experiences to be able to see our life's path in a larger context. To heal our wounds and trauma, we must be able to see life as much larger than the story we are working through. Paula D'Arcy shares in her book *Gift of the Red Bird* an example of this. After losing her husband and 2-year-old daughter, Sarah, in a drunk-driving accident, she felt shattered. When we hear such a tragic story, our first thought is, "My God, how could anyone be whole again from that?"

As I matured, I had to ask that question about my mother, who endured the loss of her 5-year-old daughter in a car accident. We can't imagine emotionally surviving such a loss. And yet we do. The human spirit is indomitable. We do go on to build a life without those dear loved ones.

Paula admits that despite her intense struggle and immense grief, she finally came to understand, after much time, that this experience was just one part of a much larger life ahead of her. Saying that doesn't minimize the trauma; it's just what we have to do.

When I began my process of healing, I couldn't see the larger picture, but stepping onto the path allowed me to see a much larger image of the life yet to be lived. Reframing our life so we can climb out of the small picture frame we are living inside is a monumental step. It has to happen for us to develop the full picture that we are destined to live.

Thank God there are gifted people who choose to walk with us to help us see more clearly how our life can become whole again. They help prepare us to walk into the love that waits for us. In that reframing, the love awaits, and it is ready to help catapult us into blessing upon blessing.

My Spiritual Practice for Today

Take little steps and begin imagining what your life will be after you move through the process of healing. What are your dreams for your life?

December 19

#NeverAgain (Pat)

Columbine, Aurora, Sandy Hook, Las Vegas, Parkland, and so many others. This is the litany of some of the terrible mass shootings that have afflicted the nation. Everyone in America has been traumatized by the all too frequent horror of innocent people—especially students at school—being gunned down. All of us have become survivors of the trauma of these horrific events. All Americans now suffer from collective PTSD. There is an increase in anxiety, a new hypervigilance whenever we are in a public place or a crowd, and a chronic helplessness and despair about the future. Sadly, this is happening particularly in our children.

Survivors of every type of trauma are particularly vulnerable to each news story about the latest shooting. You may find yourself reliving your own trauma, feeling unsafe and helpless, depressed and hopeless. It is important during these difficult times to take especially good care of yourself. Minimize your exposure to traumatic news images. Resist the compulsion to focus over and over on the horrors of the mass shootings. Remind yourself of the progress you have made in healing your own trauma. Pray for the survivors and the victims' families. Choose to trust in the soul's resilient light and the ultimate triumph of love even in the midst of this darkness.

The students of Parkland and the families of Sandy Hook and Columbine are showing us one powerful way to respond to our collective PTSD. They are refusing to be victimized by their fear and are courageously speaking out in holy anger, demanding change to protect us all. Whether you agree with their solutions, you have to admire their determination to turn their loss and trauma into powerful words and actions to help prevent these awful mass shootings. They are demonstrating to us that none of us needs to be a victim.

You may or may not be called to do something similar. You can use their courageous example to step out of the shadow of your trauma to find your voice and your own soul-inspired protest. In your own way, you can join the swelling chorus chanting the powerful prayer and anthem, "Never again."

My Spiritual Practice for Today

Observe how you are being affected by the mass shootings. Find ways to better protect yourself from being further traumatized. Ask your soul how you are being called to respond.

December 20

Next to Normal (Pat & Sue)

Next to Normal is a powerful rock musical, alternately funny and challenging, about a woman struggling with bipolar disorder. Among the questions it raises is, "What is normal?"

We frequently get this question from our survivor clients. You want to know what is normal and how do you become it. Like many survivors, you may feel that you are not normal. You feel that your trauma has rendered you somehow abnormal and uniquely, irredeemably less than others who are supposedly the normal ones. You long to be normal, and yet you have little idea how to get there.

We hate to disappoint you, and we have to say that we have come to the conclusion, after many years as therapists searching for normal ourselves, that normal does not exist. There is no such animal. Each individual is so unique and each person's story and makeup is so gloriously varied that one definition of normal is not possible. It's also not desirable.

It's so much better that you abandon the false yardstick of normal and seek to be the wondrously unique person you already are. All you need to be is yourself, your best self, and your healthy self. The best measurement for progress is how healthy you are becoming in your own singular fashion. Seek to be healthy, or the closest you can come to healthy, rather than normal—whatever that is. You will be different than others who you might consider normal (surprise, they aren't normal either!). That is okay. You will be you.

As actor Ben Platt said in his 2017 Tony acceptance speech, "Don't waste any time trying to be anybody but yourself because the things that make you strange are the things that make you powerful." So please don't try to be normal. Simply be your unique, powerful, healthy, best self.

My Spiritual Practice for Today

Choose today to give up the compulsion to be normal. Reflect instead on how to grow into the healthiest, best edition of you. Think of one step you can take in that direction today.

December 21

Winter Solstice (Pat)

Winter solstice is a holy day for many spiritual traditions and cultures, especially more ancient ones that were better in touch with nature and the rhythms of the seasons than we moderns are. The winter solstice is a celebration of light triumphing over darkness. The promise of the return of the sun even on the longest, darkest night. It is a reminder in the midst of winter that the light of the sun triumphs and nature will reawaken in the spring. Even early Christians acknowledged the solstice when they decided to celebrate Christmas, the birthday of Christ the Light, four days after the solstice.

In ancient times, special feasts and holy places marked the solstice. One of these places is Stonehenge in central Britain. Imagine that you are at Stonehenge before dawn on December 21, the year 1025 BC. You are surrounded by your family, your tribe, and a magnificent circle of stones towering over you. It has been a long, cold night, and you are anxiously awaiting the sun to warm you. A hush comes over the people, and then you see it, the sun and its brilliant rays rising above the stones. You are filled with awe and ecstatic with joy, for you know what this means. Your people have learned from close observation that these stones align with the start of the return of the sun. You celebrate and feast all day, and then gather again just before sunset within the circle of holy stones. You watch the sun set exactly over the sunset stone, perfectly aligned to mark this moment. You are a little saddened to see the day end and the sun leaving. You may be a little frightened as the darkness of the longest night settles in around you.

Yet you are filled with hope and confidence because the alignment of the stone and the sun promise you that the sun with its life-giving light is starting its return. Winter and its leanness will end; spring with new life is on its way. The light, sinking beneath the stone, sinks into your heart and soul, the promise of the triumph of light over darkness renewed.

My Spiritual Practice for Today

Celebrate the solstice in whatever way that fits for you. Reflect on its reminder that the light of your soul has and will triumph over even the long, dark night of trauma.

December 22

It's Just A Story (Pat)

Much of fear is just a story. All of shame is just a fairy tale. Fear and shame are stories that your trauma taught you to tell yourself and others. They are very powerful tales. And they are not true stories. They are lies, false narratives, and total fiction. It's as if an evil witch or wizard sat inside you after your trauma, cast a spell, and weaved an unholy tale about you and your trauma that you could not refuse to believe. It's time for you to stop believing. Your shame story is not really true. Your fear story is at least heavily exaggerated. Break the spell, cast out the witch and the wizard, and stop retelling their story to yourself and others.

You can choose to see the distortion and the lies in your fear and shame stories. This is a good beginning, and yet it may take some time to break the spell and fully realize that the stories you have believed are not true. Then you will be ready to write a new story, a new script for your life. Your soul will guide you.

Your fear story can be rewritten as a true story about your courage and resilience in surviving your trauma. You can see that you are brave and much stronger than you thought. Your shame story can be recast as a story of self-love and self-compassion for what you have endured and transcended. Your new screenplay will reflect the truth of your ultimate value and worth. You will write yourself into your own life movie as the hero or heroine, gifted and blessed in so many ways unique to you alone.

A fear story begets more fear; however, a power story begets more power. A shame story sustains your shame; a soul-esteem story breaks the power of shame and introduces you to the beautiful truth of your magnificence.

My Spiritual Practice for Today

Begin to question the veracity of your fear and shame stories. Where are the lies? What is the fiction that your trauma made you believe? Imagine what your new soul-inspired story will be like. If you are ready, write it.

December 23

Feasting on Delight (Pat)

Holiday meals are festive celebrations of life. Gathered with family or friends around a sumptuous banquet, you share the fruits of the cook's loving preparations and feast on the delights Mother Earth has brought before you. At these special meals—and really at every meal—you celebrate the essential goodness of life.

Festival banquets are also a symbol in many cultures of God's presence with the people and the abundance offered and given to them in many different ways. This is one description from the Old Testament (Isaiah 25:6–9): "On this mountain, the Lord of hosts will provide for all peoples, a feast of rich food and choice wines, juicy, rich food, and pure, choice wines." It goes on to say how God will heal the people of their wounds and dry their tears at this holy banquet.

You can feast every day at the banquet of delight that is always around you. You can be mindful of the goodness of life at special and everyday meals. You also can feed your mind daily with delight when you focus on the goodness and beauty around you and allow yourself to fully enjoy the pleasures and soul satisfactions offered you daily. Trauma may have trained you to look for the darkness and the dangers. However, you are in charge of what you feed your mind. You can feed it the junk food of negative, despairing thoughts or the sumptuous food of delight.

There is always delight available to feed yourself with. All you have to do is look for it with the eyes of your soul. You will find delight in so many places: in the clear, sharp light of a winter day, in the smile of your beloved, in the twinkle in the eye of your mischievous child, in a rainbow after a storm, or in the brilliant colors of the setting sun. Stop gnawing and noshing on negativity. Learn to feast on delight.

My Spiritual Practice for Today

Stop several times a day to look for delight. Allow your senses and your mind to feast on soul-satisfying food. At the end of the day, nourish yourself by picturing in your mind and reliving the best delight of that day.

December 24

Silent Night (Pat)

"Silent night, Holy night, All is calm, All is bright." These are the opening lines of the beautiful, traditional carol that describes the serenity of the night when a new light was born into the world. These words also describe what you as a survivor will experience when you reclaim the nighttime from the darkness of your trauma.

For many survivors, their abuse occurred during the night. This may make the night a fearful time, with your anxiety increasing as the sun sets and darkness creeps in. You may also struggle with sleeping soundly. Sleep is an act of letting go of control, of vulnerability and trust. It works best in darkness. This can be very threatening to some survivors.

Everyone needs and deserves a silent, holy night, when all is calm and quiet, and all is bright and luminous. You need a moment in your night when you feel the peace of your soul and reflect on your day, become filled with gratitude for the day's blessings, and be enlightened by its lessons. To experience this, you can reclaim the night from the fearful memories of your trauma. You will make night holy and sacred, serene and silent, a blessed time of rest, reflection, and quiet preparation for peaceful sleep.

My Spiritual Practice for Today

No matter what holiday you celebrate, Christmas, Hanukah or winter solstice, it is likely a celebration of the light overcoming the darkness. To reclaim night for yourself, find a quiet place and turn off all screens and sources of noise. Place one unlit candle on a table. Turn out all the lights. Consciously welcome the darkness and the silence, imagining only peace, blessing, and love coming to you and surrounding you. Reflect on the blessings of the day now ending. If your mind tries to return to any painful memories, focus on your peaceful breathing and your present blessings. When you are ready, light the candle and say, "In God's name, through the power of my soul, I reclaim this night for myself as sacred and healing; now and each night from this time forward." Then silently gaze at the flame of the candle, seeing it as the light of your soul permeating every corner of darkness, making night safe, holy, and bright.

December 25

Christmas—A Festival of Light (Pat & Sue)

He has made the night of our darkness, the night of our lack of understanding, the cruel night of our fear and our hopelessness into Christmas, the Holy Night! In the Word made flesh God has sent God's last Word, God's most profound Word, God's most beautiful Word into the world. And that Word means: "I love you, O World, O Humanity! Light the candles! They have more right to be here than darkness.
–Karl Rahner

It is thought that early Christians picked December 25 to celebrate Jesus's birth to coincide with the Romans' celebration of the return of the sun after the winter solstice. For Christians Jesus is the light of the world. The Jewish feast of Hanukkah is also known as the Festival of Lights and is celebrated around this time.

The triumph of light over darkness is a universal, all-humanity spiritual theme. Jesus, as well as Buddha, shows us the way to enlightenment. Abraham, Moses, and the Jewish prophets lit up the world with their faith and teachings. Mohammed and the Koran bring light to millions around the globe. Hinduism celebrates Diwali, their Festival of Lights in the autumn. So this Christmas, focus on all of the ways light is brought into the world and make it a personal and universal Festival of Light.

My Spiritual Practice for Today

Today is a day for you to celebrate the soul light that has come into the darkness of your trauma and has dispelled it. Look within you. Look all around you. See the light that has come into your life in so many ways. There may still be some darkness, and Christmas is a day to focus only on the light. See the light in children's eyes today. See the light in your beloved's eyes beaming love to you. Tour some light displays. Spend silent time in front of the Christmas tree or the menorah with all the rest of the lights out. Reflect on how light has come into your life this past year. See how the light of your soul has dispelled the darkness of shame and fear. Behold how your soul has birthed new joy and gratitude within you. Give thanks for all of the ways you have been enlightened. Have a merry and light-filled Christmas!

December 26

A Slight Shift of Emphasis (Vicki)

Brother David Stiendl-Rast, a Benedictine monk and author, teaches gratitude in a most profound way. There is one sentence that I hold close and have memorized.

> *It takes only a slight shift of emphasis, and the point of aloneness in dynamic stillness becomes the point of consummate union.*

These simple words remind me always that I have the power to become more in every second of every day. It is my choice to overcome a negative feeling or behavior that is not life giving. I know that it takes only an infinitesimal shift of emphasis within my consciousness to change the outcome of a moment or a day or a lifetime.

We can live resistant to becoming more by choosing to wallow in dysfunction and to transmit our pain to others. We can also wake up one morning and realize that living in the midst of chaos is no longer serving us. Sometimes we simply have to walk away from toxic people, even family members, in order to deal with our own "shit." To move from victim to survivor to thriver is a heroic walk and takes mammoth courage. We have the power. We have the free will to make this decision for ourselves.

Imagine that one moment we are stuck in the muck; then, if we choose, we can be pulled toward the one that can open the gate and reveal a deeper understanding of who we are and what our potential can be. It can bring us toward consummate union with our God. The notion that a slight shift of emphasis can indeed change the world is one that starts with each human heart.

My Spiritual Practice for Today

Take brief moments of negative thoughts today and practice what Brother David says. Practice consciously shifting the emphasis from a negative, damaging mind-set to a positive, spirit-filled mind-set.

December 27

Unless You Become Like a Little Child (Sue)

One day I was fixing lunch in the kitchen. My grandson Jason, then 3, was outside on the patio. I heard him calling to me, sounding very excited. "Granny! Granny! Come look!" When I joined him on the patio, Jason motioned me to drop down on my belly (in those days I could do that—LOL). As my body adjusted to the hardness of the concrete, my eyes were doing their best to focus on what he was seeing. Jason pointed his chubby little finger and exclaimed, "Watch him!" Sure enough there was a single small ant walking along the edge of the patio with a crumb of bread gripped in his mouth. The tiny ant struggled with his prize, dragging it to the anthill we could now spy amid the blades of grass uphill from us. "There! He made it!" Jason exclaimed. Then to my amazement, the next ant in the relay line found the piece of bread, broke off his own crumb, and began the journey back to his anthill home. Jason had seen the ants and dropped down to study this amazing process. I was so grateful that he had invited me to enter into his world of childlike wonder and discovery. How blessed it is to be a granny!

Jesus said, "Unless you change, and become like a little child, you will not enter the kingdom of heaven" (Matthew 18:2–3). He does not mean that you will not go to heaven. Jesus is saying that you have to do what Jason and I did if you want to experience the joy and peace of abiding in the place of wonder and grace offered to us. You are invited to rediscover your childlike spirit—perhaps your inner child—and learn again how to see the small mercies, the small wonders, the tiny packets of joy and inspiration that lay all around us. These are things that only children—or adults who become childlike—notice and absorb.

If I had been seeing as an adult that day with Jason, I would have stepped right over the ants or maybe even unwittingly stepped on them. Jason opened my eyes to truly see the many small miracles right before our eyes.

My Spiritual Practice for Today

Who or what can make you get down on your belly and open your eyes?

December 28

The Courage to Be Vulnerable (Pat & Sue)

The spiritual life is full of paradoxes. One of the greatest is that to be strong in the Spirit, you have to learn to be vulnerable. Vulnerability means that you have the courage to be visible, to let yourself be seen by others. Vulnerability is a vital component of intimacy of every kind, with trusted people in your life and with your soul and God. The word "intimacy" can be broken down to "in to me you see," revealing both the meaning and process of letting others get close to you. This is understandably intimidating for survivors. Trauma has closed off your ability to be vulnerable because your vulnerability was taken advantage of by your abuser or by the traumatic situation. Your self-protective instinct tells you to put up stout walls to defend yourself and never be vulnerable again. This is a necessary stance for a time. Eventually it isolates you, cuts you off from love, and makes you susceptible to further hurt.

Your soul invites you to risk and dare to be vulnerable. You are encouraged to, bit by bit, make the powerful choice to be visible again. What feels scary and weak will bring you the greatest emotional and spiritual strength. Vulnerability with your soul and with God is the gateway to many spiritual gifts: awe, wonder, and mystical experience; inner peace and freedom from fear and shame; access to your inner wisdom, intuition, and creativity; a deeper relationship with your soul and your Higher Power; and to love itself.

Where better to relearn to be vulnerable than by opening yourself and making yourself known to your soul and to your God? You can also start to be vulnerable and open to your trusted soul friends. As you respond to this invitation to vulnerability, you will gradually install windows and doors into the walls of your castle, and it will be much stronger, safer, and brighter than when you were all walls.

My Spiritual Practice for Today

Is there anything that you have tried to hide from your soul and your God? Ask for the grace of courageous vulnerability to open yourself up, and let this part of you or your life be visible to your Higher Power. Imagine yourself being bathed in the warmest, most welcoming light as you do so.

December 29

It's a Marathon (Pat)

A teacher who was traumatized by the shooting at Columbine High School nineteen years ago was quoted as advising students and teachers from Parkland in Florida, "Remember that your healing is a marathon, not a sprint." This is good advice for all survivors.

Your healing is a process that takes time, sometimes a great deal of time. So be gentle and patient with yourself. Give yourself space and time for healing to unfold. Don't pressure yourself with unreasonable expectations. Pace yourself like a good marathoner. Stay with your healing process, and yet don't rush it. It is happening. It will unfold as it is meant to be.

A better metaphor for your healing is a pilgrimage. One of the things on my bucket list is to someday make the Camino de Santiago (Way of St. James) pilgrimage. It is a walking pilgrimage of many weeks. Its length varies for each pilgrim, depending where each one makes his or her start. Its purported goal is the shrine of the apostle St. James in the cathedral of Santiago de Compostela in northwest Spain.

The actual goal though is your soul. It is a pilgrimage to reconnect or more deeply connect with your inner light. It is a time to renew your Spirit, to reevaluate your values and the direction of your life. This happens each day of the walking, not just when you arrive at the cathedral. It happens as you talk with fellow pilgrims. It happens as you stop to meditate. Being close to nature and more alive in your body draws you closer to your soul. There are revelations when you stop for dinner and share a meal and a bottle of local wine. There are revelations when you trek alone.

So accept that your healing is not a sprint. It is a Way, a pilgrimage to return to your True Self. As John Wayne might say, walk slow, Pilgrim, be mindful, and be grateful for each moment along your Way.

My Spiritual Practice for Today

What are your expectations for your healing journey? Are you pressing and asking too much of yourself? How can you be more patient and gentle with yourself?

December 30

What is My Call Now? (Pat)

Why have I been saved from cancer? Why did I go through all of this suffering during my treatment? Why am I still alive?

I don't pose these questions as a form of self-pity or even a philosophical inquiry; rather I ask to discover what is the vocation, the call from God in all of this? For what have I endured and survived? What will come from this for others and myself in the present and for the future? What is my call now after surviving what I went through? These questions continue to rattle around in my mind and bubble up from my soul, especially when I meditate.

A call is an invitation, a passion, a desire, a choice, and a commitment all rolled into one. The invitation is from your soul and from your God. The spiritual phenomenon of call is not limited to recognized spiritual leaders like priests, ministers, rabbis, and imams. Everyone has a call and a calling. Your call is not from some esoteric, mysterious spiritual experience. It is earthy, real and rooted, and grown in the soil of your life experiences, surprisingly even in the seedbed of your trauma. Your call will blossom and be seen and heard as you cultivate a new sense of purpose and mission arising from the suffering of your trauma. The call may be to something new, some new direction in your life. Or it may be a call to a deeper recommitment to whatever you are doing now. The call may be to something small, medium, or really big. It doesn't matter. It is all big, all valuable, all useful, if it is your call.

As I continue to listen to my post-cancer trauma call, I am still not entirely clear about what I am being called to. I learned many things from my experience that I would like to use to help others. At present I'm unsure what that will involve. I do sense a deeper commitment to my writing as a way to share some of this. And I certainly have a better understanding and compassion for what my counseling clients are enduring. I sense, though, that I am being called to something more. So I continue to listen.

My Spiritual Practice for Today

Ask your soul for an awareness of your call. What do you hear? To what new or current calling are you being invited?

December 31 (A.M.)

What Kind of Future? (Pat)

What kind of future do you envision and plan for yourself? A new branch of psychology called prospective psychology has discovered that the large majority of our thinking each day is about visualizing and planning for our future—the future of the next moment and the future of years from now. Research has also shown that it is not past painful events that determine how well we feel and function. Rather it is whether we can envision a basically positive future and believe that we are competent enough to produce it. If we see a satisfying future for ourselves, we will be happy and at peace. If we create in our minds a dim, negative, and scary future, we will likely suffer from depression and anxiety.

Your brain uses your memory of past events, including trauma, and your image of yourself to construct your personal future vision and plan. Abuse and trauma can rob you of confidence in yourself and any belief that your future could be hopeful. It's vital to realize that trauma has created a distorted and inaccurate image of yourself and the life you can create for yourself. Many people drive the car of their life forward by looking in the rearview mirror. A dangerous way to drive!

Your past does not have to be prologue for your future. It may be necessary to look back for a time to heal the hurts of the past; then the challenge is to stop looking into the rearview mirror and look out the windshield of your life to the present moment and the future you are driving into. Then you can see the choices you have, decide where you want to turn, and select the direction you want to take. You can even reconstruct the very road you are driving on.

My Spiritual Practice for Today

Reflect for a few minutes on what sort of future you envision for yourself, both your picture of tomorrow and your dreams about the longer vistas of your life. How much of it is shaped by trauma? Choose to let go of the negative, trauma-based future, and begin to create a future based on the hope, joy, and prosperity that your soul desires for you.

December 31 (P.M.)

The Mountain Meditation: Your Past Year (Sue & Pat)

My Spiritual Practice for Today

We invite you to do the Mountain Meditation one last time this year. This time the theme is your journey through the last twelve months. Bring to the mountain everything that has been healing for you in the past year. Bring everything that you are grateful for from this year now ending. Let your soul and the Spirit guide you about what to bring. To enter into this meditation, find a comfortable sitting position. As you read, pause, close your eyes, and imagine the scenes described.

Picture yourself on a beautiful beach. See the waves, the sand, the brilliant color, and the vastness of the ocean. Feel the sun and the wind on your skin. Hear the crash and whoosh of the surf. Turn around now, and face away from the sea. This time pack your backpack with all of your experiences of healing from the past year and all that that you are thankful for. Notice how it feels to carry this.

In front of you is a beautiful forest. See yourself walking along a trail into the forest. Appreciate the coolness and the shaded light. You reach the edge of the forest and see an open meadow filled with multicolored wildflowers. The trail leads you through the meadow to a clear, flowing stream with a bridge across the dancing water. Stop for a moment to enjoy the light sparkling on the water.

Now look up from the bridge and see a shining mountain before you. Following the trail, you ascend the mountain. You climb above the timberline through the clouds to the top of the peak. Look around you at the glory of creation. Then you notice a large boulder to sit on and rest.

From the other side of the peak, your spiritual guide comes and sits down with you on the boulder. You can discuss whatever you want. Unpack your backpack and lay its contents out before your spirit guide. Listen for what is said to you about what you have brought. If you receive anything, embrace it and put it in your backpack to bring it down the mountain to the outside world. Ask for a word of encouragement or guidance from your spirit guide.

When you are ready to leave, thank your Higher Power. Slowly hike back down the mountain, over the bridge, through the meadow, through the forest, to the beach, and to the edge of the vast ocean. Open your eyes. Record and reflect in your journal.

Appendix I

Five Pathways to Healing the Spirit from Abuse and Trauma

All abuse, all trauma, is an assault on the human spirit. All survivors of abuse and trauma suffer not only psychological damage, but soul damage as well. Your soul itself cannot be weakened or broken. However, abuse and trauma can rob you of your connection to your soul, can obscure your vision of your soul's light within you, and can block your hearing of its soft whispers of wisdom and guidance. All of this can cloud, or even block, your experience of your essential and eternal value and worth. This is what makes your spirit feel broken. This is what needs restoration and healing.

The Five Pathways provide a spiritual GPS, a road map, for your healing journey. It is a pilgrimage to the center of your True Self, to the mending of your spirit, and to the reclaiming of your soul from the effects of abuse. The Five Pathways will empower you to navigate the healing roads and inner landscapes you need to travel. Each pathway involves personal soul work and provides the necessary spiritual tools and soul experiences to guide you along the path of your healing process.

The Pathway of Spiritual Courage

Abuse and trauma inflict paralyzing fear and debilitating shame. These are at the root of many emotional and psychological problems. Fear and shame can also become a sickness of the soul when you are controlled by fear and are oppressed by the shame belief that you are bad, defective, worthless, unlovable, or even evil. On the pathway of spiritual courage, your soul works to liberate you from the oppressive power of fear and shame. Your soul leads you to peace and trust, bringing you to the truth that you are a magnificent person of infinite value. Spiritual courage is the soul-empowered determination to overcome fear, to discover who you really are, and to stop allowing fear and shame to rob you of your precious self and freedom.

On this pathway your soul will:

- lead you past your fears to let go of the past, surrender the future, and live in the peace and joy of the present moment
- encourage you to tell and retell your story to trusted soul-friends and, in the telling, move from victim to survivor to thriver
- break the bondage of shame by discovering your True Self, God's precious child, a magnificent person of infinite value and worth

The Pathway of Holy Anger

Just anger about your abuse or trauma is holy, healing, and empowering. It is a spiritual antidote to the shame and helplessness caused by abuse. Holy anger works with spiritual courage to affirm and empower you to live in the sacredness and beauty of your soul. Until you tap into the holy energy of your just anger, abuse still owns and controls you, and the trauma still defines you. Your soul, through holy anger, endows you with the power to break free from the wounds and life-traps caused by abuse and trauma.

On this pathway your soul will:

- use the energy from your anger to rediscover the sacredness and greatness of who you are and stand firm in that truth
- rediscover and restore inner strengths that abuse hid from you
- endow you with the power to change what is wounded, unjust, unhealthy, or abusive in your current life situation

The Pathway of Sacred Grief

Some things are so sad only your soul can do the crying for you. Grief and sorrow about what you have lost from abuse and trauma is painful, and yet can be a blessing. The spiritual purpose of grief is to slow you down and pull you inward for a time. This allows you to own and mourn your losses and discover their spiritual meaning. Grief gradually renews your shaken and broken spirit, and then reenergizes you to reinvest in your life in a new and more deeply soul-directed way. Grief is your soul's way of calling you to a time of spiritual retreat.

On this pathway your soul will:

- invite you to move deeper inside yourself, and to slow down for a time of inner spiritual reflection on your life's journey
- help you to name, feel, and mourn what you have lost as a result of your abuse or trauma
- guide you to restore the lost pieces of your broken spirit and begin to reorient and reenergize your life in new meaning and purpose

The Pathway of Forgiveness

Forgiveness is first for the forgiver, for your healing as a survivor. The purpose of forgiveness is to set your soul free from the abuse and the abuser, to let it fly and soar. Chronic anger turned to bitterness weighs down your soul and blocks it from fully expressing its love, peace, and desire for mercy. Forgiveness allows you to hold the memories of the abuse and trauma in your mind, heart, and soul without bitter resentment. Then you are no longer controlled by these painful memories. Forgiveness is a process, a journey, that your soul will bring you to when you are ready. Forgiveness is empowering. Forgiveness is freedom. Forgiveness is the path to a new and joyous life.

On this pathway your soul will:

- provide you the grace and ability to forgive; you need only to be willing to be willing to forgive
- empower you to let go of your anger and break the chains that bind you to the abuse and the abuser
- place the abuse and trauma fully and finally into the past
- enable you to see the trauma and abuse, and even your abuser, in a new light

The Pathway of Transformation

There are surprising gifts of the spirit that are hidden in your experience of abuse and trauma. What have you gained, how are you stronger because of the abuse? What inner wisdom, creativity, or awareness has come from the abuse?

How has your trauma broken you open to a deepened spiritual journey that might never have occurred without the abuse? These are the soul-expanding questions of the Transformation Pathway. On this pathway your soul is bringing forth from the depths of your suffering a new consciousness that can awaken new purpose, meaning, mission, and even service in your life.

On this pathway your soul will:

- reveal to you the spiritual gifts hidden in the depths of the trauma
- shed new light on the abuse and illuminate new purpose and meaning arising from your suffering
- kindle within you a life mission and service resurrected from the ashes of the abuse and trauma

Copyright 2018 Patrick Fleming and Sue Lauber-Fleming
From *Shattered Soul? Five Pathways to Healing the Spirit after Abuse and Trauma* (WordStream Publishing, 2011)

By
Patrick Fleming, Sue Lauber-Fleming, and Vicki Schmidt

Appendix II

The Spiritual Laundry List

A Spiritual Laundry List for Adult Children from Dysfunctional or Abusive Families

The Grease, Grit, and Grime: We seem to have several spiritual characteristics in common as a result of being raised in a wounded, dysfunctional, or abusive household.

We have imaged our Higher Power, the God of our understanding, in a distorted way due to our childhood experience of our dysfunctional, addicted, or abusive parent (or other significant adult).

We find it difficult to discover and experience the God of our understanding or, at times, even perceive within us the existence of a Higher Power at all.

We have come to believe that God is not faithful, that God is as unpredictable and untrustworthy as our wounded and abusive parent or other abuser.

We have come to believe that God's love is conditional and that we have God's acceptance only if we are perfect.

We think that our Higher Power demands more of us than we can give or handle, just as we once felt overwhelmed by the needs of our dysfunctional families or by the trauma of our abuse.

We find it difficult or impossible to trust our Higher Power.

Our spirituality is grim and lacks hope, joy, or serenity; we find it difficult to be hopeful or trust in the gift of love available to us.

We are consumed with the past, anxious about the future, and are unable to simply be in the moment with God, with another person, or with God's creation.

We fear being abandoned by our Higher Power and so resist being drawn closer to God.

We struggle with major commitments, or even becoming aware of our life-vision, purpose, and journey.

Our spirituality is based on a sense of shame and unreasonable guilt and is dominated by "shoulds."

Our spiritual growth is impeded by self-sufficiency, and we resist the need for God and others, since as children we could not depend on our addicted or abusive parent.

We find it difficult to be grateful.

We have become addicted to religion.

Our spirituality has become excessively centered on self and lacks compassion or empathy for others.

The Wash, Rinse, and Polish: By choosing the spiritual healing journey, we learn that we can live our lives in a more meaningful manner; we can learn to change our attitudes, habits, and old patterns, including our old patterns of relating to our Higher Power, to find serenity, purpose, and happiness.

We learn that God is good and loving after all. We discover that our Higher Power does not possess any of the negative characteristics that we experienced in our abuser.

We learn to see our abusers as human beings, let go of the anger and bitterness we once projected from them onto our Higher Power, and choose forgiveness.

Our spiritual healing frees our will; we find that we have choices in our spirituality; we can choose to experience our spirit, our soul, and our Higher Power in new and life-giving ways.

We choose to surrender our lives and will to the God of our understanding.

We accept that we are accepted by God; we accept that we are accepted and loved not for what we do but simply because we are!

We let go of the delusion and control of shame and perfectionism, stop "shoulding" upon ourselves, and begin to adopt personal values, which are reasonable and lead to balance and wholeness.

Our spiritual journey includes chosen companions with whom we share our soul and whom we allow to affirm and challenge us.

Through a balanced program of prayer and meditation, we develop an authentic and personal relationship with our God and invite God into every area of our lives.

We discover our poverty without God and daily live in our need of God.

We learn and experience the gift of being in the present moment with our God and with God's creation.

We recover a childlike sense of wonder, joy, and awe about the magnificence of ourselves and all of creation.

We develop a grateful heart and live in thankfulness for the many gifts that we have been given and that surround us always.

Our spirituality reveals to us that we are a person of great and infinite value; this knowledge about ourselves leads us to more fully value and love others in our life.

Our soul leads us to live in a new sense of purpose and mission that enhances and deepens our lives and the lives of all with whom we come into contact.

Recommended Resources

Any healing from the psychological and spiritual wounds of abuse and trauma is a journey best made with helpful and supportive companions. It does not have to be, and should not be, done alone. Today we are blessed with many local, regional, national, and international resources for survivors of all kinds of abuse and trauma. They include support groups, support organizations, counselors, pastors and spiritual directors, and retreat and treatment centers.

We provide here a limited list of such resources that we are most closely connected to in order to help you find the most helpful companions for your journey to wholeness in body, mind, and spirit. You will find similar resources in your own community and network.

Twelve-Step Support Groups

Survivors of Incest Anonymous (SIA): www.siawso.org; 410-893-3322

Co-Dependents Anonymous (CoDA): www.coda.org; 888-444-2357

Al-Anon (especially ACA [Adult Children of Alcoholics] meetings): www.al-anon.alateen.org; 888-4AL-Anon (888-425-2666)

Hotlines and Support Organizations

Rape, Abuse, Incest, National Network (RAINN): www.rainn.org; 800-656-HOPE (800-656-4673)

Adult Survivors of Child Abuse (ASCA): www.ascasupport.org

Survivors Network of those Abused by Priests (SNAP): www.snapnetwork.org; 877-762-7432

Office of Child and Youth Protection, U.S. Catholic Bishops, Victim Assistance Coordinators: www.usccb.org/ocyp

Pandora's Project (rape and sexual abuse): www.pandys.org

www.isurvive.org: online support community for survivors

Institute on Violence, Abuse, and Trauma: www.ivatcenters.org

National Domestic Violence Hotline: 800-799-SAFE (800-799-7233); www.thehotline.org

Suicide Hotline: 800-SUICIDE (800-784-2433)

Professional Resources

International Institute for Trauma and Addiction Professionals (IITAP): www.iitap.com

Spiritual Directors International: www.sdiworld.org

Spiritual Directors and Retreat Centers: www.findthedivine.com

American Association of Christian Counselors: www.aacc.net

Society for Advancement of Sexual Health: www.sash.net

Acknowledgments

Soul Light was conceived one day several years ago when Sue and I were at the annual conference for therapists sponsored by IITAP (International Institute of Trauma and Addiction Professionals). I had spent the day in professional training, while Sue had spent much of the afternoon hanging out in the conference bookstore with Corrine Casanova, then the editor of Gentle Path Press. When Sue and I met in the lobby of the conference center, Sue excitedly announced to me: "We have our next book, and Corrine and I have already decided that we will write it." Sue and Corrine had hatched the idea for this book during a casual conversation about what kinds of books were needed and not yet available. They decided a meditation book for survivors of trauma would be a valuable contribution. At first I felt a bit overwhelmed and intimidated by the prospect of writing and compiling this book, and yet I quickly jumped on board with Sue and Corrine.

So I first want to thank Sue and Corrine for their inspiration. Corrine, thank you also for your early support, guidance, and patience as this project unfolded. I want to thank Stefanie Carnes, PhD, and the whole staff of IITAP and Gentle Path Press for your expertise, support, receptivity, and flexibility. Thank you for believing in this book and wholeheartedly embracing it.

Words cannot express the gratefulness that I feel toward you, Sue, my best friend, wife, *anam cara*, partner, co-therapist, and co-author. Thank you for forty years of fun, adventure, spiritual journeying, support, challenge, work and love that we have shared.

Soul-felt thanks to Vicki Schmidt for her willingness to share her journey of courage, healing, and great soul with us in life and in this book. You are a precious soul-friend as well.

I want to thank everyone in my family for the incredible outpouring of love I received from you during my battle against breast cancer. Without you I would not have won the war and likely would not still be here.

Finally, I thank the many survivors of all types of trauma whom I have been graced to counsel over the years for sharing your story with me and allowing me to accompany you on your journey of healing. You taught me so much about courage and soul and Spirit. I have received more from each of you than I was ever able to give. I remain in awe of you. Your witness and strength of soul and spirit is the true inspiration for this book.

—Patrick Fleming

God's love is amazing! Thanks for this opportunity to journey so intimately with my best friend, co-author, challenger, adventurer, spiritual mentor, and husband, Patrick. You are truly open to Spirit and to allowing the "writer" to be heard! For this I am grateful!

And where would I be without my children, Joe, Mary, Gerry, Cindy, and Louise, and their amazing spouses, Angie, Arnie and Jack? From the time they were little, I have learned from and laughed and cried with my children, and I continue to be humbled by their unconditional love for me. Thank you, Jason, Molly, Christopher, John, Sammi, Michelle, Nicole, Kevin, Maggie, Erin, and Kate. You are the best grandchildren ever! My three great-grandchildren, Emery, Belle, and Shep, are the icing on the cake. All of you bring smiles, joy, wonderment, new perspectives, challenge, excitement, awe, hugs, and lots of love. Each one of you is a sacred blessing and sparks in me a great zest for life.

As a woman of strength and courage, I thank my family, my dear friends, and all of those who have gone before me for the model you have provided in responding to the challenge called life. All of these relationships and inspirations and everything that I have learned from my clients, especially my fellow survivors, have brought me to this sacred place of being me.

Vicki, I am grateful that you joined us in the healing work of this book. Thank you for your courage in sharing your sacred stories and experiences.

Thank you, Corrine Cassanova, for being a catalyst in the birthing of *Soul Light for the Dark Night*.

Life is great. Change is constant. And love flows from heart to heart.

—*Sue Lauber-Fleming*

Writing is both a solitary effort and a community effort. I offer my grateful thanks to my dear friend Barbara Fuhrwerk, who read and edited each of my contributions to this book. Proof, Barb, that your forty-seven years of teaching junior high language arts is the gift that keeps on giving. I dedicate my portion of *Soul Light for the Dark Night* to my mother, Donna Schmidt, who passed away June 13, 2017. I cherished her faithful love and presence in my life.

—*Vicki Schmidt*

About The Authors

Patrick Fleming is a CSAT supervisor and psychotherapist practicing in St. Louis, Missouri. He has a master of divinity degree and years of pastoral experience as a hospital chaplain and spiritual coach. His work has focused on integrating spirituality into psychological counseling with sexual addicts and survivors of childhood abuse and trauma. In recent years, this has included treatment of clerical sexual offenders and abusers. Patrick is the principal co-author of two books: *Shattered Soul? Five Pathways to Healing the Spirit after Abuse and Trauma* (WordStream Publishing, 2011) and *Broken Trust: Stories of Pain, Hope, and Healing from Clerical Abuse Survivors and Abusers* (Crossroad Publishing, 2007).

Sue Lauber-Fleming is a psychotherapist and personal coach in St. Louis, Missouri. She is also a psychiatric nurse and has had extensive pastoral experience as a hospital chaplain and chaplain supervisor. She has been a consultant to several religious organizations in the St. Louis region. In her counseling work, Sue has centered on the psychological and spiritual healing process of women survivors of abuse of all kinds, especially those who are victims of clerical sexual abuse. Sue co-authored *Shattered Soul? Five Pathways to Healing the Spirit after Abuse and Trauma* (WordStream Publishing, 2011) and *Broken Trust: Stories of Pain, Hope, and Healing from Clerical Abuse Survivors and Abusers* (Crossroad Publishing, 2007) in which she told her own story of emotional and spiritual healing from childhood clerical sexual abuse. With her husband, Patrick, Sue is a cofounder of Double Rainbow Counseling, Coaching, and Consulting, dedicated to integrating healthy spirituality into the psychological healing processes of counseling and recovery.

Vicki Schmidt lives in Springfield, Illinois. She considers working with St. Mother Teresa of Calcutta from 1981 to 1995 to be a great highlight of her life. She has been involved with ministry with the poor most of her life. She has served as executive director of Theresians International since 2000. Vicki was a contributing author to *Broken Trust: Stories of Pain, Hope, and Healing from Clerical Abuse Survivors and Abusers* by Patrick and Sue-Lauber Fleming (Crossroad, 2007). Vicki co-authored a second book with the Flemings entitled *Shattered Soul? Five Pathways to Healing the Spirit from Abuse and Trauma* (WordStream Publishing, 2011).